CONFLICTING WORLDS
New Dimensions of the American Civil War

T. Michael Parrish, Series Editor

Albion Winegar Tourgée (1838–1905)

Photograph by Mathew Brady, from PictureHistory

UNDAUNTED
RADICAL

UNDAUNTED
RADICAL

THE SELECTED WRITINGS AND SPEECHES OF
ALBION W. TOURGÉE

EDITED BY MARK ELLIOTT AND
JOHN DAVID SMITH

LOUISIANA STATE UNIVERSITY PRESS · BATON ROUGE

Published with the assistance of the V. Ray Cardozier Fund

Published by Louisiana State University Press
Copyright © 2010 by Louisiana State University Press
All rights reserved
Manufactured in the United States of America
LSU Press Paperback Original
First printing

Designer: Michelle A. Neustrom
Typefaces: Adobe Caslon Pro, text; AT Sackers Roman, display
Printer and binder: Thomson-Shore, Inc.

LIBRARY OF CONGRESS CATALOGING-IN-PUBLICATION DATA

Tourgée, Albion Winegar, 1838–1905.
[Selections. 2010]
Undaunted radical : the selected writings and speeches of Albion W. Tourgée / edited by
Mark Elliott and John David Smith.
   p. cm. — (Conflicting worlds)
Includes bibliographical references and index.
ISBN 978-0-8071-3593-8 (pbk. : alk. paper) 1. African Americans—Civil rights—History—
19th century. 2. United States—Race relations—History. 3. Abolitionists—United States—
History. 4. Reconstruction (U.S. history, 1865–1877) I.
Elliott, Mark Emory, 1969– II. Smith, John David. III. Title.
   PS3088.U54 2010
   813'.4—dc22

                                                            2009040747

To Emory B. Elliott, Jr.—M.E.
To Tessa Riley Andrusyszyn—J.D.S.

CONTENTS

ACKNOWLEDGMENTS

The editors would like to thank those people and institutions who provided invaluable assistance in the preparation of this volume. Our thanks go to the Chautauqua County Historical Society, Westfield, New York; the Schomburg Center for Research in Black Culture; Donna Toscano, Debbie Killen, Kathy Sheridan, and Dennis Schwab of Wagner College, who assisted with the laborious work of transcription and scanning from imperfect original documents; Perry McKenzie of the University of North Carolina at Greensboro, who copyedited the entire manuscript; Lisa F. Andrusyszyn and Barbara J. Black of the University of North Carolina at Charlotte, who provided valuable editorial and secretarial support; Carolyn L. Karcher and Otto H. Olsen, who offered their enthusiasm and editorial advice; and David W. Blight, whose initial suggestion sparked this project. The editors would also like to thank Conflicting Worlds series editor T. Michael Parrish as well as Rand Dotson, George Roupe, and Catherine L. Kadair of Louisiana State University Press for their interest in our work and for navigating the manuscript through the publication process. Linda Webster prepared the index. Mark Elliott would like to thank his family for its love and support, especially Kimberly Lutz, Zachary Elliott, and Nicholas Elliott. John David Smith thanks Sylvia A. Smith for her love and support on yet another project.

UNDAUNTED
RADICAL

Introduction

Albion W. Tourgée was among the foremost champions of racial equality in the nineteenth century. Though he was hardly the only white American of his time to believe that all men, regardless of race, were born equal and deserved equal rights and consideration, few could match the intensity and consistency with which he publicly proclaimed this doctrine. His creed was forged during a time when the nation was torn apart by the Civil War and confronted by the daunting social consequences of emancipation. In the 1860s, Tourgée joined with radicals like Thaddeus Stevens, Wendell Phillips, Lydia Maria Child, and Charles Sumner in believing that the future of American democracy would be secure only when equal justice and equal citizenship were guaranteed for all Americans, including former slaves. Over the next three decades, Tourgée argued on behalf of racial equality relentlessly, with increasing sophistication and depth, undeterred by fierce opposition. Although his name may not be familiar to Americans today, his writings offer some of the fullest articulations of color-blind citizenship as an ideal, and provide a penetrating look into the early debates about race and American citizenship that have continued into our time.

Tourgée is probably best known to students of Reconstruction as the author of the powerful historical novel *A Fool's Errand* (1879). A best-seller in its day, it remains a perennial favorite among assigned readings for college-level courses that deal with Reconstruction. The novel, drawn from his own experiences as an Ohio transplant in North Carolina, offered a gripping and historically accurate account of a Radical Republican in the South who allied with former slaves and battled to uphold the law against the political terrorism of the Ku Klux Klan. The book's success, along with the popularity of its sequel, *Bricks Without Straw* (1880), transformed Tourgée into a nationally recognized public figure and spokesman for southern Republicans. The present collection of writings and speeches, however, demonstrates that Tourgée's contribution to the national dialogue on race and citizenship went far beyond these two novels.

Tourgée continued to be an outspoken activist for black advancement and civil rights until the 1890s, and he left behind a wealth of books, essays, lectures, and newspaper articles on the subject of equal rights. Among his achievements, he founded one of the nation's first national civil rights organizations, framed the nation's first successful antilynching law, and brought the first challenge to segregation before the United States Supreme Court in the 1896 case of *Plessy* v. *Ferguson*. By the 1890s, many Americans considered Tourgée the new William Lloyd Garrison for the fervor with which he espoused racial equality. Much as they treated Garrison, unsympathetic whites also demonized Tourgée as a maniacal instigator of sectional hatred.

An astute, even prophetic, social critic, Tourgée has not received his due attention as an important public intellectual of the late nineteenth century. First, his work is a record of dissent against the rising tide of segregation, racial disfranchisement, lynching, and damaging racial propaganda and mythologies about slavery and the Civil War and Reconstruction. Though historians often portray postwar proslavery and pro-Confederate ideas as having gone virtually unchallenged by northern whites, Tourgée's writings, and their public visibility, demonstrate not only that vigorous resistance was possible, but that it constituted an integral part of the historical debate. Moreover, his writings offer profound insights into the legal, political, and social ways in which nineteenth-century Americans understood both "race" and "citizenship" and how the contested memory of the Civil War and Reconstruction shaped Americans' views of the past and present. Finally, Tourgée's writings present an unflinching analysis of the hard choices reformers had to face to pursue momentous egalitarian reforms, reforms whose success depended upon a delicate mix of political principle and shrewd strategic calculation.

This collection of Tourgée's best writings seeks to disseminate his ideas to a wide audience and to demonstrate the importance of his views on a broad range of subjects. It highlights his significance not only for students of history, but also for those in literary studies, legal studies, religious studies, and cultural studies. Literary scholars have long included him among the select few authors who portrayed issues of race and African American history in complex ways. Legal historians have shown an increasing appreciation for Tourgée's visionary insights in the *Plessy* v. *Ferguson* case. In addition, Tourgée figures prominently in some historical accounts of the Social Gospel movement, though the Christian ethics that permeated his work often have gone unnoticed by literary and legal scholars.[1] Placing these writings side by side,

1. Tourgée's religious ideas have been examined in Ralph Luker, *The Social Gospel in Black and White: American Racial Reform, 1885–1912* (Chapel Hill: University of North Carolina Press,

this collection will demonstrate the interrelation of Tourgée's literary, legal, and religious thought.

Tourgée's writings address many questions, including the proper constitutional interpretation of the Reconstruction Amendments; the validity of his generation's social scientific racial and economic theories; the cultural politics of North-South reconciliation; the ethics of corporate capitalism; the Social Gospel movement; and the philosophical underpinnings of American democratic citizenship. Before surveying the specific documents selected for this collection, it will be useful to examine the facts of Tourgée's life in more detail.[2]

Tourgée's worldview reflected the values of his upbringing in Ohio's Western Reserve, a notorious hotbed of abolitionism and religious radicalism prior to the Civil War. Though he never embraced radicalism in his youth, Tourgée lamented the "crying sin" of slavery as a young man and was impressed by the courage of abolitionists who endured public ridicule and often risked their lives in their unrelenting agitation for the abolition of slavery. At the age of twenty-one, responding to Lincoln's first call for troops in April 1861, Tourgée dropped out of the University of Rochester to enlist in the Union army. After suffering a severe injury at the First Battle of Bull Run, he spent a year recovering before reenlisting with the 105th Ohio Infantry in August 1862. Tourgée's experiences in the war radicalized his politics. After observing slavery firsthand in Kentucky, he assisted fugitive slaves who sought from the Union army protection and assistance escaping from their masters. In the spring of 1865, after the war had ended, Tourgée led a group of northern transplants to Greensboro, North Carolina (including his wife, her family, and several other families), where he hoped to aid African Americans in the transition from slavery to a free-labor economy.

Tourgée had a remarkable career in North Carolina. Most notably, he served an influential delegate to the 1868 state constitutional convention, he coauthored the state's revised civil codes, and from 1868 to 1874 he served as a superior court justice. While attempting to uphold the egalitarian reforms of Reconstruction, he witnessed the brutal politics of resistance by white conservatives and barely escaped becoming a victim of Ku Klux Klan violence himself. During Reconstruction Tourgée was deeply involved in North Carolina's black community, helping to found freedmen's schools (where he and his wife

---

1991); and Ronald C. White, Jr., *Liberty and Justice for All: Racial Reform and the Social Gospel (1877–1925)* (San Francisco: Harper & Row, 1990).

2. The biographical details provided in this introduction derive from Mark Elliott, *Color-Blind Justice: Albion W. Tourgée and the Quest for Racial Equality from the Civil War to* Plessy v. Ferguson (New York: Oxford University Press, 2006).

Emma both taught) and facilitating the purchase of land and the construction of better housing for blacks. The Tourgées even adopted a destitute ex-
slave and raised her and her sister in their home, to the horror of local white
conservatives.

In 1879 Tourgée fictionalized his experiences in North Carolina in *A Fool's
Errand*, a work that catapulted him into national literary fame. This book offered a sympathetic rendering of Reconstruction from the perspective of the
much-maligned "carpetbaggers," "scalawags," and freedpeople, and it had a
direct political impact on the Republican Party, which remained committed
in principle to the protection of African American rights in the South. Its
call for massive federal aid to public schools helped spark a major piece of
proposed legislation that ultimately fell short after a decade-long struggle to
enact it.

Partly because of his firsthand disappointment with the overthrow of Reconstruction and partly because of his own obstinate personality, Tourgée remained tenaciously committed to egalitarian principles long after most Radicals had abandoned them. As this collection shows, Tourgée spent the rest
of his life reflecting on and writing about the issues of race and American
citizenship. As a best-selling author with political clout, he used his notoriety
to promote his views on racial equality, and when that failed, he took direct
action as an early civil rights leader. In 1891, he founded the National Citizens'
Rights Association, an organization that based its assault on Jim Crow on the
idea that the Fourteenth Amendment had established a "national citizenship."
Eventually Tourgée came to serve as lead counsel and primary legal strategist
in Homer Plessy's historic constitutional challenge to the Louisiana Separate Car Act. In his brilliant brief before the court, Tourgée presented several
compelling arguments about the nature of American citizenship. These included his points that "the law should at least be color-blind" (a phrase bor-
rowed from him and made famous by Justice John Marshall Harlan in his
Plessy dissent) and that "whiteness" in America functioned as a form of legal
property that inherently advantaged some and disadvantaged others.

By the end of his life, Tourgée's writings had lost favor with the American
public and slipped into obscurity. This anthology is an effort to exhume them
and to introduce them to a broad readership. Bringing together private letters,
obscure newspaper articles, and previously overlooked speeches with selections from his better-known articles and books, this collection offers the most
thorough presentation of Tourgée's arguments to date. The editors selected the
documents with an eye toward capturing the range of issues Tourgée ad-

dressed concerning race and citizenship and to show how Tourgée addressed these issues to different audiences—northerners and southerners, whites and blacks, public and private individuals. The editors have organized the documents into five sections for thematic as well as chronological coherence. A brief overview of each section follows, situating the documentary selections within the context of Tourgée's life and work.

I. THE ORDEAL OF RECONSTRUCTION

The first section traces the development of Tourgée's political views during the violent and tumultuous period of Reconstruction. These sources make clear that Tourgée held a deep democratic sensibility from the outset of his career, which caused him to distrust elites—including his own Republican Party leadership—and cast his sympathies with the poor and disenfranchised. Believing that enforced ignorance was the South's primary means of excluding the poor and oppressed from power, Tourgée possessed a boundless faith in the democratic stimulus of free public education—an outgrowth of his own rise from obscurity through academic achievement. These documents also demonstrate the inescapable tension between moral principle and political strategy that local conditions forced Tourgée to negotiate. At heart, Tourgée preferred what might be termed a "politics of conscience," akin to that practiced by those abolitionists who refused to moderate their principles for the sake of political gain. Yet Tourgée understood that Reconstruction's success depended upon savvy political maneuvering and coalition building. The South could not be transformed into a democracy in one fell swoop; each step had to be undertaken cautiously and with the full realization of powerful cultural constraints that had to be overcome.

Campaign documents such as the "To the Voters of Guilford County" (doc. 1) show that Tourgée often struck an artful balance between moral principle and practical politics. Advocating an array of egalitarian and humanitarian reforms, from the abolition of corporal punishment to the establishment of free public schools, Tourgée carefully avoided direct appeals to black equality that might prove divisive. He emphasized class revolution instead, hoping to unite poor white and black voters against the planter aristocracy by framing the conflict as one of the property-owning few versus "the people." His strategy proved effective; in the fall of 1867 Guilford County elected him to the 1868 North Carolina constitutional convention. Yet, once ensconced in the Convention, Tourgée switched tactics and boldly advocated black suffrage, not merely as a political necessity—which it was—but as a fundamental moral principle. Tourgée's "Speech on Elective Franchise" (doc. 3), delivered on February 21, 1868, forcefully argues his point that racial equality was the guiding principle of Reconstruction. Speaking directly to the native white southerners who made up the vast majority of the Republican delegates at the Convention, Tourgée endeavored to inspire their permanent commitment to black equality. So insistent was Tourgée's tribute to the war contributions of black soldiers, in fact, that the conservative press reported derisively that "in listening to his tribute to their valor and patriotism during the war, the uninformed hearer would have thought the nigger alone 'crushed the rebellion.'"[3]

Despite his enthusiastic public support for black suffrage, Tourgée privately had reservations about enfranchising all blacks at once, believing it wiser to follow Lincoln's suggestion to limit suffrage to the educated or property-holding citizens of both races. This would be more palatable to white conservatives and would provide incentive to poor whites and blacks alike to become educated as soon as possible. As Tourgée made clear in later statements, such as his published letter to North Carolina newspaperman E. S. Parker in 1875 (doc. 7), he anticipated that black enfranchisement would be used as an *alternative* to a lengthy period of federal control over the former Confederate states. A longer period of federal control, in his view, would enable blacks and poor whites to become enfranchised gradually as they gained education and acquired property, allowing the interracial Republican Party time to solidify and lessening the desire of political terrorists to target black voters. Tourgée believed that enfranchising blacks without maintaining sufficient federal protection of their rights or granting them education would doom Reconstruction to white terrorism, intimidation, and political scandal. As Tourgée explained in "Root, Hog, or Die," the policy of enfranchisement without federal protection "was not giving the colored man a fair showing, though it professed to be based on that very idea" (doc. 8). Whether or not a longer period of federal control—perhaps lasting a decade or more—would have been more successful, the measure of radicalism for Tourgée was not black suffrage but rather greater federal control over the rebellious states.

Tourgée's writings also provide vivid eyewitness testimony to the struggles of southern Republicans on the front lines of Reconstruction. In 1869–70, while he served as a justice of the state superior court, Ku Klux Klan terrorism reached its zenith. Black and white Republicans became the Klan's victims,

3. *Raleigh North Carolinian*, February 22, 1868. The editors thank Professor Carolyn L. Karcher for bringing this article to their attention.

including Tourgée's close friend state senator John W. Stephens, who was murdered in April 1870. As the letters reproduced in this volume show, Tourgée personally faced threats and intimidation by the Klan and its sympathizers (docs. 4, 5). Determined to confront the challenge from the Klan head-on, he remained in North Carolina even after 1870 when Republicans fell from power, refusing to alter his jurisprudence and defending the reforms of Reconstruction as an outspoken Republican minority leader at the state constitutional convention of 1875. Tourgée's struggle to maintain egalitarian reforms against the wave of counterrevolution testifies to the strength of his convictions.

After the fall of the Republican governments in North Carolina, Tourgée began to see wisdom in moderation. No longer positioned to initiate new reforms, North Carolina Republicans now fought to secure the political gains of the Reconstruction period in the face of a reactionary Democratic Party that sought to undo the work of Reconstruction. In the final documents of this section, Tourgée reflects upon the mistakes of Reconstruction and warns against provoking further counterrevolution. His harsh assessment of the late Charles Sumner's Civil Rights Bill (finally passed in 1875), then recently passed by the U.S. Senate but awaiting confirmation in the House, is a case in point (doc. 6). Though on the surface the bill would appear to have supported Tourgée's long-professed goal of eradicating racial prejudice from the South, he nonetheless feared (with prescience as it turned out) that the legislation would have the opposite effect, antagonizing conservatives and mobilizing voters to defeat the Republicans, himself included, in the 1874 election. He proposed instead: "[L]et the South forget the negro for a bit: let him acquire property, stability, and self-respect; let as many as possible be educated; in short let the race itself get used to freedom[,] self-dependence and proper self-assertion; and then let his bill come little by little." Faith that blacks would "prove themselves" through individual achievement and that time inevitably would bring better conditions grew popular among blacks and their supporters after the fall of Reconstruction. During the 1880s Tourgée's approach to the problem of race and citizenship rested on the presumption that temporarily at least, maintaining conditions that allowed for gradual change was the wisest strategy.

II. REMEDIES FOR RACISM

The second section picks up Tourgée's career in the 1880s after he had achieved notoriety for his two Reconstruction novels and had established himself as a popular author and respected political commentator in the North. Tourgée's writings in this period exhibit a new confidence and maturity, the fruit of literary success and the warm reception of his political views by Republican Party leaders. This period of Tourgée's career reflects his belief that he could work within the political system, relying especially on personal connections in Washington to promote his political causes.

Tourgée exerted a great deal of energy in the 1880s promoting his plan that vigorous federal aid to public education in the South offered the best hope for the amelioration of race prejudice and the democratization of southern life. This issue raised the question not only of what the federal government owed to the former slaves, but also of whether American citizenship included the right to free public education for everyone. The promise of participatory citizenship, indeed, stood at the core of Tourgée's democratic philosophy. Alongside a strong national commitment to equality of opportunity for all, he believed that the health of American democracy depended upon practicing what Progressive Era reformer Jane Addams later called "democratic social ethics"—the duties and obligations of citizens to act in ways that respected the equal moral value and rights of other citizens. Time and again—on issues ranging from immigration policy and black recolonization to the growth of corporations and reparations for slavery—Tourgée's proposed remedies for racial and economic oppression derived from his notions of the rights and duties of American citizenship.

In 1881 Tourgée's detailed plan for legislative action to support public education for blacks, published in the *North American Review,* helped to shape the inaugural address of incoming Republican president James A. Garfield (doc. 9). Garfield's support sparked a decade-long debate in Congress during which a series of education bills failed to pass both houses, defeated each time by a cross-sectional alliance of Democrats and Liberal Republicans. In the midst of these debates, Tourgée published a book-length study, *An Appeal to Caesar* (1884), undertaken at the request of Garfield, that expanded upon on his original proposal for education through a penetrating historical and sociological examination of racism in America (doc. 12). Deliberately moderate in its conception, Tourgée's analysis sought to appeal to both moderate white southerners and northern Liberal Republicans who favored "limited" government and feared government involvement in education at the local level. He challenged the pseudo-Darwinian rationale of his opponents, who based their arguments on social-scientific assertions of black inferiority, while nevertheless appreciating Charles Darwin's genuine scientific contributions. *An Appeal to Caesar* proved to be a critically acclaimed book, and its warm reception kept Tourgée's hope alive for the amelioration of oppression against black Americans in the decade that followed Reconstruction.

Some scholars have viewed the "education solution" to racial strife as motivated by a conservative, even white supremacist, desire to establish white cultural control over blacks and to divert black resistance into manageable, peaceful forms. Indeed, the mantra of "industrial education," popularized by the white missionary and educator Samuel C. Armstrong in the 1870s, and championed by his prize student Booker T. Washington at the turn of the century, openly pandered to these desires by promising to educate blacks in a manner fit for their subordinate position in society. Tourgée's views on education, however, which included sharp criticism of "industrial education," differed in substantial ways from others of his time, and ought to be classed with those of Washington's foremost critic, W. E. B. Du Bois. Although Tourgée feared violent revolution and hoped that advancement through education would avoid a "race war" of colossal magnitude (which he feared would end in an unmitigated disaster for blacks and whites alike), he predicted that education would enable blacks to break free of white control and make distinct contributions to the "front ranks" of American society. According to Tourgée, education brought empowerment, not subordination. "Knowledge is power, whether for good or ill," Tourgée wrote in 1892. "Every colored man or woman who has learned to read and write makes the race just so much harder to control—so much the more dangerous to oppress" (doc. 25).

While the educational remedy for racism did not stray far from the dominant discourses of American citizenship, arguments that emphasized uplift, assimilation, and civilization, Tourgée moved beyond his contemporaries in his insistence upon giving equal respect to African Americans and their viewpoints. Few, if any, other white social critics endeavored as much as Tourgée to comprehend the contemporary "race problem" from an African American perspective and to convey that vantage point to others in an empathetic fashion. "The negro's view of the destiny of his race differs essentially from that of *any white man*, no matter what his specific inclination toward the colored race may be," Tourgée insisted in 1883.[4] He maintained that no solution to the "race question" could be found that failed to take the "negro's view" into account. For example, an excerpt from Tourgée's 1889 novel *Pactolus Prime* of-

---

4. A. W. Tourgée, "The Negro's View of the Destiny of His Race," newspaper clipping from unidentified source, ca. 1883, item 10828, Albion Winegar Tourgée Papers, Chautauqua County Historical Society.

fers an especially rich dialogue between strongly opinionated black characters and a variety of white authority figures on the subject of reparations for slavery (doc. 14). This novel prompted Tourgée's contemporary African American literary critic Anna Julia Cooper to remark, "[I]n presenting truth from the colored American's standpoint Mr Tourgee excels, we think, in fervency and frequency of utterance, any living writer, white or colored."[5] Indeed, Tourgée worked as hard as anyone to understand the African American experience, and he succeeded far better than most of his contemporaries.

Significantly, in the 1880s Tourgée wrote in books, essays, speeches, and hundreds of newspaper editorials on a wide variety of topics that did not directly address the "race problem." Considering a few selections of his writings on related issues—including immigration policy, the theory of evolution, and the corporate reorganization of the economy—contextualizes and clarifies his stance on race. In this period, for instance, Tourgée examined the relationship between Christian social ethics and democratic culture. The Social Gospel movement, which sought to extract the universal values in Christianity and apply them usually to class-related social problems influenced Tourgée deeply. He believed that the humanitarian core of America's democratic principles evolved from Christian religious doctrine, and thus his democratic social ethics drew heavily from this Christian foundation. Tourgée's social gospel novel *Murvale Eastman, Christian Socialist* (doc. 15) offers the fullest explication of his view of corporate capitalism; it demonstrates how Tourgée's radical position on racial injustice fits within a larger view of democratic citizenship.

This section of the anthology concludes with one of Tourgée's finest and most important speeches, "The Negro's View on the Race Problem," one that marked another watershed in his career (doc. 16). Celebrated in the black press afterwards, Tourgée delivered this talk before a national conference of distinguished white "authorities" on the "Negro Question" at Lake Mohonk, New York, in June 1890. Designed to forge a cross-sectional consensus on the "solution" to racial strife in the South, the conference's Quaker organizers excluded blacks from participating, fearful of alienating the southerners in attendance who might have had to share close quarters with persons of color at the remote mountain retreat.[6] In his address Tourgée posed a blister-

5. Anna Julia Cooper, *A Voice from the South* (Xenia, OH: Aldine Printing House, 1892), 190.

6. For a discussion of the politics of this conference, and the rationale behind the organizers' decisions, see Leslie H. Fishel, Jr., "The 'Negro Question' at Mohonk: Microcosm, Mirage, and Message," *New York History* 74 (July 1993): 277–314; and Luker, *The Social Gospel in Black and White*, 24–28.

ing challenge to the accommodationist tenor of the meeting, exposing the unexamined racial assumptions of the organizers and critiquing the shameful acquiescence of the religious community to the rampant racism north and south. Despite his lecture's title, Tourgée never presumed to speak for blacks, but rather "to show how [the Negro's view] may be arrived at" by sympathetic whites. This speech highlighted the vast differences between Tourgée and the white liberal mainstream, especially on the issue of "industrial education." According to Tourgée, mechanical education for blacks circumscribed their potential for upward social mobility and accomplishment and, further, served to perpetuate the rigid racial hierarchy of the existing social order. This speech also marked Tourgée's abandonment of federal aid to education. Dismayed by repeated congressional compromises on this proposal, he explained his opposition to Senator Henry F. Blair's education bill (which finally met defeat in the Senate in 1890), effectively ending the New Hampshire politician's decade-long campaign for federal aid for schools for the freedpeople. Hereafter, Tourgée's politics eschewed gradualist measures and favored uncompromising protest and direct action instead.

III. HISTORY AND PUBLIC MEMORY

While Tourgée's vision of the Civil War as a radical, even revolutionary, event infuses most of the writings in this collection, the third section singles out a few of his most revealing contributions on the meaning, history, and memory of the sectional conflict. Historian David W. Blight describes Tourgée's writing as "the literary equivalent of Frederick Douglass's oratory in the development of the Civil War memory in the late nineteenth century."[7] Tourgée, like Douglass, understood the degree to which racial politics were tied to the public memory of the war. Drawn from the span of his career, these documents highlight the elements of his radical interpretation of the war and his insights into the politics of reconciliation in post-war American culture.

Popular novels provided a favorite medium for those who wished to shape historical memory in the nineteenth century. Hoping to influence the literate middle classes of the North, Tourgée wrote several historical novels of the Civil War and Reconstruction that sought to drive home what Blight terms the "emancipationist" memory of the war. Depicting slavery as the cause of the conflict, and emancipation as the war's redeeming consequence, these novels

7. David W. Blight, *Race and Reunion: The Civil War in American Memory* (Cambridge: Belknap Press of Harvard University Press, 2001), 218.

turn on the "awakening" of whites to the injustices of racism and slavery. They
celebrate the contributions of slaves and African Americans soldiers to the
war effort. Tourgée's first novel, *Toinette* (1874), provides a perfect example
of his technique, particularly in the chapter "Types" excerpted here (doc. 17).
Depicting a real event—Lincoln's visit to Richmond following its capture by
Union troops in April 1865—Tourgée dramatizes the scene by making Senator Charles Sumner (who was not actually present) Lincoln's companion.
Contrasting Lincoln's innate conservatism and humble southern origins with
Sumner's radicalism and elite New England Brahmin background, Tourgée shows how Lincoln, and through him the nation, had been converted
to the cause of abolition. As the men view manifestations of the momentous
changes the war has wrought, including a regiment of U.S. Colored Troops
on the march and the ruins of Richmond, Tourgée captures with skill and
complexity Lincoln's hesitant embrace of black citizenship and his ultimate
conviction in the moral righteousness of it. Written as a "grand allegory of the
nation's second birth," in Tourgée's words, this scene illustrates the forces that
served as catalysts of a new national identity in the form of a new trinity—the
"poor white" president, the fanatical "theorist," and the slave-turned-soldier.

By the 1880s, themes of reconciliation and white supremacist nationalism began to dominate public memory of the war. Tourgée both contributed
to and critiqued the emerging constructed memory of the war in its various
forms. One of the most inventive of his creations was a series of essays in
the *Chicago Daily Inter-Ocean* in 1885 entitled *The Veteran and His Pipe* (doc.
18). Written from the perspective of a (fictional) one-armed veteran, these
essays bemoan the decline of national morals in the pursuit of wealth and
recall the higher ideals of those who fought the Civil War to redeem the nation from the injustices of slavery. Full of bitter satire, Tourgée's debilitated
veteran embodies the "forgotten" soldier, who feels disparaged as a "bummer"
for accepting his modest pension only grudgingly paid by the federal government for his sacrifice to the nation. His lonely soliloquies, addressed to a
fallen comrade's smoking pipe that the veteran has dubbed "Blower," cover a
range of topics including the evolution of Memorial Day and the mythifica-
tion of such figures as Lincoln and Confederate generals Robert E. Lee and
Thomas J. Jackson.

Tourgée also called attention to the rise of "Lost Cause" romanticism
in fiction. One of Tourgée's most quoted essays, "The South as a Field for
Fiction" (doc. 19) surveys the literature about slavery and the Civil War, and
warns of the dearth of southern blacks or northern writers tackling the sub-

ject. While northern writers tended to avoid the subject for fear of offending white southerners, those same southern whites dominated the field with unabashed vindications of the Confederacy. Tourgée also called upon African American novelists to provide their essential, but heretofore missing, perspective in the historical drama of slavery and its downfall, predicting that one day black authors would dominate the field. Another selection, "The Literary Quality of Uncle Tom's Cabin" (doc. 21), published soon after Harriet Beecher Stowe's death in 1896, discusses both the extraordinary achievements and the shortcomings of Stowe's great 1852 antislavery novel. Significantly, critics often compared Tourgée's fiction with that of Stowe, though not entirely with justification, and his name became inextricably linked to hers in the late-nineteenth-century literary world. This short piece of literary analysis reveals a great deal about the impact of *Uncle Tom's Cabin* on Tourgée's fiction. His writings frequently employ the techniques of realism while at the same time presenting race and slavery as symbol and metaphor in the manner of Stowe.

IV. RACE AND CITIZENSHIP IN THE REACTIONARY 1890S

After the defeat of Blair's education bill in 1890, Tourgée began a new phase of his career as a leading civil rights activist, relentlessly opposing racial segregation, lynching, and disfranchisement. He returned to radicalism because of the upswing of racial violence that spread from the South to the Midwest in the 1890s. Capitalizing on the sentiment that spurred on the wave of southern lynchings, white supremacist politicians began to propose harsh new measures curtailing black rights. Southern legislatures met, redrafted their state constitutions, and reinscribed black subordination in the form of Jim Crow laws. In the face of this racial reaction, Tourgée defended equal citizenship in what might be judged the last stand of Radical Republicanism of his generation.

Tourgée's main public platform for this crusade was his remarkable column "A Bystander's Notes," published weekly in Chicago's leading Republican newspaper, the *Daily Inter-Ocean*. While he addressed a wide range of subjects, Tourgée's column drew national attention for his relentless focus on the plight of blacks. Years ahead of Ida B. Wells's celebrated antilynching articles in the *New York Age,* in his column Tourgée reported minute details of lynchings and other forms of racial violence. Recalling his battles twenty years earlier, Tourgée regarded organized mobs, such as the rural midwestern White Caps, as "nothing less than Northern ku-klux," and he offered penetrating analyses of the impact of racial strife on democratic values. Several of his columns appear here, starting with his first antilynching articles in 1888 (docs. 22–24). Throughout the 1880s and 1890s Tourgée continued to put unrelenting pressure on the Republican Party to live up to the commitments of Reconstruction.

In the 1890s Tourgée did more than write articles of social protest. In 1894, for example, he framed a visionary antilynching law, adopted in Ohio thanks to the tireless efforts of Harry C. Smith, a black state congressman and general editor of the *Cleveland Gazette* (doc. 29). This law may have contributed to the subsequent reduction in the occurrence of lynchings in Ohio, and it withstood two constitutional reviews by the state supreme court. More famously, Tourgée took a leading role in the constitutional challenge to Louisiana's Separate Car Act of 1890, which required all railroad cars to provide "equal but separate" accommodations for blacks and whites. Louis A. Martinet, the radical editor of the *New Orleans Crusader*, who took the initial lead in organizing a local protest movement against the law, brought Tourgée into the case.

To mobilize public support behind their constitutional challenge, the two men agreed to launch a national civil rights organization, with Tourgée as its president, which he announced in "A Bystander's Notes" on October 17, 1891. Conceived as an interracial organization, the National Citizens' Rights Association declared itself opposed to all violations of citizens' rights, regardless of color, but targeted the oppression of blacks as the most pressing threat to citizens' rights across the country. The organization later published the thirty-two-page pamphlet *Is Liberty Worth Preserving?* (doc. 25) outlining its principles and strategies. It distributed twenty-five thousand copies of the publication at the 1892 Republican National Convention in Minneapolis.

The Louisiana test case became the focal point of Tourgée's movement against the reactionary tide of the 1890s. His legal team's strategy evolved through a lengthy correspondence among himself, Martinet, and local criminal attorney James C. Walker. Tourgée suggested that they choose a plaintiff light-skinned enough to "pass" for a white man in order to exploit the ambiguous legal and scientific basis for "race" as a reasonable classification of citizens. On June 7, 1892, in a planned incident, Homer A. Plessy, a New Orleans shoemaker of seven-eighths "white" ancestry, agreed to serve as plaintiff, allowing himself to be arrested for violating the Separate Car Act. However, by the time the case made it to the U.S. Supreme Court docket in the fall 1893, then known as *Plessy v. Ferguson*, Tourgée had begun to entertain serious doubts about its outcome. His October 31, 1893, letter to Louis A. Martinet (doc. 28) analyzed the inclinations of the various Supreme Court justices and advised his clients that the case would certainly fail without a successful mobilization of public opinion in their favor. Though its attempts to revive the abolitionist spirit in the North failed, the New Orleans Citizens' Committee nevertheless pressed Tourgée to move forward with the case. In 1896, the Court upheld the Louisiana law as constitutional, prompting the rapid spread of "separate but equal" segregation statutes throughout the South.

Tourgée delivered his argument before the Supreme Court in two forms, both reproduced here (docs. 30, 31). Scholars have studied his written brief, entered into the docket in the fall of 1895, extensively.[8] Scholars, however, remain largely unaware of the fact that on April 13, 1896, Tourgée appeared in court and delivered an oral argument to elaborate on a few of the key points from his brief. Except for a few sentences recorded by a *Washington Post* reporter, none of Tourgée's court remarks heretofore have made their way into print. Significantly, Tourgée's papers include a meticulously prepared typescript argument imprinted upon forty-five note cards that he brought into court and surely intended to read. Whether the justices allowed him to read the entire prepared text remains unknown; the eight justices in attendance probably would have interrupted, interrogated, and cut off Tourgée at will during the hearing. Nevertheless, this never-before-published text sheds important light on Tourgée's closely studied brief, underscoring his use of Homer Plessy's "race" and amplifying his view that the Fourteenth Amendment had transformed American citizenship by nationalizing it and prohibiting laws that create or perpetuate racial or caste distinctions.

V. CODA: LETTERS FROM BORDEAUX

The closing section of this collection captures Tourgée's final statements on the "race problem." In 1897 President William McKinley appointed him U.S. consul to Bordeaux, France; thereafter Tourgée began a self-imposed pub-

---

8. For more critical views on his brief, see C. Vann Woodward, "The Birth of Jim Crow," *American Heritage* 15 (April 1964): 52–55, 100–10; David W. Bishop, "*Plessy v. Ferguson:* A Reinterpretation," *Journal of Negro History* 62 (April 1977): 125–33; and Harvey Fireside, *Separate and Unequal: Homer Plessy and the Supreme Court Decision That Legalized Racism* (New York: Carroll & Graf Publishers, 2004), 120–21. More positive evaluations of Tourgée's arguments include Sidney Kaplan, "Albion W. Tourgée: Attorney for the Segregated," *Journal of Negro History* 49 (April 1964): 128–33; Charles A. Lofgren, *The Plessy Case: A Legal-Historical Interpretation* (Oxford: Oxford University Press, 1987); Brook Thomas, ed., *Plessy v. Ferguson, A Brief History with Documents* (New York: Bedford Books, 1997); and Michael Kent Curtis, "Albion Tourgée: Remembering Plessy's Lawyer on the 100th Anniversary of Plessy v. Ferguson," *Constitutional Commentary* 13 (Summer 1996): 187–99.

lic silence on controversial public issues. Nonetheless Tourgée maintained a
regular private correspondence with McKinley and his successor, Theodore
Roosevelt, offering frank, unsolicited commentary on various topics. These
letters reveal that following the *Plessy* decision Tourgée became utterly demoralized, repeatedly acknowledging that he had lost faith in the peaceful
resolution of the "race problem" in the United States and in the moral capacity of Western civilization. Despite his rejection of his nation and its values,
Tourgée's fundamental belief in the equality of all persons, regardless of race,
remained unchanged. Leaving the means of its accomplishment to the agency
of God, he believed that one day this truth would be vindicated.

During his time as McKinley's consul in Bordeaux, Tourgée kept up a regular correspondence with the president. From President James A. Garfield's
administration forward, Tourgée took it upon himself to advise Republicans
who occupied the White House, hopeful that his opinions might have some
influence. For example, on November 23, 1898, he wrote to McKinley (doc.
32) responding to the November 10 Wilmington, North Carolina, race riot in
which white supremacists killed at least twenty-two blacks in an armed uprising against the city's biracial Republican majority, forcing Republican leaders
to resign from office and scores of blacks to flee for their lives. This successful
coup d'etat left Tourgée stunned and demoralized. Instead of offering his customary advice, he lamented that "no organized resistance to [white violence]
is possible" and deemed the situation "beyond remedy by any human means."
Tourgée even recanted his earlier "naïve" belief that education, Christian ethics, and moral progress would inevitably generate civic acceptance and racial
justice. Still, Tourgée never doubted the falsity of white southerners' increas-
ingly bold assertion that "white supremacy" was natural and inevitable and that
white violence signified a necessary step in the reassertion of the "natural" order.

Tourgée's August 6, 1900, letter to Ferdinand Barnett echoed his deep-
ening pessimism (doc. 33). A longtime ally of Barnett, editor of the *Chicago
Conservator,* and his wife, Ida B. Wells-Barnett, a vocal civil rights activist,
Tourgée could not encourage them in their determined quest for racial justice.
While criticizing the accommodationism of black ministers and other leaders, he nevertheless predicted that it would require "martyrs by the thousand"
and at least one hundred years to overcome the current wave of white reaction. This letter testifies to the demoralization of the movement for equal citizenship during what historian Rayford W. Logan termed the "nadir" of race
relations in American history.

A slight revival of hope for Tourgée occurred in 1901 when Theodore
Roosevelt, newly ascended to the presidency, inadvertently made interna-

tional headlines when he entertained black leader Booker T. Washington at the White House. Harshly criticized for this act, especially by the southern press, Roosevelt received a letter of support from Tourgée, then consul in Bordeaux, who interpreted the incident as a symbolic blow against racial prejudice and Jim Crow segregation (doc. 34). Tourgée regarded Roosevelt's willingness to treat Washington as a social equal as "one of the momentous acts of history, the effect of which no man can measure." Urging Roosevelt to stand firm against his critics, Tourgée nevertheless reminded Roosevelt of the political dangers involved in his alleged social transgression and recounted his own career of disappointment as a champion of racial equality. The mixture of pessimism and encouragement must have perplexed Roosevelt who, nonetheless, was "touched and pleased" by the letter.

The final document in this collection (doc. 35) is one of Tourgée's last statements on the race problem, written a few years before his death and fittingly summing up many of the themes of his long career as an activist for equal rights. In a letter to a former University of Rochester classmate, E. H. Johnson, Tourgée responded to *The Leopard's Spots* (1902), Thomas Dixon's wildly popular first novel on Reconstruction. In what amounts to a thirty-eight-page essay on the history and memory of Reconstruction, Tourgée analyzes the falsifications of Dixon's work and reflects in deeply personal and philosophical ways on the meaning of his own career as a champion of racial equality. In light of Dixon's success, however, Tourgée marked each page of his letter "*Personal & Confidential*" and asked Johnson to keep his views quiet lest they provoke further backlash from white southerners—or even cost him his position at the Bordeaux consulate. Thus, until its publication here, Tourgée's scathing attack on Dixon has never before appeared in print. The history of Reconstruction would continue to suffer from great distortion and defamation after his death, while Tourgée and his writings became discredited, relegated to the margins of American literature and social criticism until the start of the Second Reconstruction of the 1960s.

TOURGÉE'S LEGACY

By the end of his life, racial inequality had once again become the legally established norm in America, and Tourgée rapidly slipped from public memory after his death in 1905. Propaganda from white southerners about the alleged "horrors" they had suffered under the years of so-called Negro Domination dogged every discussion about race and government policy from the end of Reconstruction until the start of the modern civil rights movement. Extremists like Thomas Dixon, who grew up in Reconstruction North Carolina, consciously set out to refute Tourgée's account of the post–Civil War decades. Dixon's Reconstruction novels became the basis for the 1915 film *Birth of a Nation*—America's first blockbuster motion picture and a work that profoundly shaped the public memory of that era for decades.

As Tourgée's works slipped into obscurity, in 1921 he received his first biographical treatment from Roy Dibble, a literary critic whose *Albion W. Tourgée* began as a dissertation at Columbia University.[9] No doubt influenced by Columbia's legendary conservative, pro-South, anti-black "Dunning school" that dominated the Reconstruction-era historiography of his day, Dibble portrayed Tourgée critically as recklessly driven by ambition and tragically ruined, in both his writing and politics, by a single-minded didactic obsession with race.[10] Though Tourgée continued to receive respectful treatment by African American scholars like W. E. B. Du Bois, Hugh Gloster, and Sterling Brown in surveys of the period, white intellectuals largely ignored him until the 1954 *Brown v. Board of Education* decision.[11] The new wave of scholarship on the history of Reconstruction and civil rights that followed *Brown* revived interest in Tourgée. Most notably in *Patriotic Gore*, his influential 1962 study of Civil War literature, Edmund Wilson proclaimed *A Fool's Errand* "an historical classic" and placed Tourgée among the most important writers of the period.[12] Otto

9. Roy F. Dibble, *Albion W. Tourgée* (New York: Lemcke & Buechner, 1921).

10. Columbia University historian William A. Dunning (1857–1922) directed more than a half dozen state studies on the Civil War and Reconstruction. On Dunning, see John Harrelson Hosmer, "William A. Dunning: 'The Greatest Historian,'" *Mid-America* 68 (April–June 1986): 57–78.

11. Two exceptions to the general neglect of Tourgée during this time were the following articles by a noted historian and a literary critic, respectively: Russell B. Nye, "Judge Tourgée and Reconstruction," *Ohio State Archaeological and Historical Quarterly* 50 (July 1941): 101–14; George J. Becker, "Albion W. Tourgée: Pioneer in Social Criticism," *American Literature* 19 (March 1947): 59–72. See comments on Tourgée in W. E. B. Du Bois, *Black Reconstruction in America* (New York: Harcourt, Brace and Company, 1935); Hugh Gloster, *Negro Voices in American Fiction* (Washington, DC: Associates in Negro Folk Education, 1937); and Sterling Brown, *The Negro in American Fiction* (Port Washington, NY: Kennikat, 1937).

12. Edmund Wilson, *Patriotic Gore: Studies in the Literature of the American Civil War* (New York: Farrar, Strauss, and Giroux, 1962). Significantly, Wilson sometimes badly misread Tourgée's ironic tone. Carter Everett analyzes Wilson's interpretations in "Edmund Wilson Refights the Civil War: The Revision of Albion Tourgée's Novels," *American Literary Realism, 1870–1910* 29 (Winter 1997): 68–75. Other Tourgée scholarship of the early 1960s includes Monte M. Olenick, "Albion W. Tourgée: Radical Republican Spokesman of the Civil War Crusade," *Phylon* 23 (4th Qtr. 1962): 332–45; Sidney Kaplan, "Albion W. Tourgée: Attorney for the Segregated," *Journal of Negro History* 49 (April 1964): 128–33; and Theodore L. Gross, *Albion W. Tourgée* (New York: Twayne, 1963).

Olsen's 1965 biography *Carpetbagger's Crusade* firmly established Tourgée's importance, not just as a novelist, but also as a principled and uncompromising radical who made significant state and national contributions to the cause of equal rights during Reconstruction and afterward. A few years later Olsen followed his excellent biography with *The Thin Disguise*, a valuable collection of documents on *Plessy* that highlighted Tourgée's involvement in the case.[13]

By the end of the 1960s, many of Tourgée's books finally reappeared in print, including a Harvard Library edition of *A Fool's Errand*, edited by John Hope Franklin, and another edition by George Fredrickson, who dubbed Tourgée "the North's leading exponent of racial egalitarianism" in the late nineteenth century.[14] Yet, in the 1970s after the civil rights movement fragmented into disappointment and frustration, mirroring Reconstruction in many ways, scholarly interest in Tourgée once again waned. As scholars began to focus on Reconstruction's limitations, lamenting the failure of its architects to impose broader reforms on the South, including land redistribution, and decrying their inordinate faith in free markets to settle labor conflict, the egalitarianism of Civil War–era reformers like Tourgée seemed inadequate. Moreover, late-twentieth-century historians came to regard Radical Republicans and abolitionists as suspect even in their commitment to racial equality because of their lack of multiculturalism and their perceived complicity in the "civilizationist" goal of moral uplift and assimilation. These historians considered the goals of radicals like Tourgée misplaced. Since the mid-1990s groundbreaking scholarship has shown how African American activists of the late nineteenth century, including Ida B. Wells, Charles W. Chesnutt, W. E. B. Du Bois, and even Booker T. Washington, reshaped the discourses of uplift and civilization in subtle and subversive ways to advance the cause of racial equality.[15] The editors of this volume believe that Tourgée's radicalism

---

13. Otto H. Olsen, *Carpetbagger's Crusade: The Life of Albion Winegar Tourgée* (Baltimore: Johns Hopkins University Press, 1965); Otto H. Olsen, ed., *The Thin Disguise: Plessy v. Ferguson, A Documentary Presentation* (New York: Humanities Press, 1967).

14. George M. Fredrickson's introduction to his 1966 edition of *A Fool's Errand* appeared as "The Travail of a Radical Republican: Albion W. Tourgée and Reconstruction" in Fredrickson, *The Arrogance of Race: Historical Perspectives on Slavery, Racism, and Social Inequality* (Middletown, CT: Wesleyan University Press, 1988), 94–106.

15. For instance, see the chapter on Ida B. Wells in Gail Bederman, *Manliness and Civilization: A Cultural History of Gender and Race in the United States, 1880–1917* (Chicago: University of Chicago Press, 1995); the chapter on Chesnutt in Eric J. Sundquist, *To Wake the Nations: Race in the Making of American Literature* (Cambridge: Harvard University Press, 1993); David Levering Lewis, *W. E. B. Du Bois: Biography of a Race, 1868–1919* (New York: Henry Holt, 1993); Wilson Jeremiah Moses, *Creative Conflict in African American Thought: Frederick Douglass, Alexander*

contained subversion of a similar kind and that he deserves to stand alongside Wells and Du Bois in the front ranks of racial reformers.

A fast-growing body of new scholarship on Tourgée suggests that the time has arrived for a more thorough reassessment of him and his views. Mark Elliott's 2006 biography, *Color-Blind Justice: Albion W. Tourgée and the Quest for Racial Equality from the Civil War to Plessy v. Ferguson,* argued that Tourgée emerged from an antebellum political tradition of "radical individualism" that demanded that conscience predominate over personal self-interest and that a higher law of justice for all men override political self-interest. A bona fide radical, Tourgée's "radicalism," according to this view, came from his insistence on granting equal citizenship and the means for upward social mobility for blacks, without shrinking from the use of governmental power to realize these goals. In 2001, in his award-winning *Race and Reunion: The Civil War in American Memory,* David W. Blight accorded Tourgée distinction as a principal defender of what he termed the "emancipationist" memory of the Civil War and as one of the sharpest critics of the Lost Cause mythology. Literary historian Carolyn L. Karcher also has helped to reestablish Tourgée's importance in the antilynching movement of the 1890s and has recently published a new edition of his overlooked Reconstruction novel *Bricks Without Straw.* Finally, Mark M. Smith, Brook Thomas, Rebecca J. Scott, Mark Golub, and J. Allen Douglas have illuminated the *Plessy* case in new ways and have clarified some of the past misreadings of Tourgée's brief that have clouded scholarship about the case. By recovering and contextualizing the broader challenge to segregation Plessy's lawyers posed to Jim Crow–era segregation, new scholarship has made it possible to view Tourgée's arguments in a proper light.[16]

Crummell, Booker T. Washington, W. E. B. Du Bois, and Marcus Garvey (Cambridge: Harvard University Press, 2004); and W. Fitzhugh Brundage, ed., *Booker T. Washington and Black Progress:* Up from Slavery *100 Years Later* (Gainesville: University Press of Florida, 2003).

16. See Elliott, *Color-Blind Justice;* Blight, *Race and Reunion;* Carolyn L. Karcher, "Ida B. Wells and Her Allies against Lynching: A Transnational Perspective," *Comparative American Studies* 3 (June 2005): 131–51; Carolyn L. Karcher, "The White 'Bystander' and the Black Journalist 'Abroad': Albion W. Tourgée and Ida B. Wells as Allies against Lynching," *Prospects* 29 (2005): 85–119; and Albion W. Tourgée, *Bricks Without Straw: A Novel,* ed. Carolyn L. Karcher (Durham: Duke University Press, 2009); Mark M. Smith, *How Race Is Made: Slavery, Segregation, and the Senses* (Chapel Hill: University of North Carolina Press, 2006); Brook Thomas, *American Literary Realism and the Failed Promise of Contract* (Berkeley: University of California Press, 1997); and Brook Thomas, ed., *Plessy v. Ferguson: A Brief History;* Rebecca J. Scott, "'There Is No Caste Here': Public Rights, Social Equality and the Conceptual Roots of the Plessy Challenge," *Michigan Law Review* 106 (March 2008): 777–804; Mark Golub, "Plessy as 'Passing': Judicial

This anthology builds upon the new wave of scholarship by making Tourgée's writings across the span of his career widely available for the first time. Tourgée's radical ideas have become relevant once again, and their history and meaning the subject of political and scholarly debate. A better understanding of Tourgée and his work undoubtedly enriches our understanding of the Civil War era, underscoring the relationship between race and citizenship. As in Tourgée's day, the question of integrating a diverse population into the fabric of American society continues to be the focus of intense public discussion in the twenty-first century.

EDITORIAL STATEMENT

The editors have sought to maintain the original intent and meaning of Albion W. Tourgée's writings as closely as possible. They have reproduced and transcribed Tourgée's texts as near to the "literal" editorial method as possible. Determined not to interfere with the integrity and flow of Tourgée's ideas, in a few cases the editors nevertheless indicate material deleted within and between paragraphs with ellipses. Material omitted between sections or chapters of texts of books and pamphlets appears as a series of six spaced dots. On occasion the editors have also inserted information in square brackets to provide essential or missing facts, letters, words, personal names, or punctuation. In addition, they have sparingly corrected and standardized capitalization and spelling, modernized punctuation, systematized capitalization, and added paragraph breaks. Inconsistent capitalization of certain keywords, including "Negro," "Nation," "State," and "Reconstruction," has been preserved to represent accurately Tourgée's original use of these terms. Tourgée added an accent mark to his last name in 1882. The editors have used the accent mark in all their references to him throughout the book, but have retained the original appearance of the last name in Tourgée's own texts. The editors provide explanatory footnotes to clarify Tourgée's references and have retained his occasional annotations, indicated by asterisks.

Responses to Ambiguously Raced Bodies in Plessy v. Ferguson," *Law and Society Review* 39 (September 2005): 563–600; and J. Allen Douglas, "The 'Most Valuable Sort of Property': Constructing White Identity in American Law, 1880–1940," *San Diego Law Review* 40, no. 3 (Fall 2003): 881–946.

I

THE ORDEAL
OF RECONSTRUCTION

I

To the Voters of Guilford (1867)*

This statement of principles appeared as a two-column broadside that Tourgée published and distributed in support of his candidacy for representative of Guilford County at North Carolina's 1868 constitutional convention. While an accurate reflection of his principles, its emphasis on class leveling was pitched to unite poor white and black voters against the planter aristocracy. This strategy proved effective, as he was subsequently elected to the convention.

Fellow Citizens:

Having been urgently solicited to become a candidate for the Constitutional Convention, and having consented to do so, I hereby offer for your suffrages, as the exponent of the following principles to the earnest and unflinching support of which, in the future as in the past, I am impelled by every incentive of justice, humanity and patriotism:

1st.   Equality of civil and political rights to all citizens.

2nd.   No property qualifications for jurymen.

3rd.   Every voter eligible for election to any office of trust or emolument.

4th.   All legislative, executive, and judicial officers of the state to be filled by the vote of the people.

5th.   A criminal code humane and Christian, without whip or stocks.

6th.   An ample system of public instruction reaching from the lowest primary school to the highest university course, free to the children of every citizen.

7th.   A uniform ad valorum system of taxation upon property.

8th.   The tax upon the poll (or more properly tax upon the value of labor) not to exceed three days' work upon the public highway or its equivalent.

*"To the Voters of Guilford," broadside, October 21, 1867, item 2428, Albion Winegar Tourgée Papers, Chautauqua County Historical Society.

9th. In addition to the provisions of Section 4th of the Constitutional Amendment, the assumption or payment by any county, city, or other political corporation, within the state of any debt, contracted in aid of rebellion, directly or indirectly, should be prohibited by Constitutional enactment.

10th. The rights of citizenship to be extended to the present excluded classes whenever the Congress of the United States shall see fit to remove their disabilities and not before.

These are the principles of equal and exact justice to all men, the marrow and essence of republican government. Incorporated in the Constitution they will order the new state a government of the people, by the people and for the people. Without them it will be government controlled and administered in the interests of the few.

Voters of Guilford, two courses are open before you. Shall the new State have an Oligarchy or a Republic? An Aristocracy or a Democracy? Shall its fundamental law respect the rights of the hundred thousand voters who do not own land enough to give to each a burial place, or consider only the interests of the fifteen hundred men who own two-thirds of the lands of the state? Shall the poor man's labor be taxed four or five percent and the rich man's property but one-third of one percent? Shall poverty be taxed higher than wealth? Shall the honest and capable, though landless voter, be allowed to hold offices of trust and emolument, or shall that privilege be granted only to "the lord of barren acres"? Shall the poor man be allowed a seat upon the jury, or is "red clay" necessary to give judgment and integrity? Shall capacity, honesty, and your suffrages be sufficient to entitle the voter to a seat in the assembly or shall the clayey Juggernaut set up his alter in the State House?

The aristocracy of slavery is dead. Shall we now build up an aristocracy of land? Shall we have a government of a few, by a few, and for a few? You have tried it once and the past seven years are its results—six hundred thousand dead are the glorious first fruits of aristocratic rule.

Poor men of Guilford & laboring men of Guilford, now is your golden moment! The tide is at the flood! Old things are passing away. Slavery, that fed daintily upon your lives, has ceased to ask its yearly hecatomb of men and women. Aristocracy, which would let "a thousand paupers die that our oligarch might live," is fighting its last battle with Democracy. Muscle is no longer bought and sold, nor brain made the subject of barter. Wealth is no longer the great I Am, nor manhood a political cipher. "The bone of contention" has become a constituent element of the Republic. "We, the people," has a new signification. Do you choose to govern yourselves or be ruled by those who still crave the name of "master"? Will you be free men or serfs? Will the "new people" have a "new" state, or the old one patched up, with its whip and stocks, its oppressive system of taxation and its tyrannic landed aristocracy!

Laborers of Guilford are you not as capable of self-government as those men who with the motto rule or ruin, did both rule and ruin all this glorious Southern land? Will you exercise and preserve the power which three hundred thousand martyrs died to place in your hands, or will you basely yield it *into the hands of our enemies!* But the cry is "Property must be protected!" That was the rallying cry of '61. "Our property! Our property! Great is Diana!" "The rich man's war and the poor man's fight" was the result. The contest which was meant to make every poor man a slave has made them free. Let then our battle cry be "Manhood, Equal Rights, Free Schools, Free Juries, Free Offices, Free Press, Free Speech, Free Men!"

For the purpose of more fully discussing the great issues which are upon us, I shall be happy to meet the citizens of the county wherever and whenever they may desire until the day of election.

Very Respectfully,
Your Obdt. Servant,
A. W. Tourgee.
Oct. 21, 1867.

2

The Reaction (1868)*

This letter was the fourth in a series of correspondence that the *National Anti-Slavery Standard* commissioned from Tourgée in late 1867 and early 1868. Entitled "The Reaction," this installment analyzed the perceived setback for the radical wing of the Republican Party in the fall 1867 elections, in which the Democratic Party gained substantially in many states outside of the South. Though widely interpreted in the press as a death knell for radicalism, Tourgée rejected this view and posited that the Republican leadership's failing moral vision had cost it the people's support. Significantly, this letter demonstrates Tourgée's deep distrust of party leadership, even in the early stages of Reconstruction, and his fidelity to the politics of conscience. Tourgée believed that a sincere commitment to moral principles would inspire a devoted following more effectively than shallow, politically calculated moderation.

To the Editor of the Standard:

It is an assertion constantly reiterated by men of almost every shade of political belief, that a political reaction has begun, and is now going on, in the minds of the American people. According to Conservative authority, the people are sickened of "nigger," "taxation," "equality," "loyal rule"; in short, justice applied to political questions. And to escape the omnipresent right and avoid commercial disaster, they are hurriedly crawfishing into the gaping maw of Democracy—that party which is never disturbed by questions of Right or Wrong, and whose acme of prosperity is only reached through the surges of financial ruin. To them it is a reaction from better to worse—from a higher to a lower political morality; a reaction which leads men to inquire upon every political question, not what is right, but what will best subserve the idea of

*Winegar, "North Carolina Correspondence. No. IV. The Reaction," *National Anti-Slavery Standard,* January 4, 1868.

government designed especially for the white man. In short a reaction which is to substitute prejudice for conscience.

The moderately inclined, constitutionally timid portion of the Republican party, men who are willing enough to be right if they are sure they can win thereby, who worship present success beyond all other gods, insist that their Congressional leaders have been too fast, too radical; that the Republican party has got ahead of the people, and that a movement to the rear is necessary, to prevent it from destruction. The party wire-pullers have sounded a retreat, and the puppets all over the country are advancing backward, each in his own peculiar manner, as circumstances or inclination dictates. Some bolt with such ready impetuosity as to outstrip their leaders and get into the very camp of Democracy, while they are yet dallying with the pickets. Others slowly and painfully drag themselves over the hindrances which time and their own efforts have placed in the backward pathway. Others, having burned their ships, have no recourse but to plunge boldly into the sea of inconsistency, only to be hopelessly choked by their own utterances. The whippers-in of every aspirant for the Republican Presidential nomination, having the same theory of reaction in mind, are peculiarly anxious to establish the fact that *their* man is moderate, or at least not offensively radical, insisting at the same time that the recent reaction (at the North, as Southern trigger-workers are fond of saying) utterly forbids all hope for the election of an ultra Radical. This reaction, then, according to the timid Republicans, is of the same nature as is claimed by the Conservatives, only a little less decided in its character. Instead of substituting prejudice for conscience, they only propose to make success the test in all political questions.

Upon this principle, a man who never expressed a political belief in all his life, and one whose chief merits is, that the most persistent quiz could never yet find out with which party even his sympathies lay, and who cannot be proven by any set or utterance to be good or bad, Radical or Conservative, man or mouse, is claimed to be the most feasible candidate for the Republican party in the coming struggle; and for the same reasons the mouths of other candidates are closed, lest they should utter some radical truth to interfere with their chances of nomination. These moderate Republicans, who dream so constantly of the horrors of reaction, whose timid souls can see only defeat in the future, unless half the fruits of the past six years of warfare is given up to the enemy, are very fond of saying, especially to colored men, and to our Southern Unionists, when they are inclined to murmur at the chaff which is offered to them, "You know our only hope is in the Republican party." As if the people were not greater than the party! As if it were not the party which was dependent upon them, rather than they upon the party! The Republican theory of the "Reaction" is, that the masses of the people, or at least of that party, have pronounced against manhood suffrage and loyal reconstruction, and that now, in order to save the party from defeat, we must perpetrate another Brobdignagian lie. We must have a candidate who shall be all things to all men, and a platform which is ditto. To the newly enfranchised "brother of the African persuasion," in North Carolina, the Republican party must stand forth still as the champion of "Liberty and Equality," the sanctified agency through which freedom came to those in bondage, while to the jaundiced negrophobist in Ohio, it must be represented as only having given a little to the colored man from necessity, and as very willing to revoke that little upon a reasonable opportunity. And this Janus-visaged party is now tried to be foisted on North and South alike, upon the special plea that the reaction in public sentiment at the North renders it imperatively necessary.

Now, the whole theory on which this outcry of "Reaction" is based is deceptive and false. There has been no reaction *among the people* in the reference to the great principles now at the issue. They gave their verdict, and sent it into the court of final appeal, sealed with the blood of hundreds of thousands of their sons. You might as well expect the tide of Niagara to reverse its flow, as to expect them to set aside that verdict. And as for us of the South, black or white, we had rather be killed than commit suicide. If our throats must be cut, we don't care about handling the cleaver. There is no reaction here, and will not be in our day, among the party of freedom and justice.

"But," says the objector, "there has been some change in the political world—you cannot deny that; for the elections show it unmistakably." Evidently there has been a change, and for lack of a better appreciation of its true character, it has been generally denominated a *reaction*. And because there could not possibly be any reaction or advance in the Conservative party, it being at the best only a sort of political backwater, it was at once concluded that it must of necessity be a retrograde movement among the rank and file of the Republican party.

Here is the mistake. What we see today is *not reaction, but the effects of reaction,* and the reaction itself is not of the present, but of the past, and was not a reaction in sentiment among the rank and file of the party, but a reaction in policy among its leaders. It began as soon as the business of the war was over, when Lee and Johnston had surrendered, and Abraham Lincoln had been borne to his prairie tomb. It was first fully developed—so far as the writer knows at least—at the Loyalist Convention in Philadelphia, in September, 1866, and was the result of the most egregious stupidity on the part of the recognized leaders of the Republican party.[1] It is resulting now just as every clear-headed and sound-hearted Radical in that Convention prophecied that it would, either in the death or thorough reformation of the party.

The Republican party in 1861 was compelled to put itself in array against rebellion. Its very existence depended on the putting down of that war against the Union. The people were opposed to rebellion because it was a great wrong, and the consequences of a still greater wrong. The enormity of the crime of rebellion, the fearful wickedness on which it was based, was so apparent that its contemplation often made the boor a hero. To the leaders of the party its suppression was a political necessity, to the people a holy duty; and when it could no longer be hidden, but was evident to all that the deeply seared conscience of the people was at least touched, that they were determined to right the wrong of the past, that the long slumbering crater showed signs of life—*then* the Republican party, mindful for the first time of the maxim that "Honesty is the best policy," concluded to adopt the role of Peter the Hermit, and preach the crusade against rebellion, on the grounds of its justice and righteousness.

Its leaders approached the limits of the crater doubtfully, and began to stir the seething mass within very carefully. Nobody was to be hurt—nothing disturbed. Love for the "erring sisters" was too strong in their hearts to allow more than a big scare. The fire in the great crater flashed and flamed. They warmed to their work and patted one another gleefully, exclaiming, "See what a fire we have builded." By-and-by the flames grew hotter and began to burn the hay-straw hobby of the sanctity of slavery which some of them bestrode; and then some tried to put out the fire by blowing on it, as they would cool a plate of soup. But others saw that the sanctified hobby tried to hinder it. So they deserted the hobby, and as they had before cried, "Down with rebellion!" so they now cried, "Down with rebellion and slavery!" and they punched away at the seething mass within the crater, thinking all the time that the great flame which swept the length and breadth of our land and licked up the chaff with which the harvests of ninety years had cumbered the soil's threshing-floor, was a thing of their own creation.

1. The Southern Loyalist Convention held in Philadelphia in September 1866 brought together southern Republicans from every state in order to rally their support against President Johnson's Reconstruction policies. Tourgée represented Guilford County, North Carolina, at the convention.

Unconsciously to itself, the Republican party at the commencement of the war rose to the dignity of a party of right against wrong, of justice against expediency, of principle against policy. Accident offered it this character, and an overwhelming necessity compelled its acceptance. It was successful during the war simply because this was its character. It inaugurated a new school of political thought in our nation. "Right or wrong" was made the test question upon all political issues. The issues presented were mostly those of direct and apparent right against unmistakable wrong. The people supported the right because it was right and they were true. In so doing they supported the Republican party, because it happened to be on the side of right, and not right because it was on the side of the Republican party. This fact the leaders of that party have never yet apprehended. They regard that mighty exhibition of popular conscience which sustained and carried on the war, as a pleasant humbug, and its rallying cry—Justice, Liberty and Humanity—as one of the most successful tubs ever thrown to that great whale, the people. This was the miserable folly and mistake of the Republican leaders during the war. They thought that they, through the agency of the Republican party, had created the spirit which saved the country from destruction. The contemplation of this imaginary feat has so absorbed the energies of the party leaders, that the Republican members of Congress have had room for but little beside self-gratulation since the close of the war. They flatter themselves with the belief—comfortable, though false—that they are and have been, constantly "ahead of the people." Well does the writer recollect the quiet assumption with which, at the Philadelphia Convention, one of our well-fed M.C.'s folded his hands over his abdominal developments, as said to him, "We were ahead of the people. If we had not stirred up the people constantly the rebellion could never have been put down. The Republicans in Congress were the leaders of the people as the generals were of the army." The writer was one of the "people," and the smoke had scarcely settled about Sumter in 1861 before he had entered the service of the United States to put down rebellion. As he sat and talked with his sleek "leader of the people," he was a scarred and crippled veteran. He wondered if this "leader" thought that his listener was one of those whom he had stirred up, or who needed his stirring up. And yet he knew that the vast body of the people were as earnest upon this matter as himself, and this idea of being "ahead of the people" was an illusion very flattering to the vanity of our Radical Congressmen, but by no means complimentary to their discernment.

From this blindness sprung the only actual political reaction which has taken place since the war—a reaction not in the sentiments of the people, but in the policy of the leaders of the Republican party. Having no confidence in the conscience of the people, regarding the war itself as a sort of campaign document for the Republican party, when it was finally over, they adopted another policy. Before the war every party was Janus-faced, one visage gaping toward the North, the other facing towards the Gulf. It was supposed that the people only supported the right when carefully wheedled into so doing by some cunning policy. Many of the leaders of the Republican party were trained in this ante-war school and were no doubt skilled in the mystery of harmonizing the needs of slavery and freedom, in catering at once for North and South successfully. They are men who, having once become settled to one mode of action, can adopt no other. As soon, therefore, as the war was over, they considered that the special pleading of the Republican party was at an end. It would not do any longer to press any political measure because it was absolutely and essentially just, but the dose of righteousness must be sugared over with a coat of policy, or, in other words, covered with a lie. The Republican party had dealt with truths during the war, it must do so no more. The people must be deceived into its support. This was the *reaction*.

In accordance with this policy the political campaign of 1866 was builded on that matchless lie, the Howard [Fourteenth] Amendment as a finality in reconstruction. Everyone knew that it must be either a shameless lie, or an absolute surrender and betrayal of all the rights of the colored men of the South, not excepting those who had fought against rebellion. This was the first fruit of the *reaction* which has periled the life of the Republican party. From that day to this it has lost ground. If they had taken the suffrage issue when first presented, and stood squarely upon it as a matter of intrinsic right, they would have been triumphantly sustained. The people would have accepted it as a right, but as a means of strengthening the Republican party they care nothing about it.

This change of policy, from What is Right to What will Win, at first puzzled the people. They could not understand why certain evidently just and proper measures did not meet the support of the Republican leaders. The fact has, however, at length forced itself upon very many of the most active and valuable men of the country, that our Republican Congressmen are more anxious about re-electing each other than about reconstructing the government, more concerned in the election of a President than in doing justice to all.

The latest exhibition of this anxiety is in the reference to the Conventions now in session in the late rebel States. Each at this time a delegation of Republican lobbyists from Washington are said to be at Richmond to prevent

the Virginia Constitution Convention doing anything which might prejudice
the Republican party. It makes no difference what may be the needs of the
people in these States, the Republican party and its interests are paramount.
It must be saved though the liberties of the people are left unprotected. Much
of the legislation which it thus sought to smother is not only very just and
proper, but absolutely essential to the future people and prosperity of the
states concerned.

Again the "reaction" cry, striking as it does the little remaining courage
from the hearts of the thimble-riggers of the party, has developed a sudden
and pressing necessity for relieving a large portion of the present excluded
classes from disability. In so doing it is not proposed to afford specific relief
to men who ought not to have been disfranchised at the first, but to offer a
reward for party work in the matter of reconstruction. There are many men
here who, according to the letter of the acts, are disfranchised, but who were
as good Union men during the entire war as the South could show, yet after
it was over honestly differed with the policy of Congress upon the matter of
Reconstruction. These men were disfranchised upon the hypothesis that they
had been disloyal to the United States, and in all cases where the reverse can
be shown are of course entitled to relief from disabilities by Congress. These,
however, are not the men whom it is proposed by "Reactionists" to relieve, but
those who have done party-work, those who were shrewd enough to foresee the
success of the party and ally themselves with it in good time. It is said these
men "must be rewarded," that they have "condoned their offences," etc. As if
work done for the Republican party, with the prospect of fat offices in view,
could condone an offence against the government of the United States!

These are a few of the measures which, if preserved in for a while longer, if
forced upon the Republican party to avoid the fancied terrors of "Reaction,"
will most certainly react upon the minds of all just and patriotic men and
sound the knell of Republicanism.

The only way to save it alive, is to come back to standard of Right and
Wrong, stand squarely upon the principles of Justice, and select a Presidential
candidate who shall represent them positively. A double-faced candidate will
complete its ruin.

winegar

3

Speech on Elective Franchise (1868)*

Tourgée delivered this speech on Friday, February 21, 1868, before a session of the North Carolina constitutional convention. Hastily prepared, Tourgée's twenty-three-page handwritten copy reproduced here may not reflect the exact words he spoke that day. Newspaper reports, however, verify the general accuracy of his prepared text. Tourgée's unequivocal support for black suffrage and resounding embrace of the principle of racial equality were designed to energize the large majority of Republican delegates who were native white southerners. While it was a fait accompli that Republicans would include black suffrage in their revised constitution, Tourgée evidently wanted the convention to undertake this unprecedented step enthusiastically—out of moral conviction rather than mere political expediency.

The *North Carolinian*, a conservative newspaper, acknowledged the impact of Tourgée's speech upon the convention when it reported that he "drew crocodile tears from his sympathetic listeners" and even became choked with emotion himself at times while delivering it. The reporter added derisively that "in listening to his tribute to their valor and patriotism during the war, the uninformed hearer would have thought the nigger alone 'crushed the rebellion'" (*Raleigh North Carolinian*, February 22, 1868).

Mr. President: The manner in which this question has been discussed has certainly awakened my surprise. The attention of the Convention has been chiefly directed to the question of the colored man's right to vote. This to my apprehension sir, is a dead issue, a settled question, it has been forever fixed and decided by the colored man himself. Not in the remote and indistinct past alone, but in the days and years that are fresh in memory of all in that conflict which the nation has yet emerged, scarred and dimmed but unweak-

*"Speech on Elective Franchise Delivered in Convention of 1868," item 801, Albion W. Tourgée Papers, Chautauqua County Historical Society.

ened, it seems but a few days sir since I was one of those who were swayed and controlled by that unmanly prejudice that has found such full expression on this floor, since I too thought the negro a kin to the brute and accepted the truth stamped upon the first page of God's revelations of one blood are all nations of the earth, with a proviso. I can remember sir, when in my folly, I recoiled at the idea the uniform I wore should ever cover a black breast, or the Flag which I served be upborn by bayonets in the hands of dusky soldiers.

I confess it now with shame, as I dwell upon it now there comes before me a picture photographed forever on my mind. It is a sunny slope in Tennessee the wreck and ruin of a bloody battle lie around. Carnage has builded his alter there and his myriad of victims is cast upon it. The sacrifice is over, and the bloody servitors have departed, the mellowed sunrise casts its glory over all. Beside a stiffened corpse which lies about with tightly folded arms and looks with glassy eyes up into the bright heavens as if appealing for the light of life again bends a young officer, my friend, he seeks for a memento to send to some loved one of the brave man by whose cold clay he knelt. With difficulty he unclasps the folded arms, looses the blue jacket and looks for his watch, it is gone, he unbuttons the vest and there between a black hide and a blue shirt stained with the blood of a dusky martyr finds the colors of his Regiment. That corpse was the Color Sergeant and that the colonel of the 6th United States Colored Infantry massacred at Fort Pillow after fair and honorable surrender, by a fiend who walks today unhung, and clamors for a white man's government.[1] If I ever forget that day and its lesson in noble manhood and ever fail to give my voice and my strength for the equal, political, and civil rights to that race which gave one hundred and eighty thousand such heroes in the darkest hour of the conflict to snatch the banner of freedom from such foes, may God forget me and mine forever. But sir this question has been settled also by the government of the United States when coming time shall hymn the glories of the present era, when our age shall be classic in history, when children shall study our literature and laws with the reverence to which we now turn to Rome and Athens, then the historian will write as the crowning glory of the nineteenth century, the recognition of the rights of manhood. Man is man is the keynote to our civilization.

And it is the highest glory of our country, that she was first among the nations of the earth, to write upon her forehead this great truth, its glory will

1. Tourgée refers to General Nathan Bedford Forrest, leader of the Ku Klux Klan in Tennessee, who had commanded the Confederate troops who attacked Fort Pillow, Tennessee, and notoriously massacred surrendering Union troops, including many African Americans.

shine back like the star of evening over the darkening orient world, and be the beacon light of promise and of joy, to the downtrodden peoples of the old world. The providence of God sweeping through the cycles of the past, like Homer's Gods through space, has turned and overturned the works of man and nations until the American people have been forced to declare amid the anguished throes of dissolution, *Man is Man.* As the great idea of Godhood and its unity filling and inspiring the followers of Mahomet giving power to their arms and victory to their valor was crystalized in that glorious aphorism which has become their watchword, *Allah Allah,* so the great idea of our American nationality and civilization is enthroned in that one word the proudest of earthly names *manhood.* There is no color before the law, black and white are citizens alike of our glorious nationality, co-laborers in working out her destiny and heirs alike with the glories purchased with their mingled blood.

But gentlemen may say that this idea is not universally adopted in the States of this Union and that we have the same right to exclude the colored men in N. Carolina as in New York. The root is dead and the branches will soon wither, you might as well try to stay the tide as the progress of this principle, it is fixed and fixed forever. The solemnity with which some delegates choose to consider this established principle, the tragic garb which they confer upon the past Hob Goblin of an extinct era is really amusing, the earnestness with which they strive to reanimate the defunct negro of our ante war politics is worthy of a better cause. Alas, it is too late, the Ethiopian plank in the Democratic platform has lost its strength. The wet nurse of American politicians will never more frighten their protégés with the blab lipped[,] broken noses[,] long heels and crooked shins of the typical African.

Proudly he stand[s] in the political arena and proclaims himself the peer of his fellow-men, glorying that God has made him such as he is, it will not do[,] the cry has lost its potency[,] the Scepter has departed from Judea, the mournful wail whose cadences have fallen on our ears is but the echo of a dead *lie.*

It is a voice from the tombs like the whining chant of the peddlers of Constantinople in the name of the prophets—*figs.*

The question is not shall any race be excluded from suffrage, but shall any men be debarred from that privilege whether they be white or black and, if so, what men?

The fundamental principle of Republican government I conceive to be that no man shall be deprived of any of the rights and privileges enjoyed by his fellow men, except so far as may be necessary to secure the rights of others.

This principle has forced itself upon the minds of every political philosopher and found expression in myriad forms. It has burst through every artificial organization of society and struggled on towards its own fulfillment, despotism could not crush it, and revolutions have compelled monarchs to acknowledge its truth, it is greater than Constitutions being the rock upon which all true government is founded.

"I have saved the Republic" was the only answer of the great Roman, when asked if he had not violated the law. The safety of the state is the highest law, was the rightest truth which the medieval philosopher could glean from all the wisdom of the ancient lore.

This truth has also been forced upon the American people as one of the eternal principles, which the omniscient wisdom has ordained and which neither men nor nations can violate with impunity. It is the pith and marrow of the war through which we have passed; its first lesson. Upon no other ground, can that great uprising of freemen which crushed the power of rebellion be justified or excused.

No legal sophistry, no self-styled Science, no superficial lore, can stand before its Damascenic edge: law, customs, interests, institutions fall before it. It is the instinct of justice more true and certain than the wisdom of the schools: It is the truth of Almighty God written in the watch fires of a hundred circling camps, the American people read the message aright, they obeyed its teachings and victory purchased upon their Standard; their deliverance was accomplished, the peon was shouted, the people were free—the nation was saved. How soon was the lesson forgotten. Rejoicing for the triumph, sorrow for the dead and pity for the conquered mingled in every heart.

The nation mourned. Her noble sons had fallen in the conflict, by hundreds of thousands, every family mourned. Every hearthstone was draped and the wreath . . . rested sweetly on a half-million of martyr-graves. The nation mourned. Its heart was tender. Mercy gleamed in every teardrop, and joy at our great triumph, sorrow for the dead and pity for the conquered, mingled in every breast. At that hour, the American people would have received the people of the rebel states with open arms, to a full commission of political privileges and rights. Those "to whom nations and peoples are but kind," saw fit to change this mood. The hand of the assassin struck the beloved head of our nation, and he was borne to his beautiful prairie tomb amid the waiting of millions of indignant mourners. It was enough. Justice resumed her sway. Without forgetting mercy the sword of justice was unsheathed. The immortal maxim of the Hero-martyr whom they mourned was enshrined in every

heart—"to do the right as God gives us to see the right." That glorious principle was made the corner-stone of future legislation. And what was the result?
How has this great lesson been crystallized in our laws?

The amendment known as the 14th Article of the Constitution of the
United States, the Civil Rights Bill and Reconstruction Acts are its glorious
first fruits. Shall our Constitution be another? That is the question we are
called upon to decide.

But against what danger are we called upon to guard? How shall the safety
of the State be secured? How shall this greatest of political principles be
applied?

The war which has just closed was indeed a war of great ideas. But those
ideas were wider and deeper than the gentleman from Beaufort seems to apprehend. It was not simply between Slavery—African servitude—and the
non-enslavement of that race. It was between the principles of free labor, free
speech and free truth and oligarchy builded upon, fed and sustained by slavery. Slavery was the mere feeder, the nurse and supporter of Aristocracy. The
basis principle of the Rebellion was not Slavery. That institution was a mere
concomitant, a companion piece of the greater, fouler, and more damnable
principle—a few are born to rule, the rest of mankind to obey—a few should
govern, the many serve.

This was the basis principle of the rebellion, the corner stone of the Confederacy, to maintain power in the hands of the few, the rights and liberties
of the many were overthrown. Color was nothing, caste was everything in the
theory of the rebellion. It was builded upon the principle that labor was the
badge of servitude, that a nation was composed of two classes only, the ruling class and the serving class, it was enunciated by the master mind of that
movement in the columns of De Bows Review in these words. "I am aware
that in order that one real gentleman may live, a thousand paupers must die,
yet I would by all means make them and make them permanent by laws of
entail and primogeniture."

This was the object and purpose of the Confederacy, the pith and marrow
of the rebellion.

Men were to be divided into gentlemen and servants, nobles and serfs,
color had not place in the creed, the poor white man was to be the compeer of
the Ethiopian slave.

Did time permit, a thousand witnesses could be produced of the truth of
this statement, I will refer to but one. It has been often noted sir, with what
accuracy the minds of the common people grasp a great truth and enshrine

it in a maxim, never shall I forget how vividly this fact forced itself upon my mind when a prisoner in one of the Confederate Bastilles, a garrulous soldier, said to me with mournful emphasis "ah! Sir, this is the rich man's [war] and the poor man's fight," it was the whole matter in a nutshell, a volume in a sentence. The war from which we have just emerged was a struggle between Republicanism and Oligarchy, between the rights of the people and the usurpations of Aristocracy, between the elevation of the mass and the exaltation of the few, between feudal theory and free principles. It was the old sophism of the divine right to rule, and the ambition of a pampered aristocracy pitted against the unerring instincts of a few people.

The war of the Revolution established and fixed upon this continent the principle of national freedom and equality of right. The struggle was not ended. The young giant was exhausted, by years of war . . . and fruit were necessary that he might be able to grapple with the great Dragon Despotism again and in more deadly form.

Meanwhile, the mighty foe had been strengthened by the same years of rest, and had become entrenched at the South, and had made Slavery the bulwark which the next battle of the war of Republicanism against Oligarchy was to be fought. The issue was made up, the battle fought[,] the rampart carried[,] one more stronghold of oppression was overthrown. Did the struggle end here? Was the accursed spirit which animated and maintained Rebellion finally exorcised by defeat? Did the few renounce their right to rule, and yield the sovereignty to the people? If so, we have, nothing more to fear. The ballot may then be safely entrusted to all, within the limits of the state. If we are assured that these men accepted in its fullness the arbitrament of war, if they were willing that the poor and the oppressed, the humble and the enslaved, should stand forth erect as when they came from the hand of the Creator and enjoy the same rights and privileges as themselves, then indeed the ends of justice are accomplished and our liberties are secure. But let us see, what was the first act of these men whom the mercy of the Conqueror had spared from destruction, was to spurn the freedman, the former slave to whom they owed a debt which eternity is hardly long enough to liquidate, spurned him with contempt and obloquy from their door. They left him desolate and alone to struggle with the world which their own enslavement had unfitted him to grapple with. Did they devise means for his elevation and education? Did they take the outcast whom they claim to be so terribly degraded, by the hand and strive to lift him up and purify, prepare him for the duties of the man and the citizen? Or did they with cowardly spite seek to drive him further into vice and press him lower into degradation? Did they grant him the rights of manhood before the law or did they shut him from the jury-box—no matter how intelligent and how honorable he might become? Did they put him upon the witness stand and allow a jury, even of themselves to decide upon his credibility as a witness or did they declare that his testimony against a white man was void? Did they allow him representation when taxed or did they put an unheard of tax upon his property and the employer responsible for its payment? Did they grant him any of the rights of a man, not to say freeman which they dared withhold? Did they grant to him the right to a voice in the formation and execution of the laws by which he was governed as did they decree that one sixteenth of negro blood should debar him from the privileges of citizenship? Did they grant them one single right or privilege civil, political, moral and educational, or did they deny them all, and then came and justify the offense, because some doctor, proscribing for his own disease had found the negro's shin to be as crooked as the paths [of] treason? But did they go further? Did they burn churches and school houses built by the toil-earned money of the newly-freed slave, and the kindly charity of earnest friends? Did they do more? Let Memphis and New Orleans answer. I shudder at the picture. It is too horrible for recital. I turn to another branch of inquiry.

Did they offer reparation of past injury? Did they restore that of which they had robbed the poor? Did they provide that the malefactor should suffer for his crimes? Did they declare that the cries of woman tortured and children maimed by inhuman monsters in unholy warfare should reach the ears of justice and punishment be meted out impartially? Or did they vote immunity to all, balk the loyal man of his remedy and permit the foulest demons who have disgraced the earth to go unpunished? Did they offer any reparation for any act committed? If so, when and what? Were they sorry for the act of rebellion or did they glory in the misery and carnage, suffering and woe which their own foul wickedness had wrought? Do they show penitence for crime or do they openly boast that their only regret is that they did not more deeply imbue souls in blood and crime, their only sorrow that the foul wickedness they inaugurated was not completed and perfected in all terrific vileness? Do they honor loyalty and treat with respect the patriot who refused to sully his fame forever by taking any part or lot in their unparalleled crime, who took his life in his own hand, and chose to run the gauntlet of guards and spies, who chose rather to match himself in cunning and fortitude with the myriad blood hounds of conscription; who left home, friends and family to the mercy of the merciless rather than become a party to the overthrow of our glorious nationality whose loyalty was tried as no people's was ever tried and came forth from the crucible pure gold: Do they honor these patriots for their devotion to the government which they now claim to serve, or do they come upon this floor and with a vengefulness worthy of Cataline ask that every such man, shall be deprived of the election franchise?

Do they even honor him who gave his strength to the unholy cause until hope was lost and success despaired of, and who at the last moment of this final hour, threw down his arms, accepted in hearty good will the terms of the conquering power and put himself in the harness, to render effective and successful the policy and laws of the government to which he owed his life and fortune or does he curse him as a renegade and a traitor, and ask that he too may be shut out from the privileges of freedmen[?]

Are they loyal or do they come upon this floor boastful only that they do not longer offer resistance to the government of the United States?

What has been their course toward the government of the United States? Have they accepted the terms offered in mercy or flung them back with scorn?

Have these men power and is that power dangerous?

Will it be increased by giving the right of suffrage?

The power of the states is exercised through the ballot.

We are told that we are not the tribunal to punish crime against the United States.

We are told that we should not go farther than Congress of the U.S.

Let us follow Congress. It is God-like to forgive. Summa justitiu est summa injuria.

Should we confer this right upon these men? Can we go before our Constituents and stand before the future and say that we have fulfilled this greatest, highest principle of government, and answer like the noble Roman, "I have saved the Republic?"

4

Letter to the *North Carolina Standard* (1870)*

This letter to the editor of the *North Carolina Standard*, published on January 28, 1870, shows the methods Tourgée's enemies used against him and his attempts to counter them. While Tourgée was serving as superior court justice for the Seventh District of North Carolina, his jurisprudence came under attack for its alleged political biases. In this case, Tourgée twice set aside the guilty verdict of a black man convicted of larceny on weak evidence for which he was accused of favoritism by sympathizers of the Ku Klux Klan. Defending his decisions, Tourgée explained his conduct in the case and proclaimed his ideal of "color blind" justice.

Editor of STANDARD,

As you are aware I am not accustomed to pay any attention whatever to the assaults of traducers, being satisfied that the majority of them are simply contemptible fabrications of feeble minded malice. Having, however, been assailed in public debate upon the floor of the [state] Senate; and also (as I am informed) in the House, as the cause and origin of all the trouble in the county of Orange, I feel bound to lay the circumstances before the public, not in self-defense, but simply that it may be seen from what the clamor has sprung. It was stated by Mr. Graham, of Orange, on Monday night last in the Senate, that the excuse offered for all the outrages committed by disguised persons in his county, *by the parties who were guilty of them,* was that they could not trust the Courts because I had *twice* granted a new trial to a colored man found guilty of larceny. This, the Senator stated, was what *the men themselves* had told him. I am not sufficiently intimate with any of these men to judge the accuracy of Mr. Graham's statement. But admitting that his faculties for obtaining information upon this point are far superior to my own, since I have not the honor of knowing "the men themselves," I wish to call attention to the excuse alleged and its sufficiency.

*"Letter to the Editor," *North Carolina Standard,* January 28, 1870.

The case referred to (as I suppose) was that of "The State v. Dennis Haines." It was first tried at Spring Term (May) 1869. Previous to this time there had been several cases of outrages committed by gangs of disguised men, in that county, one of which the "Steele case" obtained considerable notoriety. Several others were reported to the Solicitor, but the Grand Jury found no bill against any of them.

I suppose that setting aside the verdict a second time, could hardly be counted an excuse for, or a cause of, the acts committed before the case had been tried at all.

Again before the Fall Term of the Court had arrived, the jail at Hillsboro had been broken open, by armed men in disguise, two men taken out and one of them murdered in cold blood not far from the town, two men hanged by the road, and numerous other acts of "wild justice," as Mr. Graham terms them, committed by "wild" men in that county. Before the second trial of this cause had come on, organized murder had become so prevalent in the county that the Governor had threatened to send troops there, to protect the citizens.

At the Fall Term of 1869—in November; the case came on for trial a second time. A verdict of guilty was rendered, and a new trial granted. Since that time, so far as I have been advised, there has been less outrages in that county than before. I cannot exactly see how my granting a new trial for the second time to Denis Hains [*sic*], in November, 1869, *could* have been *an excuse for*, or *cause of* the murder committed, upon the tenth of August or sixth of October preceding.

This much as to the setting aside this verdict. Now let us consider the act itself. Immediately after the remarks made upon the matter in the Senate, I wrote to Henry K. Nash, Esq. of Hillsboro,' the defendant's counsel, and asked him to put in writing his recollection of the entire case. This morning I received his reply. His recollection differs from my own in one immaterial point, I give it, however, entire, and accept it as a fair, clear and lawyer-like statement of the case. The following is his letter:

HILLSBORO, Jan. 25, 1870.

Hon. A. W. TOURGEE:

Dear Sir:—I received your letter of the 24th inst. this morning and reply at my earliest convenience as requested.

I have regretted to see the comments made by some of our public journals upon your action in the case alluded to by you, because I thought at the time, and still think it was right and proper. The facts in the case are, as I recollect them, that Dennis Haines, colored, was indicted at Spring Term, 1869, for larceny. The State introduced Mr. Jas. Parks, of this place, as a witness, who proved that some months before his house of business was entered and a pair of boots, shoes, leather, and other articles were stolen therefrom. That he had never seen or heard of any of the articles since, except the boots which he recovered, and had only heard of them some four or five weeks after the larceny.

Mr. A. W. Cheek was then introduced by the State, who proved that some three or four weeks after hearing of the larceny, being in the city of Raleigh, he saw the boots identified by Parks in the store of Mr. Upchurch, and recognized them as the boots lost by Parks, and upon returning to Hillsboro' he reported this fact to Parks. Mr. Upchurch proved that on or about the day that Cheek recognized the boots the defendant, Dennis Hains, [*sic*] brought them to him openly, and in the day time, and pawned them to him for $5, saying that he was on his way down the country, and as he returned if he had the money, he would redeem them. The boots were worth $9. Before the defendant returned they were delivered to Mr. Parks. This was the case for the state—no evidence was offered by the defendant and the case was submitted to the jury under the charge of your Honor.

The charge of the Court was to the effect, that the only evidence against the defendant was his possession of the boots several weeks after the larceny. And his being found in possession of the stolen goods, did not raise such a presumption in law of his guilt, as would justify a verdict of guilty in the absence of any other testimony.

The jury returned a verdict of "guilty," whereupon I, as counsel for the defendant, moved the Court to set aside the verdict and grant the defendant a new trial, on the grounds that it was against the charge of the Court and that there was not sufficient evidence to sustain it. This was done and the defendant bound in his own recognizance to appear at the Fall Term of the Court to answer, &c. The Court also directed that if at the next Term no further evidence could be introduced by the State, that the solicitor enter a *nol. pros.* At Fall Term the case was again called for trial, counsel having been retained to appear with Solicitor. It was announced by the State that additional evidence had been obtained and the second trial was had. The State introduced Mr. Parks, Mr. Cheek, and Mr. Upchurch, who all proved what they had proved on the former, neither more nor less.

Washington Lay (colored) was then called by the State, and asked if he knew the defendant? He said, "he did." He was then asked if he knew how he made his living? He said, "he did not." This was the only additional testimony to that given on the first trial. The case was then argued by the counsel and then submitted under the charge of the Judge which was in substance the same as in the first trial. The Jury after retiring, returned with a verdict of "Guilty." I again moved the Court to set aside the verdict and grant a new trial, and in reply to the State remarked that the fact of another Jury having convicted the defendant on the same evidence should not weigh with the Court if the conviction was an improper one, for the fact that it was as much the duty of the Court to protect the innocent, or those not convicted, according to the law, and the evidence, as it was to punish the guilty. I also said, that I was afraid that prejudice, unknown to the jurors themselves, had entered the jury-box, for that I did not believe a white man would have been convicted upon the evidence in the case, and under the same charge from the Court. I may have been wrong in my opinion of the law, as applicable to the case, but I thought I was right then and am of the same opinion still.

Your Honor, after hearing the motion argued, promptly set aside the verdict, and granted the defendant a new trial, and in so doing, did what I think was eminently right and proper.

I have written this statement hastily, but think I have omitted no material fact. My own conclusions are as I have stated above.

Very respectfully,
Your obedient servant,
HENRY K. NASH

Entertaining the same opinions with Mr. Nash, as to the law of the case, I had only this alternative,—set the verdict aside, and grant a new trial, or be guilty of a great and glaring injustice to the defendant. Believing that the evidence was legally insufficient for conviction I acted accordingly. Had I done otherwise I should have avoided the clamor and abuse that has been heaped upon me, but I should have despised myself forever, as one who did evil in the seat of justice from a cowardly fear of the slanderer. I shall continue to act upon my own sense of justice, my own apprehension of the law, and my own conviction of duty entirely unmindful of whether the same please friend or foe, or accords with the administration of "wild justice" in the county of Orange or elsewhere or not. I prize my own self respect too highly to do otherwise, and believing as I do that justice should at least be "color blind," I shall know no man by the hue of his skin.

A. W. Tourgee
Judge Superior Court 7th Jud. Dist.
Greensboro, N.C. Jan. 28, 1870.

5

Letter to Senator Joseph C. Abbott (1870)*

This letter to U.S. Senator Joseph C. Abbott, written on May 24, 1870, was published in the *New York Tribune*, August 3, 1870. Tourgée informed Senator Abbott of the murder of his close friend Republican state senator John Walter Stephens and offered shocking testimony to the extent and brutality of Ku Klux Klan violence in his judicial district. Tourgée also urged Senator Abbott to support legislation to empower strong federal action against the Klan. Soon afterward, on May 31, 1870, the U.S. Congress passed the first Enforcement Act, which struck back at the Klan by making it a felony to attempt to deprive another person of his civil or political rights as defined by the U.S. Constitution. This letter circulated widely on Capitol Hill that summer, influencing many in Washington, and eventually made its way into the *New York Tribune* in August. Tourgée was dismayed when the *Tribune* published his letter without his authorization.

Greensboro, May 24, 1870.

My Dear General,

It is my mournful duty to inform you that our friend John W. Stephens, State Senator from Caswell, is dead. He was foully murdered by the Ku-Klux in the Grand Jury room of the Court House on Saturday or Saturday night last. The circumstances attending his murder have not yet fully come to light there. So far as I can learn, I judge these to have been the circumstances: He was one of the Justices of the Peace in that township, and was accustomed to hold court in that room on Saturdays. It is evident that he was set upon by someone while holding this court, or immediately after its close, and disabled by a sudden attack, otherwise there would have been a very sharp resistance, as he was a man, and always went armed to the teeth. He was stabbed five or six times, and then hanged on a hook in the Grand Jury room, where he was found on Sunday morning. Another brave, honest Republican citizen has met

*"Justice Albion W. Tourgée to Senator Abbott, May 24, 1870," *New York Tribune*, August 3, 1870.

his fate at the hands of these fiends. Warned of his danger, and fully cognizant of the terrible risk which surrounded him, he still manfully refused to quit the field. Against the advice of his friends, against the entreaties of his family, he constantly refused to leave those who had stood by him in the day of his disgrace and peril. He was accustomed to say that 3,000 poor, ignorant, colored Republican voters in that county had stood by him and elected him, at the risk of persecution and starvation, and that he had no idea of abandoning them to the Ku-Klux. He was determined to stay with them, and either put an end to these outrages, or die with the other victims of Rebel hate and national apathy. Nearly six months ago I declared my belief that before the election in August next the Ku-Klux would have killed more men in the State than there would be members to be elected to the Legislature. A good beginning has been made toward the fulfillment of this prophecy.

The following counties have already filled, or nearly so, their respective "quotas:" Jones County, quota full, excess 1; Orange County, quota full, excess, 1; Caswell County, quota full, excess, 2; Alamance County, quota full, excess, 1; Chatham County, quota nearly full. Or, to state the matter differently, there have been twelve murders in five counties of the district during the past eighteen months by bands of disguised villains. In addition to this, from the best information I can derive, I am of the opinion that in this district alone there have been 1,000 outrages of a less serious nature perpetrated by the same masked fiends. Of course this estimate is not made from any absolute record, nor is it possible to ascertain with accuracy the entire number of beatings and other outrages which have been perpetrated. The uselessness, the utter futility of complaint from the lack of ability in the laws to punish is fully known to all. The danger of making such complaint is also well understood. It is therefore not unfrequently by accident that the outrage is found out, and unquestionably it is frequently absolutely concealed. Thus, a respectable, hard working white carpenter was working for a neighbor, when accidentally his shirt was torn, and disclosed his back scarred and beaten. The poor fellow begged for the sake of his wife and children that nothing might be said about it, as the Ku-Klux had threatened to kill him if he disclosed how he had been outraged. Hundreds of cases have come to my notice and that of my solicitor, in which we have hardly ascertained the names of the parties suffering violence.

Men and women come scarred, mangled, and bruised, and say: "The Ku-Klux came to my house last night and beat me almost to death, and my old woman right smart, and shot into the house, 'bust' the door down, and told me they would kill me if I made complaint," and the bloody mangled forms attest the truth of their declarations. On being asked if any one knew any of the party it will be ascertained that there was no recognition, or only the most uncertain and doubtful one. In such cases as these nothing can be done by the court. We have not been accustomed to enter them on record. A man of the best standing in Chatham told me that he could count up 200 and upward in that county. In Alamance County, a citizen in conversation one evening enumerated upward of 50 cases which had occurred within his own knowledge, and in one section of the county. He gave it as his opinion that there had been 200 cases in that county. I have no idea that he exceeded the proper estimate. That was six months ago, and I am satisfied that another hundred would not cover the work done in that time.

These crimes have been of every character imaginable. Perhaps the most usual has been the dragging of men and women from their beds, and beating their naked bodies with hickory switches, or as witnesses in an examination the other day said, "sticks" between a "switch" and a "club." From 50 to 100 blows is the usual allowance, sometimes 200 and 300 blows are administered. Occasionally an instrument of torture is owned. Thus in one case two women, one 74 years old, were taken out, stripped naked, and beaten with a paddle, with several holes bored through it. The paddle was about 30 inches long, 3 or 4 inches wide, and 1/4 of an inch thick, of Oak. Their bodies were so bruised and beaten that they were sickening to behold. They were white women and of good character until the younger was seduced, and swore her child to its father. Previous to that and so far as others were concerned her character was good.

Again, there is sometimes a fiendish malignity and cunning displayed in the form and character of the outrages. For instance, a colored man was placed astride of a log, and an iron staple driven through his person into the log. In another case, after a band of them had in turn violated a young negro girl, she was forced into bed with a colored man, their bodies were bound together face to face, and the fire from the hearth piled upon them. The K.K.K. rode off and left them, with shouts of laughter. Of course the bed was soon in flames, and somehow they managed to crawl out, though terribly burned and scarred. The house was burned.

I could give other incidents of cruelty, such as hanging up a boy of nine years old until he was nearly dead, to make him tell where his father was hidden, and beating an old negress of 103 years old with garden partings because she would not own that she was afraid of the Ku-Klux. But it is unnecessary to go into further detail. In this district I estimate their offenses as follows, in the past ten months: Twelve murders, 9 rapes, 11 arsons, 7 mutilations, ascertained and most of them on record. In some no identification could be made.

Four thousand or 5,000 houses[1] have been broken open, and property or persons taken out. In all cases all arms are taken and destroyed. Seven hundred or 800 persons have been beaten or otherwise maltreated. These of course are partly persons living in the houses which were broken into.

And yet the Government sleeps. The poor disarmed nurses of the Republican party—those men by whose ballots the Republican party holds power—who took their lives in their hands when they cast their ballots for U. S. Grant and other officials—all of us who happen to be beyond the pale of the governmental regard—must be sacrificed, murdered, scourged, mangled, because some contemptible party scheme might be foiled by doing us justice. I could stand it very well to fight for Uncle Sam, and was never known to refuse an invitation on such an occasion, but this lying down, tied hand and foot with the shackles of the law, to be killed by the very dregs of the rebellion, the scum of the earth, and not allowed either the consolation of fighting or the satisfaction that our "fall" will be noted by the Government, and protection given to others thereby, is somewhat too hard. I am ashamed of the nation that will let its citizens be slain by scores, and scourged by thousands, and offer no remedy or protection. I am ashamed of a State which has not sufficient strength to protect its own officers in the discharge of their duties, nor guarantee the safety of any man's domicile throughout its length and breadth. I am ashamed of a party which, with the reins of power in its hands, has not nerve or decision enough to arm its own adherents, or to protect them from assassinations at the hands of their opponents. A General who in time of war would permit 2,000 or 3,000 of his men to be bushwhacked and destroyed by private treachery even in an enemy's country without any one being punished for it would be worthy of universal execration, and would get it, too. How much more worthy of detestation is a Government which in time of peace will permit such wholesale slaughter of its citizens? It is simple cowardice, inertness, and wholesale demoralization. The wholesale slaughter of the war has dulled our Nation's sense of horror at the shedding of blood, and the habit of regarding the South as simply a laboratory, where every demagogue may carry on his reconstructionary experiments at will, and not as an integral party of the Nation itself, has led our Government to shut its eyes to the atrocities of these times. Unless these evils are speedily remedied, I tell you, General, the Republican Party has signed its death warrant. It is a party of cowards or idiots—I don't care which alternative is chosen. The remedy

1. Tourgée claimed that the *New York Tribune* transcribed this number incorrectly from his original letter (now lost), in which he estimated four hundred or five hundred houses had been broken open by the Klan.

is in our hands, and we are afraid or too dull to bestir ourselves and use it.

But you will tell me that Congress is ready and willing to act if it only knew what to do. Like the old Irish woman it wrings its hands and cries, "O Lawk, O Lawk, if I only knew which way." And yet this same Congress has the control of the militia and can organize its own force in every county in the United States, and arm more or less of it. This same Congress has the undoubted right to guarantee and provide a republican government, and protect every citizen in "life, liberty, and the pursuit of happiness," as well as the power conferred by the XVth Amendment. And yet we suffer and die in peace and murderers walk abroad with the blood yet fresh upon their garments, unharmed, unquestioned and unchecked. Fifty thousand dollars given to good detectives would secure, if well used, a complete knowledge of all this gigantic organization of murderers. In connection with an organized and armed militia, it would result in the apprehension of any number of these thugs *en masque* and with blood on their hands. What then is the remedy?

First: Let Congress give to the U.S. Courts, or to Courts of the States under its own laws, cognizance of this class of crimes, as crimes against the Nation, and let it provide that this legislation be enforced. Why not, for instance, make going armed and masked or disguised, or masked or disguised in the night time, an act of insurrection or sedition? *Second:* Organize militia, National—State militia is a nuisance—and arm as many as may be necessary in each county to enforce its laws. *Third:* Put detectives at work to get hold of this whole organization. Its ultimate aim is unquestionably to revolutionize the Government. If we have not pluck enough for this, why then let us just offer our throats to the knife, emasculate ourselves, and be a nation of self-subjugated slaves at once.

And now, Abbott, I have but one thing to say to you. I have very little doubt that I shall be one of the next victims. My steps have been dogged for months, and only a good opportunity has been wanting to secure to me the fate which Stephens has just met, and I speak earnestly upon this matter. I feel that I have a right to do so, and a right to be heard as well, and with this conviction I say to you plainly that any member of Congress who, especially if from the South, does not support, advocate, and urge immediate, active, and thorough measures to put an end to these outrages, and make citizenship a privilege, is a coward, a traitor, or a fool. The time for action has come, and the man who has now only speeches to make over some Constitutional scarecrow, deserves to be damned.

Yours respectfully,
A. W. Tourgee

6

Letter to Martin B. Anderson (1874)*

This letter, written to his mentor, University of Rochester president Martin B. Anderson, addressed Tourgée's chances for election as U.S. congressman in the upcoming 1874 election. Evaluating Republican prospects in the election, Tourgée harshly criticizes the Civil Rights Bill proposed by recently deceased Massachusetts senator Charles Sumner. He feared that if passed, the bill would become effective propaganda for the Democratic Party. It prohibited racial segregation in most public accommodations, including hotels, theaters, railroad cars and streetcars, and public schools. While the bill reflected "good doctrine" and "fine theory," Tourgée warns that it will destroy the public school system in the South because white southerners would rather close public schools than see them racially integrated. Subsequently, Tourgée lost the Republican nomination to moderate William F. Henderson, a white North Carolina native, who subsequently lost in a nationwide Democratic landslide victory in the fall 1874 elections. For the first time since the Civil War, the Democrats captured both houses of Congress, thus ensuring the end of further Reconstruction legislation. Many historians attribute this electoral reversal in the southern states to the widespread reaction against the Civil Rights Bill. When the lame-duck Republican Congress finally passed the bill in early 1875, it dropped the provision to include public schools to appease moderate white Republicans, especially those in the South.

Greensboro, N.C.

May 11, 1874

My Dear Doctor:

Your letter is rec'd and places me under new obligations for your kindness. You would hardly write so coolly of my election—I suppose—if you knew the situation fully. I am hardly sure of the nomination. It is admitted that I am the *only* man who has a ghost of a chance to carry the Dist[rict], but a man

*Albion W. Tourgée to Martin B. Anderson, May 11, 1874, item 1739, Albion Winegar Tourgée Papers, Chautauqua County Historical Society.

whom I run off four years ago, after he had brought up a nomination by one vote, proposed to have his revenge now. It is surely possible he may defeat the nomination. If he does not, he will do his best to defeat me and one cannot carry too much weight in a Dist. like this. My hope is, if I cannot be elected, to make a caucus which shall be remembered. . . . *I* believe I can carry the Dist.—but *I honestly think* I am the only one who does believe it.

The worst thing will be the Civil Rights Bill—Sumner's Supplementary— I know the maxim *De Mortis Nihil* & etc, but I have no use for those who prescribe for disease without knowing their nature. Sumner knew no more of the actual condition of the colored man here than he realized his condition on the Gold Coast. The bill—with all respect to its author, is just like a blister plaster put on a dozing man whom it is desirable to soothe to sleep. The most important thing in the world is to let the South forget the negro for a bit: let him acquire property, stability, and self-respect; let as many as possible be educated; in short let the race itself get used to freedom[,] self-dependence and proper self-assertion; and then let his bill come little by little if necessary. Of course, if it becomes law, it will constantly be avoided. No man can frame a statute which some other cannot avoid. For all its beneficent purposes it will be a dead letter. For its evil influences it will be vivid and active. It will be like the firebrands between the tails of Sampson's foxes. It is just pure folly and the results from what I have long claimed, that the people of the North and our Legislators, will not study the people of the South reasonably. They will not remember that a prejudice 250 years old (at least) should only be legislated against when *positively harmful,* and should always be let alone when it only conflicts with good doctrine—fine theory.

It will utterly destroy the bulk of our common schools in the South. These States will throw them aside at once and the people, except in those where there is a colored majority, will approve. They are not over-fond of Education here at the best. Our poor white people have to be fed a heap of soft corn to get them to take much stock in it, and the old slave owners *et cet,* do not see any great need in general education. A tax for free schools is as unwelcome as a vapor bath in dog days. If we get this fool's notion imposed on us, good-bye schools in the South. It simply delays—puts back—the thorough and complete rehabilitation of the South ten or twenty years. It is the idea of a visionary quack who prescribes for the disease without having made a diagnosis.

But pardon me, I did not mean to write all of this. If I ever do get to that Canaan of my aspirations I will surely come up and hear you talk finances till you are either satisfied with my proficiency or give me up as a hopeless cause. . . .

7

Letter to E. S. Parker (1875)*

In the fall of 1874, North Carolina conservatives regained a majority in the state assembly, and, in the spring of 1875 they called for a constitutional convention, where they hoped to undo the reforms incorporated in the 1868 state constitution. This letter, published in the *Greensboro New North State* on June 18, 1875, offered a statement of Tourgée's political philosophy and clarified his stance on black suffrage. Since Tourgée had been a prominent member of the 1868 convention, his views on these matters were solicited by editor E. S. Parker, who had asked Tourgée whether he regretted any of the 1868 reforms. Tourgée may have been positioning himself to become a candidate for the upcoming constitutional convention. After this public exchange, voters elected Tourgée to the 1875 convention, where he fought to preserve the 1868 reforms.

Dear Mr. Parker:

Your favor of yesterday is received. . . . In answer to your question, I am not aware of any change in my political faith, nor even an inclination to change. If I were to write my political creed it would be Lincoln's favorite aphorism. "A government *of* the people, *by* the people and *for* the people," including in the term "people" the entire population of the United States. You know, for we have often talked freely of these matters, how broad and deep the foundations of my faith in the people lie. I have no faith in politicians, aristocrats, or classes of any sort. The whole, with the counter-checks of variant interests and conflicting views, is far more likely to do justice and promote the true interests of all, than any part or class. I consider the elements in this definition of American Republicanism to be as inseparable as the Holy Trinity. That theory, plan or idea of government which brings the government most nearly to the people—the whole people—allows them most directly to control and direct it, does away with political "middlemen," damns privileged classes, and

*"A. W. Tourgée to E. S. Parker," *Greensboro New North State*, June 18, 1875.

trains the people most rapidly and effectually in the management of public affairs for their own good—that theory is the one to which I give my unfaltering adhesion. Whatever smacks of political Phariseeism—standing upon the street corner and thanking God that we are not as other men—that I repudiate. It matters not how honest a man may be in that view—it matters not how much he may honestly pride himself upon Caucasian complexion, or his *unmixed* Anglo-Saxon-Norman-Celtic lineage, the very assumption of exclusiveness, or superior right to rule or govern in our own land, is repellant to my instincts, my conviction, and my deliberate belief as to sound policy.

On the other hand, it is well known to you and many others of my personal friends, of both political parties, that I have never fully approved the measures known as the Reconstruction Acts—not from the principles on which they are based, but from what I deemed their insufficiency to secure the end aimed at. This desired end I understand to be the erection of self-regulating republican government in the territory of the late Confederacy in which the equal rights of all citizens, shall be secured and maintained and their highest interests promoted. I entertained this idea of the insufficiency of these measures at the time of their adoption, and have seen no good reason as yet to change it. Indeed, any views in regard to the operation, and results of this policy have been fulfilled with singular accuracy. I *do* hold this to have been "a serious error" on the part of the Republican Party which was then in power—an error in policy, mind you, not in principle. I hold it to have been the duty of that party to have taken such a course, to have so legislated, as to have set at rest forever that host of unpleasant issues—not to say dangerous ones, which are crowding the near future of the South for solution. At the same time, it was a movement, an experiment in the direction of popular government, equal right and universal manhood. While therefore I thought it insufficient and illy-considered in its details, I cheerfully co-operated in the endeavor to secure its success and am heartily glad that I did so.

What plan I think would have been better is immaterial now, as were my convictions then. It has been stated that I thought the negroes should have been educated before they were allowed to vote. In one sense this is true and in another false. I think an ignorant man has the same right to his share in self-government as a wise one. These States, even now, offer a significant illustration of this truth. Had their rehabilitation been left to the 38% of our adult population who are educated, that is not illiterate—the colored man would have now no rights at all, legal or political as opposed to the white citizen, or, in other words, none "which the white man is bound to respect." Fortunately in this State this is not a mere matter of speculation and belief; we have the proposed Constitution of 1865 to justify this conclusion. At the same time, I think that the government owed both the education and training in the duties of civil life, to the slave, and an education to the 24% of illiterate whites whom slavery had kept from knowledge, both as an act of justice and of policy, having a wise regard to its own future. The whole nation was responsible for slavery—there is no shirking that. The nation permitted, encouraged, protected and nurtured it. It justified the Southern man in investing his money in, and building his future upon the basis of slave property. It was responsible, therefore, for the ills which sprung from slavery and was bound in honor and good conscience to repair them, so far as was possible. The greatest evil arising from slavery and continuing when the slave was made a citizen in a governmental view, was the ignorance and inexperience of civil and political duties, which it produced. That the nation should have remedied as speedily, thoroughly and safely as possible, and until it was in good degree remedied, it should never have given the reins of government unreservedly into the hands of communities thus constituted. How could this have been done? By some modification perhaps of the territorial plan by which the internal affairs of these States might have been administered under the supervision of the national government. I think by this means both the extravagance and the lawlessness of the past and the danger of the immediate future might have been avoided.

But, it is urged, that this course would have taken so long a time, perhaps a generation. Ah, there is the trouble. We have no faith in time! We think that the railroad and telegraph have annihilated time and space! Milton wrote that one of the attributes of Hell was the power to compress eternity into an hour. The Republican Party and Congress got an idea that they also had this power. Hence this "serious error." You remember somebody's idea that if a Yankee had had the contract of creation he would have finished it all up in five days and gone fishing on Saturday? It was so with our Republican Congress at the close of the war. They wanted to do the work of a generation in a day.

I tell you Captain, I cannot get over the impression that our children will be fitter men to settle this "hash" than we who have looked into each other's faces over a glimmering gun barrel or pricked at each other's throats with bloody sabers. We are good friends, and find each other pleasurable companions, but there is a heap of human nature in us yet. You know that the law counts a man not precisely indifferent who has merely "formed and expressed an opinion." How would it hold one who had fought for his opinion for four years?

I doubt if this generation will see the end of those questions which a majority of the nation fondly believe to have been settled by the war. I seriously fear that the struggle is not only unconcluded, but also that it has not yet reached the climax of intensity.

I have no idea that my views in regard to political matters past, present or to come, are of any importance, but since you were so courteous as to ask an expression of them, I could not do justice to your inquiry and my own convictions more briefly. I remain with the highest respect,

Yours,

A. W. Tourgee

8

Root, Hog, or Die (ca. 1876)*

Around the time of the 1875 North Carolina constitutional convention, Tourgée began to publish retrospectives on the policies of Reconstruction. These articles, appearing mostly in obscure newspapers and journals, rehearsed in expository form many of the points he later made in his Reconstruction novels, *A Fool's Errand* and *Bricks Without Straw*. In this article, he responded to the Liberal Republican movement made up of critics who sharply criticized Grant's Reconstruction efforts and espoused a laissez-faire philosophy in regard to the South. After being nominated by the Liberal Republicans, Horace Greeley ran for president in 1872 against Ulysses S. Grant and famously declared that the federal government's only obligation to former slaves was to allow them to "root, hog or die" in nature's struggle for life.

Reconstruction has been a failure. It is useless to deny this fact. It has not only been a failure, but one of so utter and ignominious a character that people are even disinclined to go back and inquire into its causes. Of course, by failure it is not meant to be said that the physical unity of the nation has not been restored, and the lately rebellious States rehabilitated with their former rights and privileges in the Federal Union. This, however, was the smallest and simplest part of the duty which devolved on the Government at the close of the war, and which was endeavored to be performed under the name and style of Reconstruction.

The word itself was one of ill-omen, in that it rushed back into the past for the type and model of what was to be in the future. By its very force it accustomed the people to the idea that the work which was to be done was but the patching up of an old garment; that it was an act of restoration rather than one of creation. It foreshadowed an attempt to put new wine into old bot-

*A. W. Tourgée, "Root, Hog, or Die," newspaper clipping, no date [ca. 1876], items 2428 and 10845, Albion Winegar Tourgée Papers, Chautauqua County Historical Society.

tles, which has been but too successfully carried into execution, with a result which can at present be inferred only from the rule in such cases prescribed and certain ominous events which have already appeared.

The duty which lay before the Government was not chiefly nor primarily to restore statal relations. That was a matter which could be done in ten minutes and by a single act of five lines. Its duty was to erect in the lately rebellious regions Republican governments, in which the rights of all should be secured, protected and maintained. Such governments had never existed here. Free speech, free thought, free labor, and free ballot, were strangers to the territory which fell a victim to secession. The very basic elements of Republican government were lacking here. Reconstruction hinted at going back to these husks. The duty of the nation was to tread them under foot, and sternly set its face to secure to every man in that new domain which its arms had just conquered from slavery, not only the rights of a freeman, but the protection and security of a freeman, and an unmistakable guarantee that he might transmit them to his children, and they to theirs in endless perpetuity.

This the nation has utterly and completely failed to do. In name, the colored man is a citizen. In theory, he has the rights of a freeman. In fact, he exercises those rights only by sufferance, and in all but two of the States he is hardly more of a citizen than when he was sold on the block, or driven a-field by those whom he served.

In this respect reconstruction is a failure in a wider and completer sense than most of those even who are subjected to its effects, at this time appreciate.

The cause of this failure is largely embraced in the philosophy set forth with more force than elegance by Mr. Greeley in the words of the subject of this article: "Root, hog, or die." Soon after the war he put this forth as the quintessence of his theory in regard to the southern blacks. He was willing that they should be clothed with the ballot, given equal rights and privileges with the whites, among whom they lived—no more and no less—and then he would leave them to stand or fall, sink or swim, survive or perish, as they might. He would have them preside over their own future, and make or mar their destiny for themselves. In enunciating this doctrine the *Tribune* philosopher was by no means putting forth any new or startling hypothesis. He was announcing no theory peculiar to himself, and evolved from the depths of his own consciousness. On the contrary, he was only giving a peculiarly striking illustration of that faculty of shrewd observation which enabled him during a long life, to keep on the crest of American public opinion without once falling into the trough, which was but a little way before or behind, even when the party—of which he was one of the leaders—was dashed on the rocks, it was too blind to see and avoid. He knew that the people of the North looked upon slavery as the sole cause of rebellion and supposed that treason must die for lack of nutriment when it was destroyed. He knew that the average American citizen drew a sigh of relief when the question of emancipation was decided, not so much on account of its giving freedom to the black as because it was thought by him to settle a most vexatious and troublesome question. It was thought that it would take the "nigger" out of politics. For half a century the curly locks and ebon integument of the African had obtruded on every platform and complicated every question. Saints could not pray and senators could not legislate in peace because of the ubiquitous "nigger." When the war was over and emancipation an accomplished fact, therefore, the average American gave a sigh of relief, and said, "Thank God, the nigger is dead! He is free now. Let him go to work and prove if he is as good as a white man." He was willing to give him a "white man's chance," and let him do a white man's work, if he could. It was, in the main, the idea of the ring and prize fighter, which we have brought from old England—"let the best man win." Greeley chose, however, to embody it in the more forcible and less elegant vulgarism of the Northwest: "Root, hog, or die."

Because this phrase exactly represented the feeling of nine-tenths of the people of the North at that time in regard to the freedmen of the south, it became a general exponent of the nation's feeling, and unconsciously, no doubt, molded in no small degree the tone and character of the legislation which constituted the reconstruction code.

The idea which underlay all this legislation, was that if the freedmen were clothed with the same powers as the whites, had the same privileges and immunities, nothing more need be done in their behalf. Some said they would take care of themselves and their future; would rise and flourish, develop and grow strong and prosperous. Others, perhaps as many, said they never could not rise; that they were a race imbecile in all the requisites of success and prosperity and predicted that they would fail and fall. But all agreed that whether they rose or fell, it should be of themselves. "Root, hog, or die," expressed the philosophy of both.

Right here occurred the errors which the few years which have elapsed since these governments were created and autonomic States erected on the ruins of the Confederacy, have shown so plainly that one can but wonder that their existence could have been overlooked. Two facts were neglected in this legislation which were fatal to its value:

1. That men who had come up from barbarism through two hundred and fifty years of slavery, could not make complete self-protecting, well-balanced, advancing freemen in a day.

2. That a party made up chiefly of these could never protect itself, nor the rights of its members, from the assaults of a party combining experience, culture and wealth, and animated by the keenest party spirit, the rancor of race prejudice, and the sting of defeat.

It was not giving the colored man a fair showing, though it professed to be based on that very idea. It was pitting ignorance against knowledge, poverty against wealth, ineptness against experience, the habit of deference against the habit of command, the weak against the powerful, and then saying to them: "Go on! take care of yourselves! root, hog, or die!"

The fruits of this error were states which were in the control of parties incompetent to their management or solidification, extravagance, corruption and all the vagaries naturally incident to ignorance and inexperience, suddenly entrusted with power. The next noticeable result is the rapid disappearance of this class as a ruling element, even where it is in the majority, and the rising of the recently master race above it, with renewed hatred and malevolence toward them. This is but a forerunner of the practical disfranchisement and de-citizenship of the colored man, until, by his own act, or by some favoring providence, he shall rise again provided with the freeman's only armor of proof—knowledge, education, experience; not because they are inferior to their brethren of lighter integuments in mental power or facility of culture, but because while they were yet babes, too weak to walk without a guiding and controlling hand, the nation said to them: "Root, hog, or die!"

The responsibility for this failure does not rest with the people of the South. No class of them urged the hasty and ill-considered legislation which characterized the period of reconstruction. The people of the North and hot-headed legislators who were ambitious to do all that was to be done in an instant must bear the blame. Neither understood the disease nor the remedy. They were willing to apply a nostrum without making a diagnosis. Who, but a people and a party who were intoxicated with success, would ever have dreamed of conferring the power of a State upon a party having not more than a tenth of the property, intelligence and experience in public affairs which was to be found in its limits? Who would expect such power to last, or the rights of the individual members of such a party to be secured from the encroachment of the compact, educated, wealthy minority? It was simply a fool's hazard. Milton said that one of the attributes of divinity is the power to compress eternity into an hour. The Congress of the United States thought for the moment that it had that power. It was mistaken, and the poor and weak of the South are reaping now the bitter fruits of its stupid error. Something more than emancipation was necessary to make the slave a self-protecting citizen. Something more than the election franchise was necessary to secure to the freedmen, the rights of the citizen. That something is intelligence, culture, development. If the nation had given freedmen of the Southern States thoroughly organized schools instead of the ballot; if it had given the stable and even-handed justice instead of Ku-Klux and white leagues; if it had waited until there was a right-minded, intelligent and loyal people, before it attempted to create loyal States; if it had waited until the freedman had grown used to liberty, and had learned something of its duties; until the master had become accustomed to yield to his late slave the rights and privileges of a citizen; until the traditions of the mart and the plantation had grown dim; if the nation had waited until these things had come to pass, there would have been no burlesque of statal organizations—mere hot-beds of future evils—scattered through the South today. The wards of the nation would be slowly and surely rising to the full stature of self-sustaining manhood, and the bitterness of hereditary hostility would be fading out of the bosoms of the nation's recent foes under the warmth of material prosperity and national advancement. As it is, the State machinery which has been put in operation at the South is but a set of engines made ready for the hands of our enemies, by means of which the results of the war may be made valueless, the fruits of emancipation destroyed, and the future of the freedmen made one of darkness, doubt and struggle; and in all likelihood, one of tyranny, resistance and bloodshed. All this is the legitimate result of hasty legislation, based upon imperfect knowledge of its subject matter, and the weathercock philosophy, "Root, hog, or die."

II

REMEDIES FOR RACISM

9

Aaron's Rod in Politics (1881)*

Tourgée published this, one of his most important essays, in the *North American Review* in February 1881. This article offers a detailed overview of Tourgée's plan for national funding for public education. It was read closely by the Republican president-elect James A. Garfield, who used his inaugural address to endorse the idea (though not Tourgée's specific plan) of aiding public education in the South. Privately, Garfield encouraged his friend Tourgée to undertake a book-length study of the issue.

Simultaneously with the nomination of General Garfield, the Republican Party had the good fortune to fall heir to a new idea. Such windfalls are by no means frequent in the political world. As a rule, government is simply an eternal repetend. The problem of yesterday is puzzled over today, and comes up for a new solution tomorrow. The life of a nation is, in the main, only an infinite series of attempts to solve the same old problem in some new way. The stock properties of all governments are matters of revenue and administration. Parties are far more frequently divided upon the question of how to do than of what to do. With nations as with individuals, the chief business of existence is to find the means of living. The struggle for daily bread is the great end of government, as well as of the separate existences whose aggregate composes the nation. When to raise money and when to borrow it; what to tax and what to spare; what to buy and what to sell; how to spend and how to save—these are the questions as to which government is most frequently concerned, and differences of opinion in regard to which usually distinguish parties. They are questions of method and detail. Right or wrong does not enter into them as a component. Policy, expediency, a question of profit and loss, is their highest element.

*Albion W. Tourgée, "Aaron's Rod in Politics," *North American Review* 132 (February 1881): 139–62.

Now and then there comes a time when the question that is uppermost in all minds is not "How?" but "What?"—when the question of method, the mere economy of administration, sinks into insignificance in the presence of some peril which threatens the very fact of existence, or some crisis when that which has been is cast off like an outgrown garment and that which is to be has not yet assumed form and consistency.

Such an occasion was the birth-hour of the Republican Party. Those who led did not know it, but subsequent events fully demonstrated that the people of the North had arrived at that point when they determined to use their power to cripple and destroy slavery. How, they knew not; neither did they care very much about the means to be employed. Like the Pentecostan multitude, they all heard and saw the same thing—all understood that in some way or other the Republican Party in its last analysis meant personal liberty. The public mind turned aside from the beaten paths of administration and addressed itself to the higher duty of deciding between a new-born righteousness and an ancient evil.

So, too, when armed rebellion stood threatening the nation's life, the struggle between parties instantly became not one concerning the economies of existence, but one of existence at all. Again, at the close of the war, questions of method of administration were dwarfed by the overtopping importance of fixing and establishing the terms and conditions of restoration, or, as we blindly though more wisely termed it, reconstruction.

Since those questions have been decided, or at least have taken on the form of legislative enactments, there has been an unremitting attempt to steer our political thought back into the old channels. Politicians and political scolds have agreed in reiterating that we must come back to the good old ways, and fight over again and again the ancient battles of banking, tariff, and currency, currency, banking, and tariff, without any disturbing influences from without. To consider the causes of revolution and counter-revolution, to trace the course of prejudice and caste, to tell the tale of violence, or balance the rights of the citizen over against a petty economy, instead of discussing the rate of interest or the system of banking, is to be "a stirrer up of strife," a "waver of the bloody shirt," a "ranter on dead issues," a party insubordinate, and a pestiferous political nuisance.

This is not strange. Politicians do not like to be jostled out of their accustomed ruts. The old issues, the everlasting conundrums, leave the lines of battle undisturbed. They make the conflict of parties as peaceful and regular as a sham battle. The ground is known, the lines are drawn, and the result is—almost immaterial. No one is out of his bearings or beyond his depth. A few dollars, a little hog-cunning, a convenient slander, and the old battle has been won and lost on the same old ground, and by the same perennial parties. A question of principle instead of method is like a bomb-shell in the midst of holiday warfare. It forces an advance over ground that may be full of pitfalls. A leader, by one misstep, may stumble into oblivion. A new political idea, therefore, is rarely adopted by any party until the last day of grace. Then it is that the people get ahead of their leaders. There is an advance along the whole line of a party which has planned only to hold its old works. Ordered to "dress" on some old issue, the people insubordinately "charge" on some new evil. Such times are crises. Old parties must clothe themselves with new ideas, or new ones are sure to arise.

Such a time is the present. The Democratic Party, ever since the close of the war, has been trying to revivify old issues of form and method. They have sought to draw the veil of absolute forgetfulness over the new departure of 1861 and all that was either causative or resultant of that struggle. They have tried to lash the American people back to the lines of the old "autumn maneuvers," to divert attention from the rights of the citizen and the security of the Republic to matters of trade and discount.

Almost by accident, as it would seem, the Republican Party gave utterance to a new political thought at Chicago, which is destined, if carried to its logical results, to make the coming quadrenniate of its power no less important and memorable than its first. If neglected, shirked, or trifled with, this administration will simply pass into history as one of those interregnums during which a party held power but did nothing—when "I dare not" waited on "I would," and politicians schemed for future places unmindful of the common weal. This thought which is destined to compel a new departure in politics, is the relation of the general government—the American nation or the American people—to the illiterate voters of the several States.

The Republican platform of 1880, for the first time in our history, pledges a party to the idea of national action in the direction of public education. The resolution in regard to it is not at all striking in its character, except in the fact that it does embrace this idea. It was evidently drawn with fear and trembling, and may be regarded as a not altogether unsuccessful attempt to make language a means of concealing thought rather than expressing it. Its history may almost be traced in its words. It is self-evidently a hesitant yielding to an irresistible demand. It is the language of the skilled politician, compelled to take a forward step in compliance with a popular sentiment which he dare not ignore. Not to go forward is to risk favor; an inch too far may be ruin to the party whose plan of campaign he is preparing. For years the popular sentiment has been growing. An unshaped, indefinite conviction has sprung up in the public mind that something of the kind is wise and necessary. Members of Congress belonging to this party have introduced tentative measures, designed to feel the public pulse rather than to effect a specific cure. The president of this very convention, with commendable pertinacity, has more than once brought the subject to the attention of his colleagues. The question is one not without difficulty. The national charter is dumb in regard to it. No party has ever gone before to blaze the way or show its pitfalls and dangers. Four years before, a like committee quietly sat down upon this feeling evidenced by petitions and sought to be made the basis of a new Southern policy. The President of the Republic, impressed with the need of doing something which had not been done before, during the first three years of his term had not deemed this question worthy of serious consideration, but within a month preceding the sitting of this convention had voiced the popular sentiment in a public address. One of the leading candidates before the convention, a statesman of unusual strength and subtlety, a politician of great sagacity and long experience, had put it forth as one of the first and strongest points of the coming campaign, in a speech of remarkable power, in which, with commendable frankness, he announced his own candidacy for the nomination. It is evident that something must be done. The trend of public thought is unmistakable. The party must say something, but not too much. The draftsman must write as the cautious hunter shot—"so as to hit it if a deer and miss it if a calf." The demon of State sovereignty rose before him, grim and terrible, stained with the blood of recent warfare, yet potent for defeat.

Thus pressed in front and rear, the politician seized his pen and, with the skill of polished statecraft, wrote:

"The work of popular education is one left to the care of the several States, but it is the duty of the national government to aid that to the extent of its constitutional ability. The intelligence of the nation is but the aggregate of the intelligence of the several States; and the destiny of the nation must be guided, not by the genius of any one State, but by the genius of all."[1]

It was well and wisely and skillfully done. The first sentence is one of infinite possibilities. Much or little, anything or nothing, may be the scope of its significance according to the standpoint of the reader. The chameleon cannot

1. These words are quoted from the official Republican Party platform adopted on June 2, 1880, at the Republican National Convention in Chicago.

rival it in unchangeable power for infinite change. It is a messenger which needs no injunction to be everything to all men. The concluding sentence, the biggest half of the resolution, was addressed with deft flattery directly and entirely to the State sovereignty gnome. The writer judged well that the repeated impersonation of the "several States," and the deft appeal to the banded "genius" of these incorporeal existences, would effectually conceal the kernel of truth hidden in his bushel of chaff. Nevertheless, the grain was there, which is bound to grow and blossom and swallow other issues, like the prophet's rod. If vigorously carried into execution by the party in power, it will change the whole face of the Southern question. If haltingly dealt with as heretofore, that party will justly lose the advantage to be gained by the priority of their declaration in its favor.

THE DANGER

As a general, abstract principle, it requires no argument to establish the truth of Madison's immortal apothegm that "a popular government, without popular information or the means of acquiring it, is but a prologue to a farce, or a tragedy, or perhaps to both."

It is to be feared, however, that very few have clearly formulated the extent and imminency of the danger arising from popular ignorance, which now confronts us.

There is a general belief that ignorance is at the root of some of our national ills, and that sometime and somehow danger is likely to result therefrom. This peril was clearly apparent to the mind of General Grant, when he recommended the desperate expedient of excluding all illiterates from the right of suffrage, by constitutional amendment. Though it evoked no Congressional action, it awakened thought, and the present state of the public mind is largely due to his action. President Hayes has rarely missed an opportunity during the last few months to feel the public pulse upon this subject, and, like many Republican canvassers during the late campaign, universally met with a hearty response from all, irrespective of party. His last message reveals his own conviction of the danger, but contains no practical suggestions on the subject. Several bills now before Congress are the outgrowth of this general feeling of apprehension.

The usual form of stating the danger to be apprehended from this source by no means discloses the imminency of our national peril. It does not consist alone in the fact that of our population some 17% is illiterate; nor even in the fact that 20% of our voters cannot read their ballots. This proportion, if evenly distributed, would perhaps hardly afford ground for apprehension, certainly not for immediate alarm. The real danger lies in the unequal distribution of this percentage of illiterates. The following table, compiled from the census of 1870, will sufficiently disclose this fact. While the recent census will considerably increase the aggregates, it is not probable that it will materially affect the relative proportions:

Voting population of the United States	7,623,000
" " " former slave State	2,775,000
Illiterate male adults in United States	1,580,000
" " " former slave States	1,123,000
Per cent. illiterate voters in United States to entire vote	20
" " " slave States	45
" " " States not slave	9
" " " South Carolina	59
Illiterate voters in Southern States (white)	304,000
" " " (colored)	819,000

From this table the following facts will be apparent:

1. The sixteen Southern States contain about one-third of our voting population, and almost three-fourths of our illiteracy.
2. 45% of the voters of the Southern States are unable to read their ballots.
3. The illiteracy of the South, plus 6% of its literate voters, can exercise the entire power of those States.
4. If this illiterate vote be neutralized by force or fraud, a majority of the intelligent voters, or 28% of the entire vote of those States, will exercise their entire national strength.

These States have one hundred and thirty-eight electoral votes, or, in other words, they exercise *72%* of the power necessary to choose a President or constitute a majority in the House of Representatives, and *84%* of a majority in the Senate.

By reason of their ignorance, 45% of the voters of the South are unable:

1. To know what is their political duty.
2. To be sure that their votes actually represent their wishes.
3. To secure the counting of the ballots which they cast.
4. To protect themselves in the exercise of their ballotorial privileges.

So that the alternative presented is between an honest exercise of power by voters who are too ignorant to have any certain knowledge whether they are right or wrong, and the suppression of their votes by force or fraud. So far as their effects upon the nation are concerned, both are alike dangerous. While this mass of ignorance may be instinctively right in purpose, it is naturally unable to judge of the instrumentalities with which it works. If suppressed, that very act discloses a purpose and intent in itself dangerous. It is simply a choice between the dangers of honest ignorance and dishonest fraud or unlawful violence. The question for the nation to answer is whether it can afford to have three-fourths of the power necessary to control the government exercised by either ignorance, or fraud, or violence. The question is one above partisanship, as the safety of the nation is above party supremacy.

The general apprehension of danger to result from either horn of this dilemma is evidenced by the fact that what is termed the "solid South" is universally regarded as a thing to be either dreaded or excused. In the late campaign, each party accused the other of responsibility for its existence, and each asserted, as one of its chief claims to support, that its success would effectually banish this *bête noir* of our modern politics. Oddly enough, too, the one claimed that the "solid South" would be broken by the election of its candidate, because that action would show an inclination on the part of the North to give to the "solid South" whatever it desired, and thereupon there would result such a struggle over the spoils of victory inside the "solid South" as would permanently destroy all of its solidarity. The argument of the other party was that the success of its candidate would evidence such a determination on the part of the North as would induce the individuals composing the "solid South" to despair of winning national control by means of this solidarity, consequently, it was argued, they would gradually sliver off court alliance with the Republicans, and, by so doing, not only protect the ignorant colored voters in the exercise of their franchise, but also compel the remainder of their present associates to court in like manner the colored vote, and so accomplish the end, by all professedly deemed most desirable, to wit, the breaking up of the "solid South" and of the colored vote of the South at once.

Both of these claims are fallacious, but they show a universal conviction that the "solid South" and the solid ignorant vote of the South are both dangerous things. The trouble is that instead of seeking to eradicate the cause, both parties have hitherto sought to "whip the devil around the stump" by shallow artifices, which, even if they were to succeed, would afford but a temporary relief. This mistake results in a great measure from a misapprehension of the relative character of the present parties at the South, and the use of the terms "the South," "Southern people," and "solid South," in different senses.

Of the white race at the South, some 24% of the voters are illiterate; of the colored race, about 90%. Of the Republican Party at the South, about 75% is colored, and the remainder white. The ratio of illiteracy among the whites of the two parties is probably about the same, for, while the white Republicans will hardly average with their Democratic neighbors in wealth, it takes a certain amount of intelligence to furnish the backbone necessary to make a Southern Republican. There are no colored Democrats, or not enough to constitute an appreciable percentage. This estimate would make something more than 75% of the present Republican party of the South illiterate and 24% of their opponents. This classification of parties dates back to the period of reconstruction, and was formed solely upon the question of accepting or rejecting rehabilitation under those measures. The lodestone which united the opposition was hostility to the political equality of the negro. All other points of difference were insignificant and trivial, except as they bore upon that one absorbing idea. Since that time there has been no material change in the strength or animus of the respective parties.

The party opposed to the reconstruction measures became what is known as the "solid South." The alliance of this faction with the Democratic party of the nation was purely accidental. They united with that party simply because the Republicans favored the reconstruction measures. The "solid South" is not solidly Democratic, but solidly "Southern"; or, what is the same thing, solidly opposed to the exercise of political power by the colored man. It did not become solid in the hope of achieving national power, but moved into the Democratic camp in the hope of achieving power by means of its already established solidarity. The "solid South" has no especial affinity for the Democracy any more than for any other Party. Its distinctive features are peculiar to itself. No defeat of the Democratic party affects its solidarity, nor is any triumph of the Republican party of any moment to it so long as no step is taken to interfere with or remove the causes of its solidarity. This faction was not made "solid" by the hope of enjoying federal patronage and favor. When it was first organized, there seemed little hope of success for it even in local affairs. Only the most far-seeing sagacity could have predicted that astonishing triumph which it has achieved. Yet, there was no hesitation, no faltering, no desertion. The number of proselytes from it during the years of Republican supremacy was surprisingly small. The most tremendous majorities did not appall or discourage them. As they did not abandon their faction when in a minority for the sake of preferment, so they will not now defy its power for the sake of favor.

This faction, unquestionably a minority, assume for themselves the term "Southern," with a sublime disregard of the weak and ignorant majority. This use of the term "Southern" has become so general that its absurdity is almost forgotten. That which is favored by this element is said to be "Southern," and that which is opposed to it, "anti-Southern." A national policy which is thoroughly approved by every member of the actual majority of the people of that section is denounced by this element as one hostile to "the South." Even as these words are written, the message of the President is spoken of by a leading journal as "meeting with universal execration at the South," while in truth no document he has ever written is regarded by the actual majority there as approaching it in good sense and statesmanship. This assumption by a faction of terms denoting the whole, and the general concurrence in their use, is the cause of endless confusion. In this article, "the South" will be used for the section, and the "solid South" to designate the faction.

If such a thing as the disruption of the "solid South," and the distribution of the colored vote between its fragments were possible, it would still be only a temporary remedy for the evil which threatens the nation's future. For a time it would lessen the danger and the political Micawber might be excused for appealing to an artifice which would give opportunity for an unforeseen something to turn up. When we consider the extreme improbability of any such disruption, and the absence of any stronger issue than the mere bait of official power which can be offered to induce the dissolution of a "solid South," which is based on race-prejudice and the traditions of the past, we may well conclude that the only remedy is to attack the citadel of ignorance.

There are two methods by which the danger may be avoided. The one is that which has been adopted by certain of the States, which is to exclude the illiterate from the ballot. This can never be honestly done, even if desirable, because in more than one-third of the States an honest majority can never be obtained in its favor. Every unlettered man will of course oppose his own exclusion from political power, unless intimidated or deceived, and there will never be found a time, should it be attempted, when there will not be intelligent voters enough who unite with them to give a majority. Who believes that such a measure could be honestly adopted in South Carolina, for instance, where 59% of the voters are illiterate? Such a movement could not consistently be inaugurated or supported by the Republican party, both because of the vast percentage of illiterates in its Southern wing, and also because it would be a virtual confession of folly or insincerity in its reconstructionary legislation. Such an admission would be fatal.

The only other method of treating this evil is that so cautiously pointed out in the resolution, already quoted, of the Republican platform of 1880—national education, or national aid to education. So that we face the inquiry, is this a sufficient and possible remedy?

THE POWER OF CONGRESS

The first question to be considered in connection with this inquiry is the power of Congress over the subject-matter.

No power to provide for the education of the citizens of the different States, or that vague thing denominated "American citizenship," or to prescribe the course or character of instruction, is provided in the Constitution. At the time of its adoption, such a thing as an organized system of public schools under State control was unknown. The whole idea of public education is one of later growth. Washington and others of his compatriots were anxious for a national university, but the systematic education of all the people, by the state or nation, was hardly dreamed of at that time. Its especial necessity, arising from the influence of ignorance upon political affairs, was not then felt, because of two things, viz.: The restrictions upon the ballot were such that very few men could compass that privilege who were not at least able to read and write. The immigration to our shores (except the pauper and penal immigration to some of the Southern plantations) had chiefly been confined to religious malcontents, who came to avoid persecution, and persons who voluntarily left their homes to seek advantage from settlement in unbroken wilds. This very fact stamps them as among the most enterprising, far-seeing, and determined of their respective classes. They were really picked men. The doctrine of the survival of the fittest never had a better illustration than in the settlement of the American colonies. This was the main reason why our early settlers, coming as they did chiefly from the middle and lower classes of England, developed so suddenly a capacity for self-government, invented new governmental forms, and adapted themselves to untried conditions with such astonishing ease. They neither understood the danger resulting from ignorance, however, nor the proportions to which it would grow in our land. They were too busy securing rights against the power of king and lords to fear any evil to come from the masses. It was one of those things which the Constitution is silent in regard to, simply because its authors had no prevision of the subject-matter. It is, however, one of that numerous class of questions which the inherent necessities of national existence have, from time to time, forced upon our attention. The department of agriculture, the coast survey, scientific and exploring expeditions, the signal service, the military and naval academies at West Point and Annapolis, and many other branches of administrative work, are beyond the purview of the written Constitution. There is no sense in saying that they are not within a strict construction of that instrument. They cannot be embraced by *any* construction of its words, because they were not within the range of its authors' thoughts, and could not have been within the intendment of their language. Of these extensions of the governmental powers beyond the purview of the written Constitution, by far the greater portion have been accepted and concurred in without controversy. Their need was so apparent, and the logic of their existence so irresistible, that they have been deemed only necessary corollaries of other unquestioned powers.

The incidents of national power—those things which are essential to its existence, development, and perpetuity—have always been held to be within the legitimate scope of both the legislative and executive branches of our national government. Out of our Constitution has grown a nation, and out of the needs of that nation, following the English precedent, has grown the doctrine of intendment, by which our Constitution is kept as flexible, as capacious and receptive as the unwritten constitution of Great Britain. The positive authorizations and inhibitions of the written instrument are, of course, in no case to be disregarded; but the silences which lie between have been peopled with incidental powers until the fabric of a compact and harmonious nationality bids fair to rise by natural and healthy growth out of the imperfect federation which our fathers adopted.

The power to provide for the education of the people, to secure the intelligence of its electors and thereby prevent its own disintegration and destruction, is one of these incidents of national existence. The right of self-preservation and defense is as much an essential of national as of individual life. The power to provide for an intelligent exercise of the ballotorial power is a necessary incident of elective government. If we are to be ruled by the ballot, the ballot-box must be kept open, free, and the power to be exercised through it must be the power of intelligence. The rule of the ballot implies supervision and the power to make all participants in our governmental control, implies the right to make them fit to do so. Manhood suffrage, equality of right, presupposes, in the power conferring such equality, the power and the right to render the recipient capable of its intelligent exercise. The safety of the republic is the highest law, and the most evident condition of its safety is, that those who rule shall have sufficient intelligence to know what they desire to do, and when they are doing it. The illiterate man who holds a ballot is like the blind man who wields a sword—he knows not whether he wounds friend or foe.

The ballot-box, controlled by ignorance, is as much an instrument of chance as a dice-box. The illiterate has, in the first place, but a limited means of learning how he ought to vote, and no means at all of making sure that he has voted as he wishes. He is the ready victim of fraud. He invites deception, and furnishes food to the demagogue. He is more to be feared than the traitor or usurper, because he constitutes the following which makes treason dangerous. The ignorant voter swells the rank and file of the army that follows at the heels of the corrupt politician. Education does not make men honest, but it enables them to detect fraud. It is a safeguard, because the bulk of mankind are honest, and if intelligent enough to distinguish the right, will follow it. The power to educate its own voters then, is, and must be, inherent in any republic, because it is only an incident of the right of national defense.

The nation's right of self-defense, the implied power to maintain itself, was not exhausted by the struggle to put down rebellion. It equally exists as to any impending evil. The national board of health, and the proposed action in regard to the cattle plague, are recent instances in which the public mind has approved the exercise of such power. Is the nation to hold its hand, permit disease to ravage a portion of the land and threaten all the rest, simply because the boundary of a State must be crossed to provide a remedy? The peril from ignorance is of precisely the same character. Fortunately it is not, as a fact, contagious, but under our system of government its evils are by no means bounded by the State, or district, in which it prevails. When it furnishes the votes which elect a member of Congress from the city of New York, or by fraud or intimidation permits a member to be chosen by the majority of a minority in Mississippi, the conduct of those representatives bears with equal weight, for good or ill, on every citizen in every district of the United States. If the blind man cut only himself he might perhaps be allowed to play with the sword, but when fifty millions more are wounded every time he smites himself, it is not only permissible for them to take measures for their own protection, but incumbent upon them to do so. It is because aggregated ignorance has become dangerous to the continuance and development of the nation, inimical to our form of government and the principles on which it is based, that the nation has the right to begin and carry on a war of extermination against it. It is not the Constitution, but the law of national existence that flows from the Constitution, which gives us this right. A nation has not only the inherent right to exist, to guard and protect its present, but also to secure its future and perpetuate its life. That right our nation is not only entitled to exercise, but it has reached a point where further to omit to do so would be hazardous and criminal.

While, if it became necessary, the nation might lawfully stamp out ignorance as it did secession, yet it becomes incumbent on the statesman to adopt that method which promises to secure the result aimed at with the least interference with the established harmony of our complex system of government. There are three possible methods of national education:

1. The assumption by the general government of the duty of educating its own citizens, without reference to the State organizations.
2. The distribution of a national fund to the various State organizations, to be by them applied and controlled, without supervision or interference on the part of the general government.
3. The appropriation of a fund in aid of primary schools in the different States, to be administered under the supervision and control of the national government.

The first of these needs no consideration, because, as has just been remarked, it is only to be resorted to when all other plans have failed. Neither public sentiment nor the imminency of the peril is such as to justify such a radical departure from the system of coordination which has existed hitherto between our State and national governments.

The second, that of placing funds absolutely in the hands of the various States for educational purposes, which is the basis idea of the bills now pending before Congress, is open to the following serious objections:

1. The experience of the nation in regard to such bequests is not encouraging. The results have not generally been at all proportionate to the munificence of the gifts.
2. Such a fund is especially liable to misappropriation. It goes into the absolute control of the various State legislatures, and being a fund not raised by immediate taxation of their own constituents, they are naturally held to a less rigid accountability for its expenditure. "Easy come, easy go" is especially true of such funds. It is almost a moral certainty that its investment or application would soon become a party question in every State, and the result would be a minimum of progress at a maximum of cost.
3. Such a fund is liable to be diverted from its legitimate purpose for the

benefit of a class or a sect. Instead of being devoted to the cure of illiteracy, it may be frittered away in costly scientific experiment or the
support of higher education for a few, which, while good enough in
itself, does not materially affect the specific evil sought to be remedied.
The bill now pending before Congress has not avoided this evil. One-
third of the fund it appropriates is to go to the support of colleges. Illiteracy is the present danger. When that is cured, there will be time
enough to think about polishing diamonds. The Louisville "Journal" is
entirely right when it says, "Let the whole proceeds go to the common
schools, and to no schools of higher education." The nation is interested in curing the illiteracy of all classes and both races. A fund given
in bulk to the authorities of a State can no longer be controlled by the
general government, and may be applied to the benefit of one race or
class, without remedy. The fund distributed to the States many years
ago was, in not a few cases, invested in Confederate bonds and used to
destroy the giver.

4. Instead of being an incentive to exertion on the part of the States and
their citizens, it is a bid for carelessness and sloth. Instead of exert-
ing themselves to supplement the nation's bounty with their own best
endeavors, the tax-payers of the State would be apt to clamor for a
reduction of the State tax for schools on account of this donation, and
demagogues would soon seek for votes by promising such relief, thus
corrupting their constituents by means of the national funds, and destroying that public sentiment which must underlie every successful
system of public instruction.

THE REMEDY

We come, then, to consider the third method, and meet at once the inquiry:
"Can the general government administer a fund in aid of public education
in the various States without assuming the control of the public schools
thereof?"

We believe it can, by means of any system which shall contain the following elements:

1. The raising of a sufficient national fund for educational purposes.
2. The distribution of this fund on the basis of illiteracy.
3. The payment of the fund directly to the officers or teachers of schools
in towns or districts, according to the number of illiterates therein, and

on proof that schools, free to all within school age, have actually been kept in operation therein for a certain specified portion of the year.

4. A thorough system of inspection and supervision of the schools thus assisted, and full and accurate reports of all matters necessary to direct future legislation on the subject.

5. Provision that the fund not applied in any particular district for any year shall be forfeited to the general fund for the succeeding year.

6. The sum allowed ought, in no case, to be more than one-third or one-half the amount necessary to maintain the school during the specified time; the balance being required to be provided either by State taxation or private subscription.

It is not intended here to discuss the method of raising this fund, nor the amount required, further than to express the belief that it should be a regular part of the national budget, and be provided in like manner with other current expenses. We should not wait for the slow process of a sinking-fund, nor seek to sneak out of responsibility by giving the income of a fancifully invested sum, the existence of which may depend on some doubtful contingency. It should be an honest fund, not raised by indirection nor appropriated by stealth. Its distribution, on the basis of illiteracy, is an idea already incorporated in at least two bills now before Congress, and strongly advocated by Mr. Commissioner Eaton for several years. It has the merit of putting the plaster directly on the sore.

The result of this would be to apply more than two-thirds of the fund to primary education at the South, so long as the present ratio of illiteracy existed there. This is not only good policy, but the highest justice. Slavery was the parent of ignorance, not only on the part of the slave, but also of the white race. Through national encouragement it grew, and the amount invested in it yearly increased until the war began. The result of the war not only deprived the South of the proceeds of previous economy by destroying the capital thus invested, but also, by making the freedman a citizen, imposed on someone the task and burden of his instruction. It is an enormous undertaking for either the State or the nation. For those States, it is quite an impossible one. They could, by the utmost reasonable exertion, hardly bring their population to the level of our present Northern intelligence in a hundred years. During that time, the nation would be constantly imperiled by this mass of ignorance. Not only is it an almost impossible task for them, but it is one which they ought not in justice to be asked to perform alone. Not only did the nation, by its laws and institutions, encourage slavery, but it shared in its profits and reaped advantage from the prosperity which it helped to bring. The merchants of the North shared the profits of every pound of cotton, tobacco, or sugar which the Southern planter raised. The Northern manufacturer had the advantage of this great market close at hand, and protected from foreign competition by a tariff which made every planter of the South pay tribute to him on almost every article he purchased. The advantages of slavery were, therefore, shared by North and South alike, and in a pretty nearly equal degree.

The evils of slavery, and the losses consequent upon emancipation, fell mainly upon the South. It is true that great losses were sustained by the North. The industries of the North so greatly exceed those of the South, and its aggregated wealth is so much more, that the burden of public debt falls chiefly upon it. Yet it is by no means just that the South should be compelled to bear alone the burden of curing the evils which the nation fostered and grew fat upon. If slavery was an evil, the nation should bear a part of the cost of its cure. If it be regarded only as a productive institution, the North should bear a part of the cost of its transformation into self-directing labor, and a co-equal political element, because it shared in the profits of its enslavement.

There is still another view of this matter. Although emancipation was a necessary resultant of the War of Rebellion, and enfranchisement an un-avoidable corollary of emancipation, yet, as political facts, both were of Northern origin, and enforced by Northern or national power. The voice of the South—excluding the colored man's vote—has never ratified either the emancipation of the slave or the enfranchisement of the freedman. By na-tional authority they were made constituent elements, not only of the nation itself, but of the subordinate commonwealths in which they dwelt. The re-construction acts were in effect as compulsory as if they had been prescribed by the commander-in-chief, with force of arms. The fact that we empowered the colored man to do by his ballot the will of the nation does not deprive those acts of their compulsory character, so far as the former constituent ele-ments of statal-power in the Southern States were concerned. Their result was to render necessary the education of the illiterate voters of the South, in order to prevent misgovernment or usurpation. Sooner or later, every man in those States will see that their only hope lies in the intelligence of their voters. Thus to compel those States to assume a vast expenditure is a flagrant instance of taxation without representation. It is what the Irishman, during the war, defined a draft to be—"a nate way of compelling a poor fellow to volunteer." Equity and good conscience, as well as the public safety, demand that the na-tion should assume a fair share of this burden.

The third proposition is intended to afford a simple and effective method of securing the application of the fund to the very purpose for which it was intended. It is the most important element of the plan proposed. Instead of giving the fund in gross into the hands of the States and making them its almoner, the nation itself takes care that its purpose is fulfilled. It secures its bounty to the people, and not to the States. It is, in effect, the plan adopted in the distribution of the Peabody fund,[2] and has there shown itself well calculated both to secure immunity from imposition and also to awaken public interest and cooperation in educational work. By this wise method of administration, the trustees have doubled, and perhaps trebled, the value of Peabody's munificent benefaction. Giving to no school enough to wholly sustain it, requiring it to be kept open a certain number of months in every school year to have a certain minimum of enrolled pupils and a certain average attendance during that time, and, above all, paying only when its work has been done, the Peabody fund has done more good by inducing others to give, than by the funds actually distributed. Its working has been altogether harmonious, both with State systems and free schools maintained by private subscription. The same system adopted by the nation would have a like effect. If the authorities of a State should refuse to cooperate with the nation, the people of the separate districts of such State might still share its benefits by a little individual exertion. It would only be necessary, in order to carry out this provision, to ascertain the number of illiterates in any specified territory of each race, apportion the fund thereto, and before giving money to any school within that town or district, to require proof either that it was open to all races, or, in States where public opinion does not allow of mixed schools, that like opportunity was afforded to the other race by other schools in such district. Of course, the details of this would require careful elaboration. No man could today draw a bill sufficiently broad and elastic to meet all the needs of such a system. Only care, experience, and the most extended study of the data furnished by full and careful reports could enable one to accomplish such a task.

From this very fact arises the necessity of the fourth proposition. Up to this point it is believed that the plan proposed has steered clear of debatable

2. Massachusetts-born banker George Peabody established this philanthropic fund in 1867. A model for philanthropic causes, the Peabody Fund began with a donation of $2 million to establish schools and train teachers in the former Confederate states and West Virginia. The administrators of the fund carefully targeted for aid communities in greatest need, expending the vast majority of the fund on former slaves. Remarkably successful, the Peabody Fund continued its work until 1914.

ground. It cannot well be denied that the Congress has a right to appropriate
funds for school purposes, since it has not infrequently done so. It will hardly
be questioned that it may distribute that fund itself, and not through the
agency of the State governments, provided the plan adopted is not intended
to favor one State more than another. In connection with this, it should be
remembered that the purpose and object of this work is neither to benefit nor
favor any State nor section. Its object is not even to favor the recipients of its
bounty. Its sole intent is to protect the nation from an insidious and deadly
peril. In this result every State, and every individual in every State, has an
equal and direct interest. As it is intended, however, to act in harmony with
State systems of public instruction, to assist, promote, and develop primary
schools, which are, in part or in whole, supported by taxation under State
laws, controlled by State officials, and managed by State authority, it may
be urged at once that the States will not submit to national supervision or
inspection of such schools. It will be noted that it is not proposed that the
government shall exercise any *control* over such schools, but only to provide
that, as a condition precedent to participation in the benefits of the fund, the
school shall have been open to the thorough inspection and supervision of an
authorized representative of the general government, who shall report upon
its methods, grade, and character. It is not proposed that he shall have any
authority, but merely be the eyes through which the Congress shall watch
over its own work, and guide itself in the future exercise of its power. These
inspectors are to be merely gatherers of data, acting under prescribed forms.
Nothing need be said about their method of appointment or compensation. It
is not intended that there should be a numerous force of paid inspectors. On
the contrary, it is believed that good men and women can be found in every
township in the land who will willingly give the little time required to visit
the schools in their district, and furnish the reports required, for the sake of
securing the benefits of the system and promoting the cause of education.
They should be appointed without regard to party or sex. Indeed, it is more
than probable that there would be no occasion for partisan feeling in regard
to the matter. Each race should be allowed at least a representation in the
supervision of its own schools, if desired.

It is not believed that any serious opposition could be made to such a system of inspection. If it is, the issue ought to be made up at once. In no State
could a party standing on such opposition long succeed in retaining power. It
is in the Southern States alone that any opposition to such a plan of national
action is to be anticipated. The mistaken ideas of the rank and file of the "solid

South," in regard to the true interests of that section, naturally incline them to oppose anything looking toward governmental action in this respect, and many of their leaders would be bitterly hostile to anything which promised to secure the enlightenment of their constituents. Their power depends in great measure on the ignorance of the masses. It is a mistake to suppose that the leaders of the "solid South" are the best men of the organization which they control. They are, to a large extent, the buccaneers, the desperadoes, of their own party; the men who were bold enough and unscrupulous enough to assume its leadership in the days of active Ku-kluxism, and head the revolutionary organizations which gave it power. They are men who gained prominence by their boldness in directing movements which touched the verge of treason, were unlawful and violent. There were many who sympathized with the purposes of such organizations who did not approve of their methods. Few cared to face danger and ostracism to oppose; but many tacitly disapproved. These are the really "best men" of the "solid South." As a rule, they are not extravagantly proud of their present leaders. Many of them—and the number is hourly increasing—are becoming more and more convinced that the education of the voter is the only chance for the permanent prosperity of their section. These would undoubtedly give in their adhesion to such a system.

The principle of national supervision, however, is vital to the success of national aid to education, because:

1. It provides a check upon fraud, imposition, or misapplication of the fund.
2. It secures material for future amendment of the law.
3. It enables the Congress to know just what sort of instruction the citizens of the nation are receiving through its bounty.

This last point is not one to be neglected. It is a very significant fact, that in nearly every one of the Southern States the text-books prescribed by the authorities openly and ably defend the right of secession, extol the Confederacy and its leaders; assail the national government and its defenders, and, in short, tend directly to diminish the respect due to the government, and justify the action of those who sought its disruption. No man can read the Southern school histories without being assured that their purpose and intent is to instill the extremest doctrines of State sovereignty and secession, both by direct argument, and by subtle depreciation of the federal government and its acts and agencies. This is altogether natural. The "solid South" is, in the main, the successor of the rebellious South, not in its present purpose, but in its underlying spirit, and largely in its *personale*. To defend rebellion is to them merely the instinct of self-justification. To uphold and justify the leaders of secession without assailing the government which suppressed rebellion is a logical impossibility. If Jeff Davis is to be glorified as a patriot and a martyr, Lincoln must, of necessity, be depreciated. If the rebellion was just and righteous, of course its suppression was a crime. That those who promoted and carried on rebellion should desire to stand in history as patriots and martyrs is altogether natural and reasonable. That they should especially desire their sons and their daughters, to the latest moment of time, to venerate their cause and glorify their efforts is by no means surprising. That their children should be even more devout believers in the righteousness of the "lost cause" than their fathers ever were is but a natural result. Hardly a man of the South has ever admitted that secession or rebellion was wrong. "It was simply a question of power," said one prominent Southerner. "The principles for which Lee fought and Jackson fell" are referred to by another as living facts. "The sword decides nothing" has become a favorite apothegm with them. Not one has expressed penitence, or any conviction of having adhered to an unholy cause, or even admitted that if they were placed in like circumstances again they would do otherwise. Their words to the coming generation are not: "My son, take warning from the errors of thy father; shun that false doctrine which led me to shed blood in an unworthy cause; beware of any pitfall of prejudice or dogma that may lead you to take up arms against the government of the United States." On the contrary, their language is: "Our cause was just; we were entirely right; our deeds of heroism were unmatched; our escutcheon was unstained; our enemies were servile and degraded, corrupt and inhuman; we were never defeated, but were simply 'overpowered' by a hireling and imported soldiery; we were *right* enough but not *strong* enough!"

Considering these things, it is not surprising that the books which are prescribed, even for the colored schools of the South, by the State officials, are largely occupied in demonstrating to the children of emancipated parents the righteousness of that confederacy whose corner-stone was slavery, and the unholiness of that government which oppressed, exasperated, and finally "overpowered" the "South." As a matter of sentiment, we cannot refrain from a certain sympathy with this feeling. When we consider it as a political fact, however, we must lay aside sentiment, and inquire of ourselves whether it promises well for the future of the country that one-third of its children are being taught to despise and contemn that government to whose crowning effort the nation owes its existence.

No one desires in any manner to reflect upon the individual motives of the Confederate leaders or soldiery. A man may be honestly and earnestly and patriotically wrong. We are willing to admit that the adherents of the Confederacy were so. Indeed, we have always clamorously insisted that such was the fact, and have thrust our forgiveness upon them unsought, by reason of it. Such, however, has never been their position. They have always stoutly insisted, not only that they were sincere, but that they were right. If this be true, then the nation was wrong, and if wrong then is wrong today, and always will be wrong until the principles of the Confederacy prevail, and the wrong of its suppression is righted. This is the unavoidable conclusion from the doctrine taught in the public schools of the South today.

It becomes necessary, therefore, to know the extent and effect of such teaching. It is believed that general intelligence in this age of free thought, fed with the utterances of an untrammeled press, is in itself a sure cure for false dogma, and the writer confidently expects that such a system of national education will soon modify, and eventually do away both with such instruction and the baser element of the feeling from which it springs. It is, however, a matter which should not go unnoted, and the government should be fully informed to what extent a system designed to secure its perpetuity is perverted to increase its peril. By no means should funds be given into the hands of State authorities to be used in strengthening such a sentiment.

The fifth of the proposed elements of this system is merely designed to prevent any district from allowing its proportion of the fund to accumulate, until it is sufficient to maintain a school for the prescribed period in one year, and then drawing and using it, without any exertion on the part of its own people to supplement and enhance its benefits; and the sixth is intended to make the law a constant incentive to local efforts to promote general primary education.

The probable results of such a system are almost too vast for estimate. Some of them, however, are hardly matters of conjecture. Among these are:

1. It would rapidly reduce the number of men who do not know where to register, where to vote, for whom they are voting, what are their rights, or what is necessary to be done to secure them.
2. It would rapidly increase the number of men who would know how they were voting, be able to see to it that their votes were counted, and whose knowledge would enable them intelligently to determine their duty.

3. It would strike at the roots of the "exodus" by enabling the laborer to guard himself from fraud by the terms of his contract, and by securing its honest and intelligent enforcement.

4. It would offer a new issue which would enable men who are not proud of fraud, and are ashamed of violence, to withhold their support from the "solid South," at least upon national questions.

5. It would afford opportunity for reorganizing the Republican Party of the South, and do away with "rings" designed simply to gather crumbs of patronage, and not inclined to court accessions of such talent and character as might interfere with the distribution of the crumbs. While it is, in no true sense, what the pending "Burnside Bill" has been termed—"a gift from the more educated to the illiterate States," but a measure of self-protection and justice merely, it is still far preferable, as a measure of wise conciliation, to that extensive scheme of internal improvement at the South, which consists chiefly in finding channels for the waters of the West, and water for the channels of the East.

6. It strikes at the very root of the sentiment in which the doctrine of State rights is grounded. The Southern man has heretofore regarded the nation as a vague penumbra, foreign, and usually hostile to the State, which is the object of his most profound adoration. His universal excuse for rebellion is: "I would go with my State against anything outside of it." This plan of State aid to education presents the national government to the eyes of all the people, constantly and persistently, and in an entirely beneficent light. They will learn to regard it, not as a thing "outside" of the State, but inside of, above, and around, pervading, sustaining, and vivifying the State.

7. By raising the grade of intelligence among the working population of the South, it will tend to promote the growth of manufactures, and so unify the interests and development of the different parts of the nation.

Other effects of perhaps even greater significance will occur to the mind which carefully considers the possibilities of such a system. There remains only to discuss the cost. In regard to this it need but be said that no money can compensate for the perils which every quadrenniate brings, by reason of the cloud of ignorance which hangs over the Southern portion of the republic.

So far as the foregoing pages are occupied with matters of method, they are of course only tentative: other and better plans may be devised, or these greatly improved; but so far as they pertain to the developments of the present and the past, to the nature of the remedy rather than the details, they are the result of long and careful study, thoughtful and unprejudiced observation, and the most profound conviction.

To any one who may be disposed to count the cost, there comes an imperative demand to estimate also the danger, to consider whether the present evil shows any hopeful signs of amendment; whether by any other means the republic is likely to be preserved; whether the results, even aside from all political considerations, will not fully repay the expenditure; whether justice does not especially demand that the nation should educate the freedman it has emancipated; and finally, whether the noble sentiment of Peabody, that "education is a debt which the present owes to future generations," does not include within its scope the nation, as well as its components, the State and the individual.

10

The Veto of the Chinese Bill (1882)*

From 1882 to 1884, Tourgée edited *Our Continent,* a weekly literary and political magazine. The following editorial appeared in his regular column on May 10, 1882. Giving rare praise to Republican president Chester A. Arthur, Tourgée applauds the president's veto of the Chinese Exclusion Bill, deeming the exclusion of immigrants on the basis of race or nationality "repugnant to all our national traditions." Tourgée nonetheless seems to accept some of the claims of the anti-Chinese supporters of the bill in regard to the alleged morally "degraded" condition of the predominately male Chinese immigrant population. Just as he did for southern whites and blacks, he urges assimilation and moral uplift for the Chinese no less than for the white population of the American West.

No more statesmanlike document has issued from the White House in many a year, than the calm, dispassionate one in which the President announced his objections to the anti-Chinese bill. In thus calling a halt in "Sand-lot" legislation President Arthur has placed himself among that noble category [of] those who dare to do right, whether it be in consonance with party behest or not. He very properly regards the veto power as one entrusted to him by the Constitution not to promote party interests nor to be used or unused according to the dictate of popular clamor; but in order that hasty legislation may be avoided and time be secured for the reconsideration of any measure which he may regard as of doubtful policy or unconstitutional character. The temper displayed in this paper is most admirable. Few would ever detect its real character if read without the opening and the concluding paragraphs. Very few of the veto messages which have been sent to Congress have been so entirely free from that self-assertive tone which has sometimes been carried to the extent of delivering very caustic lectures to the legislative branch of the

*"The Veto of the Chinese Bill," *Our Continent* 1 (May 10, 1882): 13.

government on the neglect of their duty or an undue exercise of their power. The language of this is earnest, calm, unassuming and entirely respectful of the opinions of the supporters of the bill. This is the more remarkable, since the legislation itself is unpleasantly suggestive of a mere attempt to make party capital by catering to an absurd prejudice.

The treaty with China gives us the right to regulate immigration from the Flowery Kingdom whenever the same may be necessary. Does the presence of one hundred thousand Celestials in a population of fifty millions render such a course necessary? It hardly seems reasonable and the act of exclusion is peculiarly repugnant to all our national traditions. The proposed remedy seems indeed, like a leaf out of the policy of the utmost absolute and arbitrary of monarchies. It is a right, which should be used only upon the most urgent and otherwise unavoidable necessity. The Chinese communities of the western coast are no doubt unpleasant facts. John is beyond question an offensive neighbor. He is industrious, economical, peaceable, but he does not readily adapt himself to our civilization. He is degraded himself and, as a consequence, degrading to others. This cannot be denied, though one cannot avoid the impression that it is not entirely on account of his vices that his exclusion is sought to be effected. But even granting all that has been urged as to his undesirable qualities, and the danger likely to result front his wholesale transportation hither, are we entirely justifiable in resorting to this remedy? Are not the evils of Chinese life on the western coast susceptible of cure by state and municipal legislation? Are their demoralizing attributes beyond the reach of sanitary and police regulations? It may be hard to frame a law that will suppress Chinese gambling halls and allow full liberty to institutions of that kind designed for the profit and amusement of the variously admixtured white race of the Pacific slope. So too it may be somewhat troublesome to close the opium-dive and leave the grog-shop in full blast. How to reach the immoralities of the Chinese immigrant without interfering with the divine right of the Caucasian to debase himself and debauch his fellows, is no doubt a difficult problem. It does seem, however, that if the affrighted virtue of the western slope should direct its energies somewhat more against the evils themselves and somewhat less against the nationality of a part of the malefactors, the nation need not to be troubled with a demand that it shall trample on its own history and abandon the basis principle on which it rests.

Of course, if our only safety is in exclusion—if that is the last resort against the destruction or orientalization of any considerable portion of our country, it must be adopted. It has been well urged by the advocates of this measure that self-preservation is the first law of nations as well as of individuals. There is no doubt but it must override theories and constitutions when they are in its way. "Delenda est Carthago"[1] is the universal logic of every nation that faces a deadly foe. All apparent wrong is made right when the plea of self-defense is once established. With nations as well as individuals, however, it must be clearly apparent before it will justify a blow. The danger must be imminent and such as a reasonably brave man would consider unavoidable by other means. When such a case shall be made out against the Chinese immigration, it will be the clear duty of the nation to grant the remedy now sought.

It is doubtful if any other bill upon the subject will pass at this session and before another arrives the question may meet with some other solution. At least it is likely to have a more thorough and impartial consideration by all classes of people, than the pendency of a general election would permit. It is a good time to move slowly.

1. This derives from the Roman war cry: "Carthage must be destroyed."

II

The Apostle of Evolution (1882)*

On May 24, 1882, Tourgée reflected on Charles Darwin's death in *Our Continent*. Surprisingly, in light of common use of Darwinian terminology by racial theorists, Tourgée defended Darwin against his critics and praised him for his fearless pursuit of truth. His comments suggest that Tourgée felt an affinity with Darwin as sincere propagator of an unpopular gospel, who was ostracized—as Tourgée had been in the South—for speaking his conscience.

"Is it right for Christian people to laud to the skies one who has done so much harm as Darwin simply because he is dead?" asks a devout friend. We are not of those who believe that death sanctifies, "the evil that men do lives after them" and ought to do so. The only value of some lives is to stand as a sign-post in the memory of those who came after pointing the pathway to destruction. A bad omen is made no better by death; only the good are set in the heavens to be remembered with blessing. Yet the question asked no doubt by many sincere believers who have lately read damning eulogies for Charles Robert Darwin in journals that have been wont to blazen his name with diatribe, involves too many assumptions to be answered in a paragraph.

Did he do any harm? Why should he not be praised? "But he was an enemy of religion!" If it be admitted, what then? Shall a man only be praised when he is right in his conclusions? Fame's list would be a short one if that were the rule. One thing in Darwin's life and character every one might share and imitate and the world be better and purer and sweeter for their doing so. He loved Nature, tenderly, truly, reverently. Her least as well as her mightiest manifestations were sacred to his touch. The poorest blade of grass was to his mind the sanctuary of divinity. No humbler child ever sat at Nature's knee and sought to learn of her. Whether he was right or wrong in his conclusions, no man, not even the blindest bigot, ever doubted that he went up to them

*"The Apostle of Evolution," *Our Continent* I (May 24, 1882): 226.

honestly, walking as he believed, in the footsteps of Nature. To him might well be applied the words that Longfellow sang of Agassiz:[1]

> "So he wandered away and away,
> With Nature the dear old nurse
> Who sung to him night and day,
> The rhymes of the universe."

There was one other thing in Darwin's life and character which the most devout might emulate. His life was that of a theorist and controversialist. Perhaps no man of our day has been more ruthlessly assailed. The Church has fulminated against him. His opponents have barbed the shafts of ridicule with malice. His name has been made the synonym of folly on the lips of the ignorant. From all quarters he has met with rancor, abuse and scorn. Yet in it all he has not answered railing with railing, scorn with scorn, or hate with hate. Not a word that he has written of another needs now to be blotted out, while strangely enough whole volumes of malignant wrath aimed at his head by those who claimed to be the followers of the meek and lowly Nazarene were better buried in the grave of the philosopher who was too great and calm and earnest to hate his fellow. Whether his theories be right or wrong, everyone who loves Nature may well thank Nature's God, for the keen eye, the skilful hand and patient heart, of the philosopher whose love never failed and whose heart never wearied in his search after truth. If he degraded man in his origin he exalted God in his works. He spat upon the sealed eyelids and we saw the things of God. He walked with us, and we heard voices in Nature unheard before. Never arrogant yet always earnest, the simple-hearted interpreter of Nature has taught us many a beautiful truth, and if he has erred in one rendering thereof, it becomes not us, blind moles whom he enlightened, to carp at his honest error.

Albion W. Tourgée

1. Louis Agassiz (1807–1873), one of the world's leading naturalists, who taught at Harvard University from 1848 to his death.

12

From *An Appeal to Caesar* (1884)*

Tourgée's book-length treatise *An Appeal to Caesar* (1884) presented his case for national aid to education in the South in its most fully developed form. Extending his analysis from "Aaron's Rod in Politics," this book offered both a lawyer's brief and a sociological treatise on race relations in the South and the transition from slavery to freedom. Widely reviewed in its day, the book provoked a variety of responses, but it was generally received with approval and respect. In the following excerpt, Tourgée ruminates on the nature of racial prejudice and the prospects of overcoming it, and he responds to several objections that had been raised against his proposal.

SOME QUEER NOTIONS PLAINLY STATED.

For himself, the author has become impressed with the truth of certain propositions; some of which persons much wiser than he may deny, and others of which they may doubt. Some there certainly are who will reject them. There may be those who, having assented to what was done when it was done, are now so sure that what they then did was in all respects perfect and complete that they do not deem it worth their while to work out the reckoning anew. Such will, of course, find nothing in these propositions worthy of consideration. There are some who will at once accept a part of them and reject the others without consideration. Of those, however, who I believe that even Wisdom may sometimes err, there are probably very few who will not find in them abundant food for very serious thought.

The propositions are these:

I. The real object of Reconstructionary legislation was to eradicate all irreconcilable differences between the North and the South and thereby avoid

*Excerpted from chapters 4, 7, and 22 of Albion W. Tourgée, *An Appeal to Caesar* (New York: Fords, Howard & Hulbert, 1884).

future conflict, establish homogeneity of sentiment throughout the country, and make the nation ONE PEOPLE, not merely in form, but also in fact.

II. The legislation which followed the close of the war, and which has generally been termed Reconstructionary, was utterly insufficient to accomplish such results either immediately or ultimately—in a decade or in a century.

III. This Reconstructionary legislation, whatever its other merits or defects, whether of principle or detail, lacked *some essential element* and must be and remain a failure, if not a farce, until that element is in some manner supplied.

IV. Every hour that we delay to ascertain and apply this supplementary remedy for the evils of the past is fraught with a danger which cannot be measured and can hardly be estimated by any examples which history has furnished.

V. If such remedy is not speedily applied, the evil that must result will be far greater than would have been likely to arise from the continuance of slavery.

VI. To give the slave his freedom, and impose upon the freedman the duties and responsibilities of the citizen, without providing for his instruction in those duties or securing him in their exercise, is not only a more perilous thing to the nation but just as inhuman a thing to the slave as to have left him still in bondage.

VII. On the one hand, to free four millions of slaves, not one in a hundred of whom could read or write, and not one of whom had the means for providing himself with tomorrow's bread; to give those freedmen an equal right with the other citizens of the several States in determining the policy and destiny not only of those States but also of the nation; and, on the other hand, to make no provision for their enlightenment, but to leave their instruction entirely to communities impoverished by war and predisposed by antecedent development and the prejudice of race and caste, as well as by the method and attendant circumstances of emancipation, to do but scanty justice to the negro—to do this thing and to leave the other undone, was not only an act of folly but of cowardly oppression to our foes, and of the basest treachery to our allies in war.

VIII. So thoroughly have the conscience and intelligence of the North apprehended these facts that, while the nation has done nothing, they have given in private charity intended to remedy this evil, *nearly a million dollars a year for nearly twenty years.* This is the instinct of a people versus the stupidity of her legislators.

IX. The turpitude of doing nothing is, in this case, only equaled by the folly of leaving the method of action to the determination of those who are, *a priori,* least favorably inclined to the results necessary to be achieved.

X. The chief reasons why, with an overflowing treasury, nothing has yet been done in this direction are the following: (a) No party has yet laid its imperative behest upon its servants that they should do this thing at the peril of disapproval for neglect; (b) No party has yet discovered any means by which it may utilize such a piece of statesmanship to enhance its chances in the next election by an appeal to the self-interest of the voters; (c) No method has yet been devised by which the same unity of sentiment can be obtained for such a measure as for the River and Harbor Appropriation—that is, by making it an engine for the election of a Republican in one district and a Democrat in another.

Anyone who agrees with these ten propositions does not need to read this book. To one who agrees with *none* of them its perusal would be a useless waste of time. To those who believe a part and doubt or deny the rest, it is hoped that it may suggest some things that shall serve either, to confirm or remove the doubt, and thereby assist them in determining upon the duty they have to perform. Whether the Nation shall seek to avoid evil or wait supinely until evil comes, it is well that the PEOPLE, who are its rulers, should decide with open eyes upon their duty and the behests they will lay upon their servants.

. . . . . .

A "TREASON OF THE BLOOD"

The sentiment of prejudice or hostility against the colored race on the part of the whites of the South is generally considered one of those "results of the war" which it is supposed need only to be let alone to cure themselves. In truth the war had little or nothing to do with the matter. The feeling which is termed race-prejudice or antipathy is not by any means peculiar to the white people of the South, nor is it in any sense dependent upon recent historical events. The failure of the Confederate cause and the consequent elevation of the negro may have brought into bolder relief the pre-existing characteristics of the contrasted races. So, too, it is unquestionable that the indiscreet exuberance of the African in the first possession of his new-found liberty may have tended to present more sharply to the minds of the Southern white people the difference of race upon which they had always insisted, and which the new political movement that followed the war may have seemed like an attempt to overthrow. It is, however, only that which has always occurred in history when two races, separated by an insurmountable barrier, have occupied the same territory, neither being subject to the other. This feeling of prejudice or antipathy existing between two distinctly marked races who are not only joint occupants of the same territory, but so closely intermingled that each constitutes an appreciable and important part of every subdivision of the community, is not in itself a matter of blame. Nor does its existence imply any lack of moral tone on the part of those who entertain such feeling. It is no fault of the Southern whites that they regard the colored man not only as their inferior at the present time, but as radically and irredeemably incapable of the same elevation and development. It is hardly surprising that, judging from the docility of this race in slavery and from the lack of inherent impulses towards civilization and development as manifested by its history, they should have arrived at this conclusion. Indeed, it seems much more remarkable that the people of the North should have so generally arrived at the contrary conclusion. Looking upon the negro as he presented himself to the eye of the ethnologist and historian in 1860, it appears now a most remarkable thing that so large a portion of the most intelligent and conscientious people of the North believed in the capacity of the colored man for self-support and ultimate self-direction. It is not at all likely, however, that anything less than the events of the war, the signal courage manifested by individuals of the colored race, and the marvelous devotion of all of them to the cause and persons of their deliverers, together with the strange and anomalous relation in which they stood to their former masters, would have induced the more conservative elements of the Northern people to consent to their enfranchisement even after their emancipation had become an accomplished fact.

The prejudice of race, whether it be a natural instinct or an acquired habit of mind, is a matter of very little importance so far as the result is concerned. Regarded from one point of view it is a disease. Looked at from another it is a natural instinctive feeling. In either case the remedy is the same. If it be an instinct, the highest intelligence is necessary to restrain its manifestation within due and proper limits and to prevent it from endangering the public peace or injuriously affecting the natural rights of those in relation to whom it exists. If it be a disease, the same modicum of intelligence is required not only to limit its manifestations, but ultimately to eradicate and destroy it. So far as this book is concerned it is a matter of entire indifference whether the prejudice of the white race for the negro is a matter of instinct or of cultivation. Whether it is an inherent ineradicable animosity planted in the breast of the white man for some inscrutable reason, or whether it is a natural and divine provision to prevent the admixture of the races and carry into effect some mysterious purpose of Providence by which the great classes of the human family shall forever be kept separate and distinct, or simply a sentiment engendered by centuries of association in the relation of master and slave, is a matter altogether foreign to the subject which we have in hand. In either case it remains a simple fact, a fact for which neither the white man nor the colored man of the South can be held morally or individually responsible, but one which should be carefully and calmly considered in all its various relations in order that serious and dangerous consequences which might otherwise arise therefrom shall be duly foreseen and securely guarded against. Whether it be a natural instinct or acquired prejudice the remedy against its dangerous manifestation is the same to wit, the intelligence of the individuals of both races. A clear perception of the perils incident to both the intermingled races from any extended conflict between them is the only thing that will restrain the superior race from oppression, or the inferior from revolt. We shall consider race prejudice, therefore, simply as a fact for which the individual affected by it is only in a modified sense responsible, which of itself constitutes no imputation upon his morality, civilization, or purity of purpose, but which needs to be recognized and understood in all its relations as well by the superior as by the inferior race, in order that serious consequences may not arise from the intimate admixture of the races and their constant exposure to disturbing and inflammatory influences.

No two free races thus distinctly separated by color and by marked natural characteristics have ever yet dwelt side by side without conflict. That they should ever do so is accounted by very many an impossibility. Every Southern writer upon the subject of slavery from the very first moment when the conflict of ideas began to stir the Western world to universal thought upon the subject, has laid it down as a basis principle that two such races cannot, by any possibility, dwell together in freedom and in peace.

Upon this subject we quote the words of Prof. E. W. Gilliam, writing from a Southern stand point and with a strong Southern bias, in the *Popular Science Monthly* for February, 1883. His views are important, not merely from the terse and epigrammatic form in which they are set, but because they represent clearly and distinctly the feelings of a man fully in sympathy with both the future and the past of the whites at the South:

> The second factor in our argument is the impossibility of fusion between whites and blacks. The latter have been, and must continue to be, a distinct

and alien race. The fusion of races is the resultant from social equality and intermarriage, and the barrier to this is here insurmountable. The human species presents three grand varieties, marked off by color—white, yellow, and black. One at the first, in origin and color, the race multiplied and spread, and separate sections, settled in different latitudes, took on—under climatic conditions acting with abnormal force in that early and impressionable period of the races's [*sic*] age—took on, we say, different hues, which, as the race grew and hardened, crystallized into permanent characteristics. Social affinity exists among the families of these three groups. The groups themselves stand rigidly apart. The Irish, German, French, etc., who come to these shores, readily intermarry among themselves and with the native population. Within a generation or two the sharpness of national feature disappears, and the issue is the American whose mixed blood is the country's foremost hope. It cannot be—a fusion like this between whites and blacks. Account for it as we may, the antipathy is a palpable fact which no one fails to recognize—an antipathy not less strong among the Northern than among the Southern whites. However, the former may on the score of matters political, profess themselves special friends to the blacks, the question of intermarriage and social, equality, when brought to practical test, they will not touch with the end of the little finger. Whether it be that the blacks, because of their former condition of servitude, are regarded as a permanently degraded class; whether it be that the whites, from their historic eminence, are possessed with a consciousness of superiority which spurns alliance—the fact that fusion is impossible no one in his senses can deny.

The conclusion at which Prof. Gilliam arrives is indisputable, as he says, "by any man in his senses" during any period with regard to which speculation may be properly and reasonably extended. Certain it is that the influences now existent will render his words as true a hundred years from now as they are today. What change may possibly be wrought in the tone and sentiment of generations more remote and under circumstances which cannot now be foreseen, it is, of course, impossible to estimate. Looking at the subject from a standpoint diametrically opposed in every respect both to the intellectual bias and political inclination of Prof. Gilliam, we are compelled to indorse his views in this respect almost without the least modification.

This feeling does not in any sense necessitate or imply a sentiment of hostility, either individual or collective, upon the part of one race toward the other. The Southern white man who says that he feels kindly toward the negro is entitled to the utmost credence, even though it may be shown by irrefragable testimony that he has exerted unlawful violence to prevent the negro from the exercise of a legal right. He simply regards the negro as an inferior, with an inherited belief which amounts almost to an instinct, even if it be not actually instinctive. He wishes only good to that inferior; has no desire to do him harm, to lessen his comfort or prevent his success, within what he deems the proper sphere of his existence. He is a Christian man, and he desires to see the colored man improve in morals, industry, and the virtues of a Christian life. All these things he may most earnestly and sincerely desire for the colored man whom he calls, with effusive and perhaps delusive warmth, "our brother in black." It is only when the necessity arises for considering this race as the equal of the white race in power, in freedom, and in opportunity, that we discover that beneath this sentiment of kindness lies the indefinable feeling that the colored man may not, must not, shall not, stand upon the same level of right and power as the white. It matters not how good, how kind, how charitable the man may be in an overwhelming majority of cases, you will find that he has, at bottom, an ineradicable hostility to the colored man as a political integer, simply because he *is* a *Negro*.

It is not strange that this feeling should exist. The very fact of difference of race and color is not one lightly to be disregarded. There are instances in the world's history in which two types of the same race have dwelt side by side for centuries, almost, without intermingling of blood. There are cases in which inherited antipathies have been handed down from generation to generation for centuries between two peoples having the same colored skin and similar casts of features, each preserving their own peculiar language, customs and habits of life, and maintaining between them an almost bottomless gulf of separation. Between the Anglo-Saxon or the Caucasian of the temperate zone and all other races, this feeling of repulsion seems always to have been peculiarly strong. There is hardly an instance to be found in which this color-line has been successfully passed over by either race, no matter how long they have lived in juxtaposition.

That the whites should not willingly and voluntarily disregard this line of demarcation is not strange. It was by no means an inconsiderable impulse at the outset, and has been greatly strengthened by centuries of association in the relation of master and slave, superior and inferior, ruler and worker. It is altogether wrong to suppose that, as a rule, the Southern slave-master was cruel to his slave, beyond the mere fact of restraining him of his liberty and depriving him of his rights. Not only the ordinary feeling of kindness which subsists between man and man prevailed with them, but the impulse of self-interest tended in the same direction. The sentiment of race prejudice or animosity is not at all akin to any feeling of personal hostility or individual dislike. It is only a mutual shrinking away from each other of distinctly marked types—a crystallization about different centers, the claim of peculiar privileges or the reverse, because of distinctive characteristics, common to great masses. It is only that feeling which marks off into two distinct bodies the people occupying the same territory, by insurmountable and invisible, barriers. Race-prejudice, if it be possible to overcome it at all, if it can ever be eliminated, will only disappear after the lapse not of years but of generations and centuries. At present it is not likely to diminish perceptibly in strength and influence upon the contrasted cases during any period that may be regarded as within the influences of the present. It may be repressed and its manifestations may be so modified by peculiar influences as to be comparatively innocuous, but there is no prospect of its elimination for centuries, if indeed it be possible that it should ever disappear.

It is worthy of consideration, too, that this feeling has another side which is daily coming to be of more and more importance. The sentiment of the colored man toward the white man according to the theory of slavery was one of filial regard and dependency. According to the theory of the slave it was one of hopeless helplessness and ineradicable distrust. The colored man since his enslavement in America could not help regarding the white man as having deprived him of certain natural rights. We speak now of the colored man as animated by the ordinary impulses of humanity. It is not worth while to consider the question whether the instinct of liberty and the impulse of self-control is as strong in the African as in the Anglo-Saxon or not. In a greater or lesser degree, varying of course with temper and intelligence, the two races are and must be controlled by the same general laws. The slave never forgot his enslavement. The colored man, whose manhood had been stripped away from his life, never forgot that the power which did this was that of the white man. He may have believed, almost, that it was right that he should be thus subjugated. There may, possibly, have been instances in which religious feeling was so strongly wrought upon as to produce in the mind of the slave the conviction that God had designed him for nothing but slavery, and there unquestionably were thousands of cases in which the attachment of the slave to the master or the master's child was stronger than the instinct of life itself. So, too, the slave would trust implicitly the master's word in all matters that did not touch his own liberty and right. Upon this subject he listened to him with incredulity. Down deep in the heart of the slave dwelt always this one thought: "I am not a free man *because* the white man has made me a slave."

This feeling grew in strength with the inevitable increase of the slave in intelligence. Though the spelling-book was a sealed mystery to his eyes, while it was a felony for any one to teach him to read and write, while instruction in the arts and sciences was forbidden him, yet it was impossible for the American negro to be brought in contact with the wonderful life of the New World without growing unconsciously in strength and knowledge; so that the slave of the period of the war differed, perhaps, quite as much from his African congener as did the master from the type of Englishman from which he was evolved.

This feeling was at the root of that wide-spread belief among the slaves that a day of Jubilee would come—that sooner or later God would in some mysterious way work out their deliverance from bondage. Already for half a century, or more perhaps, it had been taking root and spreading throughout the whole mass of the colored population of the South, leavening the whole body with a hope of something in the future distinctly favorable to the race, as such. When the War of Rebellion began, it had not yet grown so strong as to demand active co-operation upon their part with the Federal power, but as the struggle progressed and they saw in its outcome the possible fulfillment of their hopes, the race attested its manhood, and, under the inspiration of this feeling, did worthy battle for that power which promised the accomplishment of their desire.

While it was true that the conflict which resulted in their freedom was between two hostile sections of the white race, and that they owed their emancipation to the Caucasian just as certainly as they had previously owed their enslavement to that race, there was still this difference: the power which freed was to them a foreign power; the power which enslaved, a domestic one. That they divided the world, into three classes, "white folks, niggers, and Yanks," was by no means unnatural or unphilosophical; and in a great degree the distinction still prevails. The power with which they finally joined hands for their own liberation was, to all intents and purposes, one outside of the life of which they constituted a part. The "white people" to them meant, and must always mean, those by whom they are surrounded and with whom the relations of daily life are to be maintained.

Between these two classes the distance has greatly increased since the close of the war, and it must continue to increase as the daily lives of the individuals diverge more and more from each other. Slavery was a domestic institution. More or less the master's chattels were a part of his household and became touched with his sentiments and feelings. The domestic servants were the depositaries of all the secrets of the family. Its most sacred mysteries were unveiled to them. These intimate personal relations served to keep out of sight during the existence of slavery that feeling of race-antipathy which the servile relation was all the time actually strengthening between those affected by these relations. When the freedman began to establish his own home-circle, to build for himself a household about his own hearth, however humble, the distance between the whites and blacks, though in fact very greatly diminished, seemed to have been as greatly increased.

One of the chief absurdities that marks the ordinary belief in regard to this matter is the general impression that in the course of a generation or so the descendants of the American slave will have forgotten all about slavery. Nothing could be more at variance with the universal testimony of history upon this point. A race which has been subjected to humiliation and oppression by another race retains the memory of wrong long after all sense of personal grievance has been lost. The fierce rage of the Israelites against their Egyptian oppressors lasted for centuries after they had escaped from the power of the Pharaoh. Even in private life, the tradition of wrong done to the father often produces a bitterer animosity on the part of the children than in the mind of the injured party. A hundred years hence the hardships and wrongs of slavery will constitute a stronger impulse to united action on the part of the colored race than they do today. It would be inconsistent with every principle of human nature if, even after the lapse of centuries, the colored orator and poet did not dwell upon the wrongs of their forefathers with a fervor and intensity that would surprise the recipient of the wrongs described. The colored man who today looks back upon slavery with feelings very far removed from unmixed bitterness will have great-grandchildren to whom the wrongs which he has suffered will constitute a ceaseless impulse to concerted action with their fellows in the interests of their race.

Besides this, it is an inflexible rule of development that the inferior class when free has always an upward tendency and inclination to rise and become, sooner or later, the dominant power. The slave has nothing to hope for and no impulse to exertion; but no sooner does he become free than the avenues to wealth and ambition open more or less clearly for him. It may be generations before the race is able to improve its new-found opportunity. It may be that but one colored man in a State has achieved financial independence in a decade, yet that one man is an example to all others, constantly stimulating them to renewed exertion. It maybe that in a whole State but one or two colored men have won their way into the mystic arena of the bar, and even these may be far from encouraging examples of forensic ability, yet never one of them opens his lips in court that his example does not inspire some colored boy that listens to do as he has done. The same inclination to stand by each other and to make common cause in matters pertaining to the race has led the people to associate together in churches of their own, their own lodges and protective unions, and the law has built for them a barrier around the schools. The freedman of the South is distinctly a negro from his birth and in every relation of life. It is the chief element in every phase of his existence. Religion, that is supposed to be the great mollifier of savage influences, has become in his case the promoter of differences. The slave, in the main, went with his master to church. In a city of ten thousand people you will find today hardly ten colored faces in the white congregations.

This mutual isolation of the races must of necessity constantly increase. Already there are but two important relations of life in which the negro mingles with the white man on anything like a basis of equality. The one is as a laborer, where, indeed, his position is not equality, but superiority. The negro is *par excellence* the laborer of the South. The white man is compelled to work beside him, and feels himself humiliated by the fact. The other place where they are supposed to meet upon the level of right is at the ballot-box, where the white man regards him as an intruder. The colored man, as he goes farther away from the wrongs of slavery with the lapse of time, will feel all the more keenly the disabilities that still remain, and will become more and more suspicious of the race to which he not unnaturally attributes the woes of himself and his ancestors. The white man, as he watches what he deems the aggressions of the colored man, his acquisition of wealth and power, and his assumption of independent relations for himself and his race, will naturally be impelled still more strongly to maintain his own actual or fancied superiority by whatever means may be necessary effectually to maintain a "white man's government" and the white man's right to rule throughout every State of the South.

If, therefore, the existing influences and forces which govern and control Southern life shall continue in their present relations, the point of general conflict must be reached sooner or later. The negro's struggles for equality of right and recognition as a potent factor in public affairs must some time become organized, general, and irresistible except by overwhelming force. At the same time the white man's resolution to keep him still in an inferior position, growing stronger and stronger by repeated successes, must eventually result in such organized repression as can be met only by organized retaliation.

Whether there is any remedy which may avert this catastrophe it behooves us earnestly to inquire. If something be not done, and done quickly, the result is inevitable.

. . . . . .

OBJECTIONS CONSIDERED

Various objections are made both to the policy and legality of any measure proposing the national aid to education, but more especially to one which does not put the distribution and application of the fund entirely within the control of the individual States. First and most important of these objections is the following:

Congress has not the constitutional authority to levy taxes or appropriate funds for such purpose.

This objection comes too late. It has already been determined by numerous precedents that the Government has such power. Under various acts nearly two billion acres of the public domain have already been appropriated for the purposes of education. Schools have been established, funds have been created for the establishment in different States of institutions of a peculiar class or character, and the whole course of the Government tends to show an almost universal concurrence in the idea that the power "to promote science and the useful arts" must include that master-key to all science and art, the general intelligence of the citizen and the prevalence among all classes of the people of that rudimentary knowledge without which neither science nor art can flourish.

But in the view which we have taken of this subject the authority of Congress to appropriate funds for the primary education of the citizen rests upon a much broader basis—the authority granted in the Constitution to "provide for the common defense and general welfare of the United States." It rests upon the same fundamental principle as the various acts and appropriations for the support of the Military Academy at West Point or the Naval Academy at Annapolis. The great controlling purpose of such appropriation is to secure public peace, promote the national power, and establish the national welfare and prosperity, by giving to its citizens an opportunity to learn the duties of citizenship, to perform the functions devolved upon them as component elements of our national power, to cement and strengthen their allegiance and devotion to the Government and the principles upon which it is founded. If there was ever a measure proposed which was clearly and unmistakably within the scope and purpose of this broad and essential power, it is the one which we are now considering. It is essential to the common defense because it tends to unity of sentiment, suppression of discord, and the removal of causes which might easily result in domestic violence.

It promotes the national welfare because it enables the citizen to comprehend and perform his duties, to protect himself against fraud and violence, to understand and appreciate the rights and privileges conferred upon him; and it strengthens his adhesion and devotion to the Government. Moreover, this constitutional objection, it will be observed, whether it count for much or little, applies just as strongly to the one plan of distribution as to the other. If the Nation has not the right to levy taxes and distribute funds through its own agencies, it very clearly has no right to apportion those funds among the different States.

The second objection is that the general government has no right to appropriate funds for the benefit of classes or individuals.

Those who urge this objection seem to be laboring under the impression that national aid to education is to be given solely for the benefit and advantage of those individuals and classes receiving instruction. Such is not at all the principle on which public instruction, whether State or National, is based. The State does not educate the citizen for his own sake. It does not bestow the rudiments of education or the elements of science for the sake of the individual. The whole theory of public instruction is based upon the principle of public benefit to be derived there from. The fact that the individual receives advantage thereby is entirely secondary and subordinate to this main object. The fact that education increases individual opportunity and power, opens to the instructed the avenues of wealth and prosperity, enables him to pursue avocations from which he would otherwise be excluded—in short, the fact that intelligence directly or indirectly elevates, strengthens, and in all respects improves the individual, while a very pleasant and agreeable incident of public instruction, would yet constitute an entirely insufficient reason for the establishment of such systems. No fact can be clearer, both from fundamental reasoning and constitutional consideration than the proposition that a government, whether State or National, has no right to tax A for the benefit of B, C, or D, or for any class or number of individuals. It is only upon the ground that the ignorance of B, C, and D is an element of weakness, expense, or peril to the State or the Nation that it becomes permissible to employ public funds for the removal of such peril or for the enhancement of public prosperity by the lessening of expenditure or the increase of productive capacity. The right of the Nation to secure the general intelligence of its citizens is even more limited than this. The State as such—the subordinate republic of our Federal Union—is interested directly in increasing the productive capacity and the power of self-support of each one of her citizens. One of the first great duties of a modern government is to provide for the support of its pauper classes. This also constitutes one of its chiefest burdens. This burden is greatly lessened by the general intelligence of the citizen which promotes his capacity for self-support by opening to him other channels and fresh opportunities for exertion. The State, therefore, is directly interested in the intelligence of its entire population. Schools are in this respect as in some others a direct investment for the benefit of the commonwealth. The general government has no such direct interest in the intelligence of the masses. The support of the poor, outside of the District of Columbia, in no case becomes a charge upon its treasury. Its interest in the citizen is not one of direct pecuniary advantage. While the prevalence of illiteracy no doubt indirectly tends to reduce its revenues by repressing enterprise and reducing the productive capacity of the masses, its interest in their development is of a higher and less material character. Still it is the interest of the general public and not that of the recipient classes which is to be subserved by national aid to primary education. As ignorance is dangerous to the public welfare, so intelligence is favorable to it. As ignorance of the duties of the citizen necessarily implies inability for their proper discharge, so intelligence presumes the faithful performance of such duties. The principle on which this measure depends, therefore, is not the benefit of any particular class but the general advantage of the entire Republic.

This objection is especially potent with those who conceive that the purpose and intention of this act is to extend some special favor to the colored race. While it might be within the purview of the powers of Congress to grant to this race special privilege or advantage in consideration of the circumstances which have attended its previous history, yet such cannot properly be accounted the purpose of this measure. More than one-third of the recipients of direct advantage therefrom will be of the white race; and the indirect advantage to accrue is in the proportion of *seven millions* of blacks to *forty-three millions* of whites. It is true that the relations which our Government has sustained to the colored people in the past, and the duties which it has placed upon the individuals of that race while yet in a state of profound ignorance with regard to their performance, have been such as should constitute, a most potent factor in inclining every right-minded citizen toward the acceptance of this policy. This duty becomes incumbent upon us not simply because education will be a direct advantage to the individuals of that race, but because the national honor is pledged—the good faith of a great people placed in pawn— with those unfortunate allies whom the Nation has abandoned in its hour of prosperity. We gave them liberty which we coupled with the duty of citizen- ship. We put into their hands the sword which we asked them to use for the national honor as well as for individual defense. We left them ignorant of the proper exercise of the power they held, defenseless before their hereditary en- emies, the sometime foes of the Republic. Yet it is not chiefly for their advan- tage that this measure of justice and righteousness is proposed, but to redeem the honor of the whole people and to secure the safety of a great nation.

Another objection made to this measure is that a large portion of the fund will be expended in the attempt to educate the negro and prepare him for the exercise of co- equal power in the Government, man for man, with his white fellow-citizens, and that such expenditure is simply a wasteful attempt to perform an impossibility.

I do not care to discuss the question. Whether the colored man is the equal, the inferior, or the superior of the white race in knowledge, capacity, or the power of self-direction has not been specifically revealed to me. I have no knowledge in regard to the matter beyond what is accessible to every other citizen. Some things are self-evident, and among these is the fact that every argument and demonstration by which the inherent inferiority of the African of the United States has been so frequently established has been shown by the irrefragable evidence of experience to be false. Year after year for a cen- tury, it has been dinned into the ears of the American people that the African could not live except in a state of slavery. Those who boasted of having con- verted him to Christianity declared his inherent barbarism to be incurable. The power of progress and development was denied him. Only the form of man, the debased instincts of the slave, and a sufficiency of the immortal prin- ciple to make him a child of grace were accorded to the colored man. We were told that he would not work; that he would starve in the midst of profusion; that idleness was not only his besetting sin but his irremediable defect; that lust and vice would make the race an uncontrollable scourge to the land; that there were but two alternatives, the state of bondage or utter annihilation. Twenty years of liberty have disproved each one of these dicta. Already there are proportionably fewer of this race maintained of the public expense than of the white race. The idleness which was to destroy has resulted in increased production of all the staples of that region. The vice which was to overwhelm society has for the most part been confined to petty crimes and misdemeanors which slavery encouraged. Having been taught by Christian slavery that the sacrament of marriage could not bind their race, cast adrift with no recognized or legal family ties, the great bulk of this despised people recognized the moral force of previous personal association, and even in this respect are not behind those classes of the whites which are affected with like ignorance and poverty. In addition to all this, in eighteen years of liberty they have organized thousands of efficient church-societies, erected all over the South comfortable houses of worship, and, with all their crudity of ideas and of practice, constitute today perhaps the best organized, most self-sacrificing body of professed Christians in the world. This power of church government, religious association, and intelligent management and direction of church affairs—the accomplishment of really great things with the most scanty means, the least possible opportunity, and under the most adverse circumstances—would seem to demonstrate that the colored man may yet constitute a factor in republican government by no means to be despised.

Whether the black man will in all respects, develop an absolute equality of power with the white is, however, a question that cannot yet be answered either the one way or the other. So far as the measure under discussion is concerned it is entirely immaterial whether he has such a capacity or not. This one thing we do know: that the Nation has recognized him as capable to perform the duties of citizenship even without the preparation and the experience which the white race had received before developing such capacity. Having conferred that privilege and duty upon him, it is an unavoidable obligation that we place before him every possible opportunity to develop whatever power he may possess. If he is not capable of competing with the white race after enjoying such opportunity, certainly no harm will have resulted from allowing him to approach as nearly to that level as he is capable of attaining. On the other hand, if it should be that his capacity is not materially different from that of the white man, certainly no Christian people can be excused and no government upon which rest such obligations as we have recognized can be held guiltless if they fail to enable him to take the initial step in the race of progress by granting him an opportunity to obtain the rudiments of an education.

There are some—more than would generally be supposed, yet, thank God, not so many as there might be—who urge against this measure that it would result in a sacrilegious disturbance of the ordained and established relations between the races, by which dominion and control has been given to the whites, and menial service and subjection decreed for the blacks.

There are not a few, especially among our Southern brethren, who do not hesitate to declare that the divine order prescribes subjection of the negro to the control of the white. They assert without any hesitation that it is the un-doubted will of the Almighty that the white man is and must forever remain the undoubted superior and the rightful controller and director of the destiny of the colored race. The belief in this peculiar dogma is, perhaps, more widely spread than one might suppose it possible that it should be. Its constant rep-etition, year after year and generation after generation, has unquestionably served to fix it in the minds of the Southern whites as a truth which, if not ab-solutely demonstrable from the words of revelation, is yet so indubitable that it may as well be accepted as divine. This was the supposed premise on which negro slavery rested its claim to recognition as a Christian institution. It was never contended that the right existed under any circumstances to enslave a white man. There were undoubtedly some instances in which it was done, but such acts were always, not only in violation of law but opposed to the public sentiment and religious conviction of the entire people of the South. The defense set up in favor of American slavery, distinguishing it from that which existed among the early Roman believers, was based entirely upon the fact that the American slave was of the African race. It was freely admitted that under no circumstances could the right exist to enslave one of Caucasian birth, but it was maintained by the great body of Southern Christians that the distinction of race and color was designed to mark a difference of right and destiny which the Supreme Being had for his own inscrutable purposes established. The same belief in a modified form still exists and actuates the conduct and convictions of a very large proportion of the Southern people. They do not admit that the colored man can ever become entitled to share in the duty of mutual control and direction that rests upon the white citizen. He is regarded as having been divinely set apart for a peculiar, specific, and inferior destiny. To attempt to enlarge his sphere of action, to seek to elevate him to the level of the white or permit him to claim as of right equal dignity authority, and capacity, is to impugn the wisdom and decrees of the Almighty. We do not know whether this belief is well founded or not. We have no spe-cial knowledge of the divine purpose in establishing distinctions of race, nor do we believe that any other human being has. At any rate the events of the past quarter of a century would seem to be sufficient to convince any one of the possibility of mistake in regard to such a theory. There was evidently some sort of error in the doctrine so universally accepted and taught at the South with regard to the divine nature of slavery. There must have been some sort of mistake in regard to the capacity of the negro for self-support. Time has demonstrated that emancipation is not the forerunner of extinction through any natural or physical cause. It is, therefore, at least possible that the related theory in regard to the purpose intended to be subserved by the distinction of race and color may also be erroneous. Where so many theories, each one resting in some degree upon the other and all of them being merely speculative conclusions from the same group of facts, have been proved false by the irresistible logic of events, it is well not to regard the other doctrines of this group of related theories with too much positiveness of conviction. It would seem to be altogether possible that the whole idea of the inferiority of the blacks to the whites might yet disappear. Whether it be true or false, however, one thing is certain, the white race can never prove or maintain its superiority simply by excluding the negro from all opportunity for growth and development.

. . . . . .

There remains one general objection to national aid to education specially applicable to the view which we have taken of the subject, namely, that education of itself is not sufficient to make a man a good citizen.

There can be no doubt in regard to this proposition. A man may have all knowledge and possess all wisdom and yet be a tyrant, a usurper, a "boss," a traitor, or a conspirator. Mere intelligence is not enough to insure the performance of public duties, any more than it is a sufficient safeguard against private crime. Knowledge simply gives to the individual the power to be a good citizen, not the inclination. It shows him how the power which he holds by means of the ballot may be exercised either for good or for evil. How he will exercise it depends very largely upon his antecedent development. Knowledge, whether it be much or little, is only an instrumentality by which a good or evil inclination acts. And while it is true that an educated man may not be a good citizen because he will not perform the duties which he understands, it is very certain that the ignorant man cannot exercise the power of the citizen with any sort of assurance that he is acting rightly. Knowledge does not of necessity make any man honest, but it enables him to detect other men's dishonesty. Intelligence does not make a man courageous and incorruptible; it only shows him how he may use his courage and how he may defend himself against fraud. Intelligence simply furnishes the motive power by which manhood may make itself effective in political affairs as well as in any other.

Political error is possible to the most highly cultured community, and it is not an infrequent thing to find the best-educated class in a community adopting some pet theory which if carried into effect would result in the most imminent public disaster. The Southern slave-owners were unquestionably a highly intelligent and well-educated class of men. They were also men of as keen natural instincts and as good and patriotic bias as could be found. Blinded by the fact of slavery, however, they became the most dangerous enemies the country has ever known.

Our Government is the first great republic of the world, indeed the first nation, to have tried the experiment of self-government on the broad basis of including within the governing power all the males of mature age. This theory is founded upon the hypothesis that the majority of all communities are right-thinking, honest, patriotic, and brave, they are supposed to be honest enough to decide (without being influenced by base motives or narrow individual considerations) what measures are for the public weal and what party is most likely to carry out and enforce such measures. They are supposed to be too honest to be willing to sell the safety and happiness and prosperity of the future for a trivial pleasure of the present. They are supposed to be earnest enough in their convictions, loyal enough to their duty and the interest of the country to be ready and willing to maintain those convictions at whatever hazard against fraud or violence.

If these basis-hypotheses on which our Government was founded are incorrect, then, in indeed, it matters little what may be the character of our controlling masses. But if our Government is founded upon the true principles of democracy, if self-government is a possibility to any great nation, then it is of the utmost importance that every individual constituting the governing power in such nation should be not only honest and patriotic and courageous, but that he should have knowledge to inform his honesty, knowledge to sustain his patriotism, knowledge to direct his courage. The ignorant man is as the breath of life to the nostrils of the demagogue. He is the material which the ambitious and unscrupulous leader uses to promote his own unrighteous ends. While intelligence may in some cases lead to abuse of power, ignorance renders almost certain its misuse. The voter who drops into the box a ballot which he cannot read is like a blind man wielding a sword; he may slay his enemy, but he is quite as likely to destroy his friend.

13

Shall White Minorities Rule? (1889)*

"Shall White Minorities Rule?" was a part of a debate on black voting rights published in the journal *Forum*. In this article, Tourgée responded to Alabama senator John T. Morgan, who had defended the exclusion of blacks from the ballot box in the article "Shall Negro Majorities Rule?" (*Forum* 6 [February 1889]: 586–99). At the time of their exchange, the Republicans held a majority of both congressional houses for the first time since 1874, and legislation to protect black voting rights in the South was on the agenda of the new Congress. Senator Morgan was among the most outspoken opponents of federal intervention in the southern states to protect black voting rights.

The "Negro question" is unquestionably the most momentous problem of our civilization. Considered with regard either to its scope or character it is almost unprecedented in importance, difficulty, and the possible peril involved in its solution. It is not a new question. Slavery and the slave trade were only its earlier phases. Rebellion, reconstruction, and Ku-Kluxism were incidents attending its partial solution. For a hundred years it has almost constantly threatened the life of the republic. The steps already taken toward its solution have cost the nation a million lives and some half-dozen billions of dollars. It still confronts us unresolved and growing every hour more perilous. In its essential elements the Negro question has remained, from the very first, substantially unchanged. The slave trade was based solely upon the claim that the white man was inherently superior to the colored man, and therefore had a right to take, hold, subjugate, and utilize the labor of the Negro, without compensation and without his consent. This was accounted a conclusive argument at that time. Might and right were then very nearly convertible terms. The strong were always in the right, while the weak were peculiarly liable to

*Albion W. Tourgée, "Shall White Minorities Rule?" *Forum* 7 (April 1889): 143–55.

error and, of course, required restraint. The sword and the stake were then approved theological arguments, and difference of faith was almost as perilous to individual liberty as a contrast in the color of the skin. Slavery held the same ground. Backed by scriptural exegesis and entrenched behind the Constitution, it held this position until the whole fabric of illusions based on the patriarchal anathema, "Cursed be Canaan," and the Apostolic injunction, "Servants, be obedient to your masters," was swept away by a whelming tide of freemen's blood. It is useless at this time to discuss the question of the inherent superiority of the white race, or whether the fact of superiority confers a right to subordinate and control an inferior race. The conscience and intelligence of today will not tolerate any such absurdity.

The present phase of the question is a controversy touching the Negro's right to exercise freely, peacefully, and effectually the elective franchise, and to enjoy without hindrance its resulting incidents. It is not fairly presented by the inquiry, "Shall black majorities rule?" The rule of the majority is the fundamental principle of our government. It is one of the incidents of the right to exercise the elective franchise, of which no individual or class can lawfully be deprived while that right remains unrestricted. Some confusion has been produced in the discussion of this question by attempting to treat the elective franchise as a privilege instead of a right. Until duly conferred it is a privilege— a privilege which no individual or class has any legal right to demand. Once granted, however, the exercise and enjoyment of it and of all its natural incidents becomes a right which the sovereign must maintain and enforce, or submit to nullification of the law. The particular point in controversy is not whether the colored man shall be allowed a new privilege, but whether lie shall be permitted to exercise a right already guaranteed by law. The proper form of inquiry, therefore, is, "Shall white minorities rule?"

The arguments advanced in support of this monstrous proposition thus far are identical with those adduced in favor of slavery and the slave trade, nullification, secession, rebellion, Ku-Kluxism—all varying phases, let us not forget, of the same idea. They are urged by the same class of our people, with the same unanimity, the same positiveness, and the same arrogant assumption of infallibility as of old. They not only boastfully admit that for a decade and a half they have nullified the law and defied the national power, but boldly proclaim their determination to continue to do so as long as they may see fit.

In order to appreciate the importance of this question, it is necessary to consider both its character and its scope. In character it is a question of relative rank between two classes of people in a republic whose laws guarantee equality of right and privilege to all. Both classes speak the same language, profess the same religion, owe allegiance to the same government, and are legally entitled to exercise, man for man, the same power in its control. The one is black, more or less; the other is white. The one has been the bondman of the other for two centuries and a half; he has been a freeman for twenty-four years (since 1865), and a citizen for twenty-one years (since 1868). Socially, they are antipodes. Intermarriage between them is forbidden in most of the States, North as well as South; yet in none of them is the illicit relation of the white man with the colored female specifically prohibited. While professing the same religion, their church relations are entirely separate. They do not worship in the same edifice, white and colored ministrants do not serve at the same altar, and white and black communicants do not kneel together to partake of the same sacraments. No colored man is ever invited to a fashionable gathering. No white woman can recognize a colored woman as a friend and intimate without losing caste with her own people. One drop of colored blood constitutes its possessor a social pariah just as much as if he were of pure African descent.

In scope the Negro question embraces the political and economic relations which eight millions of our people must sustain to the remaining seven eighths of our population, as well as to the people and government of the States in which they arc chiefly to be found. South of the Potomac and Ohio rivers, and westward to Kansas, the Negro constitutes one-third of the population. Three-fourths of the entire colored population are to be found in eight States—Virginia, North Carolina, South Carolina, Georgia, Alabama, Florida, Louisiana, and Mississippi. In these States there is one colored man for every white one. In three of them, South Carolina, Mississippi, and Louisiana, there are one-fifth more blacks than whites. In these States the population is very intimately intermixed. On every plantation and in almost every house both races are represented. Few white families are without colored kindred. In churches, schools, and social gatherings, however, they are distinct. Politically, the white race is exclusively dominant. All executive and judicial positions are filled by white men. In the eight States named there are less than half a score of colored members of the State legislatures. The colored race increases in numbers in these States much faster than the white race. Since 1790 they have increased 564%; in the same time the whites have increased only 343%. The whites of these States show a much greater tendency to migrate than the blacks. In 1880 24% of the native white population had removed from the State of birth; but only 15% of the colored natives are to be found in other States. There are no existing conditions which are likely to change these proportions or tendencies. Alabama and Georgia will probably show more blacks than whites in 1890, and Florida, North Carolina, and Virginia in 1900. The colored race is not likely to emigrate in any great numbers, because there is no region in which the training which slavery gave is likely to win success in competition with that developed by free labor and the universal employment of machinery in agricultural processes. There will never be any white immigration to these States sufficient sensibly to affect the proportions between the races. In 1880 there were 30,000 fewer whites of northern birth in these States than in 1860, and 3,000 fewer of northern birth than in 1870. Of the latter—whites of a northern birth, that is—there were in all these eight States only 52,000 in 1880, and 55,000 in 1870, or less than three-fifths of 1% of the population. This proportion is not likely to be greatly increased, because the northern white man cannot compete with the southern Negro as a manual laborer. The Negro will work more hours for less money, wait longer for his pay, live in cheaper houses, endure more hardships, claim fewer privileges, and increase more rapidly than the northern or foreign white laborer. The numerical relations of the races in these States are not likely to be greatly modified in favor of the white race, and the distribution of the colored race throughout the country is not likely to be sensibly disturbed during the next generation. While the ratio of blacks in the whole country is not likely to be greatly increased, in the eight States named every indication points to a greatly-enhanced numerical proportion. Its future scope, therefore, may be defined with almost the same accuracy as its present limits.

In its present phase, the Negro question is not one of sentiment, so far as the colored man is concerned. He asks nothing as a Negro. On the score of "race, color, or previous condition of servitude" he makes no demand, asks no favors. It is as a citizen merely that we are called on to consider what rights and privileges he is entitled to exercise, and how far and in what manner it is just, politic, and safe to permit them to be restricted, abridged, or revoked. Like most political questions, it presents a mixed issue of policy and principle. What is best to be done must depend to a great extent upon what we have the right to do. These elements cannot be separated, and must both be allowed due weight in the final decision.

Even if the claim of inherent superiority of the white race be admitted, it does not follow that it constitutes a sufficient ground for the disfranchisement of the inferior race. The world has moved since it was recognized as a fundamental principle that a divine right to rule inhered in particular classes.

The chief function of government at the present time is to protect the weak against the strong. The past has shown conclusively that the white man of the South is not a fair or just guardian of the interests of the colored man. In two hundred and fifty years, while the Negro lay prostrate and helpless, appealing simply to the kindness, gratitude, and charity of the white Christians of the South, not one single act designed to ameliorate his condition or brighten his hope was placed on the statute-books of any of these States. On the contrary, the last days of American slavery were infinitely worse than the first. Even the shreds of privilege the slave had at first enjoyed were stripped from him, and the faint gleams of hope that once had gladdened his eyes were excluded. It was made a felony to assist him to escape or to teach him to read, and the master was forbidden to liberate him by will. There is nothing in their past history to show that the southern people would so control the course of government as to promote the interests of the Negro if abandoned to their care, and nothing in their present attitude or declarations to show that they desire the elevation or development of the race they ask to be permitted unlawfully to subordinate. "Ignorance may struggle up to enlightenment," says Mr. Henry W. Grady, in a recent self-reported speech; "out of corruption may come the incorruptible; but the supremacy of the white race at the South must be maintained forever, simply because it is the white race and is the superior race!" There is no doubt that in this he expresses the conviction of the majority of the white race of the South; and a people who within thirty years punished as a felon the man who uttered the name of liberty in the slave's hearing or taught him to spell it out himself, would not hesitate to destroy the Negro's opportunity for development in order to keep him weak, dependent, and manageable. Not because the Negro is ignorant or incapable do they object to his exercise of the right of suffrage, but because he is a Negro, and as such they will spare no pains to keep him weak.

But even if the inherent superiority of the white race is admitted, and a consequent right to rule not denied, the means by which alone the rule of white minorities can be secured must make the proposition a most serious one. There are but three methods by which it may be accomplished. Two of them would require an appeal at least to the forms of law; the other presupposes a steady and persistent defiance of law. The most direct method would be to restore the term "white" as an essential qualification for citizenship in the State constitutions. Such an amendment could no doubt be easily adopted in all the States of the South by the same means by which the will of the majority is now nullified. This method would have one great advantage over any other—it would save the need of a frequent display of deterrent force, or the habitual recourse to fraud to defeat the will of the duly-constituted majority. This habitual appeal to unlawful force, or the habitual perjury of some thousands of election officials, cannot but exert a deleterious effect on public morals in an American commonwealth. An insuperable objection arises in the southern mind, however, to this method of eliminating the power of the Negro as a political factor. The representation of those States in the House of Representatives and the Electoral Colleges would be reduced in exact proportion to the number thus excluded from political power. Now, however much the southern man may object to the Negro as a political force, the southern politician is desperately fond of him as a political counter. It is as essential to his peace of mind that the Negro should be counted as a constituent, as that he should be disfranchised as a citizen. The simple fact is, that he desires the Negro's constituent power in the government to be added to his own, in order to give him the same advantage over his peer, the white man of the North, which he enjoyed during the slave epoch. This method of securing power for the white minorities of the South, therefore, is hardly thought worthy of consideration by southern political leaders. It would reduce the electoral strength of the South by about fifty votes, thereby doubling the number of electoral votes which must be obtained at the North in order to enable the "solid South" to elect a President or control national legislation.

Another method in which the derived result might be temporarily attained by apparently legal means, is by imposing an educational qualification upon the voter. Such a course would probably command the approval of a majority of the people of the North. They would no doubt be willing to punish the Negro still further for the crime of having been kept in compulsory ignorance by his white Christian brethren for two centuries and a half, in order to conciliate the white people of the South, and get rid, for a time at least, of the unpleasant and annoying Negro question. There is one difficulty in the way of adopting this plan, to wit: 45% of the voters of the eight States in which the matter is most pressing are unable to read their ballots. In three of them more than 50% are illiterate. Of course, these men will never knowingly vote to disfranchise themselves, and no amount of iron-clad assertion would convince either them or the world that such an amendment of the existing constitutions was fairly adopted. There is another difficulty, too. One-fifth of the white voters of these States cannot read the ballots they cast. It would be a very unpleasant thing to disfranchise so large a proportion of the white voters, especially as fully one-fifth of the colored vote would still remain duly qualified. With the amazing increase of intelligence among the Negroes during the past twenty-four years, it is evident that this expedient would be but temporary. While the proportion of colored illiterates is rapidly decreasing, illiteracy among the whites shows hardly any diminution, if indeed it is decreasing at all. Already in one of the counties of South Carolina the census reveals a greater number of colored people who can read and write than of whites. In Kentucky there are more white men who cannot read and write than there are blacks. For these reasons an educational qualification, which is the most popular remedy among northern theorists, the southern politician perceives to be utterly impracticable.

There remains only the alternative of deterrent violence or neutralizing fraud, which is frankly admitted to have been in operation for a dozen years or more, and which, it is unmistakably intimated by such men as Mr. Watterson, Senator Eustis, Senator Morgan, and Mr. Grady, is to be indefinitely continued as a means of perpetuating the rule of white minorities. This answers all the required conditions. It saves the Negro as a constituent and neutralizes him as a factor in government. This is what southern writers mean when they insist that white minorities at the South shall be left to deal with the Negro question in their own way. This was the demand which slavery always made, and the apprehension that it might not be allowed was the sole excuse for secession and rebellion. There are two obstacles in the way of the successful operation of this plan in the future. The first is the inequality it establishes between the power of the white voter living at the North and one dwelling in a southern State. New Jersey and South Carolina have each seven congressmen under the present apportionment; but six-tenths of the enumerated constituents in South Carolina are colored. These being neutralized in accordance with this plan in order that the white minority may rule, the vote of a white man in South Carolina is made just two and a half times as potential in national affairs as that of a white man in New Jersey. Now, while the people of the North might perhaps consent to sacrifice all the rights and a good many of the lives of the colored people of the South in order to conciliate the southern whites, they will never willingly surrender one iota of their own individual power to secure this desirable result. This was in fact the straw that broke the camel's back in the case of slavery, and the resulting impurity under this plan is much greater than it was in the slave epoch.

Another difficulty in the way of this indefinite continuance of unlawful usurpation, is the uncertainty that exists as to the course the Negro himself will pursue in regard to the matter. Thus far the Negro has been counted only a silent factor in the problem to which he has given a name. Slavery no more thought of asking him how he enjoyed his condition than the owner does of inquiring whether his horse prefers to go on the road or disport himself in the pasture.

The discussion of the present phase of the problem was started by the grave inquiry of an eminent ecclesiastic, "What shall we do with the Negro?" Is it not about time that we asked ourselves, "What will the Negro permit us to do with him?" To this inquiry the advocate of the inherent right of white minorities to rule responds with his usual confidence in his own infallibility: "Just let us alone; we will take care of him; we understand the Negro; leave us to manage him." This confidence is very largely based on the docility and submissiveness of the colored race in the past. The man who advocates continued unlawful repression seems not to realize that a race which has been a perfect type of humility for centuries when in a position of abject servitude, invariably shows altogether different qualities when once it has set its foot upon the lower rung of the ladder of opportunity. As a slave, the colored man had no reasonable chance, even if so disposed, to offer collective organized resistance to the will of his oppressors. He was not allowed to learn to read, lest he should find how to resist; nor to write, lest he should be able to communicate seditious plans to others. He could not go upon the highway without a written pass, nor meet three of his fellows, even for prayer, except in the presence of a white man. He had neither friends nor allies. There was no potential sentiment in the outside world to which he might appeal, and no arm that would be stretched out to save him from extinction in case of conflict. The laws of the several States in which he was enslaved gave his master power to take his life at pleasure. Numbers only added to his weakness. Now the circumstances are very different, and it is possible that conclusions based on the Negro's patient endurance of wrong as a slave may be altogether fallacious as an indication of his future course.

In view of this, it is well to consider briefly who and what the American Negro is. In the first place, he is an American. Since 1807, when the slave-trade was abolished, very few African Negroes have entered the United States. In the second place, he is not a heathen. A larger people of the United States than of any equal body of whites in the country are actual members of a Christian church. It may be well to remember, too, that very few of them are pure Negroes. Hardly ten in a thousand of the colored people of the United States, if their pedigrees were traced, would be unable to show some strains of white blood. Indeed, it may be doubted if, taken drop for drop, there is not pretty nearly as much white as colored blood in the veins of those ranked as Negroes in this country. And this white infusion, it must be remembered, represents the very best stocks of the South. Hardly a noted family can be named that is not as fully represented on the colored side as on the white. The statesmen, politicians, soldiers of the South—almost all who have added to her fame or ministered to her pride—have given something of their vigor to swell the ranks of the subject race. This is one of the chief causes of its remarkable numerical increase. This fact alone makes it dangerous to count on the indefinite submission of this strangely-composed race under gross and flagrant wrong.

There are other qualities which the colored man has displayed that should incline the enthusiastic advocates of the supremacy of white minorities to pause and think very seriously before they decide upon an indefinite perpetuation of this policy of unlawful and defiant despoliation of political rights. Twenty-four years ago the five millions of newly-enfranchised freemen were not worth all together five million cents. They were naked, helpless, inept. They had hands, and a sort of dull, incomprehensible power to endure; that was all. Within a decade they had $12,000,000 in the savings banks alone. They lived on wages and flourished on conditions that would have exterminated the northern white laborer in a generation. Today they claim a valuation in the southern States alone of $100,000,000. In Georgia they own nearly a million acres of land. The six millions of Negroes who confront six millions of whites in the eight coastward States between Maryland and Texas, perform by far the larger part of the productive labor in them. Probably not a fifth as many of the Negroes live without labor as of the whites. Two-thirds, at least, of the cotton, tobacco, sugar, and rice of the South never feels the touch of a white hand till it reaches the market. Fully half the ordinary mechanical laborers of those States are black, yet they furnish but a third of the paupers and only half the defective recipients of public charity. In 1865 hardly one in a thousand knew the letters of the alphabet; in 1880 more than twenty in a hundred above the age of ten years could read and write. These are miracles of which it is worth our while to take note.

One instance of what they have achieved may give a better idea of the qualities of the race than many columns of statistics. A single Christian sect—the African Methodist Church—which has not a white man among its members or any organic relations with any white church organization, reports a membership of 460,000; it has 12,000 places of worship, numbers 10,000 ministers, has 15,000 Sabbath schools, supports its own denominational papers, has missions in the West Indies, Mexico, and Africa, and its reported contributions foot up more than $2,000,000 annually for the support of church work. Men who accomplish such results will not always submit to wrong, even for the dear Lord's sake. Christianity is not drawing the white and black races nearer together, but separating them farther than ever in habits of thought, and developing and solidifying the manhood of the Negro with wonderful rapidity.

We often hear the idea advanced that what is termed the "race question" will disappear from politics just as soon as a proper issue is presented. No race can separate into parties or factions while its rights and liberties are assailed by another on the ground of race alone. Their rights must be freely admitted before they will dare to surrender whatever power there may be in cohesion. To do otherwise would be an act of stupendous and incredible folly. One might as well expect a herd of sheep to separate in the presence of wolves. Their only hope is in union. So, too, we hear it said that when the present generation dies off slavery will be only a dream to the colored man. Such is not the lesson of history. The farther a people recede from bondage, the keener is their appreciation of the wrong and the more intense their hate of the oppressor. The horror which the American Negro feels for the institution of slavery will become greater rather than less for several generations at least. When did the Jewish prophets cease to anathematize the Egyptian oppressor? Such antipathies were curable only by continued and undeniable recognition of the right.

"But what can they do?" is the triumphant inquiry which greets the objector who calls attention to these things. "We have the arms, the skill, the experience, the wealth; what can they do?" Truly, the question is not an idle one, yet history clearly teaches that whenever an inferior class, intimately intermingled with a dominant and oppressive caste, becomes both intelligent enough to organize and desperate enough to resist, it is sure to overwhelm the arrogant and better-equipped minority. No man can say when the limit of endurance will be reached if this policy is continued, but that it will be reached in the near future is just as certain as that a boiler will explode if the safety valve is fastened down and the fire kept up. When that day shall come, the advocates of a policy of forcible repression and unlawful subjection will find that the battle is not always to the strong.

Should a conflict arise tomorrow, the odds would by no means be entirely with the white race. Their very wealth might constitute a source of weakness. Black eyes and black ears would take note of every white man's movements. In every camp there would be spies; in every household informers. While the

Negro has not so heroic a record as the southern white man, it should not be forgotten that there are 50,000 still living who wore the federal blue and fought for the freedom of their race. Besides that, in a strife such as must result if the occasion for it is not carefully and wisely avoided, it is not valor alone that counts, nor excellence of equipment that assures victory. In such a conflict a box of matches is equal to a hundred Winchester rifles!

In the meantime, neither the nation nor the world would sit still and witness the *auto da fé* of a race. Eight millions of people cannot very long be kept in a subordinate position and despoiled of their guaranteed rights by a minority, however superior and arrogant, of election officials. It is quite probable that the North might not awake to its duty in the prevention of evil until blood had been shed. Thus far it has entirely failed to realize its responsibility. It has left the Negro to his fate, in seeming unconsciousness that the wrongs of the past must be atoned for either by justice or by disaster.

The solution of the Negro question is of all the problems of civilization the simplest and yet the most difficult. The trouble is not with the Negro, who has always been content with half a chance in the world's scramble, but with the southern white man, who is not willing that any one should differ with him in opinion or dissent from him in practice; who is the traditional if not inveterate enemy of free thought and free speech, and is so confident of his own infallibility that he would rather appeal to arms or become a cowardly and disguised murderer, than submit to the control of a lawfully-ascertained majority of legal voters. There cannot be any security for our institutions or any guarantee of our domestic peace, so long as the question of depriving a majority of the qualified electors of any State of the rights which they are solemnly guaranteed by law through any unlawful means is coolly discussed as a living issue in the great organs through which popular thought finds expression. The remedy is a simple one—justice and knowledge. These are all the Negro asks. The superior white race should be ashamed to grant him less. It is not a question of sentiment, nor entirely one of right. As a matter of policy, it resolves itself into an inquiry as to what the American people can afford to do or leave undone—whether we can afford even negatively to admit that white minorities have the right not only to rule, but to nullify and subvert the law of the land, boldly, defiantly, and persistently, in order to bar a lawful majority from the exercises of political power, merely because the minority demand it.

14

From *Pactolus Prime, or the White Christ* (1889)*

Originally serialized in the *Chicago Advance* from December 13, 1888, to March 14, 1889, the novel *Pactolus Prime* is among Tourgée's most inventive and ambiguous works. Tourgée hoped to shock readers with the heretical views of race, Christianity, and American democracy expressed by his mysterious, embittered title character. Some readers, such as Anna Julia Cooper, took Pactolus Prime to be a mouthpiece for Tourgée's own radical views. In the selection below, Pactolus and his assistant Benny argue on behalf of economic reparations to blacks for slavery. Staging a Socratic dialogue on the subject, Tourgée has their view challenged by a number of prominent men, including an unnamed Supreme Court justice.

III. A PROFESSOR OF THE BLACK ART

PACTOLUS PRIME was the bootblack of the "Best House." Most of the hotels in the national metropolis are "houses" of some sort. The style serves to mark the evolution of the hostel. The inn or tavern became first a "hotel," then a "house," and finally has dropped all descriptive modifiers, and bullies the traveler with the puzzling uncertainty of a name alone. Our grandfathers found "entertainment for man and beast" at the "Wayside Inn"; our fathers at the "Grand Hotel," while the aspiration of our own younger days was to put up in style at the new "Monument House," and we now instruct the cabman, with a bit of cockney flavor in our tone, to drive us to "The Brunswick." The one thing to be thankful for about Washington caravanseries is that they have not yet ceased to be "houses." It sounds provincial, but it implies comfort and a certain amount of liberty. The guest of the hotel which sports a single name, as if it were the one distinctive thing so-named on earth, is apt to be a pris-

*Excerpted from chapters 3, 6, and 7 of Albion W. Tourgée, *Pactolus Prime* (New York: Cassell Publishing Co., 1890).

oner who submits to being bullied at extortionate rates for the honor of indit-
ing his letters on its specially embossed paper.

The Best House needs no description. Everybody knows its character and
location. It fronts on two streets and one avenue; is accessible from each; has
the most unpretentious of entrances; innumerable tiled corridors; a spacious
office; a magnificent dining-room; a bar notable alike for its ornamentation,
its service, and the quality of its decoctions; smoking-rooms, billiard-rooms,
writing-rooms, and half a thousand sleeping-rooms. Where the army of servants work or lodge or what is the number of them, none knoweth save he
who bears the imperial title of "Manager." Him the guests seldom see, but his
authority is represented and his dignity suffers no diminution in the person
of the "Clerk," who in the category of the modern hotel officials ought more
properly to bear the title of "Lord of the Bed-chamber," he having the care,
and being responsible for the safety and comfort, of the guest, asleep or awake.

The bootblack's stand was in the basement, adjoining the public wash-
room. The "stand" consisted of four chairs placed upon a dais raised a couple
of steps above the level of the floor. There was a pivoted iron foot-rest in
front of each of these, and behind them a window, the lower sash of ground
glass, the upper one showing a whitewashed area wall with its railed enclo-
sure above. Through this railing one had a glimpse of the street and sidewalk.
The pavement sloped backward from the front of the house, pretty sharply,
on the side-street. At the upper edge of the window one barely saw the knee
of the passerby; at the lower, the vision extended almost to the middle. Only
the faces of dwarfs and children were ever visible. Pactolus Prime loved to
watch this queer procession of toe and heel in the intervals of his work. His
calling—it was something more than avocation to him—had made him observant of feet, and especially of foot-gear. He noticed the shape, the make of
the shoe, the play of the instep, the swing of the leg, and the turn of the ankle
with discriminating knowledge. He probably knew more men and women
by their feet—or rather by their shoes—than any other man in the country;
more indeed than most men know by memory of faces. Most of the accustomed passers-by and all the regular patrons of his stand he knew by name.
Many a man would have gone another way had he known that observant eyes
rested on his boots as he strode by Prime's window, and many a lady would
have blushed had she known that her feet were recognized by one who had
never seen her face.

Pactolus Prime had occupied this "stand" twelve years. Every guest of the
great hotel knew him, and many more, for he had blacked boots somewhere

in the city, years before he became a feature of the Best House—just how many nobody seemed to know, and he was little inclined to talk about himself. Indeed, beyond the fact that he was not only the bootblack of the Best House, but the best bootblack in any house—North or South, or East or West, and so conceded to be by the traveling public whom he served—very little was known of him or his life. He rented his stand, hired his own assistant, boarded himself, lived somewhere in the suburbs, was always at his post by daylight and usually remained until dark. His assistant stayed until nine or ten at night, and came later in the morning—there was not often more than one could attend to until after eight o'clock. Two days in each week Pactolus Prime himself remained until ten and his assistant left at noon. One or two days in the week he took a holiday, and in the afternoon was usually found in one of the galleries at the Capitol, listening to the debates. Here he always occupied the same seat unless it chanced to be filled on his arrival, and then sat in the one nearest to it which he found vacant. Nearly everybody in Washington knew him by sight, and many members of Congress and high officials of the government, by name.

He was not a man of many words, but his deeds were unexceptionable. No boot ever left his hands until its luster was perfect, and no customer departed from his stand with any removable dust upon his clothing. Sometimes he talked with his customers, but never about them. If he heard what they said of each other, he never repeated it. He never answered inquiries about them, either. No matter how recently he had tapped a gentleman's foot to show that his work was done, he could never be made to remember when he had last seen him. He baffled all questions by an unhesitating denial of recollection; his assistant by the denial of knowledge. No detective had ever learned anything from him to a patron's disadvantage, and no assistant of his had ever been called to testify as to the whereabouts of a customer at a particular hour.

But if he said little, he well knew how to make others talk, and was considered a very superior man for one in his station, by those who loved the sound of their own voices. So, too, though he would not gossip, he was always eager to listen to the discussion of public affairs, and never hesitated to express an opinion thereon. He was not exactly a politician, but had his own ideas, was considered a close observer, and not seldom proved himself a sound adviser. Statesmen were not ashamed to consider his warnings, and more than once sporting men had risked their money on his political predictions with noticeable advantage. He knew the "blue-book" by heart, and needed no mark of rank to enable him to give any accustomed patron his proper title. He was

familiar with the status of most of those upon the civil list, and the aspirations of many who desired to get there. Perhaps a majority of the guests of the
great hotel, at one time or another, confided to him something of their hopes
or fears; and not a few condescended to ask his advice—some of them his aid.
He paid more for his stand than many of the clerks in the Departments receive as salary, yet the proprietor leased to him at a lower figure than he would
to another, because of the prudence which made him popular with the guests.

Nobody knew whether his profits were great or small, unless it was his
assistant. He never boasted of good fortune nor bewailed bad luck. Some
thought he must have grown rich, others wondered how he could live and pay
the rent he did. It was whispered among the guests that he was a good man to
apply to in an emergency. The clerk, after a peculiarly piteous appeal from an
unfortunate player or unexpectedly embarrassed wayfarer, sometimes dropped
a hint that Prime might help him out of his trouble. He often raised small
sums, sometimes very considerable ones, to accommodate people in such unpleasant predicament. He always acted cautiously, yet he had been known to
obtain money on all sorts of pledges, watches, diamonds—even horses and
patents which were not regarded as absolutely good security for the sums
advanced. If these ventures ever resulted in loss no one knew it, neither the
profit, if any there were. Some thought he ventured his own money, some
that he was another's agent. There was a general belief that he was very fortunate in these ventures, and among gamblers there was a superstition that it
brought good luck to borrow of him. It was noticeable that he could never be
induced to serve one whom he had once refused.

This was about all the clerk, proprietor, or any employé of the "Best House"
could have told about Pactolus Prime, for though he was a man of mark in
his way, he lived his own life and seemed to have neither family nor intimates.
Those whom he served usually spoke of him as "Prime;" some called him
"Uncle Prime," or simply "Uncle"; one or two addressed him as "Pactolus";
while to the servants at the hotel and his assistant, he was always "Mistah"
Prime. Though respected by all, he was very far from being popular with the
colored element of the city's population. Indeed, he seemed to be shunned
rather than sought by his own people, except in emergencies when the interests of the race were clearly at stake.

His appearance was very striking—full of incongruities that attracted attention yet were hard to define. At first sight and at a little distance, he seemed
an old man; on closer inspection one detected neither wrinkles nor muscular
deterioration. In his prime he must have been above the medium height, slen-

derly rather than strongly built. He was stoop-shouldered, but his chest did not lack depth. His arms were long and his hands narrow, with white, hard nails that somehow seemed out of place upon the fingers of one in his condition. A racial expert—one of the old slave-traders, for instance—would have found it hard to reconcile those nails with the color of the hands, according to the theories that prevailed among the sagacious dealers in human flesh of a generation ago. The sense of narrowness in his figure was perhaps increased by the fact that his right leg seemed to turn inward at the knee, or rather turned outward below the knee, until the foot was almost at a right angle with its fellow. It dragged after the other in walking, and was used as a sort of fleshly ratchet to hold what the left had gained, instead of being sent forward to conquer space on its own account.

But the countenance of the bootblack of the "Best House" was even more noticeable than his form. A narrow, almost pinched face, growing broad across the eyes, with a high forehead, a straight nose having that flexibility of nostril which is claimed to be indicative of the Caucasian, thin lips, and a peculiar leaden-gray complexion that seemed singularly pervasive of his whole being, were the things which first attracted the attention of a stranger. Closer observation showed that the same blue-gray tint seemed to be even intensified upon the lips, which lacked all trace of redness, so that the rows of short, even teeth showed with startling whiteness between them. After a time, one became conscious, as he studied the physiognomy, that a part of its strange effect was due to the entire absence of hair. His head was bald—not partially, but absolutely. The black knitted cap he wore could not conceal that fact. There was no trace of beard, and even the great, round, silver-mounted spectacles could not hide the absence of eyebrows on the somewhat prominent forehead. These glasses effectually concealed his eyes, except when the light was good, as it seldom was in the wash-room of the great hotel.

Such, as near as words can picture him, was the man who came down the stairs, turned up the lights in the wash-room, and began to undo the package he had received from the clerk. When he had taken off the cover of the box and undid a light paper wrapping, he took out an overcoat made of rich material, with a fur lining and furred sleeves.

"That's a nice coat," he said, after examining it carefully, "and it was kind in Ben to get it for me. He ought not to have done it, though; he don't get wages enough not to have plenty of use for his money without buying such a present as that for me. I had about made up my mind to offer him a better chance, and this opens the way to do it."

There was hardly a trace, in this monologue, of the negro dialect which had been noticeable in his conversation a little while before, but on the contrary a smoothness and accuracy of enunciation which showed that the bootblack of the "Best House" had not associated with the brainiest men of the nation without learning the refinements of speech that prevail among them. He took out a card which he found in one of the pockets of the coat and read:

"For PACTOLUS PRIME, ESQ.

CHRISTMAS GIFT."

"What does he want to tag the 'Esquire' to it for? The idea of calling a man of my complexion 'Esquire!' No one but a nigger would think of doing so. It doesn't mean anything among white men, but no white man would ever use it in addressing a nigger. If it does not mean rank, it at least means equality. 'Christmas Gift,' too! Well, I'm glad he's a nigger. I should hate to get a present that really meant consideration from a white man. There's no danger, though," he added with a quiet laugh. "I suppose I'll get the worth of that coat in extra fees today, but it will all be flung to me like a biscuit to a dog after a good day's sport. That's a white man's notion of kindness to a nigger."

The white teeth, showing between the drawn blue lips, made the man's sneer horribly sardonic. He threw the coat on one of the chairs, took out a bunch of keys, opened a drawer in the dais, and spread out on the platform the instruments of his vocation—a half dozen brushes, a sponge, a scraper, and a bunch of cotton waste. Then he lifted out a flat marble slab, took it over to one of the washstands, sponged it off, and bringing it back wiped it dry with the shreds. After that he put on it a small quantity of blacking with a spatula, moistened it with liquids from two or three different bottles—ejecting them with a quick jerk through quills set in the corks—worked it evenly and carefully with the spatula, testing its consistency now and then until he seemed satisfied with the result.

"Queer, nobody ever found out the secret of this mixture," he said, as he watched it drip from the edge of the spatula. "Ben mixes it almost as well as I do, but I don't think he has any idea what it's made of. I've made a good thing by it and there's a fortune in it yet. Everybody thinks the excellence and durability of our 'shines' depend upon the way the work is done—and there's a good deal in that, too—but all the pains in the world wouldn't do it with any other blacking ever invented. I've thought sometimes I'd patent it, but if I did I'd have to reveal the secret. I'm going out of business pretty soon, but I'll give it to Ben; and he—well, maybe he'll find as good a man to give it to when he comes to retire. To retire! Think of it! A bootblack retiring—as if he was a banker! A nigger bootblack, too!"

The man laughed at his strange conceit, looked at his watch, then at the window where the day was beginning to show, and turned his attention to preparing another portion of the liquid whose virtues he had commemorated for the use of his assistant.

. . . . . .

VI. AN ASSESSMENT OF DAMAGES

"I am afraid, uncle," said the minister very gently, as Phelps and the reporter disappeared, "that you are too impatient—your people I mean; you want everything at once."

"Did anybody ever owe you money?" asked Prime.

"Unfortunately, yes," answered the other with a smile.

"When did you ask for payment?"

"When it was due, of course. I've never had enough to grow careless in that respect."

"Was it ever refused?"

"Well," said the minister, still smiling, "it has often been neglected."

"I suppose when payment was neglected you ceased to ask or desire it, didn't you?"

"I have sometimes ceased to ask—never to desire."

"And why did you cease to ask?"

"Because I grew hopeless, I suppose."

"Did it make you especially happy to be deprived of what you had a right to receive?"

"Certainly not, but—"

"Wait a minute! If the amount thus unjustly withheld from you had embraced every cent you had earned in your whole life—the entire earnings of your parents and their parents for two centuries and a half, depriving them of every luxury, every opportunity, every privilege, every right—everything in fact except the barest necessities of existence—would you think you ought to be called 'impatient,' if you began, after waiting uncomplainingly so many years, to speak a little roughly of your debtor?"

"I suppose not; but you see—"

"One word more," said Prime respectfully, as he finished brushing the coat of his reverend customer and turned to begin work upon the boot of another who had already taken the seat, "I don't want to hurt your feelings, sir, nor to say anything you might consider disrespectful, either to yourself or your profession, but I have more feeling in this matter than you might suppose."

"Very naturally," rejoined the other, waiting to continue the conversation. "You are a colored man."

"Well, yes," said Prime, glancing up with a sardonic grin, his white teeth showing through the dark lips, "I am so taken and accepted; but then you are white, so the interest should be mutual."

"I hardly see it," said the other inquiringly, "you naturally feel the wrongs your race has suffered, or which you fancy they have suffered, more keenly than we."

"In other words, you think the one who suffers is more likely to remember the wrong than the one who perpetrates it. Very likely. It doesn't seem as if it ought to be so, does it? Seems as if it ought to be just the other way—the man who does wrong ought never to be able to forget it. Perhaps that would make us all too unhappy, though. Well, I'll tell you, sir, how I feel about it. I feel as if Christianity—the followers of the white Christ—had robbed my people of two hundred and fifty years of bodily toil and rightful opportunity, taking the proceeds to add to their own wealth, their own luxury, the education of their children, the building of churches and colleges—whatever they chose which was to their own exclusive advantage. Not a dollar nor a cent came back to us in any form. We gave and you took; that is all there is of it. You said, 'Blessed be the name of the Lord,' as well you might; and we were expected to say the same in order that we might be allowed the credit of having souls. You—American civilization, American Christianity, sir,—took our money,—the honest wages of our toil,—and no shuffling or evasion can avoid the responsibility. As Mr. Phelps said one day, 'it's a debt that can't be barred by any statute of limitation.'"

"Well," interrupted one to whose finely shaped boot Benny was giving a final touch, a thin-faced, positive man whose fingers worked nervously while his eyes flashed angrily as he spoke, "I wish you niggers would find out just how much the country owes you, or how much you would be satisfied with, and let us pay you off and quit fussing about it! I don't seem to have heard of much else in my day except the wrongs of the nigger, and I'm tired—sick of the whole matter! I'd like to have the account settled and be done with it!"

"You would find it a pretty hard one to state, and harder still to pay off," said Prime solemnly. "Such claims as ours grow fast and draw big interest."

"Oh, we wouldn't be particular about the amount," said the last speaker. "I don't think we would even ask credit for any counterclaim or set-off, if we could only stop the race's whining and have them own up that they were satisfied for once. I've had enough of it myself. I'd like to see the account squared and start fresh, with the understanding that each race was to keep up its own end hereafter and ask no favors. It wouldn't be long before you'd get tired."

"You would be the first to get tired of such a bargain," said the old man confidently.

"How so?"

"In trying to square the account."

"Why, how much do you suppose the whole value of the Negro's work in the United States as a slave would amount to?'" asked the other defiantly. "During the whole time, I mean, from the day the first slave was landed at Jamestown until the last one was set free?"

"A good deal more than you would care to pay."

"Well, how much?" said the other, taking out paper and pencil. "Out with it! Let's come down to figures. I'm a traveling man and accustomed to narrow margins. Come now, set your price!"

"Well," said Prime as he finished with another customer, "I 'spose ten cents wouldn't be too high a price for a day's work, would it, over and above such board, clothes and attendance in sickness as we received?"

"Well, probably not," answered the traveling man with characteristic promptness, and evident surprise at the moderation of the demand.

"And I s'pose it wouldn't be out of the way to estimate three-fifths of each life as work-time, at that rate, leaving out two-fifths for infancy, old age and sickness?"

"I should say that was a liberal basis on which to estimate it," interposed the minister.

"Well," said the drummer, squinting up his eyes as if making a close bargain, "considering the price per day, it can't be called unfair. That is certainly low—too low. You'll fall behind at that rate, old man. We'll pay you off at your own price and not feel it. About a cigar a day less, for each smoker in the country for a week or so, would make it all right, I should say. Put up your figures, man! Say fifteen or twenty cents a day, anyhow!"

The drummer spoke in a confident, bantering tone, shifting his cigar from one side of his mouth to the other by the motion of his lips, as he spoke, but Prime answered quietly:

"No, ten cents will do and that'll be a heap more than we'll ever get."

"How much would it amount to? I suppose you have looked the matter up, you speak so confidently."

"Figure it out yourself," said Prime. "You kept us ignorant on purpose that we might not know what was our due and how it was taken from us. It isn't a hard sum. Benny here worked it out the other day, all by himself, so it must be easy, for he's a nigger, gentlemen; he couldn't do a hard sum! Tell 'em about it, Benny."

"Oh, it's not difficult," said the young man, with a flush on his fair face. "You see there were two hundred and forty-seven years of bondage; there were twenty-six slaves at first and five millions at the last. Making it an even progression, counting only three hundred days to the year, and throwing off two-fifths of the whole for childhood, old age and sickness, and putting the rest at ten cents a day, and it would amount to *more than ten billions of dollars!*"

"What!" exclaimed the commercial man. "It can't be! Do you want the earth?"

"You can work it out by yourself if you think I have made a mistake," said the young man proudly.

The salesman's pencil flew over the pad. The others waited in silence for his decision.

"Well, I vow!" he muttered, as he added a cipher and marked off the decimals, "I wouldn't have thought it!"

"Is he right?" asked the minister earnestly. "Right!" exclaimed the expert, "he's fully a half billion below the truth!"

"You don't say," murmured several of the bystanders.

"We'll throw off the odd half billion and take the rest in long-time bonds at two percent interest, if you please. That's fair, isn't it, Mister?" said Prime, addressing the man of samples.

"Uncle," said the other, as he put up his book and pencil and slipped down to be brushed off. "You've got me! You're right! We're your debtors and aren't likely to get square with you, either! I'm with you; send in your account! Blamed if I ever snarl at a nigger for grumbling, again!"

"But the ground of indebtness hasn't been half stated yet."

"Don't want to hear any more; I've had enough. Good-by, uncle."

He dropped a liberal douceur into the young man's hand, shook his head when offered change, and had disappeared up the stairway by the time another was seated in the chair.

"I must go too," said the minister apologetically. "I had never thought of the matter in this light before. Your people certainly cannot be blamed for feeling that they have been bitterly wronged; but—was it Christianity that did it, my friend?"

"It was Christian men and women who did it—the earthly exponents of the Christian idea—and they received the advantage," answered Prime.

"But Christianity is not responsible for all that is done even by its votaries."

"Why not? You hold Mahometanism responsible for all the ills of Turkish life and government, and credit heathenism with the woes that befall the people who practice idolatry. In like manner, Christianity is responsible for every evil it permits to exist among a Christian people—or that results from a Christian government. This amount is only a tithe of what Christianity owes my people. Who shall estimate the damages for lost opportunity, to say nothing of violated right? Who shall state the money value of two centuries of enforced ignorance and depravity? What sum could compensate a people for the stain of universal illegitimacy, the denial of fatherhood, the violation of maternal right, the debasement of female virtue, the utter effacement of all family ties and family relations, the refusal of even a family name."

"I—I don't know," said the minister blankly. "I never thought of it in that light before. Good-morning, sir."

He seemed to forget the color of the old man's skin as he bowed respectfully to Prime and went slowly and thoughtfully up the stairs.

Several customers had come and gone during this conversation. The hands of the bootblack and his assistant had not been idle. The knitted cap had been pushed back on Prime's head, showing the clingy scalp almost to the crown. The sweat beads stood upon his brow. The right side of his face twitched nervously, and the words flowed from his lips as if he were uttering the stored-up thoughts of a lifetime. Those who were accustomed to his usually quiet demeanor were surprised at the feeling he displayed, while his assistant glanced up at him now and then with a look almost of reverence.

"I wonder if he is right," mused the minister as he walked along the street toward a church whose echoing chimes invited a thronging multitude of well-dressed worshipers. "Who would have dreamed there could be such a difference in the views that may be taken of the Saviour of Mankind and the Message which ushered in the Christian Era! Can it be that he is right? Those are terrible truths which he recounts; can it be that the followers of the Christ have made Him seem to be only the friend and Saviour of the white man? Is Prime right in calling Him the 'White' Christ? Will we never learn the Master's lessons? Will the rich and strong and brave who profess His name, never learn to put themselves in the place of the weak and poor and timid? Must His very name be a thing of terror and distrust to those for whom He died? It is hard enough to be black without having the curse of eternal hopelessness added to it! It must be difficult to reconcile such an apparent curse with the idea of Divine mercy! And then to think, to feel, to believe, that the Christ— the divine and universal lover of humanity—to think that His church is but the cult of the wrongdoer—the oppressor! God help us! How little we know of each other's burdens and how our own acts may make heavier the load our neighbor bears! Yet what can we do? God help us—*it is a terrible problem!*"

The good man brushed aside a tear as he went up the marble steps, and his face was very sad as he passed through the vestibule of the great church thronged with happy faces and full of the soft echoes of half-suppressed but joyful greetings. The hymns and prayers seemed full of the idea of the "White" Christ! His heart stood still with horror, even as he listened to the songs of jubilee, as he thought what would have been his own religious status had the *Man* Jesus Christ been black, and the circumstances of his life and that of Pactolus Prime been reversed. He was a good man, and tried faithfully to picture to his own mind the terrors of such a transformation. Yet how far below the fact did the wildest effort of his fancy fall!

VII. SOME EXPERT TESTIMONY

"Tell, Uncle," said the man who took the commercial traveler's place, "I am not an expert accountant, but you can't humbug me with such figures as we've been having here. I know something about the facts of history, and something about niggers too; and when you come to talk about the white people of this country being indebted to the colored man, I tell you it's all nonsense. When a nigger got his board and clothes, house and firewood, and a doctor to attend him when he was sick, he got all his work was worth, and generally a good deal more."

"He raised what he ate, didn't he?" asked Prime sharply.

The bystanders smiled at the evidently pertinent inquiry.

"Why, of course; all but the sugar and coffee and whisky and tobacco and things of that sort," boastfully answered the undismayed assailant.

"And how much did the slave's sugar and coffee and 'things of that sort' average a year, do you think?" asked Prime blandly.

"Well—not a great deal, that is true," was the careless reply.

"How many masters furnished such luxuries?"

"Not so many, perhaps; though many furnished tobacco, and molasses, and most of them allowed deserving slaves to raise truck for themselves, with which to buy little things of that sort. This amounted to the same thing as providing it. You see it was the master's land they worked, the master's time they used, and the master's niggers that did the work. So you may as well say the master furnished them."

The man spoke with such positiveness as to make himself offensive to the listeners, as their countenances clearly showed. Prime did not seem to mind it, but said quietly, as lie finished mixing a new supply of blacking on the marble block:

"In other words, you mean that after the bondman got through his day's work, they allowed him to use the time he otherwise might have wasted in rest or recreation—which a free man would perhaps have employed in reading, study and self development—in cultivating a crop to buy himself the ordinary creature comforts."

"Of course," said the other with a sneer, "he wasn't sent to school!"

"No," answered Prime, "and he was prevented by law from learning anything that is taught in the schools, wasn't he?"

"Well, sometimes."

"Sometimes! Was it not a crime—a violation of the statute law—punishable as a felony, to teach him to read or write?"

"Yes, that was the law, but it was not always enforced. There were a good many who allowed their slaves to learn to read and write."

"How many slaves did you ever know who had such acquirements?"

"Well, I've heard of quite a number."

"How many have you known?—how many could you name?"

"Not many; one or two."

"I have known more than that number," said Prime frankly. "I suppose I could recall a half-dozen. I was one myself. But they were not numerous; they did not average one in a thousand—hardly two in ten thousand."

"Oh, there must have been more than that!"

"Fortunately, the matter is not left to be guessed at. There were a few, a very few, who slipped by the sentinel who stood with a flaming sword at the gate of the garden in which grew the tree of knowledge; but two years after the close of the war it was next to impossible to find a score of grown colored men in many of the counties of a half-dozen States, who could read ten lines intelligibly. That I know, and I think it a high estimate to say that two in ten thousand of the five millions of slaves could read and write when liberated. Even these few were the result of unlawful indulgence on the part of individual masters, or of exceptional enterprise and daring on the part of the men themselves. They were unlawful trespassers in the field of knowledge, and liable to the severest punishment if their offense was discovered. If they dared acquire knowledge they were compelled to conceal and deny its possession."

"The masters could not afford to educate their slaves."

"Why not?"

"Why not!"

"Yes, why not? The free men of the North educated themselves by their own labor, didn't they? And had a surplus to invest in homes and luxuries, besides?"

"Of course."

"If an average laborer at the North could support himself and family and educate his children, besides earning a surplus for investment or luxury, why should not the men who enjoyed the proceeds of the slave's labor have been able to afford him at least the rudiments of an education?"

"Yes," said the questioner hesitatingly, "but it was the States that educated the people of the North."

"Exactly, but the State schools were supported by the tax-payers, and the tax-payers represented the results of labor, didn't they? Then why should not a Christian State that added the labor of the slave—aye, even the slave himself, to its taxable aggregate—why should it not have educated his children?"

"Now, Uncle, what is the sense of talking in that way?" burst out the objector angrily. "You know it would not have done to educate the slaves. They would have been burning and killing the white people in no time if they had been educated. Why, man, it would have needed a regiment in every county to keep them down, and you know it. But what's the use of fussing about the matter now? Slavery is dead and gone. You are just as free as I am. What do you want to keep harping on what two-thirds of the people now living know nothing in the world about, except by hearsay?"

"If a man robbed you, I suppose you would say nothing about it?"

"Not if there were no chance for me to get back what I had lost—certainly not after he was dead and gone."

"Not if you saw his children flaunting the fruits of his wrong in your face, and boasting of it every day?" exclaimed the old man, straightening up while his customer put his other foot upon the form.

"Who's got the money the nigger earned?" angrily shouted the other, shaking his folded newspaper in the old man's face. "Can anybody trace it? Does anybody know how much it is? Where is it deposited? In what is it invested? I am tired of these indefinite statements. If a man can prove his property, he has a right to take it, not otherwise. That is the law!"

"That is the law; but it is not equity, and our case is in equity.[1] We do not

1. Here Tourgée's character alludes to one of the most famous pleas of the 1880s for the protection of full civil rights for the former slaves: George Washington Cable's "The Freedmen's Case in Equity," *Century Magazine* 29 (January 1885): 409–418.

ask to follow that which is ours, *in specie.* Our demand is for an equivalent, or a partial equivalent, for what has been wrongfully taken from us and converted to the use of the taker."

It was Ben who spoke. Up to this time he had taken no part in the conversation, and his words were greeted with applause by most of those present.

"Well done, youngster," said a gruff man upon whose boot the young man was at work. "You haven't studied law for nothing, but when one tries to apply the rules of equity to the practice of peoples and nations, I am afraid he will run foul of a good many obstacles."

"But the rules hold good though they cannot be enforced, do they not, Judge?" asked the young man respectfully.

"Oh, of course; they must if they are, as we are fond of declaring them to be, 'what the common reason of mankind approves as just and true.'"

"In equity then," the young man continued, "those who received the labor of our people unjustly, became trustees for us by their own wrongful act, and it is not necessary that we should follow and designate our own. The trustee *de son tort*[2] who mingles the trust fund with his own becomes a debtor to that amount."

"True enough," said the gruff man with kindly condescension, "but where is the fund? Who is the *tortfeasor?*[3] What estate will you subject to the slave's claim?"

"It seems to me, sir," said the young man, looking frankly up into his interlocutor's face, "that the slave's labor has gone into the national wealth—that immense aggregate we have recently seen paraded before the world's eyes with so much boastfulness—I don't know how many billions it is—and that all this is, in equity, charged with whatever sums may be necessary to recompense our people, so far as may be, for the wrong done them in the past."

"That is a bold claim, young man," said the jurist, in a tone which of itself expressed warm commendation. "If the principles of equity could be applied to national affairs, or rather to collective relations, it is not easy to see how such a claim could be avoided. One objection would be that there is no means of making any distinction between the slaveholder or his descendants, and those who remonstrated against the injustice of slavery and opposed its continuance."

"It is the duty of *all* the people to see that the law wrongs no man, is it not?'"

"Very true," said the judge affably, "but you understand that in our dual system of government the people of one State are not responsible for what the people of another State may do, except within certain limits."

2. Latin, "of his own wrong."

3. Latin, "wrongdoer."

"I understand that," said the young man, "at least I have tried to understand it."

"That is as near as anybody gets, my son," answered the judge, laughing. "I've been trying a long time to make out the puzzle, and am free to confess that it doesn't grow easier. I suppose it will take another hundred years to decide just where the boundary lies between state and national power and state and national responsibility for the rights and privileges of the citizen. For myself, I must say I never approach the subject without feeling like a surveyor setting out to find a way through an unexplored wilderness."

"Of course, I don't know much about the matter, Judge," said the young man modestly, "but it seems to me that the people of all the States are estopped from denying their responsibility for slavery and, therefore, their moral liability for its results. You see slavery prevailed in every one of the original thirteen States, and although hundreds of slaves fought in the Continental armies to secure the independence of the Colonies, yet when these Colonies—these sovereign peoples if you please—came to form 'a more perfect union,' each one of them agreed that every other one might hold men in bondage, take from them every right and privilege, even to life itself, simply because they had more or less of colored blood in their veins. They stood by consenting, and—"

"Like Saul at the stoning of Stephen, eh?" exclaimed the judge. "There is something in that, certainly. But how about the new States?" he asked, seemingly desirous of drawing the youngster out.

"They derive their powers and privileges through the action of the older States, and are morally as well as legally, subject to the same responsibility. In other words, they are only convenient extensions of the original thirteen. Now the fact that any of these States at a subsequent time abjured the doctrine of slavery and found their hands tied by the Constitution so that they were unable to interfere with it in others, does not relieve them from responsibility, because they themselves assented to this restriction of their power. They not only submitted to have their hands tied but helped to tie them."

"But, of course, you cannot hold the whole people of a State responsible for the wrong-doing of a part of them," said the judge gravely.

"Not unless the wrong is a result of some public act or neglect, but in such cases the courts frequently hold the whole responsible for the resultant injury, do they not? For instance, if a State takes a man's property, the whole body of the people is taxed to make the owner whole. So too, if property is destroyed in a riot, the municipality which did not afford sufficient protection is responsible for the damages."

"Well said, young man, well said," exclaimed the judge heartily, as he relieved the groaning chair of its burden of flesh and stepped gingerly off the platform. "Mr. Phelps has reason to be proud of his pupil. I hope to see you at the bar very soon, sir, and do not doubt you will have occasion to express your views upon these matters more effectually when I am dead and gone."

"That isn't all," said Prime eagerly; "I ain't a lawyer like Benny, but I've thought a heap about this matter, Judge, and I reckon justice is about the same thing whether she's seen through your glasses or mine."

"Well, as she is always represented as blindfolded we may infer she is not particular about her appearance and doesn't care who sees her—though it seems inconsistent to speak of her as a woman if that is the case," answered the judge, with humorous complaisance.

"I don't know about that," said Prime seriously. "But this is what seems to me to put an end to any such claim. They all shared in the proceeds of the wrong. It could not be otherwise, you see."

"It's a great question—a great question," responded the judge as he started to leave. "God has a strange way of keeping his accounts—the debit and credit of right and wrong between races and peoples—and settling them according to His own notions. He holds the scales between them as courts do between man and man, only a great deal steadier. Our equity is only a faint reflection of His justice, but the procedure in the Heavenly Chancery"—he pointed upward with the fat forefinger of his left hand, an awkward but impressive gesture, and shook his great head as he glanced round upon the listeners— "the procedure up there is different from ours. There's no shuffling, and the judgments entered there are always enforced—always enforced, gentlemen!"

The little group were silent as he turned away and climbed the steps with a ponderous strength which concealed the effort it must have required. The respect which had kept others silent while he took part in the conversation was not so much due to the exalted position which he held, as to that innate respect for his moral and intellectual qualities which has been the bulwark of the American judiciary.[4]

4. The Supreme Court justice depicted in this scene is probably Stephen Johnson Field, a distinguished senior member of the court whose dissent in the Slaughterhouse Cases (1873) Tourgée admired. Field served as an associate justice of the United States Supreme Court from 1863 to 1897, and sided with the majority against Tourgée in the *Plessy* case seven years after the publication of *Pactolus Prime*.

15

From *Murvale Eastman, Christian Socialist* (1890)*

Originally serialized as "Nazirema or the Church of the Golden Lilies" in the *Chicago Advance* from October 1889 to July 1890, this novel represents Tourgée's fullest sustained treatment of economic injustice and the inequities of corporate capitalism. Just as with the race problem, Tourgée addresses the problems of capital and labor in the novel through the lens of social ethics and the rights and duties of citizenship. The following excerpts are taken from the preface to the book, in which Tourgée describes the social problems he intends to address, and from chapters 10 and 11, in which the character Murvale Eastman, minister of the Church of the Golden Lilies, explains his philosophy of "Christian Socialism."

PREFACE

Inheritance and environment are not only realities, but are the most important elements of every life. The thought of yesterday fixes the tendency of today; the conditions of today are the background against which every life is projected.

The impulse of our yesterday was one of achievement; the most notable miracles of the world's history have been accomplished within a century. Self-government has not only grown to be a fact, but has inspired a universal impulse for control. The individual clamors for self-direction, equality of right, of privilege, of opportunity.

In the mean time, today's conditions—its material tendency and development—have opposed the fulfillment of yesterday's aspiration. The most tremendous forces have moved with unprecedented energy toward the subjection of the individual. During the last half-century, the segregation of capital in a few hands has been equaled only by the restriction of opportunity. A

*Excerpted from preface and chapters 10 and 11 of Albion W. Tourgée, *Murvale Eastman, Christian Socialist* (New York: Fords, Howard, & Hulbert, 1890).

few already control one-half the valuation of the country: the many must be content with the other moiety. But fewer still control the opportunities for labor—the avenues of profit. Not only is the ratio of self-employers rapidly diminishing, but the proportion of employers to employed has already become so small as to awaken universal alarm. Organization has practically eradicated the individual. The small manufacturer has almost disappeared. The small dealer has been absorbed. The small manufacturer has become a foreman; the small merchant an agent.

During the last ten years the manufacture of pig-iron has increased three hundred percent in the United States, but the number of establishments engaged in its production during the same time has diminished more than one-fifth! Transportation, by far the greatest business of the country, is controlled by fewer individuals than any other. There are many railroads, but all are parts of or dependent upon a few "systems." Probably less than a score of men actually control the transportation of the United States, the earnings of those engaged in it and the profits of those dependent upon it. So much power over the comfort and prosperity of so many has never before been wielded by so few.

But what exists is as nothing to what promises to be. Protecting the future on the lines of the immediate past, and the dullest mind perceives that the concentration of power by reason of the control of opportunity must, in a very brief period, increase the ratio of dependency to an extent perhaps never equaled in any civilized country. Already a new feudalism has been developed in which power is transmitted, not by blood, but by bequest, and in which vassalage is secured, not by an oath of allegiance, but by dependency. The barons of wealth are today more potent in molding the destinies of others than the feudal lords ever were or ever could be. The strong arm is potent only as far as the sword can reach; the controller of opportunity cables his will around the world and grapples his dependent by the throat even at the antipodes. Feudal strife reduced the number of lords but rarely increased the privileges of the feudatories. In like manner competition between the great lords of production, of trade and transportation, lessens the number of controllers of opportunity but increases the power of the remainder.

With these conditions come others—moral and political, social and intellectual, which color every life—high and low. Those who serve and those who control are being separated by sharper lines and more inflexible barriers. "What shall the end be?" is the universal refrain of thought today.

The past offers no parallel; it knew no similar conditions. The conflict between the many and the few has heretofore been one of personal right; the citizen has been evolved from the serf; the freeman from the slave. To this end all the forces of civilization have been shaped. The present is not a question of personal right, but of just opportunity. Wage-earning is not slavery, but when it becomes a fixed condition it is one of sheer dependence. The control of opportunity means the subjection of the individual just as much as did the control of his energies, but it does not trench upon the domain of personal right. No individual laborer has a right to demand work and wages of an individual employer. It is a question between society and the employer as to the control of opportunity.

We have simply come upon a new era. The maxims of the past are no longer safe landmarks. The social bases of the past are too narrow for the demands of the present. The domain of personal duty has been enlarged. The relations of the individual have been extended. The area of mutual obligation has been amazingly increased. The citizen has become responsible for direction as well as allegiance. The function of government has been newly defined. The wisdom of the wisest ancient monarch is folly today. It is no longer a defensible theory that "what is good for the hive is good for the bee"; the converse, rather, is the measure of policy. The welfare of the governed is acknowledged to be the supreme function of government. Already the "wealth of nations" has proved a delusion. The individual is the pivot of progress. Personal independence is the test of social forces. A nation may grow rich beyond all precedent, and at the same time individual opportunity be constantly restricted and the area of self-direction and control be rapidly diminished. The man who labors for himself is a master; he who is dependent for opportunity upon another's will is half a slave.

It is against this background of fact that the author has sought to trace certain characters. He claims for his work only that the background is a real one, and the figures such as one meets in real life, shown under familiar conditions. He has not sought to indicate specific methods of amendment or predict particular results, but merely to point out the spirit which must animate and precede any successful effort at amelioration. The general purpose is the most important element of social progress. "Where there is a will, there will always be found a way," is an adage peculiarly true of popular impulses. Method is secondary, and depends largely on the agencies the popular will must employ and the conditions under which it must act. The moral tendency from which amendment must arise, is a fact; millennial possibilities and specific remedies are at best but dreams.

"We cannot do without Christianity," said Matthew Arnold, "and we cannot endure it as it is." He uttered half a truth. We have applied the basic principle of Christianity to half the relations of life: the result has been personal liberty—the equal right of every individual to control his own energies. Is the world ready to apply the same immutable principle to another field of human relation—the field of opportunity as well as freedom of endeavor? This is the question formulated in these pages, simply because it is the paramount question which is struggling for answer in these our times—the most real fact of every life.

. . . . . .

CHAPTER X. ACHRYSALID'S RETROSPECT

When Murvale Eastman reached his lodging and sat down to his luncheon, he could hardly realize that scarce an hour had passed since he pronounced the benediction over the bowed heads of his congregation. Not so much had happened in the meanwhile, but somehow he felt as if he had lived a long time in that brief interval. This is often the case. The soul does not measure time by seconds, nor yet by heart-beats, but by modifications in its own quality and character. The watches of the world may stop; the planets may cease to measure the flight of time; the body may retain its pristine vigor—but in an hour, a moment almost, the heart may grow old, the man be transformed.

It is this fact that the mere scientist is sure to neglect in his estimate of humanity. He says of a man, of a people, or a race, given food, climate, and physical conditions of a specific character, and certain results will follow. Presently the conditions are all fulfilled and the results do not follow. Why? Simply because the mightiest part of the human being was left out of account in the scientist's estimate. So, too, that pessimistic philosophy which calls itself "realism" in art and literature, always is, and always will be, at fault when it tries to solve the riddle of humanity. It says human nature, human character, is a result of the operation of natural laws. So it is, but those laws are not all physical, nor purely mental. The soul must be taken into account if one would comprehend humanity or truly portray character. Impulse, affections, sentiments, convictions, emotions—these are more potent than all other forces in shaping the man and, if general in their application, the multitude. Every man's knowledge, almost every man's experience, is full of transformation scenes. It is a literal fact that "love works miracles" so do hate and fear and the continuing power of cumulative ill. There is in truth no miracle about it. It is in these soul-forces, even more than in physical laws and conditions that the secret of progress and the highest truth of human life lie hid. In a man or a people, the crises of sentiment or conviction are more important than physical

conditions in determining character or prescribing the lines of truthful delineation in literature or art.

"A live dog is better than a dead lion," is an artistic as well as spiritual
truth. The artist who forgets the soul may carve with unerring skill the "dead
lion," but he who with many faults of line and curve portrays the "live dog,"
will ever rank as the greater artist, when the whimsical dictate of fashion is
forgotten.

Murvale Eastman was conscious that some such change had been taking place in himself. The man who had first entered the pulpit of the Golden
Lilies, only two years before, seemed to him strangely unfamiliar, almost a
lifetime away in thought, sentiment, character. He was eminently a healthy
man, however, in body, brain, and soul. There was no more morbidness in his
thought than flaccidness in his muscles. So he ate his luncheon with hearty
relish wondering if he really was the self-same man who had hesitated to do
so commonplace a thing as to speak his own thought only a few hours before.
Was it hours or ages? And was he the Murvale Eastman of that remote past
or was that only a vision, a remembrance, an impression from some other
state of existence?

The bells of the Golden Lilies did not ring for evening service that night,
but the crowds that pressed through its artistic portal found the pastor already
in the pulpit, and the organ sending out a low, quavering strain of dreamy
restfulness. When the time for opening had come, the crowd was still pouring
in through the open doors, the pews were crowded, and people sat on chairs
in the aisles, until the great auditorium could hold no more. Some even stood
around the walls, and there were little groups about the doors that led into the
vestibule. They were an eager and excited throng, for the story of the morning sermon had gone abroad through the city and created a sensation. Many
had come merely from curiosity, some in hope, and some to see a man who
was foolish enough to take the course the pastor of the Church of the Golden
Lilies was reported to have adopted. Much to his own surprise Murvale Eastman felt neither pride nor trepidation. If many came, it but enhanced his
responsibility; and whether many or few he felt no longer any question in
regard to his duty. The one soul that would listen almost breathless in the
darkened study to his words occupied quite as much of his thought as the sea
of faces the electric lights lit up.

When the organ strain had ceased and the opening prayer had been made,
he told the congregation that the services would be brief because of the accidental presence, in an apartment of the church, of one whom it was not

deemed wise to remove at that time, and whose safety might be endangered by excitement. The door into the study was ajar, and somehow every one in the vast audience seemed suddenly to be aware that a critical scene in the tragedy of life was being enacted in the darkened room beyond.

A hymn was softly sung by the choir, and in the wondering hush that followed, the minister announced his text in the simple, unpretentious manner which had marked his morning discourse.

"'*The Sabbath was made for man.*'

"Not merely," said the speaker, "for his individual refreshment, not merely for physical or spiritual recreation, but for the welfare and advantage of mankind. To that it was particularly consecrated, and to that it should be especially devoted."

CHAPTER XI. A NEW DOCTRINE

"Christianity," continued the minister, looking over his Congregation and for the first time becoming aware of that alert expectancy which greeted his words, so different from the contented, matter-of-course attention which had usually been accorded his pulpit utterances, "Christianity is emphatically the religion of humanity. Earth and man are its themes. Justice for the strong and mercy for the weak—these were the lessons Christ inculcated. He was not concerned with forms and ceremonies. He established no church; he organized no cult; he prescribed no form of worship. 'The Twelve' and 'The Seventy,' what were they? They named themselves and assumed rank afterward; but the Master—thank God, he had not time nor inclination for such trifles! To him they were simply two bands of disciples to whom he had taught his great lessons of human betterment. Peace, righteousness, charity—these were the grand ingredients of his message.

"Peace: 'Whatsoever house ye shall enter, say, Peace be within these walls.'

"Righteousness: 'Whatsoever ye would that men should do unto you, do ye even so to them.'

"Charity: 'Love thy neighbor as thyself.' 'Do good to them that hate you.'

"These are the cardinal points of Christ's religion as we learn it from Christ's words. Of creed and prayer there is hardly enough to enable us to guess the desirability of profession and liturgical form.

"The *formal* part of Christianity is of man. However ancient, however worthy of regard the organization of the Church may be, it must be admitted that the *machinery* of Christianity is of human devising or was communicated through human agencies. It is intended to promote Christianization, the conversion of sinners, the profession and encouragement of Christians. The Master's purpose, that to which *his* thought, self-sacrifice, and devotion were given, was the *betterment of human conditions.*

"'Come unto me all ye weary'—'smitten with toil' is the radical significance of the Greek word he uses—'and I will give you rest.' 'My yoke is easy and my burden is light,' is his message to those same toilers. What does the Master mean by these words addressed to his disciples? Evidently that the adoption of his principles, his philosophy of human relations in government and society, would make the condition of the toilers, of the masses, more tolerable. His disciples fully understood this to be the prime purpose and idea of the Master's life. But how it was to be carried into effect they did not know. It was the central mystery of that revelation which has been unfolding like a flower from the hour he taught on Olivet until the present. His disciples comprehended its purport, but not its operation. They could not. The human mind does not ripen in an instant. The Master's words required the light of ages to be cast upon them before the world could grasp their significance. He did not embarrass human weakness by prescribing methods. He did not say *how* this yoke was to be made which should make the world's great burden light. That he left to them, to us, to find out.

"The disciples showed their appreciation of this message by establishing a communistic association immediately after his crucifixion. Probably his personal followers had practiced community of goods during his life. How long it continued we do not know. The believers of Macedonia and Achaia proposed, Paul tells us, to make 'a community of goods with the poor saints at Jerusalem.' We have translated it 'a contribution,' which originally meant the same thing, *to wit,* an equal share of a common burden, but has now come to mean a mere voluntary dole.

"In a more or less perfect form the communistic idea probably attached to the Church in Rome in its early days. There is little doubt that the Christians of the Catacombs were communists—not, I judge, compulsorily, but voluntarily. This early Christian socialism, indeed, seems always to have been voluntary. Freedom of thought and action was the first great lesson the disciples learned, and they learned it well. 'They that believed,' we are told, 'were of one heart.' 'Neither said any of them aught of the things *which he possessed was his own!*' 'They had all things in common.' 'Neither was there any among them that lacked.'

"This is the picture of Christian communism after the Pentecostal outpouring of the Holy Spirit. How like an echo it seems of that earlier Scripture, 'The earth is the Lord's and the fullness thereof!' Even then, however, it seems to have been purely voluntary. Those who chose entered into this community for mutual aid and support; those who did not, retained their individual possessions. The sin of Ananias and Sapphira was not in retaining the value of their lands. 'While it remained,' said the sturdy fisher-disciple, 'was it not thine own? And when thou hadst sold it, was it not in thine own power?' They desired to share the benefits of the community of goods, without performing the one condition that entitled them to support out of the common fund, *to wit,* the surrender of what they possessed. Their act was fraudulent; that was their crime.

"This experiment, under the direct control of the Apostles, was a failure. We do not know how long it lasted nor why it failed; but we have certainly a right to infer that if community of goods and obliteration of individual possession, attempted under the direction of the immediate disciples of the Christ, proved a failure with the early devotees of the new religion, it at least was not the means by which the Master expected his benign purposes toward men to be carried into effect. Christianity, even more notably than Judaism, is a religion of individualism. There are but two essences in it, Man and God—the Individual and the Creator, the Finite and the Infinite. There is no machinery, no substituted representative of the Divine Will. The Master says nothing about obedience to the Church, and gives no man or set of men the power to command another's obedience or relieve another soul of doubt or responsibility. Christ's words were uttered to all men, and must be obeyed by each for himself, according to his own conviction.

"Community of goods implies not merely a lessening of individual burdens, but a restriction of the domain of individual duty. The tendency of Christianity is in exactly the opposite direction, toward the expansion of individualism and the extension of individual responsibility. All healthful progress in the Church and in the civilization that Christianity has colored, has been in that direction. This was only a first experiment by which Christian believers sought to find out a way to carry into effect Christ's teachings as to human conditions. They sought for a way by which man might cast the greater part of his individual duty upon his fellows collectively. They failed because, though they heard his word, they did not comprehend its import. They were in error, just as in the common belief of that time that Christ would come again while one of the Apostles was still alive. Since that, there have been many experiments in the same direction. They all failed, as such experiments will always fail, because the crown and glory of humanity is individualism, and Christ's religion is always, an appeal to the better elements of humanity.

"After that, for ages we find the Church insisting on alms—'charity,' we call it when we try to stretch the blanket of our good works so as to make it cover the Divine requirement—provision for the aged and poor, as the sole measure and limit of Christian duty as regards the physical conditions of others. This is, in the main, the present position of the Church: each man has a right to hold whatever earthly possessions he may lawfully acquire; he has a right, within certain limits, to bequeath his accumulations to whomsoever he may elect. The duty of society is to give every man a fair education; to care for the infirm and enfeebled; to punish and restrain criminals. As to preventing impoverishment—making the yoke easy and the burden light to those stricken with toil, the doers, the burden-bearers of society, we acknowledge no duty of betterment, of sympathy, of regard or encouragement in this direction. The rich man is more welcome in the Church than the poor man, and the rich Christian finds himself under no obligation to see that his schemes to obtain wealth do not result in the impoverishment of others.

"Attention has sometimes been given to the idea of equalizing conditions. Methods have been proposed to keep the poor from growing poorer, and to make it easier for some of them, at least, to grow richer. The purpose is no doubt akin to the fundamental idea of the Founder of Christianity, that it is the duty of the strong to assist the weak—*not* to devour them. It has assumed various forms in the development of civilization, sometimes through governmental action, sometimes through voluntary association. Both are merely approximations to the Christian ideal, that the duty of the strong is to help the weak. 'Bear ye one another's burdens' did not mean prayers and sympathy and tears alone; not merely offering food and shelter to those whose burdens have already crushed them. It meant, and it means today, that the strong should devote a part of his strength to enabling his weaker brother to carry his burden more easily, more successfully, more profitably, if you will. If Christianization were the only aim of Christianity; if it stood on a level with Mahometanism, and had for its sole function the conversion of mankind to its tenets, it would still be the most profound wisdom that should adopt this principle as a rule of action, since it is the surest method of securing the acceptance of the religious system it represents, by the masses of mankind.

"Society punishes crime and feeds the man in absolute need of bread. Government goes farther sometimes, and conditions the power of the strong so that it shall not oppress or discourage the weak. It not only relieves want, but seeks to prevent dependency and depression. Bankruptcy laws, homestead exemptions, laws against usury, the limitations of corporate privilege, the regulation of traffic—these and many other laws are intended solely to prevent the rich from using the power of accumulated wealth to make the poor poorer, more dependent, and consequently less peaceful and contented citizens. This is not done for the benefit of the weak alone, but for the common welfare and advantage.

"The *social* function of Christianity is not merely to relieve want or exercise 'charity,' *but to incline the hearts of men in their individual, corporate, and political relations to refrain from doing evil, and induce them to assist rather than oppress the weak.* It is well to organize 'charity' to relieve destitution, but it is a thousand times better to practice that charity—'kindliness' is the true rendering—'Love thy neighbor as thyself'—which tends to prevent destitution. Thus far the Church has neglected to a great degree the consideration of this phase of human duty. We have reversed the Master's lesson, and given more prominence to the divine than to the human element of Christianity. Christianization has been its chief aim; the betterment of human conditions only an incident. Yet the Master has laid down one rule by which alone the value of Christian belief may be measured: 'By their fruits shall ye know them,' and the 'fruits' of Christianity are not merely the graces of Christian character, but the practice of Christ's teachings in regard to Christian duty.

> "'Religion is no leaf of faded green,
> Or flower of vanished fragrance pressed between
> The pages of a Bible.'

"Profoundly convinced of this, I believe it is the present duty of the Church to turn away for a time from 'the mint and cummin' of religious theory, forget for awhile—'the selfishness of salvation,' and consider what we may do for human betterment, to lessen human woe, to increase the sum of human happiness, and advance the standard of human duty; to labor, in short, for human elevation on earth both as an end and as the surest method of effecting the eternal salvation of man.

"Thus far we have allowed the discussion of these questions to remain chiefly in the hands of those who are hostile to Christian belief, sometimes mere buccaneers who fly the flag of human betterment in the hope of advantage by some great eruption. The Church has no right to allow its enemies to outstrip it in the study of the means by which civilization may be fully consecrated to the improvement of human conditions. No set of ranters, whose only idea of progress is the disruption of Society and the destruction of all that the past has achieved with such lavish expense of blood and tears, should be allowed to claim credit for being more interested in the welfare of society than is the Church, which should not set limits to progress, but point out new lines of advance. The Church should be the support of Society—not as it is, but as it ought to be—the staunch, unflinching champion of all there is of good, and the unrelenting enemy of all there is of evil in it. It does not do its duty by singing hymns with half-shut eyes or dreaming dreams of heavenly bliss. Wide-open eyes are needed—eyes that smile upon the good in life and seek out and blast with the heat of fierce disapproval all that is bad.

"'The Son of Man is Lord also of the Sabbath,' said the Master, and this Sabbath, this rest-day, this green oasis in the arid desert of heated life, he expressly consecrates, not to religious speculation, not to formal worship or the rhapsody of religious emotion, but to *Man:* 'The Sabbath was made for man.' Not merely for the physical or spiritual enjoyment of man, but to his advantage and benefit. As the Lord of the Sabbath devoted his life on earth to doing good but so he demands that his followers, of all classes and conditions, shall make the welfare of their fellows the first and highest object in life, after their own wants and the comfort of those dependent upon them. *This is Christian Socialism.*"

The pastor saw a flash of gratified expectancy sweep through the audience as he uttered these words. A couple of reporters who had secured places at a table just at the right of the pulpit, exchanged glances as their hands flew over the pages of their note-books, and each in his own peculiar manner marked the pastor's words as an effective head-line in their reports. An exultant "I-told-you-so" expression came into the eyes of some who had listened moodily to his words, while a pained, apprehensive look passed over faces which had been lighted up with approbation and hope. Both the apprehension of his friends and the exultation of his enemies was short-lived. The speaker continued:

"The Church has no right to permit this term, which should mean the science of practical amendment of social conditions, to be appropriated by men whose only notions of progress are either impossible changes of human nature or the overthrow of all existing social conditions. Christian Socialism should 'hold fast all that is good,' while bending the energies of all believers to the attainment of that which is better. It demands a nobler ideal of duty toward humanity as well as a higher standard of individual character. For eighteen hundred years the Church has devoted its Sabbaths mainly to the

work of Christianization, the inculcation of doctrine, the assertion of theological dogma, the contemplation of divine excellence, and the portrayal of
Christian graces. Profoundly convinced that the true interests of the Church,
the cause of Christianity, and the spirit of the Master's teachings demand that
we should follow his example as well as study his precepts, your pastor has
decided to devote the morning service during the ensuing year to the consideration of Christian Socialism, the study of the relation of the Christian
believer to the conditions attaching to today's life and affecting tomorrow's
welfare. In this effort to trace more clearly the line of Christian duty he asks
the cordial cooperation of this church and congregation, and on their joint
endeavor invokes the blessing of Almighty God."

16

The Negro's View of the Race Problem (1890)*

On June 4–6, 1890, Tourgée participated in an important conference hosted by Quaker Albert K. Smiley at his famous mountain retreat in Lake Mohonk, New York. Bringing together leaders from both sections and political parties, this gathering amounted to a national summit on what was termed "The Negro Question," and it included among its participants former president Rutherford B. Hayes, General Oliver O. Howard, General Samuel C. Armstrong, Dr. Lyman Abbott, and the Reverend A. D. Mayo. Conference organizers excluded blacks from attending the meeting in order to secure the participation of southern white leaders. Tourgée electrified the conference with his pointed—even accusatory—remarks, which he designed in part to protest the meeting's exclusion of blacks. Tourgée later declined an invitation to return for the second annual meeting in 1891, swearing off attending any future white-only gatherings. The following excerpts from the conference transcript include a comment Tourgée made during a discussion of "industrial education" for blacks and his prepared address in full as he delivered it under the above title.

Judge Tourgée: So much has been said this morning about the industrial deficiencies of the colored people of the South that I have been greatly surprised at the omission of any reference to the other side of the question—their industrial excellences. I have always been less impressed with the industrial needs of the colored man than his industrial achievements. From 1865 until 1880, I had a peculiarly good opportunity for observing his qualities both as an agricultural and mechanical laborer, having first and last had some hundreds in my employ, and during much of the time each year traveling in different

*"The Negro's View of the Race Problem," in *First Mohonk Conference on the Negro Question. Held at Lake Mohonk, Ulster County, New York, June 4, 5, 6,* ed. Isabel C. Barrows (Boston: G. H. Ellis, 1890).

parts of the State in which I then lived. As a result of constant study of their conditions since emancipation, I do not hesitate to say that *the colored people of the South have accomplished more in twenty-five years, from an industrial point of view, than any people on the face of the earth ever before achieved under anything like such unfavorable conditions.*

The manner in which they live and the things they do not do have been alluded to here as if they were racial qualities, and not fortuitous, resulting conditions. I was much impressed with the suggestions of more than one who has spoken,[1] as to what they should be taught to do, as if they were industrial babes. I would like to see any of their advisers give the colored man lessons in the management of a mule, or teach him to raise a crop of corn or cotton or tobacco, or work a bad hillside at the South. In those forms of industry which they have had an opportunity to acquire, they have shown an aptitude and success which are simply amazing, when we consider their previous lack of opportunity to learn management, thrift, and economy. The Northern man is always prompt to criticize their agricultural methods; yet the Northern farmer who goes South and relies upon his own judgment and his own labor is very generally a failure.

So, too, in comparison with the "poor whites" of the South, the landless cropper-class, it is unquestionable that the Negro has excelled them greatly in industrial progress since his emancipation. In five of the heaviest cotton-growing counties of five States of the South, it is estimated that from four to six percent of the heads of families among colored people live now under their own roof-trees. In the regions where agriculture is more varied, the proportion is much greater. Probably six percent is a fair average. Now, if, under the conditions prevailing in 1865, two in a thousand had housed themselves in twenty-five years, it would have been regarded, by the observant political economist, as nothing short of an industrial miracle. I have no doubt that five times as large a proportion of them have become home-owners and self-employers as of the "poor whites," who most nearly approach them in educational and financial conditions, and with whom alone they can be justly compared.

Indeed, they already stand above the average of the white race in some industrial conditions. There is only half as large a percentage of paupers among them as among the whites of the eight States of the "black belt" of the South,

1. The panel consisted of two other papers, "Industrial Training," by General Armstrong, and "Industrial Schools for the Negroes," by Rev. R. H. Allen.

and the proportion of paupers among the whites of the South is much less than at the North. It has been claimed that the reason of this is that the old masters support the aged and infirm who have been slaves. No doubt, this is sometimes true; but, even in slave times, it required special statutes in every Southern State to prevent the masters from abandoning such infirm slaves to live by their own devices, and it is not reasonable to suppose that the white man would support the infirm freedman and send the disabled ones of his own race to the poorhouse. It is simply a remarkable economic fact which establishes beyond controversy the remarkable economic value of the colored man as an industrial element of American life.

Something has been said about the frequent absence of the surname among the Negroes of the South. In "Bricks without Straw," I fully discussed the cause and character of this, to us of the North, singular feature of the freedman's character. It is a terrible unconscious testimony against the treatment American Christianity has accorded our "brother in black." It was natural that the freedman should be a little lax in the matter of names. The slave had never been allowed a surname—could not have one, indeed, because he had no father. The law expressly forbade it. He was always a *nullius filius*,[2] and was indicted, tried, and hanged simply as Jim or John. And it must be remembered that indictment and trial was the only legal privilege the slave enjoyed. He could be hanged, but could not be married; and his master changed his name as often as he chose. Why should not this man, new-born to self-control, make some experiments in nomenclature? He was a good way behind us, who have been fooling with our names for centuries, and have not always gotten them entirely satisfactory even yet. This is not a racial peculiarity, but an eternal testimony against injustice. At the close of the war there were set free 5,000,000 of men, women, and children, without a husband, a wife, a lawful father, a legitimate child, or a legal family name among them all! They were without homes, without money, without lands, tools, seeds, or stock, without education, without experience, without inheritance, without the impulse of generations of thrift and intelligence. Yet, without a family name, except one of his own selection, with wages hardly one-third those of the agricultural laborer of the North, the Negro accomplished industrial results which must make any observer of facts who can lay aside prejudice and forget theories, utter, with profound amazement, those words first of all flashed through the electric wire, "What hath God wrought!"

2. Latin, "son of no one," having no legal right to inherit.

THE NEGRO'S VIEW OF THE RACE PROBLEM

I trust I may be pardoned in advance if, in my remark, my religion and my politics should become not merely "mixed," as Dr. [Lyman] Abbott feared that his might, but even if it should appear that my religion is mostly politics; for I trust it will also become apparent that my "politics" is not altogether at odds with what we term "religion." I confess I have never been able to distinguish between them. Without religion, politics is simply the hot-bed of iniquity, the stamping-ground of devilish impulse; and, without politics, religion is as dead as "faith without works." When Christianity quits the field of political relation or politics discards the tenets of Christian philosophy, I have little use for either.

I have sometimes thought that the Christ I worship is not the Christ whom many revere. I cannot look upon him as merely a weak, tender, pitying nature, who stood beside the seething tide of human life and tearfully dropped anesthetics on its woes. My Christ is he of the knotted whipcords, who pitied human woefulness less than he hated the evil conditions from which it springs. I love to think of him as a man, and believe in his divinity because he neither shunned the woes of humanity nor excused its evils. I love to think that he lived in a cabin not much better than those we have heard so much about at this conference; that he probably sat upon the floor, ate his food with his fingers, found his friends among the poorest poor, and would not be patronized by the rich; who pointed out the one golden possibility of human nature and formulated the one principle by which humanity may hope for betterment here or salvation hereafter, yet would be flouted as a tramp today by his most respectable followers. I love to think that he knew human woe and its causes, and based upon such knowledge the remedy he prescribed for its cure. I love to think that the sandal-strings chafed his feet, that the dust and grime besmirched his body, and the salty sweat-drops crept beneath his eyelids and dropped from off his beard, while he strode along over the sun-parched hills of Judea, doing good, and implanting in the hearts of humble followers an undying zeal for humanity. I love to think that the seamless coat he wore was often in need of washing, and that, like the colored man when freed from bondage, he had nowhere on earth to lay his head.

To my mind, the Christ was not more a savior than a politician—studying first the facts of human life, tracing the causes of evil, imposing on everyone the duty of considering the welfare of others, and making "Do unto others as ye would that they should do to you" the golden key by which alone the gate of heaven may be unlocked. I do not believe that this divine thinker, on whose heart the burden of human anguish forever rested, meant mere sympathy when he asked the weary to come unto him *because* his yoke was easy, and shouted down the centuries the universal and inexorable command, "Bear ye one another's burdens." He meant not pity, but healing—the amelioration of human conditions—and made that the sole lesson of human duty, the universal principle on which collective as well as individual conduct is rightly based, the truest policy, the grandest selfishness, whereby the highest happiness is made to depend on individual effort to uplift humanity. This, to my mind, is Christianity, the kernel of civilization, the mainspring of popular government, the only "practical" politics—no more to be fully achieved by us than the purity of the Christ-life, yet ever to be striven for as the one pearl of price in the world's social philosophy.

So far as I am concerned, therefore, religion and politics cannot be separated in the consideration of the "Negro Question." The rule of duty imposed upon us as individuals, upon the American Church, upon the American Republic, upon Christian civilization, as regards the American Negro, is simply that we shall treat him as, in reversed conditions, we would desire him to treat us. That is the sole measure of right betwixt man and man, nation and nation, race and race, class and class. It is the golden coin of righteousness, bearing the Christ-stamp, and issued from the mint of Truth upon the Mount of Olives. All imitations or substitutes are false, hollow, spurious.

So the first thing to be learned about the Negro Question by those who would solve it truly is the Negro's view of the race problem. I do not mean by this the view which an uneducated individual Negro may entertain, nor even that which any single educated representative of the race might formulate, but the general sentiment, inherent and inevitable as the result of past events and present conditions, of the colored race in the United States, regarding their present, past, and future relations to the residue of the American people. Such general ideas common to races, peoples, and classes are very subtle in character, sometimes difficult to trace, always hard to formulate, and frequently almost impossible to define. They are latent forces, which are often entirely incomprehensible by other peoples who have the closest visible relations with them. No doubt Pharaoh and the more intelligent and cultivated classes of Egypt believed they fully understood the character of the degraded tribes they had held in bondage for four hundred years; but it is doubtful if one of them dreamed of that fierce tide of theocratic nationalism which burst from Moses' lips as he gazed upon the waves that engulfed Israel's pursuers.

It is not probable that one in a thousand of the Jewish people had ever uttered such scorching maledictions as centuries afterwards fell from the Hebrew prophet's tongue, when he told again the story of the bondage in Egypt. Yet they no doubt found an echo in every Israelitish heart, and these hissing curses are unquestionably the true expression of the Jewish view of the period of the sojourn in Egypt. The Irishman's idea of the Irish question has required some centuries to formulate, perhaps it is not yet fully formulated, but one can get some idea of it by tapping any average Irishman and analyzing the results. You will not find it in the words he uses, but in the spirit he manifests—in what he tries to say rather than in what he says.

So the Negro's view of the race problem must be inferred from conditions and human as well as racial proclivities, even more than from individual testimony. The testimony of observers must always be construed, too, with regard to their bias and relation to the race. And the testimony of the race itself must be read in the light of its own past experience. Both these facts we have almost ignored. We have sought testimony *about* the Negro from his avowed friends and confessed enemies, and think we shall obtain the truth by "splitting the difference" between them. The testimony of the Negro in regard to his past and present conditions and aspirations for the future is worth more than that of all the white observers that it can be packed upon the planet. The man who wears the shoe knows better than anybody else just where it pinches. He may not know how to remedy the defect, but the cobbler will never fix it unless the wearer tells him just where and how it hurts. We wise white people may know more about remedies and their methods of application than he, but the Negro owns the bunion, and his testimony is worth more than that of all the rest of mankind upon what hurts it, and his view of how and where the race question pinches him is the first prerequisite of any sensible attempt at a cure.

The Southern white man almost universally asserts that he knows the colored man better than anyone else, because he and his forbears held him for a dozen generations as a bondman. Yet, if history teaches anything, it is that the gulf between the master and the slave is the hardest of all social chasms to span, and the master's estimate of the bondman's interest, character, and rights, the farthest possible from the bondman's notion of the same. Thus we find the colored ministers of Charleston deliberately asserting in a public address, only a few years ago, that "the slave-owner knew no more about the Negro, *as a man,* than if he had lived on an inaccessible island in mid-ocean." With such differences, how shall I dare attempt to give the Negro view of the race problem?

I have only the right to express an opinion, and have a right to have an opinion only because I have studied this question from this particular point of view for a quarter of a century—because I first dissected, out of actual Negro lives, the spiritual elements from which were synthetically constructed "Toinette," "Nimbus," "Uncle Jerry," "Pactolus Prime," and half a dozen other characters, in which this very idea is the distinguishing quality. Anyone who reads my works will perceive at once that this peculiar phase of this problem has been a matter of special study with me. For instance, "Nimbus," the leading character of "Bricks without Straw," is first introduced engaged in a disquisition upon the subject of names, which has been discussed here, and in regard to which one of our friends pretty broadly intimated that my statement that the slave was not allowed to marry or have a surname was untrue because in his father's family Bible there was a record of the births, marriages, and deaths of his slaves. I do not question that man's sincerity: he could not have intended to make a false impression on your minds; but he forgot that marriage is something more than *permitted cohabitation,* and that a name is no name at all unless the bearer has a legal right to it. He knows very well, and would not dare deny, that such entries as he describes, even though made in a family Bible, had no more the quality of a family record, so far as the slave was concerned, than the pedigree of a thoroughbred horse. He knows that in every State of the South the marriage of the slave was an *impossibility,* and that no slave *could* have a surname because he *could not* have a legal sire. Bastardy was forcibly entailed upon five millions by Christian laws. I do not say this to wound his feelings or cast any imputation on his ancestors. Every American citizen was responsible for the sin of slavery. All shared in its advantages, and all are morally bound to aid in remedying its resultant ills. The Negro view of these things is not that of the sometime master, however; and, the farther he gets away from those conditions, the less excuse will he find for the white Christian's relation to his nameless sire, and to the mother whom our laws degraded to the status of a *dam.*

My study of the Negro began when he was still a slave, but when the fetters were already dropping from his hands. Fleeing from a Confederate prison, I sought his aid with confidence, and tested not only his faithfulness, but his sagacity. As a soldier, I saw him shed his blood for the flag which had meant only bondage and oppression for his race, though already growing radiant with the promise of liberty. During fifteen of the early years of his freedom (1865 to 1880), I studied him as an employer, a citizen, a lawyer, a judge. I was thoroughly familiar with his status in every portion of one of the Southern States, and since that time have studied it in every State of the South, keeping always uppermost in my mind *his* view of his past and his hope for the future. I have studied him, I will admit, with growing appreciation. He is a new type, a new MAN. He has sloughed off the African, and is first of all things an American—American in instinct and aspiration as well as largely in blood. In some respects, he understands the white man better than the white man understands himself. As a race he has not yet come to a full formulation of his view of the past or a complete realization of the relations of the present. But the elements are readily discernible to one who studies him *as a man*, not as a mere appendage of the white race. I have not always understood him. I am not certain that anyone can who has not suffered with him. I have never been so sure as many of our friends what was the very best thing *to be done for* the colored man; but I have never doubted that the most exact justice and the fullest recognition of his equality of right must be the prime elements of any successful policy which has for its purpose the elevation of the race and the development of his individual manhood. Wrong is never cured by fresh injustice, and manhood is never ennobled by being compelled to wear the brand of inferiority.

I have not always been quite sure that the teaching we are giving the Negro is the very best, either for him or for ourselves. It has occurred to me that God and Mammon are queerly mixed in the ideal we commend to him. Praise God and make money seems to me a fair paraphrase of the advice given him even here. I doubt the good results of the prescription. Remember, he may take us literally. There is danger that such an education may produce hypocrites and misers. Men are needed, I think, more than ministers; example rather than exhortation. I may be wrong, but I have thought wise expenditure a more important lesson for the race today than rigid economy. To my mind, every rich Negro is an evidence of bad teaching. No Negro has a right to be rich while so many of his people are ignorant and unformed. But what can we expect? They are black and "inferior." Freedom did not make them wise and perfect, as it no doubt would if they had been white. They have taken us at our word. They are better economists than we ourselves. They live with less expenditure than any equal number of white people. A larger proportion of them have become land-owners than of any equally impoverished and unprepared class of whites in a like period, a smaller proportion of them are supported by public charity, a larger number of them have become rich, and their aggregate possessions are greater than any equal number of illiterate, landless whites without inheritance or fortuitous discovery ever accumulated in twenty-five years. Not a single white teacher who preaches the gospel of economy to the colored man can begin to live on what the majority of his hearers deem abundance. It is the lesson of wise and fruitful expenditure that should be most earnestly enforced. The race needs heroes and patriots and martyrs rather than millionaires. And they will have heroes and patriots—men who will joyfully live and die for their fellows—when they have learned to honor devotion to the right, and when individual self-sacrifice for the collective good is accounted a better thing than successful accumulation.

So far as the peaceful and Christian solution of the race problem is concerned, indeed, I am inclined to think that the only education required is that of the *white* race. The hate, the oppression, the injustice, are all on our side; and every Negro who wins the honors of his class in a Northern college, becomes a cashier in a national bank at Topeka, writes a story which New England people read, publishes a newspaper which white people are compelled to peruse, wins a membership in the Boston Press Club, becomes a dry-goods clerk in Chicago, or so good a ball-player that a crack club has to secure his services lest another should—each and every one of these colored men is a missionary sent of God to the white people of the United States, to teach them the fundamental truth of Christianity.

There are three elements of the race problem in the United States—the white man of the North, the white man of the South, and the Negro. The problem itself consists chiefly of the views which these three elements take of the Negro and his relation to the others. The Northern white man's view of the Negro is easily stated. He regards him either with complete indifference or as a mere object of compassion—one of those "weaklings" whom Dr. Harris informed us we were not required to treat with justice—who is to be supplied with a nursing-bottle, and encouraged to suck it as peaceably as may be. He is at best only an object of charity. Such a thing as duty or a bond of reciprocal interest and obligation existing between them is hardly thought of. Some go so far as to say, and sometimes, perhaps, even to *believe,* that there is no race problem—nothing to be done to wipe out the memory of past wrong or give assurance of future opportunity.

With few exceptions, the white man of the South regards the colored man as a predestinate inferior, to be governed, controlled, and treated as such, to be educated and trained for a secondary and subordinate position. This does not necessarily imply unkindness or intended injustice. It only means the assertion of inherent superiority, and by inference the right to prescribe what constitutes justice to the Negro, what privileges shall be granted to him, and what degree of subserviency shall be demanded of him. This was the hypothesis on which slavery rested. It is the view which colored all our past civilization. It overthrew the presumptions of the common law, and in the name of Jesus Christ pronounced, by the authority of the churches, the ban of eternal subjection against the superstitious child of Ham. Civilization is rarely heedful of the rights of those whom it can make tributary to its lusts of greed, and Christianity takes on always something of the hue of the life of which it becomes a part. Right and wrong are relative terms between the weak and the strong, but never reversible. What it is right for the strong to do, it is wrong, perhaps even sinful, for the weak to contemplate. Whitefield urged the introduction of slavery into Georgia as a Christian duty, and advocated the importation of Negroes in order that they might be Christianized with the same fervor that their deportation is now urged—that they may be re-heathenized.

Do not let us be too ready to blame the Christianity of yesterday, either. Thus far Christian nations and races have generally treated subject peoples very much as if Christ had not taught a better way. Protestant civilization has been lavish of religious teaching, of Christian charity, but wonderfully scant of justice to peoples of dusky skin. American and English ships lay side by side to batter down the Chinese forts, in order to open a way into the Flowery Kingdom for English opium and American missionaries. We are shocked at the brutalities of the Arab slave-traders on the head-waters of the Nile, but for every slave the followers of Mahomet steal out of the jungles of Africa Christian civilization, with arms and rum and robbery, is today sending ten of the children of the Dark Continent beyond the reach of hope. The Christianization of Africa has only just begun; but in two hundred years how many millions of Africans have suffered death at white Christian hands? Such will always be the character of our civilization as long as we try to keep our politics and our religion apart—as long as we try to limit the Golden Rule to individual relations and fly the skull and cross-bones at the mast-head of the Ship of State. It is merely substituting a new measure for Christian conduct in lieu of the one Christ prescribed. Instead of treating the man of dusky skin as we *know* we would wish him to treat us in like conditions, we simply make it the measure of our duty that we shall treat him as well as we can afford to do, without interfering with our own comfort or prejudices, or as well as *we* think he ought to be treated. Even we who are met here to discuss the Negro, to deplore his infirmities, to magnify our charity, to extol our own excellences and determine what ought to be done with and for him, do not regard his opinion about the matter as at all important. We do not ask him what he thinks of his condition. Not one in all this assembly has put the question, "In his condition, how would we wish the residue of the American people to treat us?" He is the poor patient, we are told, who is shut out of the council of the wise physicians for his own sake. He is not even allowed to detail his own symptoms. Why should he? The physician has a theory: why should he trouble himself about facts? We do not promise justice, but are overflowing with mercy. We forget to acknowledge that every kindness done the Negro in our land has been only a scanty patch, half-hiding some hideous wrong. We congratulate ourselves on what we have contributed for his mental and religious development, but quite ignore the fact that for every dollar we have given for his enlightenment he had before given a thousand for our enrichment. We boast of the public school system of the States of the South, in which so many colored children are being educated; but we forget to acknowledge the fact that the public school system was planted in every Southern State by the vote of the Negro, in direct opposition to an overwhelming majority of the whites, and that two white children enjoy its benefits to one colored one. We extol the public spirit which divides the public school fund of the States of the South between the schools of both races, though the Negro pays but a small proportion of the taxes, but are as silent as the grave in regard to the equally important fact that it is the unrequited labor of the colored man which created the major part of the valuation on which the white man pays taxes.

Yet we are the friends of the Negro; we wish to aid, assist, develop the race. This is our openly professed purpose in assembling here. Are we willing to apply the rule which Christ of the dusty gabardine prescribed, even to our charitable efforts, and proclaim a desire to undo the wrong of the past by justice in the future?

To the Negro in the United States the race question is one of color only. He is what he is, and all his conditions are what they are, merely because a white Christian people have prescribed such conditions for him because he has more or less colored blood in his veins. That is why he was imported. That is the reason he was held in service without recompense. That is the reason he was not allowed to marry or have a family. Because of this he was prohibited by law from learning to read or write. Because of this he was prevented from taking or holding property. Because of this every obstacle was put in the way of his progress from barbarism to civilization. *We* do not, we cannot, realize this fact of color. We have even been told here that "there *is* no race problem!" I wonder if the man who made the statement ever tried to apply the Christ-rule to the relation of the races in this Christian land. Did he ever think what it would mean to have in his veins even a few drops of that blood which Christianity for centuries taught was the indelible mark of the Divine curse? Did you ever think, sir, how much it would take to hire anyone in this audience to assume the burden of a black skin for a lifetime? Where would have been your career of honor, sir, if your cheek had shown a trace of African bronze? Nay, where and what would the pastor of Plymouth Church [Dr. Lyman Abbott], who sneers at a "race question," have been if God had made him black or brown or even saddle-colored? Did he ever think how easy it is for a white man to be good, and how much more grace it must require to save a Negro? If offered the choice, would he not prefer Cranmer's doom to such a fate? Would he think there was no "race problem" then?

In all the prayers that have been offered at this Conference I have not heard one word of thankfulness that *we* are white. I do not suppose any man here dare utter such a prayer in public; yet, excepting only life and the hope of salvation, this is the most priceless blessing we enjoy. Wealth, honor, knowledge, civilization, love—all of these are trivial things to us in comparison with the blessed fact that we are white! What father here would not rather face a childless age than see this mark upon the brow of a son? What mother would not become a murderer in heart, should she see this stain upon the cheek of her first-born? When you realize these things, you can begin to guess how the nerves of a race must quiver at the thought of the brand our Christian civilization puts upon them. When we can realize the horror of such a metamorphosis, we can imagine the feeling of a cultured Christian woman, who has been mentioned here as a model of devoted womanhood, when she said, "I would lie down and be flayed without a murmur if I might only rise up white!" Not that she thought the white race superior, but because the sting of imputed degradation and inferiority never ceases to thrill her nerves and wring her heart with anguish. Let us never forget to thank God that we are white, even if we are ashamed to go before him on our knees and thank him that we are his favorite children, the pets of his mercy, and the superiors of those to whom he gave darker skins! Especially let us never forget that this is the prime factor in the Negro's view of the race question, and will continue to grow more important to him as he increases in knowledge, refinement, wealth, and sensibility, unless we make some radical improvement in our white Christianity.

Another fact that must continue to affect the Negro's view of the race question and of the relations he sustains to the white man in the United States is the character of his past. It is easy for us to excuse *ourselves* for the

wrongs of slavery, but, day by day, it is growing harder for the colored man
to do so; and it is simply to state a universal fact of human nature to declare
that a great and lasting wrong like slavery done to a whole people because of
race or creed grows blacker and darker for generations and ages as they go
away from it. The educated grandchild of the slave who looks back into the
black pit of slavery will find little excuse for the white Christian civilization
which forbade marriage, crushed aspiration, and after two centuries and a half
offered the world as the fruits of Christian endeavor five millions of bastard
sons and daughters—the product of a promiscuity *enforced by law and upheld
by Christian teaching!* Slavery will be a more terrible thing to the Negro a hundred years hence than it was to the calloused consciousness of his nameless
father, and a more shameful horror to your grandchild's soul than it was to the
aching heart of Garrison.

We say—perhaps we sometimes even *think*—that, because slavery no longer exists as a legalized form of society, we may dismiss it from our thought,
and no longer consider it as a factor of our civilization. In truth, the conditions it bequeathed are far more difficult and delicate than those attending
its existence. It is a living force in the white man's thought and in the colored
man's life. The lessons it taught to both races are ineradicable by law, and are
beyond the control of mere reason. The white man of the South thinks he
would rather perish from the earth than be accounted only the equal of the
colored man, while the Negro is fast coming to an appreciation of the fact
that subordination is only a longer name for subjection. He dare not yield his
claim to equality of right and opportunity, even if he would. These irrepressible conflicting tendencies are the heritage of slavery, and the American people who planted and protected this upas-tree must see to it that they do not
bring a still greater evil. What ought *we* to do? Let us try to imagine ourselves
colored men, with dusky wives and children, and then answer with the fear of
God before our eyes!

A good deal has been said here about the character and quality of the Negro's religion. I always wonder that a white Christian dare cast any imputation
on the Negro's faith. For one, I am glad that he has *any* faith at all. To me, the
fact that the American Negro is *ever* a Christian is the greatest of miracles
that has been wrought since the grave yielded up its dead. Remember in what
school he was taught Christian truth! Look at his surroundings as he must
view them! Think that his first religious lessons were that God had created
him to serve the will of his white Christian brother; that the earth and its
fullness belonged to the white man, and that the Negro was added merely to

promote his pleasure and advantage; that the white man was allowed to own, occupy, and possess all he could acquire, but it was a sin for the colored man to assume control of his own body and brain; that marriage was a holy ordinance to the white man, but a forbidden privilege to the Negro; that home and family were sacred to his white brother, but forbidden by Christian law to the slave; that the white man was expected to die in defense of the virtue of his wife and daughter, but that the Negro's cabin stood forever open to the ravisher; that knowledge was the key-stone of the white man's religion, progress, and liberty, but that Christian laws forbade the colored man to learn to read the word of God! Remember that, for generations, the laws of Christian American States forbade three colored men to meet together for prayer unless a white man were present to see that they did not prejudice the Almighty against "the superior race." Remember these things, and think what *must* be the Negro's view of them, and, when next you lift your heart in prayer, forget not to thank God that these five millions of our brethren, born naked, fatherless, homeless, nameless, and ignorant out of the womb of slavery, came forth not vengeful savages, but peaceful believers, whom even their unprecedented wrongs did not move to strife!

Nay, if you wish a lesson in Christian devotion and self-sacrifice, read the story of the African Methodist Church, every one of the half million members of which is the child of a slave—who twenty-five years ago were not worth twenty-five cents apiece outside of the clothes they wore—and see the reported aggregate of more than $2,000,000 paid by them for religious and charitable purposes in one year. No other church has ever begun to equal that under like conditions of poverty and difficulty. Strike off half, and it still remains a miracle. Halve it again, and the Christians of the Catacombs may well hail them across the intervening ages as their closest exemplars!

We have commented here, in this Conference, with that freedom which springs only from conscious rectitude on the morals of the Negro. I do not suppose that in this respect he is without fault, but I leave to any fair-minded man or woman to answer if he is not better than we have any reason to expect to find him after the training of two centuries of Christian slavery. Remember that the white man's example has bleached not only the Negro's morals, but his skin, until one of the most prominent slave-traders of the South testified that hardly one in a thousand of the colored people in the United States is of unmixed Negro blood!

But even here there is room to note something to the credit of the brother in black; and we ought to give even the devil his due, despite "race, color, or previous condition." For two centuries, Christian civilization encouraged and compelled mere promiscuity among the slaves. As soon as they became free, this unhallowed relation became offensive to our eyes, and men and women who had previously "taken up with each other," as the courts phrased it, were required to register themselves as man and wife, or abandon their previous relations. For this registration they were also required to pay a good round fee. In several counties embraced in my judicial district, I investigated the proportion of those who assumed and those who renounced the old relation. The former was surprisingly large, ranging from 94% to 97%, according to the estimates of the best-informed parties. I suppose in the whole eight counties it would have reached 90% at least. Let the marriage bonds be dissolved throughout the State of New York today, and it may be doubted if as large a proportion of her intelligent white citizens would choose again their old partners.

But, before we utterly condemn the Negro for incurable immorality, let us ask where in all this republic can be found a white jury who would give above a sixpence damages for the seduction of a colored woman by a white man, or render a verdict in favor of a colored woman suing a white man for breach of promise of marriage, no matter what the testimony.

I must say one word in reference to what is known as the "Blair Bill," the defeat of which has been often referred to here with regret. I suppose my views in regard to national aid to education are well known. I do not think the government of the United States deserves to exist unless it makes provision for the cure of that ignorance which it fostered in whites and blacks alike at the South, in its insane desire to perpetuate slavery. One who loves the flag for which he fought can say nothing more emphatic. I believe I was the first man who proposed the appropriation of national funds to the schools of the country, in the ratio of illiteracy. Thirteen years before the "Blair Bill" was first introduced, I had presented to Congress the Memorial of the Republicans of North Carolina, asking that such aid be extended. "A Fool's Errand" and "Bricks without Straw" had been written with the sole purpose of calling the attention of the American people to education as the only hopeful remedy for Southern conditions. Other volumes followed; and I doubt not that many of those here present signed the petitions I afterwards circulated upon the subject, and which are yet preserved in bound volumes in the Congressional Library. That I am a firm believer in national aid to State schools cannot therefore be doubted. Yet *I* do not hesitate, in the name and on behalf of the colored people of the United States, to express here the most profound gratitude that this measure failed to become a law. Why? Because it was the most amazing piece of injustice which ever resulted from unwise methods linked to kindly purpose. Two-thirds of the illiterates of the South are colored: one-third of them are white. The schools for the two races are everywhere separate. The "Blair Bill" proposed, in effect, to pay over to each State one dollar a year for eight years for every illiterate in it. Two-thirds of the funds would therefore have been paid by the United States on account of colored illiterates. But it was required to be *distributed per capita;* and, the schools being separate for the two races, the *colored* schools of the South would have received one-third and the *white* schools two-thirds of the fund, though the colored schools represent *two-thirds* of the illiteracy. A child can see that it is precisely equivalent to the United States paying four times as much for the enlightenment of a white illiterate as for the education of a colored illiterate, besides giving the whites of the South control of even that modicum of the national gratuity. I was forced to oppose this bill, despite its seductive title, both because I cannot approve injustice and because I do not believe that God ever made a people good enough to be entrusted with another people's right and interests. I regard the defeat of that measure as another evidence that God is on the side of the colored man, and has heard at length his long neglected appeal for justice, saving him in this case even from the folly of his friends.

No doubt that many warm friends of the colored man, and even many of the colored people themselves, were sorely hurt by the failure of this measure. It is not always easy to perceive that bad methods may be just as harmful as bad purposes. But, if the measure had passed, within a year or just as soon as its working was generally understood, every colored man would have been stirred to righteous wrath by an injustice all the more galling because unintended; and it is better—a thousand-fold better—that a people should suffer injustice for ages than welcome it for an hour.

I have sought, in these remarks, not so much to define the "Negro View of the Race Question" as to show how it may be arrived at by any candid mind. I have confidence in the future, because I believe in an overruling Providence. I am not one of those optimists who believe that whatever is is right, nor one of the sort of "fools" who believe that what is cannot be made better. To do justice is the highest function of civilization; to atone for wrong, the noblest phase of Christian endeavor. When Grant lay dying on Mt. McGregor, he wrote upon the margin of one of his proofs this sentence, "No nation can do wrong without paying the penalty." If he had done nothing more, this apothegm should have made his name immortal. It is the perfect flower of the

seed planted on Olivet. God keeps account between nations and peoples as
well as between man and man. History is but a record of his judgment upon
them. The Negro is not only "here to stay," but is here to offer the American
Christian republic a chance to atone by justice in the future for the sin of the
past, and thereby escape the wrath of that God to whom a thousand years are
but a day. It is all very well to look to the future; but he who tries to separate it,
from the past is as foolish as one who seeks to run away from his own shadow.
Yesterday, Today, and Tomorrow are an eternal repetend. Today is what it is
because Yesterday was what it was, and every Tomorrow must be what all its
Yesterdays shall make it. This is God's law of human evolution; and man's will
is as powerless to change it as it is to make yesterday what it was not. Prophecy is not so much a foreknowledge of what shall be as a clearer comprehension of what *has been,* and he who would foretell the future will look forever
in the mirror which reflects the past!

I have not wished by these remarks to give offence or disturb the harmony
of this meeting; but I could not consent that he who fought with me for the
land we love should be without one to speak for him in a council where the wise
men of another race have met to consider *his* welfare, condemn *his* faults, and
determine what duty the white Christians of America owe to eight millions
of people who served faithfully for two centuries, paying in advance the tui-
tion of their children in the school of civilization. I believe that, if the trustful,
reverent spirit of that race were here present in some perfected type, looking
without malice upon the past, clearly discerning the conditions of the present,
and desiring only the common welfare in the future, it would present for your
consideration not only the complacently admonitory "platform" your committee have reported, but resolutions something like these, as expressive of the
Negro view of this most important of all the questions confronting American
civilization:

Resolved, That this Conference recognizes with solemn and profound conviction the hand of an all-wise God in that mysterious chain of circumstances
by which the African was brought to these shores, absorbed the rudiments of
civilization, was miraculously freed from bondage, learned the way of salvation, was exalted to citizenship, given equality of right, and linked irrevocably
with the destiny of the republic; that, as in all this He that seeth the end from
the beginning has baffled human wisdom, overruled human greed, and made
the wrath of man to praise him, we humbly invoke his guidance, and implore
him to show the American people what there is for them to do in the further
unfolding of his righteous purpose.

Resolved, That the American nation and the Christian world have reason to be profoundly grateful that a people numbering eight millions, but recently emerging from the shadow of a wrong the woefulness of which no human mind can measure, laying aside the instincts of the savage, have crowded to the altar and the schoolroom, asking only to be shown the way of life, and to be allowed to take a man's part in the world's great battle for human welfare. And we desire to express our profound thankfulness that he has soiled his new manhood by no vengeful acts of bloodshed or violence.

Resolved, That the unrecompensed labor of the colored race during two hundred and fifty years, the proceeds of which went to swell the aggregate of our national wealth, which cleared the lands and helped to build the churches and schools of the South, enhanced the profit of Northern industries and helped to make the American republic invincible in power and unprecedented in prosperity, constitutes the American Negro an actual and meritorious cred-itor of American civilization, whose claim can only be discharged by recogni-tion of his rights as a man, and the fullest and freest opportunity to gather for himself the fail fruits of that Christian civilization of which we boast, and which we profess to exemplify.

Resolved, That we note with grateful wonder the marvelous fact that a race only twenty-five years out of bondage, from which they came naked as the child from the mother's womb, without education, without experience, with-out accumulations, have so well used their new opportunity that already they pay one-twentieth of the taxes of the States in which they constitute a moiety of the population; that more than one-fifth of their number over the age of ten years are able to read and write, and that from six to ten % already sit be-neath their own roof-trees; that they pay a larger proportion of their incomes for charitable and religious uses than any people known to history. And, when we reflect that this has been done upon a rate of wages ranging from one-third to two-fifths of that which the Northern farm laborer receives, and has been accomplished on the lot embers of civil strife, we are constrained to ad-mit that we see in this race, new risen to the light of manhood, a people wor-thy of recognition as a constituent element of American life, and rivals and worthy competitors both in the worship of God and in the service of man.

Resolved, That, while we recognize the wisdom and justice of the Southern States in devoting an equal proportion of their school taxes to the educa-tion of colored youth, though the colored race pays so small a portion of the same, we perceive in it only another instance of that wise foresight by which the rich, and especially the landholder, of other States pays for the education of the poor and landless, in order that their children may be peaceful and self-supporting citizens rather than criminal and impoverished burdens upon society. And we feel bound to call to the attention of those of our Southern brethren who deem this burden onerous that a very large proportion of this tax is the result of a valuation created by the Negro's labor during two centuries and a half of bondage.

Resolved, That, while we heartily commend the efforts of the white people of the South for the education of the Negro, we should not forget that the white youth of the South, the American people, and the Christian world owe an immense debt to the race which, in the very hour in which it crept from the chrysalis of slavery to the new estate of citizenship, planted by their voice and votes in the fundamental law of those States the free public school system, never known there before, and then opposed by three-fourths of the white voters of those States, whose blessing and beneficence twice as many white as colored children enjoy today.

Resolved, That the nation, whose Constitution, laws, courts, and power upheld and protected the system of African slavery, became thereby responsible for the wrongs *it* inflicted, and is today a trustee *de son tort* of the educational privileges denied the slave. The duty of the nation to aid in curing illiteracy is therefore not merely an obligation of policy, but one having the highest moral sanction. Yet we are constrained to congratulate the colored people of the United States on the defeat of a measure so flagrantly unjust that it gave to the white schools of the South from two to five times as much for each white illiterate as it gave to colored schools for each colored illiterate.

I thank you for your kind attention, and beg to say that, in my opinion, nothing would so surely and swiftly tend to the peaceful solution of the Negro problem which today afflicts us as the candid and unshrinking acknowledgment of the undeniable facts stated in these resolutions; and the cheerful recognition of the first and most needed step toward the moral, social, and religious development of the Negro which the people of the United States can take is to admit that the Negro is entitled to that first, last, simplest, grandest, and richest boon which man asks in Christ's name of his fellow-man—justice.

III

HISTORY AND PUBLIC MEMORY

17

From *'Toinette: A Tale of the South* (1874)*

Tourgée's first novel, *'Toinette: A Tale of the South,* appeared under the pseudonym "Henry Churton" in 1874. Subsequently, it would be republished several
times under revised titles and, later, with a revised conclusion as *A Royal Gentleman* (1881). The story focuses on a slave girl, "'Toinette," who becomes the concu-
bine of her master and escapes to the North during the Civil War. The following
selection, however, deals with Tourgée's historical portrait of the fall of Richmond. Describing Lincoln's famous visit to the city, Tourgée depicts the scene as
a symbolic moment that encapsulated the war's larger meaning.

CHAPTER XXXIV. TYPES

It was the 4th of April, 1865—five days before the end came and the heroes
surrendered to kindred heroes at Appomattox. Richmond was the seat of empire no more. The brave men who had upheld the glory which for a time she
knew were either buried in the harsh arid, bloomless soil of wasted, desolated
Virginia, or were the disheartened victims of the unsuccessful struggle. The
truculent horde, who had thronged her streets while war promised even a du-
bious hope of plunder, had vanished.

The city, queenly in its location and advantages, had gained nothing by
Confederate rule. The metropolis of the rebellion, it reaped only a sorrowful
prominence in disaster from its fall. Want and misery, disease and crime, had
walked hand in hand with prodigality and profligacy while blood flowed for
its safety. The poor had grown more abject and dependent, the vicious more
abandoned and depraved, while the rich had reveled in fictitious wealth.

There had been a marvelous show of opulence. The ordinary means of es-
timation had almost failed. The unit of value had shrunk first to one decimal

*Excerpt from Henry Churton [Albion W. Tourgée], *'Toinette: A Tale of the South* (New York:
Fords, Howard & Hulbert, 1874).

place and then to another in quick succession. What represented value by the legal fiction was more plentiful than many of the ordinary articles of daily use. Only the gifts of God were so abundant. Luxuries of the table were sometimes worth more than money, bulk for bulk.

Want at times had pressed so close that bands of women, gaunt and hunger-pinched, defied the hand of power, bore down the guards about the public stores, broke locks and bolts, and, shouting like frenzied bacchanals, possessed themselves of food. Aye, even tore the clothing from their limbs there in the garish light of day—the chill winter day—to make extempore sacks in which to bear a portion to their children.

Around this regal city for four years had raged the combat of which it was itself the prize. More than once the camp-fires of the enemy had gleamed in the eyes of its affrighted citizens. Once it was almost begirt by their lurid glow. They were the funeral torches of the mightiest of those now dead. In their glare the soul of Jackson had departed. Then, in her suburbs, within sight of the windows of Libby even, were seen the blue-coated cavaliers making good their way along the streets of the city. A few more sabers might have conquered.

During all these months and years her artisans had toiled night and day. That grand old giant, the turbid, growling James, fitly god-sired by the testy king, had given them his aid. The furnace-fires glowed, the millwheels turned, the burrs rolled, ceaselessly, and the busy spindles whirred like points of quivering light. All was action, effort. But the war-god had swallowed up the results. Instead of growth and prosperity, decay and destruction had set their marks upon the haughty capital. To crown all came the flame. Poor Richmond! No heart exulted in thy downfall while looking on this ruin! Pity drowned all other thought!

The little great man whom accident had made the head of a mighty political movement; whose audacity was equal to the task of attempting to outrank such men as Jackson, and Lee, and a host of others, upon whose brows was written immortality—this seemingly successful pigmy had betaken himself to dishonorable flight with the gold which he had hoarded. Already was opening the fathomless chasm of impenetrable obscurity in which his innate mediocrity was finally to seek its level, along with the fit companions whom his jealous imbecility had associated in his administration. Fortune turned terribly against this miserable gamester at the eleventh hour. From others she had taken kingdoms and power, and given them instead—renown. Many whom she has shabbily treated in life she has immortalized in death. This man had been her favorite always heretofore. He had won upon the weakest hands. Merit, ability, learning, devotion, all were nothing before his barefaced luck, and ever-winning impudence. He was made the head of the Confederacy with overwhelming unanimity, though a thousand overtopped him in all the requisites of leadership. But the scales turned at length, and he fell so low that his humblest enemy could not but pity him. War and defeat brought him neither death nor glory. Ignoble in his fall as he had been unworthy in his rise, he whined and paltered, sniveled for sympathy in his woes, fed on the charity of the people he had ruined, and sank fussing and fuming into that deepest hell, a living tomb—the oblivion which engulfs a worthless life before, the mantle of charity is cast about the memory of the dead.

The slender, gray clad figure, erect and lithe, which had so long been known to dwellers in the city as "the President" was gone, and in his stead there came one of a different order. The elegant and courtly chief of the Confederacy—the lordly planter of Great Bend, the favored child, nourished and cultured by the Government he had endeavored to subvert—to the last moment retained the trappings and the pomp of power. He was an aristocrat—one of the few selected and ordained to rule—whose mission it is to govern. He boasted that he belonged to a class who were born to command, even as the slave was born to serve. He knew that a thousand must live and die as paupers, or slaves, in order that one "gentleman" might exist, yet he counted them cheap, even at that price.

For those who waged the war which his class had inaugurated—who did the fighting, while they reaped the profit and the glory, if profit or glory resulted from the struggle—the great substratum of the people, "the poor white trash"—he had the most sovereign and supreme contempt. They were the clods upon which he walked, the stones which paved his pathway to renown. They were but as the dust of the balances to such as he. Yet from this class came the Avenger.

Two days before, in the gathering Sabbath twilight gloom, the hoof strokes of the flying Aristocrat had awakened the wondering echoes of the almost deserted streets. Now, along the same roughly paved street, in the mild sunlight of the April afternoon, came the tall, angular form, and coarse, dark features of "the Great Uncouth"—that man into whose hands the destinies of millions had been committed; whom Liberty had chosen from her myriad sons and consecrated, half against his will, to the fulfillment of her noblest, holiest work—Abraham Lincoln—the "rail splitter" of the Sangamon country—the "poor white" of the Kentucky "knobs,"—walking in triumph along the way his high-bred opponent had ridden in defeat.

Unaccompanied save by the friend on whose arm he leaned, and the wondering lad who clasped his hand, along the streets of the fallen Capital, paced this strangely compounded being; the head of a conquering army, yet not of it; the ruler of a victorious people, yet desirous only that victory should be forgotten; in the proudest of earthly positions, yet clothed with humility; the chosen instrument of chastisement and vengeance, yet overflowing with mercy; the appointed victim of disappointed hatred and ambition, yet anxious only for peace and reconciliation; the representative "poor white," the embodiment of a triumphant democracy, gazing on the ruined seats of a defeated oligarchy "with malice toward none, and with charity for all." Since the Nazarene wept over Jerusalem, time has not limned on the canvas of history another scene to compare in its elements of moral grandeur, and in completeness of detail and surroundings, with Lincoln entering the Capital of the Confederacy before the glare of the contest had paled, or its thunders were hushed.

He strides absently along with a sad, pitying look upon his face—grand in its very uncouthness, scarred and furrowed by the buffetings of fortune— regarding with strange inquiry all that surrounds him. His shambling, uncertain gait is strong and rapid. The friend who walks beside him pants with the fatigue of unaccustomed exercise. The great, grim presence knows it not. The boy begs him to slacken his walk. He hears him not. He does not heed the half curious, half sullen stare of the loungers in the streets, among whom the rumor of his identity is already afloat, nor the occasional cheer of knots of freedmen who thus tender their thanks for the indefinite bliss, which they have hardly tasted—the freedom which is linked forever with the name of Lincoln. He hears and lifts his hat, absently and silently. In thought, as usual, he is questioning the future. He is asking of toppling walls, decaying houses, and neglected, half-paved streets what lesson they have to give him of the future, of this land whose destiny he would trace and shape aright.

Thought stamped upon his homely features long since the index of a mighty query, and his life has been one of ceaseless questionings. He has not delved much in books, nor worshiped science and philosophy, but of men and events he has ever sought the reason of their existence and development. His genius was not formative but extractive. From laurel and thistle he gathered alike the truth they bore, and it became at once, by instant assimilation, a part of himself. He did not meditate—continuous, consequential thought was irksome to him. He did not see events afar off; but he caught the signs of their approach, he read the storm-signals of the near future with a wonderful accuracy and ease. Man or nature never passed unchallenged before his eye.

Perhaps it was from this natural bent of his mind—perhaps it was the stupendous questions with which he had to deal, but for some reason, certain it was that after he assumed the Presidential chair, the mind of Mr. Lincoln seemed constantly groping after the Infinite, feeling after the Omnipotent. The truth that was to be wrought out by the Rebellion, the purpose which existed in the Infinite Mind and in accordance with which that mighty conflict began and proceeded, seems to have dawned upon his mind only by piecemeal. Day after day and month after month, he hesitated and shrunk from the course which the first battle of Bull Run made inevitable, as thousands of minds had clearly discovered before. Even in the fall of 1862, when he saw the path of freedom, clearly defined and opened before him, his cautious mind built up a bulwark of hypothetical threats behind which he might retire in case it should become necessary. It was not necessary. Indeed, that public feeling which he feared (was it the creature of that Omniscience which he distrusted?) very soon so blocked up his backward path that he could not but go on. As the future showed, this indecision was his greatest source of strength.

And now another and a greater question faced him. The Rebellion was virtually ended. In a few days as he believed, the Confederacy would be a thing of the past. The reconciliation of the hostile moieties of the republic was a far more difficult and delicate task than the prosecution of the war, which was to restore the ancient unity of its territory.

As he crossed on foot, that April day, over the turbid waters of the James, the river spoke to him. It was the remonstrance, sullen and angry, of unused power or unimproved opportunity which it had for two hundred years been crooning to the dwellers upon its banks. The quick-eared child of nature heard and comprehended its complaint as he leaned over the parapet and looked at the swollen torrent. Then he turned and gazed sadly at the lone island where so many thousands had died for the cause which would render his name immortal. He passed on and saw the scath and havoc of the flame. The last footprint of the departing war-fiend. His brow was troubled and dark. His deep, anxious eyes were filled with brooding care. His right shoulder drooped more than its wont, and he stooped from his grand height as if borne down by the burden which was laid upon his life. The "poor white" was walking among his kindred. The problem of his birth came before his manhood for solution.

As he strode along facing this great problem, questioning eagerly all that passed before his eyes in that hour of a nation's second birth, the sound of music was heard—the fife and drum—and a marching column passed before him, at its head the starry banner. In column by platoon, it swept along the broad and silent thoroughfare.

Blue-clad, but dusky-faced, the steel-crowned ranks pressed forward to the time of that weird melody, which burst spontaneously from patriot hearts when freemen first mustered for the struggle with slavery, and moved the people ever onward to the fulfillment of its own wild prophecy.

As they passed on in the long, swinging step, this grandly measured air inspires the uncertain groping figure, which stood upon the curbstone and gazed at them, as if he would grasp from the strange medley its true significance. The deep, yearning glance rested on those sable soldiers of liberty, as they passed, with kindly questioning. There was no love in his glance, no gratitude—scarcely respect—only grave, kindly wonder. He gazed at them as a chemist might at a new element which he had cast among the discordant contents of a bubbling crucible, uncertain of its effects—expecting little from its action—caring nothing for its fate. It was a column of Weitzel's colored troops proceeding to their quarters as the garrison of the city. Suddenly the associations of the place and time became too much for the impressionable soldiery, and from a thousand throats burst the wild anthem of liberty, and the glorious chorus,

"Our God is marching on,"

swelled from end to end of the swaying column.

Some subordinate, as he passed, recognized the potent presence on the curbstone, and brought his detachment to the "Shoulder arms," in token of respect, as they passed. Those in the rear imitated his example, and an extempore review was the result.

The "Poor-White" President did not take to ceremony and parade as kindly as the aristocrat who had fled before the power he represented. He had not been taught in childhood to receive reverence himself, but to yield it to others. The lordly wave of the hand—the courtly nod of the superior—never came naturally to the uncouth genius of the new West. Yet he felt this tribute of respect. He knew that it was to him—the man, Abraham Lincoln—and not to the ruler, that it was offered. He would return the greeting. And he did it, as he did all things else, in a way peculiar to himself—not with the touch of the visor, which the Regulations prescribe; but by taking off his hat with a grave courtesy, and standing uncovered while the soldiery passed. And as he stood there, and watched the allies whom freedom had armed in her own defense, the darkness and the boding care faded out of his eyes, and only kindly sympathy and trusting hope shone there instead. Why was it? Had he solved the problem which the future presented? Perhaps, dimly.

The companion of the President was also a man of historic name—a name linked inseparably with every great question and phase of our national progress for many a year.[1] His mind had stamped its impress upon every measure of the party of freedom, and his burning eloquence had scotched, like a tongue of flame, the infamies of slavery. No danger could daunt, no suffering subdue, this leonine child of the East. His voice might be hushed by the brutal hand of the desperado, but his eye never lost its defiance, nor did his spirit quail before the haughty, power which ruled the nation with a rod of iron. He, too, was not an originator. He did not go before and show the way to coming ages and peoples; but he had the skill of the Indian hunter for the trail, which other minds had made. He had conned the lessons of history to exhaustion. He adopted instinctively that course of thought which those furthest in advance of their fellows had indicated as the truest and best. He was not the engineer who followed the compass of thought through the dark wilderness of coming events and marked out the path of future empire, but he came in the very front of the onward march of events. His eagle eye discerned the "guides and pointers" which showed the line of right, and he made plain and broad the way in which the nation should walk. To him the slightest vestiges of truth and freedom were apparent. He traced their faintest footsteps as the ordinary mind pursues the simplest formulas of mathematics. His ruthless logic and keen analysis, united to an eloquence whose overwhelming force was like the lava-tide which bursts from fierce Vesuvius, swept away all obstacles, and showed the pathway clear and unmistakable, to the dullest mind and most unwilling feet.

His mind was not groping and tentative, like his companion's. It was not speculative, not assimilative, but demonstrative. He was a prophet who had just witnessed the fulfillment of his own predictions. Others before him, it is true, had traced the line of thought which had pointed to the end they had just witnessed. The flying enemy, the conquered capital, the vanished power, had all been foreshadowed by other minds—the pioneers, whom truth had sent into the wilderness—but he had most clearly demonstrated it; had marked it so plainly that he who runs might read. Even those who would not see it could not ever afterward hide it from their sight.

1. Though Massachusetts senator Charles Sumner did not accompany Lincoln to Richmond, this character appears to be Sumner, who by 1865 had become a close advisor and friend of the president.

It is said, that very early in the war when the great, troubled heart of the President had pondered the course he should adopt in an important crisis through all the tedious watches of a sleepless night, he came very early in the morning to this accomplished co-worker and said: "I have determined on my course. I shall do so and so. Is there any authority for it?"

And the Scholar had answered doubtfully: "I will consult the oracles and learn."

And thereupon, he read and pondered the sages of the law, and found that the collected wisdom of the ages pointed to the same conclusion to which the instinctive prescience of the Pioneer had led.

Thus the heart and conscience of the West linked hands with the knowledge and culture of the East to accomplish the great work which was set before them.

During the entire struggle this bold, positive, decided mind supplemented the hesitating, fearful, doubting one of the President, not by leading or controlling but by confirming. It is doubtful if the keen, questioning frontiersman did not generally go before the polished child of the East, but while he was running the course again and again, in doubt and uncertainty, perplexed with difficulties and variations, this other great mind of a different order came to his aid, and so confirmed his conviction and cleared his view, by citing the examples and precedents which history affords, that he could no longer hesitate.

He was the Fanatic.

Did he, too, learn in that hour of the completest triumph which is ever vouchsafed to man—the triumph of ideas to which he has devoted life and strength—as he looked upon the wreck and scath of that war by which that triumph had been wrought, did he learn that lesson of abounding charity which had wrought out its perfect work in the heart of his great chief? Did he learn that abstract right might be the sorest evil in the concrete, and that the most grievous wrong might be linked with elements of the noblest manhood and most admirable virtue? Were the seeds in that hour planted in his bosom which in the future should fructify in statesmanship inspired and impersonated with the divine message of Christianity shrined in that holiest of words, "Forgive." Perhaps, but he is of sterner stuff than the compatriot whom Providence has made his chief in position, though of less commanding intellect. He is of the fine white marble of Carrara, on which the graver must work long and patiently to trace his chosen design.

It was all there in its appropriate symbols—the grand allegory of the nation's second birth—the Poor White President—the Fanatic of the regal mind and leonine mien—the ranks of armed freedmen, and the conquered Capital devastated by fire and awaiting its further doom, half-sullenly, half-hopefully. Away to the southward the arm of the Laborer, the silent Hammerer, was pounding away at the lordly crest of the flying Cavalier. All were types, and grand ones in their way, of the Past and Future, of which that moment was the connecting and dividing Present.

18

From *The Veteran and His Pipe* (1885)*

The Veteran and His Pipe appeared originally as a weekly series in the *Chicago Daily Inter-Ocean* from April 25 to September 19, 1885, and later was published as a book of collected essays. One of Tourgée's most colorful works, these essays feature an imagined one-armed Union veteran who speaks to his smoking pipe, dubbed "Blower," about the meaning and legacies of the Civil War. The following selections are from three separate essays of the series, "A Double Anniversary," "Freedom and the Right," and "Memorial Day."

A DOUBLE ANNIVERSARY

April 14, 1861—The Surrender of Fort Sumter
April 14, 1865—The Assassination of Abraham Lincoln

It is a strangely eventful day, Blower,—the anniversary of death and life. Many, perhaps the great majority of those who think to note its recurrence count it perchance the saddest of all those landmarks by which our national growth is marked, or individual achievement commemorated. But we will celebrate it, Blower, as a feast of thanksgiving and a festival of rejoicing. Twenty-four years ago today the nation awoke to the new life of its most glorious epoch. The blow had fallen on the evening of the previous day. At midnight tolling bells began its proclamation to a wondering people. With the dawning came fuller knowledge of the thing we feared. The echoes of the guns of Moultrie were yet sounding the knell of peace over our broad land. The sunshine of the Sabbath morning looked down on strangely contrasted scenes. The South was hoarse with exultant shouting. The emblems of rejoicing floated there from every hilltop. The cannon's sulphurous breath and the bonfire's smoldering embers told of the night's wild jubilee of exultation. The church bells pealed

---

*Excerpted from Albion W. Tourgée, *The Veteran and His Pipe* (Chicago: Belford, Clark & Co., 1886).

out joyfully. The matin hymns were songs of victory. Miriam's exultant chant echoed from thousands of lips that smiled with the joy of accomplished success and anticipated triumph. Thanksgiving was the theme of every pulpit. The light of conquest was in every eye, the joy of victory in every heart.

Where the nation's power was still supreme, and her glory esteemed above section and self, the scene was widely different. How well we remember it today, Blower. The chill, gray sunshine looked on clouded brows! Eyes were dull with weeping, or red with sullen rage! Men wore grave faces and were strangely silent! Women's cheeks were pallid, and they wept stealthily! The sabbath bells sounded full of solemn foreboding as they called a stricken people to the house of prayer. The sanctuaries overflowed with worshipers! The nation bowed before its God, and prayed that the blood-red cup might pass its lips, or grace be given to bear its woe! The Merciful heard and answered! The nation drank of the red wine of slaughter; but a richer, stronger life than she had ever known before swept through her veins!

Twenty years ago today another scene in the great tragedy of our national life was enacted. On that day the stroke was given which transformed an exultant nation into a weeping, grief-stricken people. The grandest life which has yet sprung from the loins of the Western world in the very hour of triumph entered, through the gate of treacherous violence, into the haven of immortality. The banners of victory flaunted gaily over thousands of happy homes when the sun went down. Smiling lips told joyful tidings by the firelit hearth. Fair cheeks flushed red with welcoming roses for the home-coming brave. Even they that mourned the dead forgot their sorrow in the universal joy. The morrow's noon saw the flaunting banners bound and draped, the fair cheeks paler than the snow, and the mourners' woe enhanced a thousandfold.

Ah! Well do I remember, Blower, how I pressed the empty sleeve against the aching heart, while your polished amber tip slid from my quivering lips, as I bowed my head upon the rough pine desk to which a veteran's duty bound me still, and wept when the morning brought us knowledge of the night's bereavement. I remember thrusting your gleaming bowl within its silken case and pushing it aside regardless of its soothing fragrance. I remember still the trace of tear-drops on the azure cuff which marked the humble service I was permitted to discharge. How often had I looked with pride on that gold-bordered bit of velvet which told of danger manfully incurred, and duty faithfully performed. Until that hour the veteran's pride had swallowed up all other thought. Our country's glory had blinded me to all weaker sentiments. The roar of battle had seemed to me the Nation's regal challenge to a wondering world and waiting future, published by the cannon's brazen lips. Laden as it might be with terror, it always brought a thrill of rapture to my heart, because I heard in its echoes the angry defiance of a free people to oppression, or the triumph of conscience over wrong.

Even the poor brave comrades who had shared peril and privation with us, whose bones lay bleaching on so many battle-scarred hillsides, had hardly been mourned. To have died for such a cause seemed more of a privilege than a hardship. They were rather to be envied than deplored, because of the beneficent glory that enshrined their memories. It seemed but natural for a soldier to die, and an infinite honor to die for a cause so holy. They had not fought for themselves, their own exaltation, nor even for their own homes or fire-sides. Their devotion was not tainted by the flavor of self. They died for the rights of man, for the perpetuity of a government founded on liberty, in deadly conflict with a republic based on the principle of slavery. These were foolish notions, as we now can well perceive, but in those days I never doubted the Moslemic dogma that "the gates of heaven swing easily before brave souls coming up from the battlefield." So the thought of conflict brought only a stern, strange joy. When we heard that thousands fell, we only thought how each death magnified our victory or added strength to our determination to avenge defeat. Strange as it may seem, I had hardly mourned the missing limb, which molders back to dust beneath the shadow of the springing pines. We were young then, Blower, and life was sweet as vernal sunshine to the springing early buds. The thought of death was all the more irksome because of life's delightsomeness. To be maimed, I knew was to be branded through the years that were to come as one in power less than his fellows—bearing in life the visible signmanual of death. Today I almost blush to own that I was then proud of the folded sleeve, because I had given the limb that filled it for the cause of human freedom. I did not once think of fame, nor of comparing myself with my fellows, whether the same had proved themselves meritorious or undeserving. I only thought that I had given up my blood to swell the rich tide that had been poured out to quicken the tree of liberty's second growth. Even the promotion that followed hard upon my hurt and bore date upon the day it happened, seemed a trivial thing compared with the high privilege I had enjoyed.

In that day, when clods were lifted to the plane of heroes, and knightly souls were fired to marvelous achievement—in all those years of conflict— there had been one, whose devotion every true heart felt had far eclipsed all others, whose tender, serious, self-forgetful spirit brooded regretfully, yet encouragingly, over every battlefield. Our "Father Abraham" had become to

every heart a presence real and benign, which represented all that was noblest
and most glorious in the struggle in which we were engaged. Strange as it
may seem to the hard, material present, the sad, plain features of the Liberator were glorified to our eyes, so that we only saw benignity, devotion and a
wisdom passing that of earth, in their calm austerity. He was to us the very
impersonation of the spirit in which we fought, "Malice toward none and
charity for all." Under its inspiration we bore "the banner of the free" from
victory to victory, counting no hardships too great, and no perils too woeful,
while we followed where it led. To us the homely features represented a new
era, which we fondly hoped would dawn when all the evils of the past had
been swept away, and peace should bring her shining harvest of prosperity. To
us he was the forerunner of an era of unmatched blissfulness—a millennium
which should cover the continent and send the reflection of its glory across
the seas. We did not fight to triumph or to slay. The tender heart that led us
on would have grieved, we fondly thought, had any impulse so low and base
nerved our arms and steeled our hearts for conflict. He was the glorified in-
carnation of a beatific future. We knew he had forgotten himself in his devotion to a principle, of which the day in which he lived was but the seed time of
the harvest which some distant morrow was to bring. His life had become so
intermingled with the nation's future, in our thought, that we hardly counted
him as mortal. We longed to see the load of care uplifted from his brow, and
note the glint of jocund sunshine in his eye once more. He was our "Old Abe,"
calm and true and faithful. The touch of earthiness was never in the picture
which our loving fancy drew of him. We never once thought of him as having any personal interest in the events that were happening beneath his ken.
It was only as the guardian angel of his country's honor and the future's hope
that he overlooked the vast arena and smiled sadly but hopefully when blood
sank into the thirsty sand.

No vulgar sentiment debased him in our fancy. If we laughed at scurri-
lous jests, which made the tour of the camps under his name, it was with no
thought that the ascription of paternity was true, but with a real gladness in the
thought that the overburdened heart did sometimes find even a momentary
relief from care in mirthful fancies. He was to us a tender leader who, while
he bore his own great burden uncomplainingly, found time to lighten ours, by
pointing us to the future, ever bright to his eyes with the fruition of a divine
hope. He was *our* Lincoln—the fruit of a marvelous past, and the precursor of
a future to be shaped and moulded by his aspirations—greater than the greatest, humbler than the lowliest!

So when death came to him in the hour of final triumph, it seemed that all other deaths had been in vain. The little we had done was naught. The heroism of our fallen comrades was but wasted manhood. With his last breath it seemed that the future's hope had departed. The free, proud, happy land which we had pictured resting peacefully beneath his placid smile, while the loitering years went by and death unwilling brought at length the crown of immortality—this dream, which had filled so many millions of strong hearts, was blotted out forever. In his grave it seemed were buried all the brightness of the future. Those who were left, however good and great they might be, seemed but base and mean in comparison with him—our immortal martyr. The sunshine was blotted out of the triumph lighted sky, and the horizon was again overcast. The shadow of the present veiled the future to our eyes.

We know now, Blower, that this was but a foolish notion—a silly sentiment. The man whose death blotted out the sunlight of that mid-April day was not exceptionally great, if indeed he was great at all, judging by our later and of course, better standards. Plain almost to uncouthness, he brought despair to the tailor's heart. Unversed in the wisdom of the schools, the highest culture yet esteems him but an uncut diamond—a possible brilliant. Counting the Nation worthy to be saved only as it represented the idea of human liberty and equal right, he is regarded by the completer manhood of today as a man of one idea whom the fever of the times cast into accidental prominence. Simple as a child, he is, of course, not to be ranked among statesmen. Little given to denunciation and a stranger to self-glorification, he is naturally little esteemed by an age which accounts fault-finding the test of wisdom. Deeming the safety of the Nation a matter above all price, he is held in little esteem by a generation of publicists to whom an economic theory outweighs in sacredness the rights of man. Even they who have written of him—saving only one or two—seem to have accounted him great only in kindness, coarse wit, and a sort of instinctive cunning in the measurement of men and the forecasting of events. They depict him as fortunate, above all other men, in favoring accidents.

Some have sought to popularize the story of his life by magnifying the superficial coarseness of his nature. Some who observed him closely saw nothing in his character, but a strange compound of the trickster and the clown. To them his greatness was but accidental and his marvelous career neither a legitimate result of previous training, nor a beneficent miracle especially ordained for the accomplishment of marvelous ends. He was simply a lucky accident of an anomalous age. There can be no doubt that these men thought they knew him thoroughly. They came very near him; knew his thought;

laughed at his jests; wondered at his success and still marvel at his fame. So far as they were capable of doing, they understood his nature, and no doubt have portrayed it truly. We cannot question the tree-toad's knowledge of the oak on which he dwells.

The new life which has grown up in the land has very generally accepted their view. The thought, which was the inspiration of yesterday is looked upon with kindly toleration today. We are told that the day of sentiment has passed, and the era of practicality begun. Gold is the criterion of value and aggregate wealth the real test of statesmanship. Patriotism is well enough as a reminiscence, but parsimony is the key-note of prosperity. Devotion to the rights of man is an innocent weakness, gain the one thing needful. The capitalist's margins are more important to the Nation than justice to the oppressed. This is the wisdom of today, Blower. It seems harsh and cold, base and degrading even, to us. But we must remember that we are of yesterday—of that recent past, which is always wrong in its strictures of the present. Today is always an iconoclast that tramples ruthlessly beneath his heel the idols before which yesterday bowed in adoration. We must be patient, Blower, and learn to see our gods debased without resentment, if not without sorrow.

Little by little we are being taught the lesson of renunciation. This very year there was found in the legislature of the state which holds his ashes as a sacred trust, *one*—thank God there is yet *but* one—who could oppose, in the name and by the authority of her people, an appropriation amounting to *less than one-hundredth part of a cent per capita—one-thousandth of a cent on every million dollars of her wealth—to provide for the adornment of the tomb of Abraham Lincoln on this anniversary of his assassination!*

It seems to us incredible. But next year there will perchance be many more like-minded with him. We may even see the day when the sentiment uttered in the legislature of a neighboring state, a few days since, shall become all but universal, and the champion and apologist, if not the leader, of the "Copperheads" of Indiana be generally looked upon as a nobler patriot, a more sagacious statesman, and a worthier citizen of the Republic than he who led her armies to victory. It is time, Blower, that we prepared ourselves to see the verdict of yesterday overthrown. What we then deemed right may yet be accounted the most grievous wrong; what we foolishly thought to be patriotism may yet be considered oppression, and what we believe the nation's highest glory may yet be held a folly bordering upon crime and hardly susceptible of excuse.

Nevertheless, Blower, we will celebrate the double anniversary once more —the birth-hour of an epoch and the apotheosis of a hero-martyr. The flag shall float a peak upon the staff above our window, shedding blessings from its beauteous folds upon the rushing, heedless passers-by. Your polished bowl shall be heaped with golden granules; and as the smoke wreaths rise above its rim, we will think upon old times, revive almost-forgotten memories, and feel again the thrill of perished aspirations. We will still believe that self-forgetfulness is nobler than greed; that patriotism is not to be measured by a gold standard; that righteousness exalteth a nation; that justice to the lowly of earth is honor to the Highest in Heaven. When the children come—the bright-eyed heralds of tomorrow—we will tell them the story of this day when the land awoke to a new life and the noblest of earth passed over to his reward. Perchance in their lives the seed sown in blood and watered with tears may spring into a fruitage all the richer for the winter of its waiting. Let us not murmur, Blower, but steadfastly believe that "the future, God's fallow, though barren it seem," shall yet out vie the past in the ripe fruits of patriotic devotion.

For many a year we used to drape the flag upon this anniversary. It was a foolish thing to do. We mourned when we ought to have exulted. We bewailed the woes of war when we ought to have magnified its blessings, and rejoiced in the glory it shed upon the land. What were the dead it left us in comparison with the fresher, nobler life it brought? Honor and glory can not be measured even by blood and pain. So, too, with him who went out from us in the hour of victory. Why did we ever weep for him? He passed away when his work was done, leaving a memory unsmirched with evil, a fame unsullied with a thought of self. The purity of his life, the unselfishness of his demotion, and the grandeur of his character are the priceless heritage of the ages. Suffering had not weakened his frame; failure had not cast its blight upon his fame; malice had no opportunity to assail. In the vigor of his strength, at the zenith of his glory, in the very hour of victory, the booming cannon told at once his death and immortality! Happy beyond compare was he in the hour and manner of his death. He did not live to see the breath of detraction wither his laurels, nor feel that the thought which inspired his life had lost all significance to the wisest and best of his countrymen. We mourn, Blower, for his great lieutenant who, languishing, still lives;[1] but for him who died in the moment when war and peace met together to exalt his fame, let us don the garments of rejoicing and chant the songs of victory.

April 14, 1885

1. Ulysses S. Grant died of throat cancer on July 23, 1885, three months following the appearance of this piece.

"FREEDOM AND THE RIGHT"

We are growing old, Blower, you and I. Yet the years that we have seen are not so many. Hardly more than two score winters have passed over the Veteran's head. Save the empty sleeve, he shows little of the scath of life. His eye is as bright, his step as elastic, and his heart as young—almost as young, it seems—as when poor Joe pressed into his hand thy polished bowl, and whispered in his ear a dying comrade's farewell message to his absent loved ones. His words as they come back to memory now seem strangely overwrought. No doubt today would deem them sadly out of place upon a soldier's stiffening lips.

"Tell them," he said, "I—died—for freedom—and,—and"—oh precious last word, let it not, be lost! How the feeble clay struggles with the dying thought! At length it comes, so faintly that the bowed ear hardly distinguishes between the whispered word, and the night wind's murmur—"and the—right!"

No syllable of sorrow! No thought of self! No murmur of disappointment! No word of consolation for the father whose hope was blighted, for the mother whose heart yet waits expectant for his coming—fondly self-deceived by every manly footstep. Nay, not even a tender message for that unwedded widow whose heart was that day sealed forever against the thought of earthly love.

There was no sorrow in his eyes. The whispered words had no touch of sadness. The stillness that follows in the wake of battle hung above the bloody field. The bright southern moon looked calmly down through the soft filmy foliage of the early spring-time. It lighted up the velvety half-grown leaves upon the giant oaks that crowned the crest on which the struggle had begun, until they seemed like silver clouds touched with the tender green of summer seas. It was here that the first few scattering shots were fired. The skirmishers had swarmed out of the wood beyond, crossed the narrow valley, and crept up the hillside toward the summit where his little force awaited them. It was only an outpost of the great army which lay behind. He was not charged with any momentous duty. The strap upon his shoulder marked only a subaltern's grade. He was only expected to give the alarm, and perhaps to check the enemy's advance an instant, while the waiting lines prepared themselves to meet the onset.

The attack was not unexpected, and though the skirmishers wavered for a moment when they met his fire, the lines which followed hard upon their footsteps swept up the slope, scarring the great trunks with wasted volleys and tainting the balmy air of spring with sulphurous fumes, which overpowered the fragrance of the jasmine, while the little force which held the summit fled, leaving their brave young commander bleeding at the foot of one of the great oaks which crowned the summit. Then the tide of battle ebbed and flowed back and forth on the broad plateau beyond. After a fierce conflict we forced them back over the ridge into the wood from whence they had come. As the sun went down the last hot line of fire flashed out upon the fleeing enemy a half mile to the southward of their morning camp.

As the night fell upon us, I traced backward the battle's bloody track in search of my friend. It is not any easy thing to do by daylight. The glare of conflict, while it photographs surrounding objects ineradicably upon the soldier's mind, so distorts distances and relations that one is always surprised when he tries to retrace the steps he has taken under fire. It needs not the flight of seasons to disguise the battle field. Even when first "Ardennes waves above them her green leaves," it is almost impossible for the soldier to designate the spot where his comrade fell. The night made my task all the harder.

The moon which hung a great red ball on the edge of the horizon when I began my search, shifted the shadows and gave to a score of other rounded hills the outline of the little "knob" on which my friend had been posted. Stark faces shone cold and white in the shadows of the half-leaved trees, and stiffened limbs made grotesque figures in the moonlight. I stopped more than once to comfort some wounded sufferer. A thin, white mist hung over the valley where the conflict had been fiercest. Voices came out of it at intervals. The low, indescribable moan that comes, from the lips of many wounded men, rising and falling in alternate wailing cadences, rose out of the silvery veil. The rumble of wheels away to the right told of trains that were struggling to the front. A lantern shining dimly in the hazy depth, showed others on a like quest with myself. The sound of a spade grating on, the stones bespoke the woefulness of a hasty burial on the battlefield. We knew the pursuit would begin at dawn, and that the offices of friendship must be speedily performed. As I passed along an unrecognized crest a groan came out of the shadow of a great yellow-leaved Spanish oak that stood in my path. I do not know why I stopped so suddenly, while my heart stood still with fear. Groans had not been rare along my way. Every soldier knows how often solitary dead are found upon the verge of the field of battle. You and I remember, Blower, finding on the very outer edge of a battle maelstrom, years after peace had drowned the din of arms, a whitened skeleton—a picket killed at his post, crouching behind a little natural mound, beneath a spreading cedar whose drooping boughs had hidden him from searching eyes. His rifle, rusty and black, lay beneath him, the hammer drawn back, the skeleton finger yet pressed upon the trigger.

I paused and listened—another groan. It is strange, Blower, but even in that muffled moan I recognized my friend. Poor Joe! He might have lived I think had help been at hand when he fell. But the hours which had intervened had drained his life. He had but few more moments and strength for few more words. He had expected me. It was a contract of long standing that after every battle we might share together, as soon as duty would permit, each should seek out the other. So he knew that I would come. Before the light had faded the sky he had traced upon a bit of paper, with a twig dipped in his own blood, a few last wishes. With the same rude stylus he had written my name in bloody characters upon the buckskin cover that encased your bowl. Poor, brave old Joe! He clasped my hand weakly; said he knew I would come; told me there was no hope, and whispering the message, "Tell them that I died for freedom and the right," fell asleep. The moon had found an opening through the leaves and looked calmly down upon his face as he breathed his last. Poor Joe! You were his dying gift, Blower. In all the years that have elapsed since then, I have never looked upon your bowl without thoughts of him. The buckskin case has long since worn away, but the red-straggling letters, "J-a-c-k," are still clear to my eyes. The touch of the worn amber mouthpiece, which his lips have pressed so often, ever brings old memories back.

He died for the right, Blower—"freedom and the right!" So he said, so he thought, brave, self-forgetful knight, who sought not adventure nor the fame of valorous achievements, but the establishment of truth! Yet, brave and chivalrous as he was, this true Sir Galahad was but a type of his time—that time to which we were proud to belong and which we still half wonderingly regret. A thousand men lay stark and cold upon that field who had rendered up their lives with gladness for the same idea—"freedom and the right"—the right of every man to equal power and privilege with other men! Say what we may, Blower, this was at the bottom of it all! One side represented the rights of man, the other the rights of the master. The one meant equal rights for all; the other special privileges for a class. It was only one phase of the mighty conflict which is as old as man—the rights of the many against the encroachments of the few.

There are some who teach today, and many who believe, that the cause for which so many died was of a narrower scope, and its upholders animated by meaner motives. We better know the story of that day, Blower; but we are getting old, and our ideas are growing sadly old-fashioned, too. To smoke a pipe and believe in human right as a practical, tangible thing—a sentiment that ought to outrank and overpower all other political ideas—are in the highest degree absurd to one who sucks rice-paper cigarettes, glorifies the Anglican ideal, and studies poetical philosophy in the sweet seclusion of his club. It is

often asserted nowadays as an undeniable truth that the sole object of the
National arms was to restore the National power, forgetful that this power
was made worthy of preservation only by the simple fact that it was the sole
representative of the idea of individual rights and equality based upon the fact
of humanity—poor Joe's "freedom and the right." Two great ideas faced each
other in the struggle—the right of man to self-direction, and the right of one
man to control and modify another's acts without his consent and against his
will. Whether it be termed "Rebellion" "War between the States" or "War for
separation," that is all there is of it.

"Freedom and the right!" The night was dim about us, under the great
oaks, when he whispered these words, but Joe's eyes already beheld the light
of an eternal day. He made no mistake in his last earthly message. If we fought
merely to preserve our national domain from dismemberment, who shall say
that we were right and they who stood over against us wrong? Who gave to
us the right "to have and hold," to compel twelve millions of people to accept,
continue and maintain one form of government rather than another—to remain a part of one nation instead of establishing a separate government? We
may claim that such right arises from the Federal compact with their sires,
but had our fathers power to bind and loose forever? Were they infallible or
their acts irrevocable? Is the right to hold territory once assimilated, always
a sacred one? Is the subjugation of a people desiring self-government essentially a holy cause?

We did not fight for "our altars and our fires." No peril threatened our
homes. It is said we fought to prevent secession. What gave us the right, the
moral right I mean, to resist with force of arms such a movement? Joe's farewell message tells it all—"freedom and the right." Because man, had a right
to liberty and life, to free access to that golden gate of opportunity—"the pursuit of happiness"—and because our nation represented this idea, it was that
we fought for "freedom and the right"—the freedom of some millions who
had been in bondage, and the rights of other millions which had been held
in abeyance by unrighteous debasement of the freeman's privilege. We fought
too, or thought we fought, for the freedom and the rights of the unnumbered
millions who should stand between our day of conflict and the hither shore
of eternity. We fought to secure infinite blessing to them and to avert infinite
woe. We counted our cause supremely holy because success could add little to
our own honor, prosperity, or ease, but offered all its rich harvest of blessing
to other ages and an alien and oppressed people. Even their freedom was not
all for which we fought, Blower. Poor Joe phrased it rightly under the gray-

green boughs of early spring, while the whippoorwill sent up his monotonous chant from the hill beyond, and the evening breeze brought the odor of the jasmine from the valley yet hidden by the powder smoke. "Freedom and the right," he said—their freedom and their rights whose liberty had been denied, and whose rights had been curtailed in the past—the freedom and the rights of man in all the future!

We thought we were right, Blower; Joe thought so. Those who died and those who lived in that strange yesterday counted the conflict righteous in its purpose, infinite in its consequences, and inexorable in its behests. Were we right? Was Joe right, Blower? Were the dead whose sweet blood nourishes oak and pine today—were they right or wrong? The question seems sacrilegious. I fancy that the fire within your bowl grows redder and hotter as my lips frame the inquiry. Yet it is a question which must be asked and answered; not by us, but by the American people; not by today only, but by many unrisen tomorrows.

If we were right, then someone must have been wrong. If "the blue" stood for righteousness, then assuredly "the gray" meant oppression. Light and darkness cannot exist. Yet it will not do today to intimate that those who stood over against us then were wrong. To impute error to them, even be it never so lightly done, accounted not only an act of folly, but a grievous wrong.

> I will not do them wrong; I rather choose
> To wrong the dead.

Why are opposites irreconcilable, or antipodes incapable of conjunction? Why should right be right, or wrong be wrong? If only we might say, "There is no right," we might escape the odious inference of another's wrong. Or if both might be in the right, there could be no ground for blame. Perhaps this may be true. Freedom may not have been exactly right, nor slavery entirely wrong. Perchance the Nation did not stand for freedom after all, nor the Confederacy mean injustice to the weak and oppression by the strong. Joe may have been wrong even at the last. Unfortunately sincerity is no reliable test of truth. Something more than honesty of purpose is needed to constitute right conduct. Honesty is always the chief ally of fanaticism, and Joe may have been a fanatic.

It is said that the voice of the people is the voice of God, but that it must be "the still, small voice," the outcome of the sober second thought which speaks the will of the Eternal—not the voice of passion nor the roar of the excited populace. Amid the tumult of arms we are told that not only the laws are silent, but the voice of reason also. It is only after the frenzy of conflict has passed away that we must look for that calm judgment of the event which shall bear the test of time and truly deserve to represent the findings of the infinite mind upon the facts of yesterday. The time would seem at length to have come. It is twenty years since the last battle-shock sent its rapturous thrill through the hearts of war-worn veterans. During that time one-half of those who then lived and wrought have gone to their eternal rest. Today sits in calm and unbiased judgment upon yesterday. A new life makes up the verdict. Was Joe right according to, this judgment?

Alas, Blower, there is every reason to believe that the Nation of today is ready to ignore the spirit and the works of yesterday. Of those who fought against us hardly one in ten thousand has admitted that they were in the wrong, or that we were in the right. The slave's freedom, as a formally accomplished fact, a state established by legal enactment, they admit. That the right to free the slave and enfranchise the freedman, inhered in the nation, or that the "freedom and the right" for which Joe fought, or any privileges based thereon, are founded in natural justice, they stubbornly and almost universally deny. They admit the failure of their hope of separate dominion, and declare their willingness to abide by the arbitrament of the sword; but twenty years have not sufficed to convince them of its righteousness, or lead them to admit that a warfare, waged in support of slavery, contained any element of wrong. On the contrary, they vaunt their submission as a meritorious thing; and boast of their forbearance in recognizing and tolerating a government reestablished, as they claim, by injustice and oppression.

One who has just been chosen to represent the power and dignity of this government at a foreign court, at a public dinner of congratulation given him by admiring friends in the late capital of the Confederacy, recently declared in a tone of proud condescension, that those who fought for secession were now loyal to the National Government, though its authority was "founded on a gross and bloody violation of public rights."

The Confederate hosts in battle array, contended that the "freedom and right" for which Joe thought he died, were in fact wrongs to which they would never submit. Today they aver that they have submitted thus far to such wrong—a wrong "founded on a perversion of public right," remember, Blower—and claim by such formal submission, to have acquired the right to practically annul the privileges conferred upon an oppressed people by the conquerors of their oppressors. Only yesterday an arrogant mouthpiece of the sentiment of the South, speaking through the pages of a great magazine— one who not content with his simple signature, adds thereto in "small caps" what no other writer deems necessary, the place of his residence—this representative thinker of the lately rebellious states declares that the "victorious armies of the North could not have enforced and maintained 'at the South' the policy of the civil rights bill"—a "bill" which today is the law of the land, and most unquestionably a part of "the right" for which poor Joe thought he was rendering up his life.

But this is not all. One can hardly blame a proud people for refusing to admit themselves to have been in the wrong. It is their right to do so, and I am not sure we do not all like them the better for it, even you and I Blower, but they have no right to expect or demand that we who fought with Joe, or the nation whose honor we maintained, shall admit their claim or recognize in them a fitness to bear rule or represent authority because of it. Yet this very thing is what we have done. The public sentiment even of the North declares against the thought of yesterday. With clamorous shamefacedness we cry out for forgetfulness and implore the shield of oblivion for our acts and motives. We insist on leaving a dead past to bury its dead. The present chooses among the men of yesterday with exceeding care, one who never yet has uttered a single word of commendation of that "freedom and the right" for which Joe died, as the Nation's executive head. Two of the great departments of government are placed under the control of men who yet stoutly maintain the moral turpitude of the National cause. Men are selected to represent the country abroad who have defiantly refused to recognize the righteousness of the results of the conflict, and thereby have even cast a doubt on their own citizenship. And worst of all, saddest of all, old friend, those of our Northern kith and kin who rejoiced when our arms suffered reverse, and mourned when victory sat upon our banners—those who mocked at Lincoln in his agony and denounced Grant in the hour of triumph—these men are singled out through all the land to typify the thought of today and represent the power and authority of the government saved from destruction by the valor and self-sacrifice such as he whose heroism we recall on this anniversary. It is hard enough to see the flag placed at half-mast in honor of one whose chosen relation to our government was that of a traitor and an enemy, who inspired from the secure shelter of a neutral territory the incendiary's torch and the murderer's dagger; but it is thousand times harder to see those who exulted in Joe's death vaunting themselves today upon the overthrow of the principles for which he fought.

Yet we will not be disconsolate, old friend. If yesterday was but half right, it will stand forever famous in history for what it believed and what it did. Joe may not have died for "freedom and the right"; nay, he may have given his life for folly and the wrong, but he did it freely and gladly; and we will ever think of his dying face glorified by the moonlight shining through the rift in the soft spring foliage as that of one wearing the halo of self-sacrifice, which alone entitles mortals to claim immortality.

April 21, 1885

......

"MEMORIAL DAY"

This is the new name, Blower, for the "festival of flowers" we have been wont to celebrate upon this 30th of May. At first we called it "Decoration Day." By that name it is designated in the statutes of those states which have made it a legal holiday, or otherwise given its observance legal recognition. For a decade and a half the heart of the nation, still warm with that patriotic ardor which inspired the soldiers of the Republic, paid homage to their valor and celebrated the triumph of the cause for which they fought, by this annual festival of flowers, and because of its triumphant and exultant character dominated it Decoration Day. The graves of departed veterans were heaped with the garlands of victory, symbolical both of grateful remembrance and patriotic rejoicing. It was a day of jubilee, on which the hero-dead were remembered with tenderness and their achievements with exultation. Such it is still for us, Blower, and forever shall be. We loved our comrades. We can never forget their virtues, and would not deserve to be remembered in our extremist hour if we should ever cease to honor their devotion.

But we can not wear the garb of woe, nor march behind a draped and trailing banner on this day. The comrades whom we loved may not be honored in sack-cloth. The shrieking pipes that wail the dead do not fitly express a ransomed nation's loving remembrance of their deeds. The soldier is most honored by the story of his exploits, and the patriot best remembered by emulation of his self-sacrifice. To dwell upon the hero's sufferings and ignore the motive which inspired his acts is to degrade him to the level of the mercenary. Fame dwells in purpose as well as in achievement. Fortitude is sanctified only by its aim. Privation is merely pitiful, unless endured for a noble end. Mourning ill-befits the memory of one who suffered bravely in a noble cause, which through his fortitude and valor has been crowned with victory. Poor Joe would count his love but ill-requited, Blower, should we go and mourn above his grave for the life cut off in the promise of its springtide strength and beauty. His grieved spirit would overwhelm us with keen reproaches, should he behold us sorrowing still for the life he gladly offered up for "freedom and the right." Ah, Blower, we know what he would say:

"Has the cause for which I died become so despicable," he would be sure to ask, "that my country recalls its triumph with sadness, and remembers the devotion of her sons with sorrow? Am I accounted so unfortunate in having died for liberty that the banner of the free is draped, and the drums exultant throbbing muffled on the one day when the nation calls my sacrifice to mind? Then, indeed, was my devotion folly and my suffering vain!"

For such comrades, Blower, I dare not weep. Tears may well fall upon the patriot's bier, but he who mourns above his verdant grave when the cause for which he fell has proved triumphant, offers insult to his memory. Yet our comrades of the ever-lessening Grand Army of survivors of that great struggle, in General Encampment assembled, have decided that the instinct of patriotism which by common consent hallowed that day when we first laid the wreaths of victory on the graves of our patriot dead, as "Decoration Day," and provided for its future observance as a day of jubilant remembrance of victory and deliverance, was for once at fault. So they have solemnly decreed that henceforth it shall not be called "Decoration Day" nor kept as a festival of rejoicing, but shall be denominated "Memorial Day," and be observed as a day of mourning for our patriot dead.

Oh! Shameful mockery of a noble impulse! As well celebrate the Savior's birth in sackcloth; pipe a funeral march before a marriage train; or require surviving veterans to wear convict stripes and march in lockstep, as to prescribe mourning emblems for this day. What have we to do with sorrow? Victors exult! They who celebrate deliverance from evil rejoice! Do we mourn our hero-dead? Then indeed are we unworthy of the devotion they displayed.

Two days in all the busy year our nation claims to celebrate in commemoration of the most notable events in its history. One also it has consecrated to the memory of its first great patriot—not choosing to mourn forever for his death—"seeking his noble father in the dust"—but electing rather to exult in the good fortune that gave to us the name of Washington as an eternal heritage of fame. The first of these American holidays marks the anniversary of our first assertion of national autonomy, made famous and immortal by the formulation of individual right on which it was predicated. The valor of our fathers made good the boastful declaration. We celebrate the fact with gay music, flaunting banners, and universal acclaim. We recount their heroism, not with tears, but with rejoicing. We do not mourn for those who fell, but exult in the sacrifice that purchased victory. To have perished in that struggle is the proudest inheritance a man of that day could leave to his children. How well we remember the story, Blower, which has come down from sire to son, of one who, ordered to "limber away," refused to leave the rocky path by which his guns were posted while he could hold the enemy in check. The commander-in-chief wrote himself to the young wife, whose tears fell upon the face of her first-born as she read his words: "Your husband's valor saved the army from destruction." Save this memory the young artilleryman left nothing for his child beyond a nation's flattering promises, which were forgotten in the very hour of utterance. But that faded scrap of paper is a precious legacy to hundreds who bear his name, and exult in the priceless boon of heroic blood. The story of toil and suffering is but the dark background against which valor and victory shine out the brighter.

Our other national feast was designed to celebrate the preservation of the nationality our fathers established, and the extension and universal application of that principle for which they gladly staked "life, fortune, and their sacred honor." As an event of history, it as far outshines the other as the nation of today excels the meager colonies of a hundred years ago in grandeur and prosperity. Our fathers formulated a new theory of government, of which they themselves took advantage, and to which they appealed in justification of the act of rebellion. Our comrades, accepting this doctrine and inspired by its spirit, overthrew armed revolt against it, gave liberty and equality of right to millions of a race our fathers had despised too heartily to heed their prayer—did what they had left undone, and transformed their boastful declaration into accomplished fact. Shall we mourn for these men, who were our comrades, while we exult in the devotion of our fathers' fathers?

No, Blower; never shall it be said that we wore the garb of mourning on that day when the achievements of our comrades are commemorated; the moments dedicated to their memory shall be full of gladness. When we wore the blue in the day of battle, we obeyed orders as a good soldier. In the Grand Army which still survives we are glad always to obey any reasonable requirement, and manifest due subordination to constituted authority. But there is a "higher law" than the edict of a General Encampment, a more potent authority than a Grand Commander's order. The dead whom we profess to honor have authority above all who live, to forbid dishonor to their memory. Our anniversary, Blower, shall be one of gladness and exultation. We will remember the old days; sing the old songs; fly our battled-scarred banner from the peak, and strew the flowers that speak of victory and rejoicing on the graves of those whose memory we revere. It shall still be "Decoration Day" in our hearts; and gratitude for a nation preserved and dedicated anew to "Freedom and the Right" shall be the theme of our exultant meditations.

Why was our glorious anniversary abolished? Why were the waving flags bound with dolorous drapery, and the veterans on this one day of their public appearance greeted with wailing dirges and escorted with funereal ceremonies to their comrades' verdant graves? Has the Nation ceased to rejoice in its deliverance? Has the birthright of liberty become a thing of shame? Do we mourn because our fathers' boastful declaration has been made a fact and wrought into the warp of our national life?

Ah, Blower it is a curious tale. They who meet on the anniversary of "Stonewall" Jackson's death, to do honor to the dead heroes of a "lost cause," most appropriately christened that sorrowful occasion "Memorial Day." The sentiment of joy could constitute no element of *its* observance. *Their* dead had died in vain. The cause for which *they* fought was lost, and the banner which had floated above their ranks was swept into oblivion. *Their* hope was inurned with their heroes. The nationality *they* had sought to establish had vanished like a dream. The luster of *their* heroes's fame must be dimmed forever by the memory of hopeless disaster and incurable wrong.

It was not Lee alone who surrendered at Appomattox. When the Confederacy yielded up its life, they who had upborne its banner in those terrible years, were compelled also formally to renounce the principle on which it was based. What its eloquent Vice-President had denominated "the great truth" on which it rested "as a corner-stone, the subordination of the black race to the white"—the right to enslave, for which so many had loyally and bravely died—those who remained were compelled by overmastering odds to yield. They who fought for the freedom of all and equality of rights for all, were victorious; while they who had made appeal to God by the device upon their battle flag to maintain and defend the sanctity and justness of slavery, suffered defeat. Through all the years that are to come these men must bear the stigma not merely of defeat, but of a cause inherently wrong. Their heroism and the sincerity of their conviction may, in part, redeem their fame, but at the best it must ever be held to have been wasted heroism—mistaken sincerity. The world may admire and pity, but it can never applaud. Their courage and fortitude are a part of the world's inheritance; but those who love "freedom and the right" in all the ages, must ever be grateful for the final overthrow of the cause their valor and their genius so long upheld.

The highest fame which it is possible for the Confederate hero to attain must ever be tainted with excuse and apology. Of their dead it must ever be

said, as in extenuation of a fault, "They *thought* they were right." Beyond that
the most daring eulogium can not go. They were brave and earnest, but misguided men. Their achievements were deeds of marvelous valor, but the hope
of liberty depended on their discomfiture. Sad beyond the power of words to
depict, is the story of their devotion and their overthrow. Sadder still, the fact
that in history they will only be remembered as the last of that brave array of
champions who, in the jarring cycles of the past, have fought and died in defense of slavery—rendering up their lives for the fancied right of oppressing
their fellows. Well is the day which is consecrated to *their* memory termed a
"Memorial Day"—a day full of mournful memories and blighted hopes. For
those who mourn these dead heroes and this ill-fated cause, the present brings
only the bitterness of regret, and the future offers no consoling hope of an ultimate rehabilitation of their fame. To them, time is but a *via dolorosa*, whose
ever-deepening gloom must rest more densely on the fame of those they
loved, as their excuse grows year by year less plausible, and the cause for which
they fought grows more and more odious to free-born millions, to whose
thought slavery will be only a horrid nightmare of an uncomprehended past.

Why was our glorious holiday, commemorative of victory rather than defeat, of glad deliverance rather than of hopeless overthrow, of triumphant battle for the right rather than of desperate struggle for the wrong,—why was
that anniversary of gladness sought to be assimilated in name and manner of
observance to this sorrowful memento of humiliation and disaster?

Ah, Blower, it is a sad story of human weakness. Strange as it may seem,
there were those, even among our comrades, who, for a little cheap laudation,
in silly deference to a sickly sentimentality, were willing to abase themselves
and strip their dead comrades of the white cerements in which they peacefully
and gloriously sleep. These men thought that the difference between right and
wrong, between devotion to liberty and the defense of slavery, between equality of right for all men and the right of the strong to oppress the weak might
be blotted out, and the Nation led to honor alike the champion of the right
and the upholder of the wrong. So they sought first to deprive the day of any
significance to the living. Only the manhood and valor of the dead were to be
commemorated. The dead were to be mourned; the cause for which they died
forgotten. There was no other way by which the desired object could be accomplished, and the future taught to honor the soldier for his deeds, regardless of his motive.

Of course, they to whom the years of conflict brought only sorrow and humiliation could not make their anniversary a jubilation. They had no reason to

rejoice. Even those who felt they had been in the wrong could not look back upon those years of havoc with feelings of genuine gladness. If either festival was to suffer change, it must be ours. So anxious were our brethren to blot out all memory of difference, to put "the blue" and "the gray" upon the same level of commendation and reverence in the eyes of posterity, that they determined that if our sometime foemen could not come up to our plane of exultation, we should go down to their level of humiliation. It was a silly notion. As if the facts of history could be changed by resolution! Right may be made wrong, or joy turned to sorrow, at the will a few sentimental enthusiasts! These men had, perhaps, the right to renounce for themselves, the merit of patriotic purpose, but they had no right to rob the lead of that which alone makes their beds upon the battle-field forever glorious. They would count poor Joe's devotion to "freedom and the right" as nothing, Blower; and call upon the country to remember and reverence, not the patriot—but the soldier! They would have us admit that the only memorable thing about our dear, dead heroes was the fact that they endured privation without murmuring, and faced death without flinching. They would ignore what made him worthy of remembrance, in order that they might do equal honor to his enemy. They would drag the hero down from his high pinnacle of moral purpose and put him on the plane of the hired bravo who fights because slaughter is his trade, and to whom the cause remains indifferent. What honor is it to say of a man that he was brave? The cur who lies upon the mat at our feet merits the same commendation. Joe's devotion was no such brutal instinct. His was the glory of self-sacrifice— the championship of right. His memory can only be rightly honored when the cause for which he fell is exalted and the halo of victory cast upon his tomb.

And they would do this, Blower—they would desecrate our festival of glory by clothing it in the garb of woe, and degrade the Nation's rejoicing in her deliverance from evil, into puerile pity for the dead, who were glorified in dying—they would do all this in the name of charity! They would invoke that sweet sentiment which was the inspiration of Joe's life—that love for the rights of others and chivalrous devotion to the cause of the weak and the oppressed, for which he lived and died—as an excuse for stripping him of his one claim to immortality!

God forgive us, Blower, if, with Joe's name on our lips and Joe's memory in our hearts, we should fail in devotion to the thought for which his blood was shed! We have no malice toward our foes of yesterday. The blood that stains the soil beneath our feet is too holy to permit our hearts to cherish aught of anger, revenge, or any form of uncharitable sentiment. We admire the courage, honor the fortitude, and respect the sincerity, of those who stood over against us in the day of conflict as much as even those who mourn in the shadow of disappointment and defeat. We are glad that such foemen were our brothers, and count our posterity happy in their joint inheritance of fame. But while we honor their valor and pity their misfortune we regret also—alas, we must ever remember and ever regret—*their error!* We can not mourn for *their* misfortune or cease to rejoice in *our* victory. Even those among them to whom the consciousness of error came with the knowledge of defeat, can not but be grateful for the disaster that brought humiliation.

God pity us, Blower, but love and charity, however sweet and fervent, cannot so gild the wrong as to make it pass current among men as the right. There is not in relapse of years any merciful medicament that will heal the fame of him who fought, however valorously and sincerely, for slavery, and raise it to the level of the humblest of those who fell in the cause of freedom. This is the gulf that lies between Joe's fame and that of the kindliest, noblest, truest of those with whom he fought, and in resisting whose impetuous valor, he died. Tears cannot obliterate it. Charity cannot hide it. As long as men love freedom, they must applaud the act of the one and deplore the attempt of the other.

For the one army of valorous dead let us hold "memorial!" services, solemn and sad, yet tender and sweet. Let us mourn their wasted manhood, and do honor to their misguided valor. But for the others—those who shed their blood for that charity which counts the rights and liberties even of the weakest and humblest of earth above life itself—let not only us and our comrades, but the nation redeemed from peril and shame, and all the liberty-lovers of earth, forever hold them in joyful remembrance! When we shall cease to heap their graves with flowers, let the garlands of fame grow brighter as the blessings which their valor bought grow richer with the coming years, making all future time their endless "Decoration Day"!

May 30, 1885

19

The South as a Field for Fiction (1888)*

This work of literary criticism remains one of Tourgée's most quoted essays. Surveying the literature about slavery and the Civil War, he notes the tendency of northern writers to avoid the subject in the interest of reconciliation. Southern writers meanwhile had come to dominate the field with works that glorified and vindicated the Confederacy. Tourgée takes some solace in the promising work of the black folklorist and writer Charles W. Chesnutt, and he predicts the rise of African American novelists who alone could provide an accurate view of slavery from the perspective of the enslaved.

More than twenty years ago, the writer ventured the prediction that the short, but eventful lifetime of the Southern Confederacy, the downfall of slavery, and the resulting conditions of Southern life would furnish to the future American novelist his richest and most striking material. At that time he was entirely unknown as a writer of fiction, and it is probable that he is now generally supposed to have turned his attention in this direction more from political bias than from any literary or artistic attraction which it offered. The exact converse was in fact true; the romantic possibility of the situation appealed to him even more vividly than its political difficulty, though, as is always the case in great national crises, the one was unavoidably colored by the other. Slavery as a condition of society has not yet become separable, in the minds of our people, North or South, from slavery as a political idea, a factor of partisan strife. They do not realize that two centuries of bondage left an ineradicable impress on master and slave alike, or that the line of separation between the races, being marked by the fact of color, is as impassable since emancipation as it was before, and perhaps even more portentous. They esteem slavery as simply a dead, unpleasant fact of which they wish to hear nothing more, and

*Albion W. Tourgée, "The South as a Field for Fiction," *Forum* 6 (December 1888): 404–13.

regard any disparaging allusion to its results as an attempt to revive a defunct political sentiment.

It is not surprising, therefore, that the literary men of the North should have looked upon such a forecast with contempt and impatience. It seemed to them to be not only absurd, but inspired by a malicious desire to keep alive the memory of an epoch which it was the duty of everyone to help bury in impenetrable oblivion. That was a foolish notion. A nation can never bury its past. A country's history may perish with it, but it can never outlive its history. Yet such was the force of the determination in the Northern mind to taboo all allusion to that social condition which had been the occasion of strife that the editor of a leading magazine felt called upon to make emphatic protest against the obnoxious prediction. "However much of pathos there may have been in the slave's life," he said, with the positiveness of infallibility, "its relations can never constitute the groundwork of enjoyable fiction. The colored race themselves can never regard the estate of bondage as a romantic epoch, or desire to perpetuate its memories. Slavery and rebellion, therefore," he concludes, "with the conditions attendant upon and re-suiting from them, can never constitute a popular field for American fiction." Time is not always prompt in its refutation of bad logic, but in this case he is not chargeable with unnecessary delay. In obedience to a pronounced and undeniable popular demand, that very magazine has given a complete reversal of its own emphatic dictum, by publishing in a recent number a dialect story of Southern life written by one of the enslaved race.

Under such circumstances, however, it is hardly surprising that the writer's farther prediction should have been regarded as too absurd for refutation. He himself is almost startled, as he looks at the dingy pages, to find himself averring, in the very glare of expiring conflict, that "within thirty years after the close of the War of Rebellion popular sympathy will be with those who upheld the Confederate cause rather than with those by whom it was overthrown; our popular heroes will be Confederate leaders; our fiction will be Southern in its prevailing types and distinctively Southern in its character."[1] There are yet seven years to elapse before the prescribed limit is reached, but the prediction is already almost literally fulfilled. Not only is the epoch of the war the favorite field of American fiction today, but the Confederate soldier is the popular hero. Our literature has become not only Southern in type, but distinctly Confederate in sympathy. The federal or Union soldier is not ex-

---

1. The source of this quotation remains unidentified.

actly depreciated, but subordinated; the Northern type is not decried, but the Southern is preferred. This is not because of any essential superiority of the one or lack of heroic attributes in the other, but because sentiment does not always follow the lead of conviction, and romantic sympathy is scarcely at all dependent upon merit. The writer makes no pretension to having foreseen the events that have occurred in the interval that has elapsed. Even the results he but imperfectly comprehended, having no clear anticipation of the peculiar forms which Southern fiction would assume. The one thing he did perceive, and the causes of which he clearly outlined, was the almost unparalleled richness of Southern life of that period as a field for fictitious narrative.

But whatever the cause may be, it cannot be denied that American fiction of today, whatever may be its origin, is predominantly Southern in type and character. The East and the West had already been in turn the seat of romantic empire. American genius has traced with care each step in the mysterious process by which the "dude" was evolved from the Puritan and the "cow-boy" from the pioneer. From Cooper to Hawthorne, the colonial and Revolutionary life of the East was the favorite ground of the novelist. The slavery agitation gave a glimpse of one phase of Southern life. As soon as the war was over, as if to distract attention from that unpleasant fact, we were invited to contrast American crudeness with English culture. Then the Western type came boldly to the front and the world studied the assimilations of our early occidental life; its product has not yet been portrayed. For a time each of these overshadowed in American fiction all the others. Each was in turn worked out. The public relish for that particular diet palled, and popular taste, which is the tyrant of the realm of literature, demanded something else. Today the South has unquestionably the preference. Hardly a novelist of prominence, except Mr. Howells and Mr. James, but has found it necessary to yield to the prevailing demand and identify himself with Southern types. Southern life does not lend itself readily to the methods of the former. It is earnest, intense, full of action, and careless to a remarkable degree of the trivialities which both these authors esteem the most important features of real life. Its types neither subsist upon soliloquy nor practice irrelevancy as a fine art; they are not affected by a chronic self-distrust nor devoted to anti-climax. Yet despite these imperfections the public appetite seems to crave their delineation.

A foreigner studying our current literature, without knowledge of our history, and judging our civilization by our fiction, would undoubtedly conclude that the South was the seat of intellectual empire in America, and the African the chief romantic element of our population. As an evidence of this, it may be noted that a few months ago every one of our great popular monthlies presented a "Southern story" as one of its most prominent features; and during the past year nearly two-thirds of the stories and sketches furnished to newspapers by various syndicates have been of this character.

To the Northern man, whose belief in averages is so profound, this flood of Southern fiction seems quite unaccountable. He recurs at once to the statistics of illiteracy, with an unfaltering belief that novels, poems, and all forms of literature are a natural and spontaneous product of the common-school system. He sees that twenty-eight out of every hundred of the white people of the South cannot read or write, and at once concludes that in literary production as well as in mechanical and financial achievement the North must of necessity excel, in about the same proportion that it does in capacity to assimilate the literary product.

Yet the fact ought not to surprise anyone. One of the compensations of war is a swift ensuing excitation of the mental faculties, which almost always yields remarkable results. This is especially true when fortune turns against a spirited and ambitious people. The War of Rebellion was a far more terrible experience to the people of the South than to those of the North. The humiliation resulting from defeat was intense and universal. They had and can have no tide of immigration and no rush of business life greatly to lessen the force of these impressions, while the presence of the Negro in numbers almost equal to the whites prevents the possibility of forgetting the past. The generation which has grown up since the war not only has the birthmark of the hour of defeat upon it, but has been shaped and molded quite as much by regret for the old conditions as by the difficulties of time now. To the Southern man or woman, therefore, the past, present, and future of Southern life is the most interesting and important matter about which they can possibly concern themselves. It is their world. Their hopes and aspirations are bounded by its destiny, and their thought is not diluted by cosmopolitan ideas. Whether self-absorption is an essential requisite of literary production or not, it is unquestionably true that almost all the noted writers of fiction have been singularly enthusiastic lovers of the national life of which they have been a part. In this respect the Southern novelist has a vast advantage over his Northern contemporary. He has never any doubt. He loves the life he portrays and sincerely believes in its superlative excellence. He does not study it as a curiosity, but knows it by intuition. He never sneers at its imperfections, but worships even its defects.

The Southern writer, too, has a curiously varied life from which he may select his types, and this life is absolutely *terra incognita* to the Northern mind. The "Tyrant of Broomsedge Cove" may have a parallel on every hillside; Mrs. Burnett's miraculously transformed "poor-white" Cinderellas may still use the springs for pier-glasses; Joel Chandler Harris's quaintness, Chestnut's [*sic*] curious realism, or the dreamy idealism that still paints the master and the slave as complements of a remembered millennial state: any of these may be a true picture of this life so far as the Northern man's knowledge or conception is concerned. He has a conventional "Southern man," a conventional "poor white," with a female counterpart of each already fitted out in his fancy; and as long as the author does not seriously disturb these preconceptions, the Northern reader likes the Southern story because it is full of life and fire and real feeling. And it is no wonder that he does, for it is getting to be quite a luxury to the novel reader to find a story in which the characters have any feeling beyond a self-conscious sensibility which seems to give them a deal of trouble without ever ripening into motive or resulting in achievement.

It is noteworthy in this revival that the Negro and the poor white are taking rank as by far the more interesting elements of Southern life. True, the dashing Confederate cavalier holds his place pretty well. It is rather odd that he was always a "cavalier," but, so far as our fiction is concerned, there does not appear to have been any Confederate infantry. Still, often the "cavalier" has come to need a foil, just as Dives required a Lazarus, and with like result— the beggar has overshadowed his patron. In literature as well as in politics, the poor white is having the best of the Southern *renaissance.* The sons of schoolmasters and overseers and even "crappers" [i.e., 'croppers] have come to the fore in the "New South," and the poor white is exalted not only in his offspring but in literature. There are infinite possibilities in the poor white of either sex; and as the supply is limited to the South, there seems to be no reason why he should not during the next half century become to the fiction of the United States what the Highlander is to Scottish literature—the only "interesting" white character in it.

But the Negro has of late developed a capacity as a stock character of fiction which no one ever dreamed that he possessed in the good old days when he was a merchantable commodity. It must be admitted, too, that the Southern writers are "working him for all he is worth," as a foil to the aristocratic types of the land of heroic possibilities. The Northern man, no matter what his prejudices, is apt to think of the Negro as having an individuality of his own. To the Southern mind, he is only a shadow—an incident of another's life. As such he is invariably assigned one of two roles. In one he figures as the devoted slave who serves and sacrifices for his master and mistress, and is content to live or die, do good or evil, for those to whom he feels himself under infinite obligation for the privilege of living and serving. There were such miracles no doubt, but they were so rare as never to have lost the miraculous character. The other favorite aspect of the Negro character from the point of view of the Southern fictionist is that of the poor "nigger" to whom liberty has brought only misfortune, and who is relieved by the disinterested friendship of some white man whose property he once was. There are such cases, too, but they are not so numerous as to destroy the charm of novelty. About the Negro as a man, with hopes, fears, and aspirations like other men, our literature is very nearly silent. Much has been written of the slave and something of the freedman, but thus far no one has been found able to weld the new life to the old.

This indeed is the great difficulty to be overcome. As soon as the American Negro seeks to rise above the level of the former time, he finds himself confronted with the past of his race and the woes of his kindred. It is to him not only a record of subjection but of injustice and oppression. The "twice-told tales" of *his* childhood are animate with rankling memories of wrongs. Slavery colored not only the lives but the traditions of his race. With the father's and the mother's blood is transmitted the story, not merely of their individual wrongs but of a race's woe, which the impenetrable oblivion of the past makes even more terrible and which the sense of color will not permit him to forget. The white man traces his ancestry back for generations, knows whence they came, where they lived, and guesses what they did. To the American Negro the past is only darkness replete with unimaginable horrors. Ancestors he has none. Until within a quarter of a century he had no record of his kindred. He was simply one number of an infinite "no name series." He had no father, no mother; only a sire and dam. Being bred for market, he had no name, only a distinguishing appellative, like that of a horse or a dog. Even in comparison with these animals he was at a disadvantage; there was no "herdbook" of slaves. A well-bred horse may be traced back in his descent for a thousand years, and may show a hundred strains of noble blood; but even this poor consolation is denied the eight millions of slave-descended men and women in our country.

The remembrance of this condition is not pleasant and can never become so. It is exasperating, galling, degrading. Every freedman's life is colored by this shadow. The farther he gets away from slavery, the more bitter and terrible will be his memory of it. The wrong that was done to his forebears is a continuing and self-magnifying evil. This is the inevitable consequence of the conditions of the past; no kindness can undo it; no success can blot it out. It is the sole inheritance the bondman left his issue, and it must grow heavier rather than lighter until the very suggestion of inequality has disappeared—if indeed such a time shall ever come.

The life of the Negro as a slave, freedman, and racial outcast offers undoubtedly the richest mine of romantic material that has opened to the English-speaking novelist since the Wizard of the North discovered and depicted the common life of Scotland.[2] The Negro as a man has an immense advantage over the Negro as a servant, being an altogether new character in fiction. The slave's devotion to the master was trite in the remote antiquity of letters; but the slave as a man, with his hopes, his fears, his faith, has been touched, and only touched, by the pen of the novelist. The traditions of the freedman's fireside are richer and far more tragic than the folklore which genius has recently put into his quaint vernacular. The freedman as a man—not as a "brother in black," with the curse of Cain yet upon him, but a man with hopes and aspirations, quick to suffer, patient to endure, full of hot passion, fervid imagination, desirous of being equal to the best—is sure to be a character of enduring interest.

The mere fact of having suffered or enjoyed does not imply the power to portray, but the Negro race in America has other attributes besides mere imagination. It has absorbed the best blood of the South, and it is quite within the possibilities that it may itself become a power in literature, of which even the descendants of the old regime shall be as proud as they now are of the dwellers in "Broomsedge Cove" and on the "Great Smoky."[3]

Pathos lies at the bottom of all enduring fiction. Agony is the key of immortality. The ills of fate, irreparable misfortune, untoward but unavoidable destiny: these are the timings that make for enduring fame. The "realists" profess to be truth-tellers, but are in fact the worst of falsifiers, since they tell only the weakest and meanest part of the grand truth which makes up the continued story of every life. As a rule, humanity is in serious earnest, and loves to have its sympathy moved with woes that are heavy enough to leave an impress of actuality on the heart. Sweetmeats may afford greater scope for the skill of the *chef;* but it is "the roast beef of old England" that "sticks to the ribs" and nourishes a race of giants. Dainties—peacocks' tongues and sparrows' brains—may bring delight to the epicure who loves to close his eyes and

2. A reference to Sir Walter Scott, whose historical romances had a great influence on Tourgée's own fiction.

3. These titles refer to novels by Mary Noailles Murfree (1850–1922), a southern author who published popular novels under the pseudonym Charles Egbert Craddock.

dream that he detects the hint of a flavor; but the strong man despises neutral things and a vigorous people demand a vigorous literature.

It is the poet of action whose clutch on the human soul is eternal, not the professor of analytics or the hierophant of doubt and uncertainty. In sincerity of passion and aspiration, as well as in the woefulness and humiliation that attended its downfall, the history of the Confederacy stands pre-eminent in human epochs. Everything about it was on a grand scale. Everything was real and sincere. The soldier fought in defense of his home, in vindication of what he deemed his right. There was a proud assumption of superiority, a regal contempt of their foe, which, like Hector's boastfulness, added wonderfully to the pathos of the result. Then, too, a civilization fell with it—a civilization full of wonderful contrasts, horrible beyond the power of imagination to conceive in its injustice, cruelty, and barbarous debasement of a subject race, yet exquisitely charming in its assumption of pastoral purity and immaculate excellence. It believed that the slave loved his chains and was all the better physically and morally for wearing them.

But then came the catastrophe, and all was changed. The man who fights and wins is only common in human esteem. The downfall of empire is always the epoch of romance. The brave, but unfortunate reap always the richest measure of immortality. The roundheads are accounted base and common realities, but the cavaliers are glorified by disaster. In all history, no cause had so many of the elements of pathos as that which failed at Appomattox, and no people ever presented to the novelist such a marvelous array of curiously contrasted lives. Added to the various elements of the white race are those other exceptional and unparalleled conditions of this epoch, springing from "race, color, and previous condition of servitude." The dominant class itself presents the accumulated pathos of a million abdications. "We are all poor whites now," is the touching phrase in which the results of the conflict are expressed with instinctive accuracy by those to whom it meant social as well as political disaster. It is a truth as yet but half appreciated. The level of Caucasian life at the South must hereafter be run from the bench-line of the poor white, and there cannot be any leveling upward. The distance between its upper and lower strata cannot be maintained; indeed it is rapidly disappearing. To the woefulness of the conquered is added the pathos of a myriad of deposed sovereigns. Around them will cluster the halo of romantic glory, and the epoch of their overthrow will live again in American literature.

It matters not whence the great names of the literary epoch which is soon to dawn may derive their origin. No doubt there is something of truth in

Herbert Spencer's suggestion, that the poets and novelists as well as the rulers of the future will come from the great plains and dwell in the shadows of the stern and silent mountains of the West. Greatness is rarely born where humanity swarms. Individual power is the product of a wide horizon. Inspiration visits men in solitude, and the infinite comes nearer as the finite recedes from the mental vision; only solitude must not be filled with self. No solitary, self-imprisoned for his own salvation, ever sang an immortal strain; but he that taketh the woes of a people into the desert with him, sees God in the burning bush. Method is but half of art—its meaner half. Inspiration gives the better part of immortality. Homer's heroes made his song undying, not his sonorous measures; and the glow of English manfulness spreads its glamour over Shakespeare's lines, and makes him for all ages the poet from whom brave men will draw renewed strength and the unfortunate get unfailing consolation. Scott's loving faith in a chivalry which perhaps never existed, not only made his work imperishable, but inspires with healthful aspiration every reader of his shining pages.

Because of these things it is that the South is destined to be the Hesperides Garden of American literature. We cannot foretell the form its product will wear or even guess its character. It may be sorrowful, exultant, aspiring, or perhaps terrible, but it will certainly be great—greater than we have hitherto known, because its causative forces are mightier than those which have shaped the productive energy of the past. That its period of highest excellence will soon be attained there is little room to doubt. The history of literature shows that it is those who were cradled amid the smoke of battle, the sons and daughters of heroes yet red with slaughter, the inheritors of national woe or racial degradation, who have given utterance to the loftiest strains of genius. Because of the exceeding woefulness of a not too recent past, therefore, and the abiding horror of unavoidable conditions which are the sad inheritance of the present, we may confidently look for the children of soldiers and of slaves to advance American literature to the very front rank of that immortal procession whose song is the eternal refrain of remembered agony, before the birth-hour of the twentieth century shall strike.

20

From *A Memorial of Frederick Douglass from the City of Boston* (1895)*

Tourgée delivered this public eulogy in Faneuil Hall on December 20, 1895. Although Frederick Douglass had died the previous February, the city of Boston held a belated memorial service for him at the request of former abolitionists, particularly those of the city's black community. That Tourgée received the honor of delivering the main eulogy reflects his stature among civil rights leaders of the day. His speech recounts Douglass's life and achievements, but also pointedly draws lessons from his biography to critique the prejudice and oppression that blacks continued to suffer in the age of Jim Crow.

The life we commemorate tonight was, in some respects, among the most remarkable the world has ever known. In sharp and swift recurring contrasts it has never been excelled. In the distance from its beginning to its ending it has rarely been equaled. If a man's capacity be measured by what he achieved, FREDERICK DOUGLASS must be ranked among the great men of a great day; if by the obstacles overcome, he must be accounted among the greatest of any time.

HISTORICAL PARALLEL

In all history there is but one parallel of his career, and that one lacks the most important element. Twenty-five hundred years ago a slave so won upon his master's love and pride that he was set free. The most cultivated people in ancient history hung upon his words in admiration. Their philosophers imitated his methods; their poets parodied his fables. He became the friend, counselor, and ambassador of the greatest king of his time. When he died Athens voted

*Albion W. Tourgée, *A Memorial of Frederick Douglass from the City of Boston* (Boston: City Council, 1896).

him a statue, and four cities claimed the honor of being accounted his birth-place. He is said to have been a hunchback, and this fact is always cited as evidence of his transcendent genius because of the added burthen it imposed. He had not only to overcome the prejudice attaching to his station, but also the aversion inspired by his uncouthness. The schoolboy of today, as he cons this story, wonders how he could rise to such heights in the face of such obstacles, especially among a beauty-loving people like the Athenians.

Yet, what were the difficulties in the way of Æsop compared with those which Douglass overcame? What was Grecian bondage in comparison with American slavery? What was Æsop's hump when compared with Douglass' color, considered as an obstacle to personal success? What was the patronage of Crœsus to the friendship of Lincoln and Grant, Sumner and Garrison, Whittier and Phillips—and all the unnumbered host of good men and women to whom Douglass' name became a household word and in whose homes he was a welcome guest? No slave was ever before so potent in the counsels of freemen. No negro ever before became so widely and favorably known among an Anglo-Saxon people.

CONTRASTED WITH ÆSOP

Æsop was freed from bondage by the favor of his master; Douglass, through the admiration of thousands of dwellers in another land who had heard his voice and wondered at his words while yet a slave, and gladly gave their money to melt the shackles of American barbarism that fettered his limbs and galled his free spirit.

Æsop became the ambassador of a sovereign, Douglass the plenipotentiary of two republics.

Athens gave Æsop a statue because of his wit; Douglass was honored because of the services he had rendered a great nation.

Three classes of the American people are under special obligations to him: the colored bondman whom he helped to free from the chains which he himself had worn, the free persons of color whom he helped to make citizens, the white people of the United States whom he sought to free from the bondage of caste and relieve from the odium of slavery.

As it was meet that Athens, the home of wit, should vote Æsop, the most illustrious of ancient slaves, a statue when he died, so it is most fit, that "in the cradle of liberty," his life should be commemorated who while yet a slave became renowned throughout the world as a champion of freedom. Every citizen of the United States is a debtor to his memory—every colored man because he relieved them, by his admirable exemplification, from the curse of incapacity which had been put upon them, as an excuse for slavery; and every white man because he did so much to take away the shame that rested on the Republic. The material ills of slavery affected chiefly the colored race; its moral blight was shared by the white people of the country as well. The wrongs of slavery attached to the colored man; its shame rested wholly with the white man. So the obligation of gratitude for its extinction is not a one-sided matter, and it is especially appropriate that Boston, the birthplace of two great revolutions for the promotion of liberty, should be the first American city to do honor to a colored man for his services to the nation which had condemned him and his people to hopeless bondage.

The chief merit that attaches to the people of the North in the great conflict in which slavery perished, consisted not in the fact that we fought for the Federal Union or resisted its disruption; but in the far nobler fact that we fought for liberty—the liberty of a poor, weak, despised people. The tramp of our legions was in tune with that most glorious of national anthems:

> "As He died to make men holy,
> Let US die to make men FREE!"

So, too, the slave who fought for his own freedom, in the field or in that great conflict that came before the sword was drawn, fought also to take away the shame of the oppressor. He who fights for his own liberty is a hero; he who strikes a blow for another's rights is the brother of Him who died for man, and fit to wear Excalibur.

A FIRST MEETING

Some forty years ago a country lad sat in an audience which an orator was addressing in impassioned tones, on an unpopular theme. The speaker was in the prime of manhood. His dark cheek flushed, his eyes flashed; his lithe but powerful frame swayed with the force of his emotion as he denounced wrong and pleaded for justice. Suddenly one of the shafts of his denunciation struck deeper than the others. There was a murmur of disapproval swelling to an angry roar, and then a storm of groans and hisses. From the neighborhood of the youngster an egg was thrown which struck the speaker on the shoulder. Other missiles were thrown also, but this one splashed up on his long wavy hair and left yellow streaks on his black beard and mustache. There was an instant's hush broken only by the boy's laugh. Then for half an hour that audience were thrilled and hushed to breathless silence, by an overwhelming tide of denunciatory eloquence rarely equaled in any age or by any orator. The speaker evidently thought the youngster who laughed had been guilty of the offence. Others thought so, too. It is not the first time a laugh has condemned the innocent. The next morning the young man called upon the orator to apologize, not for the egg, of which he was guiltless, but for the laugh, which he regretted. It was not a pleasant call. The orator was still sore over the indignity that had been offered him. The affront was one apologies could not cure. He told the wondering boy a furious tale of insults he had suffered because he was a colored man pleading for justice to his people. The interview ended peacefully, however, as if in apology for its rough beginning.

A PLEASANT ACQUAINTANCE

This was my first meeting with FREDERICK DOUGLASS. It was the beginning of a pleasant but desultory acquaintance. When we next met, the flood of battle had swept away the legal estate of slavery. I was a dweller in a southern state, he was my guest. Around us were scattered the fragments of a disrupted social and economic system—a slave-civilization to which men were trying to fit the garments of liberty. The result was grotesque—it is still grotesque. Wise theorists made it a scarecrow, and those who had little comprehension either of liberty or justice as the heritage of the colored man, have shred away the patches and left it a ghastly skeleton. He was seeking in wonder and amaze to penetrate the future and read the destiny of his people. He had known two phases of American life in the slave-republic—the slave-life into which he was born; the free life to which he had fled. How to reconcile the fragments of the one with the triumphant confidence of the other was the problem that confronted all. He knew what had been in the old slave-epoch; the young man realized more keenly, perhaps, the character of the new one. Neither was confident of what would be. From that time until just before his death, we met occasionally as our paths crossed, here and there. Our acquaintance was always candid, earnest, thoughtful—never continuous or intimate. I shall speak of him tonight, therefore, not as one having special knowledge of those qualities which appear only in personal relations, but as a public man in his relations to the epoch in which he lived, the institution he helped to overthrow, the race whose obloquy he bore, the nation he helped to redeem from ignominy, and the people whose destiny he left unsolved. I shall consider only the man whom the world knows, in the light the future must regard him.

THE THOUGHT THAT UNDERLIES A LIFE

Emerson has noted the value of the man who stands behind a thought. There is also a value to be estimated of the thought that lies back of a man's life. Every man is, in a sense, chameleonic. He gives back, more or less clearly, the color of his day. If he is careful only of his own comfort or seeks only his own advantage, he reflects but little of the life which is the light of his world. Its rays fall upon him and glance off without any added flash or fresh throb of interest. If, however, its glare enters his soul, fires his brain, and animates his being, he becomes transparent, like the little creature whose flesh absorbs the sunshine so that we see his heart-beats through the glowing walls.

This was true in an especial manner of the man we are assembled to commemorate. The thought of his epoch was his thought—he had little outside of or beyond it. From the past he had received only life as his inheritance. His present had nothing to offer but one dominant, controlling idea. This entered his soul and filled it. No wonder the thought of his time was of himself—himself and his fellows and liberty—their relations to the dominant class in the land of his, birth, to the State, to the government, to Christianity, to God. In the church, on the rostrum, in the Congress, in the Legislatures of the country, in the city mart, and in the country store—wherever men were assembled—the one object of all-absorbing interest was the colored man, his character, qualities, capacity, and the relations which God and nature designed that he should hold to his fellow-mortals of a lighter hue. In a sense, this was no new question. The only new thing about it was that there were those who contended that the theory which had so long prevailed in regard to it was not the true one; that the wisdom of the ages was not only incorrect, but that its conclusions were incontestably based on false premises.

. . . . . .

A HOPELESS PROSPECT

Fate hung about the young child's neck two burdens, either of which might well suffice to break the spirit of the strongest man—he was a slave, and bore the mark of African blood in a nation of Protestant white people, boastful of their liberty. Either of these curses was enough to crush hope out of the bravest heart. Made slaves at birth, how few of our children would break their fetters! Given a trace of color, how few of our greatest men would ever have been heard from! It needs something more than talent, and learning, and eloquence to open the door of success to a colored man, and make him welcome on the platform, in the clubs, and in the homes of men who count their hue a mark of divine and exclusive favor. If, at the Christmas-tide which is so near, the Holiest should come again, in hue and likeness of a negro, even if the heavenly radiance still shone about His head, I fear me He would meet a very chilly welcome in the churches and homes of our land. Clad in a colored integument, there lives not today a single man who could attain to the highest eminence in our government, or receive a call to a fashionable church—no matter what his attainments or how Christ-like his character! What, then, shall we say of the prospects of the young child about whose gum-tree cradle the twin pythons of Slavery and Caste reared their horrid heads, twined, and hissed to drive away his hope and dissipate even the dream of aspiration? How shall we measure his success and estimate his power? . . . .

American slavery was the greatest crime of the ages: first, because of its utter hopelessness; and, second, because the intelligence and inventiveness of the American people had been applied to the refinement and perfection of the legal-relations of the slave, until there was literally no chance for the palliation or amendment of his condition. The State could make him free indeed. This had been done in five of the original colonies. That curious piece of legislation by which slavery was excluded from the Northwest Territory, had saved the whole region west of Pennsylvania and east of the Mississippi, from the contamination of its presence, though even here it held sway over men's hearts and minds. The nation was kept half-free and half-slave by the most nicely adjusted system of checks and balances the ingenuity of man has ever devised. Slavery being based on race and color, the presumptions of the law in favor of liberty were reversed to secure its perpetuity, and the teachings of religion were made the cloak for legalized violation of all the laws of God and nature. While the half-free North had rid herself of Slavery, Caste held sway throughout its length and breadth. Equality of opportunity, which is the touchstone of liberty, was denied to all having traces of colored blood.

THE ABOLITION EPOCH

Almost contemporaneous with the "second birth" of the slave, thereafter for all time to be known as Frederick Douglass, the American people began to awaken to the enormity of that greatest of all crimes against God and man, American slavery.

The New England Anti-Slavery Society had been organized five years before the foot of Douglass touched free soil; the national society, a year or two later. Garrison had established the "Liberator," and was beating it into the hearts of men with palpitant strokes that slavery was the sin of sins, and crime of crimes. Phillips had just dedicated the powers which were to thrill the world, to the cause of human liberty and righteousness. Whittier was tuning the harp whose lays were to make him for all ages the prophet-poet of Liberty. Birney had already begun that career which was to drive him from his southern home. Garret Smith was preaching liberty in that strange confusion of rich metaphor, overflowing kindness, and inconsequent conclusion, which marked him one of the worthiest and strangest of patriots and philosophers. Elijah Lovejoy had just given up his life for liberty, and Owen, kneeling on his brother's grave, had just vowed eternal war against Slavery. Thousands more, bursting the green withes of prejudice, were pressing forward, eager to give life and strength to the conflict of freedom. Boston was the storm-centre, for here the fiery heart of Garrison sent forth the flaming sheets which flew over the whole land and, in every home they entered, kindled a fire, which nor time nor tyranny could ever smother. Even yet, thousands of hearts glow and flutter in breasts, now weak and shriveled, at the memory of his utterances. The ferment had begun which was to culminate in years of strife and bloody expiation—a struggle not yet ended!

Douglass still in bonds, caught the echoes of this conflict. He had the slave's fear of being thrust back into the Gehenna from which he had fled. He had the slave's intuition that his safety lay in silence and obscurity. For years, he looked with apprehension in the face of every white stranger whom he met, fearing he might bear the warrant for his arrest as a fugitive. By night and by day, the nightmare of recaption and reënslavement followed him. He was determined to die rather than submit. He had muscles of iron, health, and strength. Slavery, harsh mother as she was, had trained him well for self-support. Should he labor in silence, win enough for his wants, and let obscurity ripen into safety? Or should he risk his own liberty to help bring his race the Jubilee—the hour of deliverance from bondage—long prayed for? No one could have blamed him if he had remained silent. The hand of the master reached to every corner of the land. Some of the States remonstrated, but the nation upheld his right.

It was no trivial matter, even for a white man, in New England to espouse the cause of liberty. Society frowned upon him; the pulpits fulminated against him. On that first year of Douglass' semi-freedom, even the Thanksgiving sermons in Boston reeked with denunciation of the crime and sin of obeying the scriptural behest to "Proclaim liberty throughout the land unto all the inhabitants thereof!" American slavery had no year of jubilee, and was far behind that Jewish bondage of twenty centuries before, in humane and merciful character. It not only pursued the fugitive slave to the uttermost borders of its jurisdiction, but it persecuted those who aided him to escape or even claimed for him the more tolerable condition of a "free man of color."

Douglass might, with general approval, have remained in obscurity, won a reasonable competence by his labor, and enjoyed as much liberty and respect as was attainable by the "free person of color" anywhere in the United States. Many had won a precarious liberty in like manner, and kept it by silence. They were not to be blamed. Not only is self-preservation the first law of nature, but the inheritance of slavery does not incline one to sacrifice for others. The slave's peril, privation, and the dwarfing effect of generations of enforced ignorance and restraint but poorly fitted the slave for self-sacrifice for the good of others, let alone the succor of his fellows. There were some who took the same risk and adopted the same course as Douglass, but more who sought safety in the obscurity which soon became insufficient to conceal his identity. He went to an "abolition meeting." He heard the woes of the slave related by those who knew them not, except through imagination and hearsay. To him the horrors of slavery stood out in all their naked enormity. He had never spoken to an audience before; that night he rose and, begging pardon for his weakness, set forth in a clearer light than any one present had ever heard it told, the horror of that bondage from which he had fled.

DOUGLASS AN ABOLITION ORATOR

Those engaged in the abolition movement were earnest people. They did not shrink from the logic of their own teachings. They welcomed the new worker in the struggle they had undertaken as having something they had not—a concrete knowledge more potent with average minds than the most clearly woven theory. They noted, too, the fire of genius under his unpreparedness. "From night to night," said one, "I watched the growth of his vocabulary and the fuller play of his imagination. It was marvelous."

He was an orator by natural inclination. There was a rumor that his father might have been one who "swayed the listening Senate" with his honeyed words. It matters not whence it came, the natural aptitude cannot be denied, and the school where he was put in training was one never excelled in the world's history. It was the golden age of American oratory—its most earnest, impassioned, and characteristic epoch. Of the masters of eloquence of that time many of the most accomplished were already enlisted, and others were being daily enrolled among the abolition forces. No wonder that Douglass' natural powers were so swiftly developed that he was soon proclaimed "a most marvelous orator, when one considers what the life was from which he came." Under such masters, and with such a theme, one must have been dull indeed not to have felt the glow of inspiration!

He had two great advantages over those with whom he wrought—little was expected of him by his first audiences, and he was a living refutation of the charge that his people were incapable of civilization and fit only for servile tasks.

The question of the colored man's capacity was the most important premise in the argument which occupied the universal thought. Politics and religion; business and science; society and economics—all were colored with the pros and cons of this subject. The right and wrong of slavery was held to depend upon it. If the negro was incapable of civilization, slavery, though an ugly thought, must be endured for the common welfare and security. On the other hand, if he was capable of even approximate attainment with the white race, slavery became at once a monster of too horrible a mien to be contemplated with anything like forbearance or approval. Volumes were written upon the subject. Science and theology went hand and hand in the service of slavery. Wrong has ever been a good paymaster, and slavery paid him who proclaimed its sanctity, and him who upheld its necessity alike, with honors and approval. So the most noted scientists avouched the negro's inferiority, basing their judgments upon the curl of his hair, the breadth of his nose, and the hue of his skin, the convolutions of his brain, the flatness of his foot. The pulpit used these demonstrations to prove the wisdom and mercy of God in fastening on the sons of Ham the curse of the drunken patriarch. There were lots of loop-holes in the reasoning of both; but they both proved what was wanted, and were accounted oracles in their day. So science and religion became the willing servants of Slavery and cast the cloak of duty and necessity over its unutterable infamies. Everybody who was of any consequence formed and expressed an opinion on this engrossing subject. Every lawyer, every statesman, every politician, every divine, almost every man and woman of any prominence in the land, was drawn into the vortex of controversy in regard to the negro's capacity for civilization and the resulting question as to whether he should be free or slave. What tomes of wasted learning were put forth! What ingenious theories were invented to reconcile God's mercy with man's depravity! How many a grandson would be glad today to obliterate the evidence of an ancestor's folly! But what is writ, what is printed, can never be recalled. Brass may melt and marble crumble, but printer's ink endureth forever and ever! O scientist! O bigot! If you wish to learn humility and avoid the shame of the world's ridicule, read the record of your predecessors of only fifty years ago, and see how feeble is the wisdom of man when he seeks to put bounds to the mercy and justice of God! Many a man in that day made swift shipwreck of a fair renown in seeking to wrest God's truth to the devil's service. The vast majority of the people, even of the North, were against the negro's right to be free, and that opposition was based almost wholly upon a profound and sincere conviction of his unfitness for civilization and lack of capacity for freedom and self-direction and control.

The Attorney-General of the Commonwealth of Massachusetts, if I mistake not, about that time declared, perhaps in this historic hall, that "one might as well talk about releasing the wild beasts in the Zoological Garden to run about the city's streets as think of freeing negroes to prey upon the white people of the country."

Under these circumstances, it was of vast importance to the Abolition movement to have one who in himself was an undeniable refutation of this claim. Nobody could question the ability of Frederick Douglass. He was an opponent whom any man had need beware of, and no champion of slavery cared to encounter him a second time. While he studied carefully the eloquence of others and assimilated with amazing readiness the best thoughts and the most striking arguments of his co-laborers, they came forth from the laboratory of his fiery brain essentially modified and not seldom greatly improved. From the first, he had the self-possession of the natural orator. An audience inspired him; interruptions only brought fresh coruscations. His humor was heightened by an artful assumption of the slave's humility, and, scathing as was his denunciation, he had a way of excusing it because of his race and lack of preparation, that somehow deprived it of offence. Even insult, he turned back on the offender in a way that not only made him the subject of general laughter, but not seldom transformed into the insulter a champion and defender. So he not only rose to the rank of one of the most noted champions of liberty, but he became also one of the strongest arguments of all those who fought beside him. Within a decade he had become one of the most popular of Abolition orators. Many times he was listened to with patience and applause, when a white orator could hardly make himself heard because of the hisses and jeers of unfriendly audiences. Yet there were times when the very reverse was true, and noble women showed their courage and devotion to liberty, by gathering around him and with their persons shielding him from the wrath of mobs whose only answer to his irrefutable argument was the cry, "Kill the nigger!"

For a dozen years before the war of words grew silent in the clash of arms, it may be doubted if there was any more effective speaker in the abolition host. His arguments had not the polish of many others; they were not so generally reported by the press, because his efforts were almost always extemporaneous in form, and the stenographer was not then omnipresent; but there was a life, a fire, a personal magnetism about him, which made even the most polished oratory seem weak and vain beside his fiery onslaught.

I was a lad of a dozen years, or less, when I first heard him at a meeting where some of the most eloquent of the white champions of liberty had also spoken. On the way home a crowd of thoughtful country people, of varying opinions, were discussing what they had heard. One of the most intelligent, a leader in his neighborhood, said "Well, you may say what you please about the others; the 'nigger' settled it with me. When a Negro who has been a slave can make such a speech as that, it is time that every one of them should be free. I am against slavery from this day."

And he kept his word.

During this time Mr. Douglass became the one colored man who was well and favorably known to the whole American people. At that time, the country-people represented the heart of American sentiment. Only one-fifth of the population lived in great cities, instead of fifty-eight percent as now. Throughout all the country regions of the North the colored man was rarely seen. There were whole counties without a single colored inhabitant. Now and then, a fugitive struggled into a community, and settled down. But in the main, sentiment of the North in regard to the Negro was based on hearsay; and very queerly, in this case, the hearsay of the interested planter was generally preferred over the testimony of the disinterested observer. To this mass of opinion, Mr. Douglass came as a concrete fact of tremendous force. Almost every one spoke kindly and pleasantly of him; thousands took him into their homes, and made him the basis of their conclusions in regard to the righteousness of Slavery. In a dozen States he had come to be known to a large proportion of the people, who had little if any knowledge of any other colored man. When the time came, he was naturally looked upon as the embodiment of all his race's interests and qualities.

AS A POLITICIAN

With the organization of the Republican Party in 1854, Mr. Douglass became at once an active and honored member. This appears the more remarkable when we consider the fact that there were no colored voters of any consequence at the North who could be said to constitute what might be termed a "following" of his own people. The "free person of color," though he could not be a citizen of the United States, nor a citizen of any State, within the meaning of that term in the Constitution of the United States, by a singular inconsistency, could be a voter in any State which saw fit to give him the ballot, and could thus become a part of the electoral power of the nation. This power was, however, conferred on him by only four or five States of the Union, and in these the colored population was very small, and the Republican majorities very reliable. So that, in fact, there was no colored vote which it was of any material consequence to the new party to secure. Besides that, the plain interest of the colored voter has always lain with the Republican Party, since through that he has obtained all the rights he has enjoyed, and to that he must still look to secure their enjoyment.

It cannot be said, therefore, that Mr. Douglass was welcomed to the councils of the Republicans because of any influence he had among those of his own race or color whose votes the new party desired to secure. The simple truth is that he was welcomed as an orator of singularly convincing power, and as a living justification of the party tendency, if not its avowed purpose. He was the first instance of a colored man being regarded as an important factor of a national party, that party being composed entirely of white voters.

As a politician, Mr. Douglass was always cautious and practical. He believed in the theory that every man should use his power as a citizen to secure as much actual betterment as possible, instead of refusing to exercise it unless he could obtain, at once, all that he desired. Had he been a white citizen of Massachusetts, with the advantages of opportunity and education her sons have so long enjoyed, I have no doubt he would have been one of her most noted political leaders. The fact that he broke away from those with whom he had been so long associated, and gave his allegiance to the Republican Party because, though not professing a purpose to abolish slavery, it did evince a most earnest purpose to restrict it, is a fine illustration of the intensely practical character of his mind.

"To such a cause as ours," he said, "a little done is worth more than ages of clamor about what ought to be done!"

It was this quality which eminently fitted him for the role of the practical statesman. He did not originate policies nor invent methods, but he had an unerring instinct as to what promised to advance the cause nearest his heart and bring the public sentiment ultimately to entertain and indorse his plea for liberty and justice for his. people. This he always kept steadily in view. Until the emancipation of the slave, politics meant nothing to him except as it bore upon that event. Very many of the leaders of the Abolition movement had imbibed the common fallacy that the only way to secure a needed reform in a republic is to demand that all other political questions shall be subordinated to it. Mr. Douglass, with a political instinct which seems marvelous now, when we consider the entire exclusion of all other interests from his thought and purpose, recognized the broader fact that a minority should always strive not merely to overcome or force a majority to yield to all their demands upon any subject, but to persuade them, if possible, to accept some of them. The tact, patience, and knowledge of human nature which he manifested at this period of his career, prove conclusively the eminence he would have attained had not caste thrown an insuperable barrier in his way. Given a white skin, and there is no limit to be placed on the political success he might have achieved.

. . . . . .

EMANCIPATION

At the close of the war, Mr. Douglass found himself in a position of the highest honor and extremist difficulty. By the white people of the North he was regarded as in an especial manner the representative of the colored people. The colored people of the South, only half-informed with regard to his peculiar relation to the long struggle which had culminated in their emancipation, as yet regarded him simply as the most fortunate of his race, whose position in the esteem of the country only showed to what others might attain. They did not realize that during all these years while he had been fighting valiantly the battle of freedom, he had been under a process of education the like of which no other man of his race ever enjoyed. From slavery to the society of men and women of the highest culture in the land; from service under a harsh taskmaster to being the honored guest in the best white homes of the land, was a transformation few men would have had the moral quality to experience without becoming giddy with an undue sense of their own personal merit. Escaping that, however, such a life was the most perfect of educational forces which swiftly removed him to an infinite distance from the life from which he had fled. He became a slave who had put slavery under his feet. He found himself, in sentiment and feeling, much nearer akin to the most refined white society of the North than to the "freedmen" of the South. They had been freed in an instant. The moral and intellectual stamp of slavery was still upon them. He had had thirty years of preparation for the miracle he lived to behold.

During all this time, his whole thought had been liberty. Freedom for all, equal right before the law; that was all he asked for those akin to him in blood and linked with him in destiny. His mind had never gone beyond this climax. He had never asked himself what would happen afterwards. Until the outbreak of the war, indeed, he never expected to see this result. He did not doubt that it would come, but looked upon it as being generations away rather than close at hand. While his caution and sense of practicality showed him the utterly delusive character of John Brown's vision of a government based on the hope of systematic cooperation of the slave-population of the South in an endeavor to destroy slavery by force, yet his despair of better results under existing conditions was such as to restrain him from giving information in regard to the same or approving the desperate venture on which this "inspired maniac" was about to engage. Had he been able to forecast even possible success, there is no doubt that he would have engaged in it most heartily. But he saw only defeat, useless sacrifice, and the contempt of all practical people. Brown was angry because he did not give entire approval to his desperate venture. It was well that he did not. Its hopelessness was the very element that gave it strength. That such a little company should embark upon so desperate a venture to secure liberty for a despised race, fixed the world's attention and made the leader's death a grand and awful spectacle. If he had been in fact, as he desired and hoped to be, the advance-guard of a popular movement to free the slaves by force of arms, his act would have been robbed of the moral grandeur on which its effect depended.

It was not, of course, possible that Mr. Douglass should foresee such result. The question in his mind was merely as to its success, and this he at once decided in the negative. He was willing to engage in anything that promised good results, no matter how desperate, but would not give his approval to what seemed destined to hinder rather than advance the end he sought.

Emancipation came to him, as to all others, as a surprise. Until the very last moment it was doubtful whether the government would appeal to this extraordinary power in order to put down rebellion. When it was done it was doubtful whether the people of the North would approve. Even if they did approve, it was a question as to what would be the legal result. Not until December 1865 was the XIIIth Amendment of the Constitution made the law of the land and slavery abolished. Even then, the problem of the future relations of the white and colored man in the American republic was but half-

solved—perhaps not even half-solved. Five millions of people who had been
slaves were made free by its provisions. Yet they were not citizens. No man
could buy or sell them or control their labor for his own advantage; but they
had no rights, except such as the several States might confer upon them; they
were not citizens, but freedmen, or, in the language of the Chief Justice of the
Supreme Court of the United States, in the Dred Scott decision, they were
"free persons of color," "mere inhabitants" of the several States, without rights,
except such as the States might confer upon them.

It was three years afterward, in July 1868 when the XIVth Amendment
was proclaimed, and for the first time in our history, a colored man became a
CITIZEN OF THE UNITED STATES.

During these years the fact developed that mere liberty, the abolition of
"slavery and involuntary servitude," was not enough to secure for the colored
man that equal enjoyment of privilege and opportunity which is the essence
of liberty. It became apparent to all observers that the long struggle for the
abolition of slavery was not the end of conflict for the establishment and
perfection of the liberty of the individual. The destruction of slavery had only
unmasked the other and more difficult problem of Caste.

A RACE REDEEMED

There was something pathetic in the feeling of disappointment which came
over Mr. Douglass as he realized this fact. He had fought so long for liberty,
had hoped for so much, and now it seemed as if the great conflict for justice
had just began. He was not a leader in the sense of one who devises policies or
methods. He did not originate. His function was to judge of what others might
offer—to pass upon the practicability of the plans of others. What was needed
to make the work of emancipation and enfranchisement complete and effectual? This was the question he was always asking, until the end came. At first
he relied on the provisions of the XIVth Amendment. They seemed to him
sufficient; but as they were bent and twisted, in the process of legal construction, he gave up that hope. Of the opinion in the case of the United States vs.
Cruikshank, he said pithily: "It is the Dred Scott case of the new dispensation."

To the clamorous and pathetic appeal of his people to be delivered from
unjust discrimination, from oppression and outrage, which they suffered because of race and color, he could only answer, "Wait, work, hope!"

It was a vague remedy—how vague he well knew, as those to whom it was
addressed fully realized. In this again, that strong and cautious self-restraint
which was a marked feature of his character showed itself most clearly. He

dreaded above all things giving any advice to his people that might work them injury. He recognized his inability to cope with the new problem. His life-thought had been fixed on liberty. He had studied slavery in all its phases. Caste, the distinction in legal right or opportunity based on race or color and having its root in legislation of a subtle, evasive, and fraudulent character— this was an enemy of a new type. The old arguments would not do. The old weapons were powerless against it. The old allies were dispersed and could not be rallied to fight the new wrong. Other men must be trained for the warfare. Other hands must forge the new weapons. Other hearts must bear the burden. Other souls must endure the scath of the impending conflict. This was the conclusion at which he arrived during the years that lay between emancipation and the time when he was called to give up his work on earth.

Once during the last year of life the old lion roused himself for battle. In the Congress in regard to the state and condition of the Negro, held at Chicago during the World's Fair, the old argument of the essential and organic inferiority of the colored race was put forth with almost as much particularity as in the old days when it was made the justification of iniquity and the excuse of oppression. At the sound of this familiar war-cry, the old soldier mustered his failing energies, and the torrent of ridicule and denunciation of this infamous standard by which it is still sought to measure his people's right to enjoy "life, liberty, and the pursuit of happiness," is said by those who heard it, to have been worthy of his best estate.

"It is the old, old fight," he said to me a few months afterwards. "The strange claim that a white, intelligent, Christian people makes of right dependent on race or color—of a right to oppress, to degrade, to subjugate, or destroy another people, merely because they are not as white or as wise or as strong as themselves. Will it never end? Will the civilized white man never cease trying to outdo the savage in barbarity? Will the Christian never learn that the colored man is only a weaker brother? God only knows what the end will be! I am waiting—waiting with my ear close to the ground to catch the sound of the chariot wheels."

. . . . . .

THE LESSON OF HIS LIFE

His memory should be an inspiration to every colored man and a warning to every white American that caste discrimination, whether it be the prop of slavery or other wrong, cannot long be justified by its results. While it may be many years or even generations before another colored man will attain the same distinctive prominence in the whole country, Mr. Douglass was not only the exponent of new conditions but the exception that proves the rule in regard to old ones. A people that can produce a Douglass under the conditions that beset his life, will unquestionably produce many who shall be his superiors in attainment and power under an improved environment. The law of the evolution of types in humanity is just as inflexible as in the lower orders of life. One Douglass born out of slavery is the forerunner of many to be born out of the semi-freedom which is all that Caste permits his race yet to enjoy.

The difficulties that beset his life can never be duplicated in all the world's life which is to be. One of the twin dragons of oppression has at least been slain. Slavery is no more. From the rising to the setting of the sun there is no place in any civilized land where oppression dare wear that name. The slave-ship, the slave-mart, the auction-block, the life which was in all things subject to another's will, the political condition which denied marriage and family, and legal offspring, which by law refused the rights of self-defense, forbade the race to possess or to inherit; to receive, to give or take; to sue or be sued; which denied the sacred rite of marriage, and in the name of Christ forced millions to an adulterous estate to gratify Christian lust and greed— this monster, which not only had survived the Dark Ages but grew daily more horrible in character and aspect with the advance of civilization, is at least no more! Not only in our land but in all the earth slavery is dead! Only the evil stench of its decay remains to offend the moral sense of man!

Caste, the twin demon, is yet to be destroyed. Let the life of Frederick Douglass be an example to those who must take up the conflict where he was obliged to lay it down, and a warning to those who would put aside and cover up the wrongs done today, in the name of science and of that new God which measures human rights, not by manhood, but by race and color, making the shallow claim of a supreme superiority the excuse for wrong. A nation, a civilization, a Christianity, which within one man's memory upheld slavery with all its horrors should hesitate to proclaim anew its infallibility. The land, which gave a million lives to destroy the demon Slavery, should beware of enthroning in its place the fouler and more dangerous Moloch, CASTE!

As slave, freedman, citizen, and patriot, Frederick Douglass' life was such as to reflect fame upon his people, credit upon those who listened to his admonitions, renown upon the nation, which finally recognized his merits, and honor on all who do honor, to his memory. Within this fane dedicated to liberty and the memory of noble sons of the Republic, no worthier life has been commemorated.

21

The Literary Quality of
"Uncle Tom's Cabin" (1896)*

Contemporary critics often compared Tourgée's fiction with that of Harriet Beecher Stowe, particularly her great antislavery novel, *Uncle Tom's Cabin* (1852). In this short piece of literary analysis, published soon after Stowe's death in 1896, Tourgée discussed both the shortcomings and extraordinary achievements of *Uncle Tom's Cabin,* and revealed much about the novel's considerable impact on his own fictional explorations of race and slavery.

The death of Mrs. Stowe invites attention again to that literary marvel which has not only outstripped all competitors for popularity but bids fair to maintain a permanent superiority over all works of fiction in power to touch the universal heart. Through its various translations and dramatizations it is beyond question that this book has become known to more persons than any other work of fiction ever published. Translated into all civilized tongues, and into some that can hardly claim to rank as such, it has met at once the approval of all types and classes, especially that of the most intelligent, unselfish and devoted.

Even if we accept the idea that popularity is no test of literary merit, we must admit that exceptional popularity can only be accounted for by something exceptional in the literary quality or the work achieving it. There are three books of English fiction which easily excel all others of that character in the number of readers they have had and in the extent and permanency of the demand for them on the part of the best elements of all peoples. There are Bunyan's "Pilgrim's Progress," De Foe's "Robinson Crusoe," and Mrs. Stowe's "Uncle Tom's Cabin." These three books stand by themselves so far beyond all others, that it may be said of them, as of the great race horse in his supreme effort, "There is no second!" The first has maintained its place for two hundred

*"The Literary Quality of 'Uncle Tom's Cabin,'" *The Independent* 48 (August 20, 1896): 3–4.

and twenty-five years, the second for one hundred and seventy-seven years, and the third for forty-five years. Yet one was written by an imprisoned tinker, another by an imprisoned bankrupt, and the third by a woman who so little realized the character of what she had done that she wondered if the book would yield her enough to buy a black silk dress!

The attempt has been made to account for the amazing popularity of two of these works by attributing it to the themes of which they treat. It has been pointed out that missionary societies and antislavery organizations have adopted them as a favorite means of propagating their ideas. This is simply mistaking effect for cause. They are so because of their popular qualities, instead of becoming popular by such use. The same explanation, in effect, has been offered for the popularity of "Robinson Crusoe." The critics tell us that on its first appearance it had the most amazing "run" ever known in the history of literature up to that time, because it "happened to strike the temper of the time." This explanation is as enlightening as if they had said it was popular because people liked it!

We are also informed by the critics that "the style of 'Uncle Tom's Cabin' is very faulty and inartistic." Just what this means it would be difficult to say; but it may be admitted that there is no fine writing, no smartness, little wit, and scarcely a trace of humor in it. So, too, there is no "elaboration of character," as the phrase is used in regard to modern fiction. There is no pessimism and not a hint of that tendency to morbid anatomy which inclines a modern novelist to take some pages to explain an act that requires but a single sentence to relate. There is nothing inexplicable about it; one feels certain from the first what the end will be, but is none the less anxious not to miss the sequence of events from which it is to result.

What then is the secret of this perpetual charm which keeps its hold on each succeeding generation? An author who addressed himself seriously to the task of answering the question so far as "Robinson Crusoe" is concerned, came very near giving an explanation when he said that "the book has a peculiar charm for the imagination, depending chiefly on an indefinable sense of reality that pervades the whole narrative." There is no doubt about the "sense of reality" which these works possess, but is it "indefinable?" Let us see what literary qualities they have in common and from them we may adduce some of the reasons for this reality and so arrive at the cause of their exceptional popularity.

In the first place, we note that each deals with a single thought, a thought that is of world-wide and undying interest. The subjects are, respectively, Sin, Solitude and Slavery, considered not as abstractions but in their relations to specific human lives, under known or clearly defined conditions. These fundamental ideas are never allowed to drop out of sight. We carry Christian's pack until he loses it. The abiding sense of isolation from even the hint of humanity fills every page of "Robinson Crusoe," until the man Friday comes to intensify by his unlikeness to the Solitary, the previous sense of remoteness.

In "Uncle Tom's Cabin" this adherence to the central theme is doubled in force by the great variety of typical lives over which the shadow of slavery is shown to be cast. It goes with the reader's consciousness from the beginning to the end. Hardly a sentence can be found which, taken in its connection, does not tend to deepen the impression. The master and mistress as well as the slave, even the child of the dominant race, show in degree according to temper and environment the scath of evil, which spares not the doer any more than the victim. Nothing is allowed to obscure this idea for one moment. If for an instant our attention seems to be drawn away from its contemplation some expected turn in the path we are pursuing brings it again into view. From Kentucky to the Red River country, from Canada to New Orleans, we are taken only to find the baleful light of greed-inspired oppression blasting every life on which it falls.

Again, it is not realistic according to modern ideas of realism. There is an astonishing lack of detail and environment in it. The particulars of slave-life—labor, separation, deprivation, torture—all are left to the reader's imagination. Only the facts are stated, and these in the most commonplace way. There is no more affecting narrative in literature than that of the sufferings of Uncle Tom on the plantation of the "typical fiend, Legree"—the universal human monster made more horrible by the license and immunity which slavery granted to him as well as to the best of masters. Yet we only learn of the brutality by its results. Through the whole book unnecessary details are excluded with a rigor that gives the effect of baldness when compared with the efflorescent irrelevancy of our modern fiction. Description and conversation all bear upon some phase of the one thought whose pathos impregnates even nature with a newer and deeper significance. Its characters are all potential types—not externally studied examples. Its white men and women are New England natures with a curious Veneer of torpid conscience. Even the saintly Eva is a New England prodigy of precocity—an impossible product of Southern life, but a very comprehensible fact of the world-life, and seems all the sweeter for its incongruous surroundings.

Not only are the white characters of "Uncle Tom's Cabin" essentially New Englanders, but the colored ones are in intellectual and moral qualities simply "blacked Yankees." This is shown in their predilection for casuistry. As a matter of fact the slave was not given to subtle theorizing. His past had effectually repressed any tendency he might otherwise have developed to discuss his hopes and fears, rights and wrongs—and men do not argue with those who have the power of life and death over them. Through all the book there is a freedom of expression, an effusive interchange of ideas between master and servant which is quite foreign to the conditions of slavery and which, no doubt, goes far to account for the fact that the man who has been a slave and comes afterward to read it, is rarely impressed, as the one who has been a free man all his life is sure to be. Perhaps the most striking characteristic of slavery was the secretiveness it imposed upon the slave nature with regard to himself, his thoughts, desires and purposes. To the slave, language became in very truth an instrument for the concealment of thought, rather than its expression. Only in moments of rapt religious excitement did he fully unbosom himself and then only in figures but half-intelligible to those not kindred in experience. Uncle Tom was not only a Yankee in his love of speculation but a Quaker in meek self-surrender. It is doubtful if slavery ever produced exactly this type of religious enthusiast. Those it did bring forth were not cool casuists, but either silent, self-absorbed dreamers, or flaming zealots; but Uncle Tom, like Eva, was potential rather than actual.

I have been much interested in tracing the effect of this book upon those who have themselves been slaves. During fifteen years succeeding the close of the War, I was a resident of the South, and had peculiar opportunities for knowing the most intelligent colored people in the former slave States. I had "Uncle Tom's Cabin" read to a large number of these, and afterward questioned them in regard to it. Almost every one of them noted the freedom of speech between master and servant. Said one of the shrewdest and most thoughtful:

"Seems like that Uncle Tom must have been raised up North!"

"Mrs. Stowe didn't know much about niggers, that's shore," said another.

A blind man, whose daughter read the book to him, gave as his comment: "She didn't know what slavery was, and so left out the worst of it."

"What was that?" I asked.

"I don't s'pose you'll understand, sah ('pears like, no white man can), but the worst thing 'bout slavery, in my jedgment, sah, was that it took away all the ter-morrers!"

He meant that it destroyed hope, aspiration, desire for betterment of individual or collective conditions. As it happened this man was also named Tom.

He was for years a familiar presence to me, and I shall never forget the look upon his face as he turned his clear, but sightless eyes toward me and gave this trenchant criticism of the immortal work to which his race is so greatly indebted.

It was this experience which first suggested to me that the popularity, and consequent influence of "Uncle Tom's Cabin," was largely dependent on its non-realistic character. It portrayed a slavery which the free man could understand and appreciate. If it had been absolutely "realistic" in its delineation of the master and the slave, it would have been to a degree incomprehensible to those who did not, and do not yet, comprehend the moral and legal character of the "peculiar institution."

Judging from my own experience, I doubt if anything like a just and true comprehension of slavery as a social institution could possibly have been imparted to the Northern mind unused to the daily study of its manifestations. Discussing the matter with a noted Southern jurist after the close of the War, he truly remarked that "Slavery is so great an anomaly to the Anglo-Saxon mind, that no one can at all comprehend it who has not lived long within the scope of its influences, and only the lawyer who has to study its legal relations can really be said to understand its character."

The ideal presented in "Uncle Tom's Cabin" is readily appreciable by an individual reared in a free community. I well remember how vividly it impressed my own young mind. I pitied the average slave owner, whom I supposed to be fairly represented by Shelby and St. Clare, almost as much as I did the slave himself. When I came afterward to study both at close range for fifteen years, I was amazed at the erroneous character of my preconceptions. That I found master and slave both better and worse than I had expected would not have been a matter of great surprise, but with the lapse of years they revealed themselves to me as essentially different—shaped by forces I had not understood—the slave a product of a barbarized civilization, the master a still stranger product of a sterilized Christianity.

Slavery is abhorrent to all free peoples, that is, those accustomed to the general enjoyment of personal liberty, but in the dominant race of a slave-holding community there is little question of its ethical propriety, and I have no doubt that had either class been truly depicted to my mind when it was still without the special knowledge derived from study and observation, hate would have been aroused rather than pity if, indeed, the narrative had not been rejected as wholly false. The question then is not whether "Uncle Tom's Cabin" was a "literary" masterpiece. The fact is that in its ingenuous portrayals it reflected the pictures that had been vague and indistinct in a million minds, but which crystallized in sharpness by its unconscious conformity, became for the nonce a national ideal, and as such accomplished results that would have been impossible to a catalog of minutely studied dialect and customs.

IV

RACE AND CITIZENSHIP
IN THE 1890S

22

A Bystander's Notes: White Caps (1888)*

The December 15, 1888, installment of A Bystander's Notes marked the beginning of Tourgée's coverage of lynching, which would become a major theme of his weekly columns for the *Chicago Daily Inter-Ocean*. Focusing on the "White Caps" of Ohio and Indiana, he ponders the implications of northern vigilantism on the political culture of the North and examines the spread of white mob violence in the context of his own previous encounters with the Ku Klux Klan.

The repulse of the mob of lynchers by the officers in charge of the jail at Birmingham, Ala., has received the attention it deserved from the public press from its very exceptional character. It is worthy of note, however, that while most of the Northern papers improve the opportunity to read the people of the South a severe lecture on the desirability of suppressing this form of lawlessness, they are almost universally silent regarding the amazing increase in this class of crimes at the North of recent years. The Bystander's attention has been especially directed toward this matter by the fact that he has always believed that the tolerance exhibited by the people of the North for the unprecedented series of outrages which marked the victorious career of the Ku-klux Klan, indicated a corruption of public sentiment which would sooner or later prove detrimental to the administration of law and the preservation of order in these States. For a long time lynchings had been very rare in the States of the North, but since 1880 almost every one of them west of New York has been the scene of at least one, and usually of several, affairs of this sort, and the tendency seems to be growing every day stronger and stronger in that direction. A table of reported lynchings during the past eight years would be very interesting reading, the lessons of which would by no means be confined to the South or the far West.

*Albion W. Tourgée, A Bystander's Notes, *Chicago Daily Inter-Ocean,* December 15, 1888.

Akin to this disregard of law which manifests itself in the rescues of criminals from the hands of the law in order to execute upon them a summary
vengeance is the regulation of private morals and the gratification of personal
malice through the agency of secret, disguised bodies of men assuming to
be for the public good for such bodies the name White Caps has become
generic, as did the term Ku-klux for similar unlawful organizations at the
South. Indeed, there does not seem to be any material difference between
the Ku-klux and the White Caps, except that the former paid less attention
to the regulation of private morals and more attention to political action and
inclination. It is, of course, possible that the present epidemic of organized
violence, especially in the States of Ohio and Indiana, may subside of its own
accord, but such is not at all likely to be the case. The history of such organizations as the Molly Maguires and the Ku-klux does not, indeed, point in
that direction.

The impunity with which the law may be defied by such organizations,
in a community where even a considerable minority are disposed to tolerate
their existence or have become implicated in their crime, has never been better illustrated than in the fact that while they have openly and boldly defied
the law, especially in the States of Indiana and Ohio, the authorities of neither
State have ever been able to punish any of the offenders and only in one or
two well authenticated instances is one of the assaulting gang known to have
received any damage. A few years ago when the Ku-klux were riding up and
down through the South, whipping, mutilating and murdering almost at will,
the people of the North cried out in incredulous wonder, "Why don't you kill
them? Why don't you shoot them? Why do you permit such things to take
place?" Now let them answer the question themselves. They have no mass of
helpless ignorance to look after. They have only intelligent men to deal with.
Yet the White Caps are said to have absolute control of one county in Indiana
and within a few days have made two or three "raids" in Ohio.

It may be said that these White Caps claim to be good citizens and to have
the interest of the community at heart. It has been customary to assert that each
victim of their lawlessness has been guilty of some real or imaginary crime, or
of a suspected purpose to do some evil. No doubt this is generally true, but it
only makes the act of the marauders more dangerous to accept this as an excuse.
The fact is, there can be no excuse for such acts of violence. The law provides
a way for the punishment of crime and the general acceptance of any pretense
as to the character of the person injured, as in any manner excusing this most
dangerous form of lawlessness, can of necessity only result in its extension

and the consequent degradation of the law as a means of personal protection. The tendency of this sort of violence is always to extend itself. It is rarely if ever self-repressive. One excuse for illegal violence readily generates another. The pretense of subserving the public good soon drops away and personal revenge or the gratification of any individual desire soon takes its place. Those who once became participants in its crimes are thenceforth under the power of the organization, and no matter how lax may be its organization the bands by which it holds its members grow stronger and stronger with every crime to which they may become, it matters not how unwillingly, parties or privies.

The States in which these forms of violence are becoming prevalent should take warning in time and provide efficient legislation for their effectual restriction. There is no knowing at what moment the disguised law-breaker may develop into the organized and irresistible enemy of social order. Thus far no common cause has offered opportunity for this solidification of the Northern Ku-klux, and the remedy should be applied before the disease assumes further proportions.

Three species of legislative enactment should be adopted without delay in the States where this curious disease of our modern civilization has appeared. The first of these should carefully define and prescribe extreme penalties for the offense of riotous assemblage for the purpose of interfering with the course of public justice, and affixing heavy penalties to the incitement by speech or writing to such assemblage.

The next should make the going about in disguise in the night-time a misdemeanor, and for any unlawful purpose or in companies sufficient to produce apprehension or terror on the part of the citizen, a felony.

The third class of legislation should distinctly extend and apply the common law of conspiracy so as to make every member of such an unlawful organization individually responsible for its deeds, both civilly and criminally, so that a man may know when he engages in such a foray or joins such an organization just what liability he is incurring. Many a man who would not hesitate to brave public opinion or risk public prosecution would not think of imperiling his estate. The example of the Ku-klux Klan should be sufficient to awaken every good citizen to a sense of possible danger from organized violence and disguised lawbreakers.

23

A Bystander's Notes:
The Kemper County Affair (1889)*

This January 5, 1889, installment of A Bystander's Notes follows up on Tourgée's earlier report of an incident of white mob violence in Kemper County, Mississippi. As more reports on the affair became available, he brought them to the attention of his readers. Intertwined with his description of the "facts" of the incident as reported, Tourgée speculates on the motives behind such attacks, and analyzes the social meaning of racial violence in the South.

Another chapter in the "race conflict" at Wahalah may be found in the dispatches of today. It will not be new to the readers of the INTER-OCEAN. The Bystander had already outlined its incidents before they were reported. It needs no prophetic vision to foretell events when the peaceful white man rises in his wrath to rebuke the savages of the negro "desperado." There is no need for law; judge and jury are easily dispensed with, and the "wild justice" that bubbles instinctively in the Anglo-Saxon breast asserts itself against the "nigger" in a way to carry terror to every black heart, and brings tears of unalloyed delight to every white-skinned Christian.

While the lads of Kemper County were ringing out the glad chimes of the Advent time, the "man-hunters" were abroad upon the hills after the fashion of "the good old-times." The crack of the rifle tells how vengeance followed the footsteps of those who were offensive to the godlike race to whom the earth has been given as an undisturbed possession—who have by Divine endowment the indispensable right to put all things under their feet—more especially "niggers." Within four days of the blessed Christmas-time the "man-hunters," not only bagged four more "niggers," but confiscated their estates. The bloody record of Kemper County in the past had been equaled, if not

*Albion W. Tourgée, A Bystander's Notes, *Chicago Daily Inter-Ocean*, January 5, 1889.

surpassed, by a score of other loyalties. Its tale of murders was hardly worthy of mention compared with a dozen other places. The leaders in its former massacres had been poorly rewarded. One of its defenders, it is true, has been exalted to the Supreme Bench, but no one has yet received a Senatorial commission with a hand red with actual slaughter. No voice echoes proudly from the huntings proclaiming the undying glory attaching to the slaughter of an imprisoned man to compare in its clarion defiance of the craven North with the glorious notes of the South Carolina candidate who hardly three months ago declared:

"I proclaim it aloud that I was one of the Hamburg rioters who dared even the devil to save the State from the radicals and keep the niggers in their place."

That is the sort of credit that Kemper County lacked. Of course the merits of those engaged in its most notable massacre were readily admitted at home, but nobody had been inclined to boast of it abroad or been recognized as a patriot or a hero by the Nation at large on account of it. I order a secure proper recognition as the most notable battlefield of that impending conflict between the white-skinned lovers of justice and liberty, and the eight millions of "nigger desperadoes" whose industry, prosperity, and growing intelligence are a constant menace to the peace of the South. It was necessary that something should be done—something new and startling—something that would keep Kemper County in the very front rank of the assertors of Southern right and appropriate and heroic formulators of Southern doctrine. Thus far the county has been notable only as the scene of a slaughter exceptionally cowardly and brutal, even in the bloody catalogue of cowardly brutalities of the Ku-klux.

With the Christmas of 1888, however, Kemper County, Mississippi, has put itself in the very van of "Southern progress." Not only is the record of its murders a most creditable one, but they have been managed with such prudence and sagacity that they are not longer spoken of as "killings," but as "disappearances!" The actual number of these "disappearances" it is impossible to ascertain. Even the bodies are not left above the ground to testify against the authors of "disappearances," but they are decently interred and the pathetic prayer upon the tomb of Shakespeare is transposed into a threat which all are required under a penalty of it into refrain from meddling with the bones deposited under the unpretentious mounds.

This is an idea of which Kemper County has reason to be proud. It will undoubtedly be adopted throughout the South in all future "race conflicts." Hitherto the custom has been to leave the ebon corpus of the defunct "nigger desperado" to cumber the face of the earth, afflict the sight of the well-disposed, taint the air, and invite the attention of buzzards. Under these circumstances it was almost impossible to avoid unpleasant publicity. Not only buzzards and "niggers," but the elements themselves conspired to invite attention to the untimely taking off of one dangerous in the public peace. It is hardly fair to expect a coroner to be entirely blind and deaf and one who was not devoid of these two senses could hardly fail to take official notice of such "disappearances." In fact they could not properly be called "disappearances" at all. Under this system a dead "nigger" was visible, or at least appreciable to sense even farther away than a live one. Kemper County has avoided this difficulty. Of course nothing may come of a coroner's inquiry, but it gives an unpleasant notoriety to little affairs of this sort, and is apt to deter well meaning Northern men from going to a particular locality and investing their money for the public advantage. It is no doubt a little troublesome to bury the dead and it is pleasant to leave the evidences of the noble white man's prowess where it can be seen of all; but the advantages of at least shallow burial of the victims of "a wild and holy justice," is too evident to need to be enlarged upon. The coroner is not likely to mind the assembling of the buzzards, and the negroes are not likely to insist on any body being executed which the white man have once honored with a decent burial. Thus far Kemper County is in the lead in the new struggle of their heroic sons for freedom, home rule, and a white man's government, which her leading thinkers declare to be her destiny.

There are some features of the Kemper County affair which should scar the eyeballs of every honest and patriotic American. They are not new, but hitherto have not been considered worthy of any attention by the body of the American people. The Bystander has called them to their consideration so often that he is half ashamed to recount them here. The first and most noticeable fact is that all of the four last victims of the patriotic "man-hunters," were peacefully engaged to industrial avocations at the time they were killed, and that all protested their innocence—not of any unlawful act, since no such charge was made against them—but even of any knowledge of any of those who resisted the attempt to "demonstrate" with them with shot-guns and Winchesters.

Both of these acts are naturally irritating to the patriotic upholders of a white man's government at the South. A negro working under an overseer is an edifying and delightful spectacle to such men, but a "nigger" working for himself is a natural and continuing insult. If a "nigger" is allowed to work for himself and enjoy the profits of his own labor, what is to prevent his buying land, making money and driving his own team on the highway while respectable white men, who can not descend to servile labor, are compelled to go on foot? Besides that it is plain, downright "insolence" for a "nigger" to deny anything a white man may charge him with. What is it but saying that the white man is a liar? Such language from a "nigger" is ample justification for his "disappearance." This is no new doctrine; it has long ago been formulated and enforced as "a part of the common law" by the courts of these States. It is written in the volumes of their reports:

"Insolence from a free white person of color to a white man will excuse a battery to the same extent as a blow from a white man."

That is the law—that is the sense of justice toward even the "free white person of color" which the courts of the South—the legal and sworn protectors and justifiers of slavery, implanted in the hearts of the Southern people. The killing of a negro who denies a charge made by a white man is only a natural result of such teaching; the sentiment which permits it, is only the natural fruit of slavery—the unjust domination of one race and the unjust subjection of another.

All that has been said above is emphasized by another circumstance which is noted in the report. It will bear thinking about, if the people of the country have any time to think about justice and right for a man with a black skin.

"ALL THE NEGROES KILLED OWNED LITTLE FARMS"

They were thrifty men, ambitious men, such men as add to the wealth and prosperity of a State. We shall see pretty soon that they were enterprising men who had taken advantage of beneficent provisions of the law of the United States, and "entered" land as home stealers. It is probable that they had nearly completed their payments, for they had put valuable improvements on the lands, houses, barns, cotton-sheds, and in one case a steam engine. Apparently they were among the best of their race.

But appearances are often deceitful. As a rule the "nigger desperado" is among the most industrious and intelligent of his people. He is almost always "well fixed." It is this that makes him impudent. As soon as he gets a little "fore-handed," he is sure to grow "sassy." Of course no white man "who is anything" can stand that. The result is that about nine out of ten of the thousands of "nigger desperados" it becomes necessary to kill every few years to protect the white race from negro rule, will be found to have been occupants of their own houses or men who were likely to become such in a short time. It is a most deplorable fact, as far as the colored race is concerned, that so many of the strongest and most promising of them should so deteriorate under prosperity as to make their taking off a matter of absolute duty. "A mere act of self-preservation" on the part of the white race!

There is another instructive circumstance connected with the death and burial of these unfortunates. They were all of them, it seems, married men; two of them had children. Even the Kemper County heart, it would seem, must go out to the widow and the fatherless about Christmas time. But the report, which is evidently intended to excuse the acts of the "man-hunters," goes on to say with brutal frankness:

"All the dead men's farms have been relocated at Dekalb (where the United States Land Office is located) *by white men!*"

It looks a little tough, but the Supreme Court of the United States long ago taught the doctrine that a "negro had no rights a white man is bound to respect"! Who can wonder that the "man-hunters" of Mississippi should be on the lookout for improved homes while they were busy bagging and burying ebon game? What business has a "nigger desperado" with the land belonging to "a white man's government," anyhow?

There is another thing that seems a little hard perhaps, at first sight, to a soft-hearted Northern man who counts it the most creditable thing of this life that he once wore the blue and helped save the country—if indeed it can be said to have been saved!

The report tells us: "Anthony Wilder, one of those killed by the 'man-hunters,' was a Union Soldier who was with Grant at Vicksburg"!

Don't stop to grow sentimental about it, old comrade. Remember that our own G.A.R. refused to organize posts and departments for colored soldiers of the South—refused to allow them a chance to wear the button, which our daughter burnishes with pride as an emblem to her father's heroism, lest the sight of it in a black man's breast should prove offensive to the tender-hearted patriots who "wore the Gray"! It is a little tough that this dark-skinned veteran should not only lose his life, but the homestead on which he was counting in the period of enlistment which gave an obviously unfair advantage over his white neighbor. What business had a nigger "with Grant at Vicksburg," anyhow? It is a strange thing, too, that it has become absolutely necessary to the peace of the Southern States to put out of the way an amazing large proportion of the few colored veterans who have been fools enough to think that the flag for which they fought would give them any protection in person, privilege, or estate, that might be in anyway offensive to the patriotic and peaceful supporters of a white man's government.

There is one more feature of this new race war, so old as to be laughable. The reporter concludes:

"It was simply a neighborhood row"!

That is all. There is peace in the New South which holds out its hands to immigration and welcomes Capital! As long as "nigger desperadoes" improve homesteads and white men "re-locate" them lands ought to be cheap in Kemper County!

24

A Bystander's Notes:
The Afro-American League (1889)*

In this November 2, 1889, installment of A Bystander's Notes, Tourgée discusses
the upcoming national convention of "colored men" to be held in Chicago in January 1890, organized by *New York Age* editor T. Thomas Fortune. The purpose of
the convention was to form an organization—later anointed the "Afro-American
League"—to represent the interest of all black Americans. Strongly endorsing
the League, Tourgée explains why he believes white Americans no longer can
speak on behalf of blacks. At the same time, he warns the League's leadership
against the pitfalls of harnessing the collective power of black Americans.

One of the recent facts touching the question of the negro's relation to our
Nation's affairs is the proposed convention for the purpose of organizing a
National league of colored men. The object of such an organization is, broadly
stated, to promote the interests of the colored race in the United States. The
first thing to be done will, of course, be to determine what is practicable for
the negro to do to promote his own real enfranchisement, secure redress of
the wrongs which attach to his condition, and obtain for himself equal and
unrestricted privilege and opportunity as a citizen and in business. From the
point of view of an outsider who sympathizes with the work to be done, believes in the necessity of its being done by the race itself in a large measure,
and realizes the difficulties in the way of its accomplishment, the proposed
organization is a matter of very great importance.

Some Republican journals have seriously discouraged this project, insisting that the Republican Party is devoted to securing equal rights and opportunities to the colored man, and that he needs no other organization to
promote his interests. "What would be thought," asks one, "if a National con-

*Albion W. Tourgée, A Bystander's Notes, *Chicago Daily Inter-Ocean*, November 2, 1889.

vention of white men should be called to promote the interests of the white race?" Well, just such conventions are called and have long been in vogue. Until within thirty years such a thing as the interest of the colored man being considered in any political convention, except by the little squad of Abolitionists who persistently camped upon a neglected corner of the political field greatly to the annoyance of the other occupants, was never dreamed of. Even now the Democratic Party boasts itself a "white man's party," and at the South never professed to be anything else.

In fact, our entire civilization has been either positively or tacitly white. In those regions where the negro has not been actually distinguished against he has rarely been regarded as a fit subject for those influences which develop and exalt.

The claim that the Republican Party is all the organization the negro requires comes with very bad grace from the organs of a party which has shown itself thus far quite unable to deal with the questions touching his rights as a man and a citizen—a party with the record of the inconsistency of 1876[1] upon its shoulders—an inconsistency so glaring that is seems impossible that any Northern Republican of average sensibility should ever ask a colored man to rely upon that party to remedy the evils which attach to his condition, at least until that crime against good faith and common sense has been retrieved.

The simple fact is that the Republican Party is just like any other party. It seeks success and, within certain limits, it advocates and does whatever its leaders and manipulators believe will secure success and avoids what they believe will endanger that result. This is the very highest merit of the party system, which progress yet devised for a self-governing people. Strong, resolute, intense men, looking over the field of public sentiment, adjudge thus idea or that to be uppermost in the popular mind, and so order an advance along this or that portion of the line of policy the party occupies, and expect the rest without abandoning their position to remain comparatively quiet in any particular struggle. It is for this reason that the Republican Party, after twenty-five years of aggressive movement along the line of individual right, thrust again to the front the old Whig principle of protection and fought its battle almost solely on that issue. It was not because it had not abandoned the principle of equal right and privilege, but because the leaders believed that success was more probable if the attack was made on another part of the line. Many

1. Here Tourgée refers to the informal deal that resolved the disputed presidential election of 1876, known to most historians as the "compromise of 1877," by which Republicans abandoned the last of the Reconstruction governments.

of its leaders, both during the campaign and since that time, have favored relegating the question of the rights of the colored man to the background. They have "had enough of the nigger," they say.

This is only natural, but it has an especial significance for the colored man. Whenever he shall make his rights and wrongs so prominent in the public mind that the leaders of the Republican Party are morally certain of defeat unless they shall earnestly and effectually seek to secure the one and redress the other, then their condition will receive its attention and remedial measures of a practical and effective character will be adopted or proposed as an issue on which it will join battle with its opponent. The purpose of such a league as is proposed, should not be either to antagonise or promote the interests of the Republican Party. That is a body quite able to take care of itself. Its object should be to so present the interest and condition of the colored citizenship of the United States to the mind and conscience of the land, that no party will dare ignore the question—to compel the leaders of the Republican Party to make the dance of the oppressed citizen their own, as they once did the cause of the slave. The hope of success is the mainspring of all party action. There may be wheels and balances and escapements, but the power which moves them all is the prospect of success. The politician may clean the works, all the bearings, and adjust the movements, but public sentiment is the key which sets them all in motion and strains the spring which is the continuing motor.

But this is not the true test of the propriety and advisability of such a measure as the League proposed. Organization is the great weapon with which the battles of modern civilization are fought. It is the common instrument by which the strong oppress the weak, and the weak resist the aggressions of the strong. It is the power which arms the hand of capital and makes the protest of labor effectual. The negro race in America represents 8,000,000 of souls having a common interest peculiar to themselves and laboring under specific disabilities. Their first duty to themselves and the world is to organize for the redress of grievances and use the power conferred upon them to compel the granting of equal privilege and opportunity to the negro as a citizen. Let them hunt for redress just as the same number of white men having a common grievance would do—*with a club.*

It is a high time the colored man took up the cudgels for the assertion of his rights himself. There will never be any more Garrisons or Phillipses to fight his battles for him. It is not desirable that there should be. Liberty is a boon that can never be given to a race or a people. It must always be won by those who would enjoy it. All that others can do is to give a race a *chance* to be free. The colored man in the United States has passed the period of tutelage. He must define and assert his strength—make himself felt—if he expects to win equal right and privilege as a man.

The first thing to be done in the assertion of his right is to show that he has power. Establish a colored league in the United States where a solid, earnest membership, large enough in half a dozen States of the North to turn the scale in an election, and the Republican Party will no longer be apathetic in regard to his citizenship at the South. Even the Democracy may begin to have some respect for him. Let the negro of the North use the collective force of his race, not to secure what is termed "recognition"—an office and a little pelf for individuals—but use it as his noble exemplars the old time Abolitionists used their power—to bring fuller liberty to his race at the South. It amounts to nothing that A, B, or C, with a black skin is given an official position in some city or State in the North. It is civil and political liberty for that race at the South that is to be achieved. And this can only be obtained by compelling by united, harmonious action backed by demonstrable power, the active assertion of the rights of National citizenship to supplement and make effective its empty definition.

If the same number of native white citizens of the United States had a like common interest and common grievance there would have been such an organization long ago. Respect is always accorded to power and to nothing but power. Weakness may awaken pity and pity may induce people to give alms; but power or the show of power is the only things that gives equality or serves as a guarantee for right.

We have organizations of Irishmen, Germans, and other nationalities for the benefit of their countrymen at home and abroad. Farmers assert their power as citizens in order to obtain their rights as producers. Workmen band together to defend themselves against associated employers. By all means let the colored men of the country form a National league to secure their rights as men and citizens.

Two objections are made thus far; the one that such an organization will be used by ambitious men to promote their individual aspirations. Very probably, that will be attempted; very likely it may be done to some extent. It certainly would if the members were white and there is no reason to believe that the colored man is exempt from such frailties. That is simply one of the things to be guarded against if possible; if not, the matter will end in failure, and the race must wait until it grows men big enough to see beyond the verge of their own shadow. It is better the negro should fall to repeated efforts at self-assertion for a hundred years, however, than that he should let another year pass by without any effort in his own behalf.

It is also urged that such a movement will make trouble for the negroes at the South. No doubt it will. As soon as the "bulldozer" sees that the colored man is in earnest in his determination to enjoy the rights the Nation has granted him, another epoch of bloodshed is about as certain to be inaugurated as the sun is to shine. It is one of the inevitable consequences of having been once subjected by unlawful force, that such a crusade is certain to be begun against them without any fear of law and in utter contempt of National authority. It will probably require several hundred, perhaps several thousand lives, to organize such a league in the States of the South. It will be deemed that they are "organizing against the whites," and the world will be asked to listen to and believe once more, that fondly cherished lie, that men of Christian character have met together in the shade of night to devise ways and means for "ravishing all the white women in the region," which has so long been declared the prime objection of "nigger risings," or to kill all the white men and burn all the white houses of a county or State. And thereupon a few "niggers" will have to be slaughtered here and there, to preserve "the peace of society," in defense of our white civilization and the assertion of Christian purity!

These things must be expected. The question to be solved is whether the colored race in America has yet developed martyrs enough . . . to make such a movement effective. It has produced thousands who have died in patient endurance of wrong, has it yet grown men brave enough to die—one—ten, a score, it may be—in every county of the South to secure their liberty? Such men will not die in vain. Those who come after them will dip their garments in their blood and press forward all the more steadily. There is nothing like the blood of martyrs to establish a good cause. They must furnish their own martyrs, however. The blood of the stranger has done all it can for the American negro. There are some who believe the race is equal to the emergency. The Bystander is one of them—but it is not certain that any very large number of the white people, even of the North, stand with him in this faith, or are even very earnest in the desire that the negro should win and wear the crown of real enfranchisement.

Three things are all-essential to the success of this plan: 1. The Method: How shall it be most wisely and surely effected? The question is a very large one, and will need serious consideration. A race which sent 30,000 refugees from bondage to freedom in twenty years with little to help them but the north star, can surely devise means for effecting such an organization. 2. What it shall do: its first work should be to gather and disseminate facts. For this it must devise agencies. With Garrison and Phillips' warfare disappeared also their weapons. The people of the North—the conscience of the country—must now be reached in another manner. How? That is the question to be decided. 3. The man who shalt direct such a movement. Such a man is born of any race, hardly once in a century. Has the negro race in the United States a man of nerve and power and self-forgetfulness enough, who is also gifted with the supreme quality of holding his tongue? Has it a man harsh, relentless and self-centered enough to ruthlessly put down the horde of self-seekers who always spring to the front in such a movement and yet have tact enough to make them all work toward one end? It needs something of Cromwell and something of Parnell, but least of all things does it need eloquence or display. Work, tact, silence, and an utter absence of self-seeking—these are the prime qualities in the head of such a league. With such qualities in a leader commanding the confidence of the colored people and the respect of the country more may be done by such an organization toward the real enfranchisement of the negro and the ultimate settlement of the race problem in two years without effective co-operation with existing instrumentalities by the colored men of the country themselves, acting distinctively and persistently as such, in furtherance of just and fair demands upon our Christian civilization.

25

Is Liberty Worth Preserving? (1892)*

Published as a thirty-two-page pamphlet, *Is Liberty Worth Preserving?* served as
the statement of principles for the National Citizens' Rights Association and
the central text for Tourgée's equal rights crusade of the 1890s. In many ways, it
summed up his view of the "race problem." After persuading the *Chicago Daily
Inter-Ocean* to publish twenty-five thousand copies of the pamphlet, he distributed most of them at the Republican National Convention in Minneapolis in
June 1892. The pamphlet named Tourgée provisional president of the NCRA and
listed among its National Council of Administration such prominent equal rights
activists as George Washington Cable, Louis A. Martinet, and Florence A. Lewis.

When Washington warned his countrymen that "eternal vigilance is the price
of liberty," and Jefferson declared, "I tremble for my country when I remember that God is just," they each had in mind, no doubt, some specific danger
to the liberties of the people they had labored so untiringly to secure. Domestic turmoil and party strife were the perils which the Father of his Country
saw forever impending over the land he loved. . . . He perhaps foresaw that
vexed questions would be left to settle themselves; that evils might be allowed
to grow until they became incurable; that usurpations might go on unchecked
and sectional pride allowed to array itself against the national interests. If he
had foreseen the very tide of internecine war that ebbed and flowed about his
tomb, he could have given no wiser counsel to those into whose hands he
surrendered the fate of the new-born Nation. Every peril that has threatened
the American Republic has come from neglect of duty on the part of the
citizen, from failure to restrict and eliminate known and recognized evils,
from permitting sectional pride to override individual right and defy national
power with impunity, and from leaving the control of public affairs in hands
of self-constituted leaders and their associates to whom self-interest is a more

*Albion W. Tourgée, *Is Liberty Worth Preserving?* (Chicago: Inter-Ocean, 1892).

potent force than patriotic obligation. The perils we have already passed and those which now impend alike have but one origin: the lack of vigilance on the part of the citizen, who has forgotten that he alone can safely stand guard over his own liberties and has left that duty to others. Washington clearly saw that unless the citizen performed his duty, his rights would be usurped and his freedom imperiled. He knew that there was no such thing as putting in a substitute in the never-ending war for liberty.

This was the practical view of the man of action. He did not concern himself with the particular questions that might arise or the particular elements of the new nationality which might thereafter become the cause of strife or the excuse for invasion of personal rights or usurpation of public power. He saw only results and the instrumentalities by which they might be affected. The philosophic mind of Jefferson, who had been the inspirer of the great experiment in self-government, looking at the elements of which the Republic was composed, despite the optimism which inspired his splendid confidence in the people, could not but tremble at her destiny. He did not think of the means, but of the cause—because God is just. He recognized that primal truth of human society, that injustice brings woe to the oppressor. It may be long delayed; but it is inevitable. He knew, too, that oppression was self-perpetuating; that a people who have usurped another's rights never willingly relinquish their hold upon them. Such an evil grows always worse and worse until some great peril or bloody crisis arises and it is forced to yield in whole or in part. What was it that Jefferson saw in the future of the Republic that caused him to tremble when he remembered that "God is just"? He saw one race oppressing another race—one people denying another people their inherent rights. We have been accustomed to say that it was of Slavery he thus wrote. That was but one form of the injustice which he dreaded. It was the principle underlying it which he feared—the denial of the inherent rights of one people, race or class by the action of another people, race or class.

The injustice which made Jefferson tremble, and the lethargy which Washington feared are both elemental in the life of the Republic today, and threaten the rights and liberties of the American citizen far more sensibly and seriously than in that early time.

THE NATIONAL CITIZENS' RIGHTS ASSOCIATION

This organization is a body of American Citizens who seek by peaceful means and lawful agencies, to accomplish two specific results:

1. To remedy an undeniable wrong.

2. To obviate a danger of unprecedented magnitude.

The wrong is the denial of the inherent and constitutional rights of citizens of the United States on account of race, color or political affiliation in twelve States of the Union. The danger consists in the results which must inevitably accrue from a denial of political right and equal civic privilege to eight millions of freemen.

PRINCIPLES OF THE ASSOCIATION

Its members are pledged to aid in the peaceful assertion of the rights of National Citizenship, by every lawful means, in every State of the Union, without distinction of race color or political affiliation.

They deny that a white citizen has any legal rights which do not attach also to the colored citizen, or that a Democrat has a right to exercise any political privilege which is not also freely accorded to a Republican. They maintain that this principle applies to Louisiana just as well as to Vermont, and that wherever the State does not afford ample protection to every citizen in the enjoyment of his legal rights, it is the duty of the National government to secure to him their peaceful exercise and full and undisturbed enjoyment.

They contend that the exercise of free speech, peaceful assemblage, unrestricted discussion of all questions affecting the public welfare, party organization, the nomination and support of candidates are inalienable rights of every citizen of the United States, which it is the duty of the general government to assert and maintain in every part of the National domain.

They believe that the peaceful exercise of the elective franchise is a right of the highest dignity and sacredness to every citizen of the United States who is a legal voter, on the security of which the whole fabric of free government depends and that this right cannot be lawfully taken away from any citizen to whom it once attaches, except as a punishment for crime, and that one race or party has no right to prevent or forbid to another race or party the exercise of any power which they themselves enjoy.

The members of the National Citizens' Rights Association maintain that it is the duty of the general government to see to it that the ballotorial power of one race or party is not ravished from it and unlawfully added to the power of another race or party; and that the ballot-box should everywhere be made as safely accessible to every voter as the letter-box to every correspondent, and its contents a thousand times more jealously guarded; that National government should not only provide an adequate remedy for the denial or impairment of the citizens' right, but should secure the same from impairment, denial or invalidation, by providing everywhere sufficient checks and guards to prevent intimidation, fraud or official malversation in regard to the effective exercise of the same.

They believe that in a large number of the States of the American Union, such rights as freedom of speech, of public assemblage, of party organization and the effective exercise of ballotorial power are no more permitted to citizens of African descent or Republican politics, than is free speech to a Jew in Russia.

"THE LAND OF THE FREE"

That this condition of affairs does exist in all except a few restricted portions of the South is evident from, (1.) The unanimous testimony of Republicans resident therein. (2.) The testimony of all colored citizens, save a fraction altogether insignificant in numbers and character. (3.) The multitudinous declarations of governors, legislators, writers and speakers of the dominant class and party, who strenuously insist upon their right and determination never to allow the colored man to exercise any political control, no matter how great may be the majority of those acting with him.

This testimony is confirmed, (1.) By hundreds of unquestioned and undeniable acts of violence and intimidation which are capable of no other explanation unless it be claimed that they result from a widespread and purposeless barbarity, which is inconceivable in any, even semi-civilized, community. (2.) It is confirmed also by the fact that in the various States, Districts and counties of this region, save a very few, no such thing as a party organization favoring equal rights for the colored citizen is known, or is allowed to exist. (3.) It is confirmed, also, by the inherited bias of the dominant class, who maintained the righteousness of slavery on the ground of a divinely ordained superiority of the white race, which not only authorized them to subordinate and control the colored race but made it a religious duty to do so. The man who could see no injustice in slavery is not likely to regard it as a wrong to deprive the colored citizen of the rights he openly declares should never have been granted him.

But even if there were, as there is not any substantial conflict of authority as to the disfranchisement and intimidation of not merely the colored citizen, but of all who favor justice and equality of right for him it is a universal principle, illustrated by all history, that the testimony of the poor and weak subject alleging injustice, is much more likely to be true than that of strong and dominant denying or excusing it.

Especially is this true when for two centuries and a half the right to oppress the subject race and the absolute denial of every right on their part has been the unceasing contention of the dominant class. A class who for so long a time denied that a colored man had any legal right whatever; or any legal remedy for any wrong, is likely at once to manifest the highest appreciation of his rights as an equal heir of National Citizenship. Indeed, it is not strange that they should be unable to see the absurdity of one rule of right for themselves and a different one for all who entertain views in any respect at variance with theirs, since the domination of Slavery was solely based on force and terror and not only the slave, but every one who advocate his cause, was held to be outside the pale of legal protection.

Besides these confirmatory probabilities, it must not be forgotten that those who thus appeal to National power for protection in their common right of citizenship are practically the only portion of the population of the section they inhabit who were on the side of the Union in the struggle for its existence. Not only did 225,000 of the colored population of the country serve as soldiers in the ranks of our armies, with marked efficiency and fidelity, but an unnumbered host of guides, scouts, spies, and laborers of dusky hue, added to the security of every camp and the efficiency of every army. There is now no longer any room for doubt, in the mind of any reasonable man, that if the colored man had espoused the cause of the South with the same fervor with which he embraced that of the North, there would be two nations shown upon the map where now there is but one.

It must be remembered, too, that the party charged with wholesale nullification of the constitutional guarantees of citizenship stoutly resisted their adoption, and has, from the outset maintained the right of the white citizens of those States to determine exactly what privileges a colored man should be entitled to enjoy within their borders.

Under these circumstances, it is only the very prejudiced or the very ignorant northern man who will dare repeat the absurd and ridiculous statement that the Negro or Republican citizen of the South is allowed the free exercise of his political rights and civic privileges in those States.

THE EFFECT OF DISFRANCHISEMENT

But the coil does not stop here. No class or people was ever wise enough or good enough to have the unrestricted guardianship and control of another class or race. The colored man, set free from bondage, was utterly naked, defenseless, helpless. He had neither tools, stock, land or seed. He was without money, script, or property, save the clothes in which he stood. He had wrought for the dominant race for two hundred and fifty years; had been denied by laws made by the Christian men the right to hold property; to defend himself; to contract marriage; to have a family name or legitimate offspring, and to learn to read and write. He could not sue or be sued, and could appeal to no court for protection of any right or a remedy for any wrong.

Freedom was almost a mockery without the power to assert and maintain its privileges. He was given the rank of the citizen solely that he might be entitled to the protection of the flag he had saved. Deprived of this guaranty of citizenship, he became subject also in other relations. He is a dependent laborer who is fixed by the employing class without power on his part to question or refuse. Accustomed to "controlled labor" these thought they had the same right to dominate the citizen they employed, as the slave they had owned. The result has been to subject him to the will of the employer to a degree almost inconceivable in a region accustomed to free labor. The evils growing out of these conditions are very great and constantly increasing. He is arrested without process; executed without conviction; assaulted without remedy; killed without peril to his assassin.

A few months ago a colored man was hanged in Mississippi. The published report said in excuse that he was "enticing laborers to go to Arkansas with the promise of better wages." It was said that "prominent gentlemen from three counties took part in the affair!" There were no arrests.

Last spring it was reported that the employees of a Louisiana planter complaining of ill-treatment made a break for Arkansas. The employer followed with an armed force. Two were shot. "The others," the report merely said, "were persuaded to return."

About the same time a planter arriving at a station in Arkansas, found one of his employees about to take the train. Refusing to return, the employer shot him in the presence of the crowd, saying that if every one would imitate his example, "there would soon be no more runaway niggers!" No attempt was made to arrest the murderer.

The planters of several states decided to pay but 50 cents per 100 pounds for picking cotton. It is starvation wages. Very few slaves could pick 200 pounds under the most favorable conditions, even with the driver's lash to spur them on. A strike was begun. Thirteen Negroes were killed at one point and several more—the press report said, fifteen—at another, enough to stop the strike at least.

During the twelve months previous to December 1891, the public press has reported seven colored men burned alive in those States, one flayed alive and one mutilated, disjointed, disemboweled and tortured by a mob for two hours before death came to his relief. Suppose they had been white Christians tortured by dusky savages, how many would it be necessary to kill to square the account?

The number of those lynched during the time, it is impossible yet to ascertain, it being nearly as difficult and dangerous to get at the facts in such cases as it was to learn the inside truth with regarded to slavery. The writer has noted more than one hundred.

There can be no reasonable doubt that these are the direct and natural results of four things:

1. The helpless and dependent position in which the colored man was left at emancipation.
2. The fact that the National government has done absolutely nothing to protect him in the right of citizenship guaranteed him by the Constitution.
3. The fact that slavery inculcated one measure of right for the white man and a very different one for the colored man.
4. The fact that organized political opposition to the party in power in those states is prevented by violence and intimidation, so that there are none of those healthful checks by which alone safety and moderation may be secured in a popular government. . . .

THE MUTUAL CONSEQUENCES

The white man is the land-owner and employer; the colored man the laborer. It is to the interest of the white man that the colored man should remain weak and dependent in order that he may continue a cheap and controllable laborer. If he is accorded the exercise of his lawful rights of citizenship he will naturally grow self-dependent, higher-priced and less manageable. Masses act always from their general interest, and no race or people ever accords to a weaker or dependent race anything more of right than the logic of their mutual relation imperatively demands.

The denial of the rights of free speech, party organization and a free ballot to the black and white Republicans of the South involves, also, their political affiliates in every State of the Union. The Republican who votes in Vermont knows that his influence in the government is neutralized by the vote of a Democrat in Georgia who has silenced the remonstrant vote which should have counterbalanced his, by violence of fraud. This was the only point in which slavery really touched the Northern man's right or interest, at least apparently; but he felt, as an ever open sore, the fact that three-fifths of the nonvoting slaves were counted in representation, and that his power as a constituent element of the National will was lessened in comparison with that of the Southern white man in just that proportion. At present, not merely three-fifths but five-fifths of the suppressed and disfranchised citizenship, is counted in representation against the Northern voter.

Injustice and oppression have never any self-remedial force. On the contrary, unchecked evil always goes on from bad to worse. For half a century the cry was that Christianity and civilization would ultimately ameliorate the slave's condition. In the meantime, slavery grew all the while worse and worse —more rigorous, more cruel, more debasing, more insolent, more defiant. What now exists at the South only shows the tendency by which the final outcome may be guessed. It must either proceed to greater hopelessness and infamy, be repressed by external power and authority, or go on until some bloody cataclysm—some appalling horror of blood and tears—startles the world with its barbarity and teaches anew the eternal lesson that justice is the only sure foundation of freedom and prosperity. Outside of these three alternatives there is but one possibility which involves a miracle greater than any ever yet preformed, to wit, that a people should voluntarily and of their own motion, abandon the claim of right to subordinate a race or class which they have oppressed for generations.

The question for thoughtful and conscientious Americans to decide today is whether it is better to allow this evil to run its course unchecked, or to stand up as freemen and demand justice as the true remedy for wrong.

We have yet fresh in our memories an example pregnant with solemn warning. If three millions of American freemen had individually but unitedly, boldly and persistently, demanded the emancipation of the Negro by lawful and peaceful methods, in 1851, there would have been no need of the mustering in of three millions of soldiers to put down the Slaveholders' Rebellion in 1861. Ink is cheaper than blood; ballots a more civilized force than bullets, and the law a nobler weapon than the sword. These are the form the National Citizens' Rights Association propose to employ.

THE DANGER

When we look back at slavery and recognize its atrocity and horror we tremble at the thought that God's justice spared a lethargic and blinded people so long. It is then that we realize the truth which Grant traced with trembling hand upon the margin of his proof-sheets while he waited for death on

McGregor, "No nation can do wrong without paying the penalty," and of that prophetic admission of the just measure of the penalty for this darkest of National sins which fell from the lips of Lincoln in those last days when the end of life and conflict were at hand: "If God wills," he said "that it (the scourge of war) continue until all the wealth piled up by the bondman's two hundred and fifty years of unrequited toil shall be sunk, and until every drop of blood drawn by the lash shall be paid by another drawn by the sword, as was said three thousand years ago, so still it must be said, 'The judgments of the Lord are true and righteous altogether.'"

God teaches humanity but one lesson concerning its duty to man and that is—Justice. Individually or collectively, but one requirement is made of any man or race or class—that they should do to other men what in reversed conditions they would wish others to do to them. This is not charity nor mercy but Justice—measured by the one sure rule of self-demand. The lesson costs a great deal to learn and needs to often be writ down large in blood and tears before nations and peoples will heed its requirement.

THE EXCUSE

It is said in justification of such injustice, usurpation and savagery, that they are "necessary for the preservation of civilization." This is the identical plea on which Slavery based the justification of its inconceivable atrocities. It was "necessary," it was claimed, that the slave who fled from bondage should be tortured; it was "necessary" that those who conspired to achieve their liberty should be burned alive; it was "necessary" that the white man who advocated emancipation as an act of justice should be lashed, mutilated, hanged. All these things were "necessary" to protect "Christian civilization" from the tide of barbarism that would overflow the land should the slaves be set free. Yet for every white man who has been killed by a black hand during their quarter of a century of semi-freedom, a score if not a hundred colored men have been unlawfully slain by civilized white Christians at the South. The civilization which was born of Christian Slavery was based on terror and repression. It had one motive, the ease and comfort, gratification and interest of the slave-owner. All that militated against those it counted "dangerous to civilization."

The present usurpation and nullification is based on the same theory; acts on the same assumption; uses the same methods; avows the same purpose and offers the same justification. Then, the Attorney General of Massachusetts declared that "to free the slaves would be to turn loose upon society a menagerie of wild beasts."

Today, a prominent divine in one of our great cities of the North declares, that the suspension of law, the nullification of constitutional guaranties, the denial of personal rights, the barbarism that puts to shame the horrors of Russian tyranny, are all "necessary" for the preservation of Christian civilization. A civilization based on injustice and upheld by terror and lawlessness is of as little value as a Christianity which stands sponsor and excusant for inequality of right among the children of God. The man who teaches such doctrine in the name of Christ, dishonors the son of God more than they who cast lots for his raiment. Such a minister should receive an immediate call to Hades. He would be very popular there and would serve the Master much better than in an earthly pulpit, since he would endanger the salvation of none of the Father's little ones by proclaiming him a God of cruelty, injustice and wrong beside whom the bloodthirsty deities of the Aztecs were white and clean and pure. A God whose cause demands injustice as the rule of National life and policy is to too monstrously vile to be conceived a possibility, even as a devil. Just such prophets of the "necessity" of crime and cruelty and injustice were the host of ministerial sophists who lulled the consciences of freemen to sleep lest they should heed the moans of the slave and be stirred to demand liberty and justice in his behalf. They would not believe that God meant justice to the Negro or that Christian ethics applied to racial relations, until the horrors of the battlefield quickened their moral natures to the truth.

It is very hard to be just to the weak and dependent. It is much easier to recognize the rights of one whom we fear, than of one who fears us. It is easy to paint the poor as brutish and degraded. Those who dominate and oppress the weak are always the "best elements of society." Why should they not be? They have lived in the light. Ease and wealth have brought opportunity for culture. They are the flowers of civilization. Want has not tempted them. Squalor has not blunted their sensibilities. But oppression has dulled their sense of justice for another race or a class. Contempt has stifled regard for others' rights. The nobility of France was the sweetest product of its civilization but justice was on the side of the Sans Culottes and Liberty sprang from the soil they watered so freely with blood. A civilization seared by the flames of slavery is one of the most dangerous elements of a Nation's life; just as the Christianity which accommodated itself to the infamies of the slave system and became the nurse and preserver of its prejudices, however sincere it may be, is one of the most serious obstacles to the prevalence of that justice which is the foundation principle of Christian duty.

The wrong is moral, legal and political. The colored man is wronged as a man, having a right to equal liberty with other men. He is wronged as a laborer, being deprived of free opportunity. He is wronged as a citizen, being stripped of lawful political power and civic privilege. He is wronged as a Christian, being denied by his white brethren the just and equal application of the Golden Rule. As a man, his appeal to other men cannot long pass unheeded. As a laborer, his cause is that of the laboring man everywhere. As a citizen he appeals to those who gave him citizenship and to those who by political affiliation suffer through the wrong done to him. As a Christian, his appeal lies to all the followers of the Christ who are learning more and more thoroughly the lesson that the tolerated evil of today is universally the blistering curse of tomorrow. Christianity, afraid to grapple with Slavery, finds itself now confronting its resultants, powerless to denounce evil without pronouncing condemnation of its past.

WHO IS FREE?

The Negro is not the only one having a distinct interest in the assertion of the rights of citizenship. Every man in the whole land who believes in the equal rights of citizens of the United States without regard to "race, color or previous condition of servitude," is touched in his own person by present conditions. No man can call himself free who has to wear a gag or put a padlock on his tongue whenever he crosses certain state lines. A party is only of slaves, which is no terror of another party that it dare not attempt to support an organization in a dozen States. No man who dissents from the views of the dominant class at the South is free to express his dissent, except in a few districts, and the Republican party which boasts of having freed the slaves could not include a thousand of its Northern members to canvass generally for it at the South this year for $10,000 a piece. The man who is not free to express his own political opinions in Mississippi is a slave though he may live in Minnesota. There is not a Republican in the Union who has a right to claim to be a freeman—he is only free in certain States. . . .

THE ELEMENTS OF DANGER

In seeking to estimate the consequences likely to result from present conditions, it is necessary to consider the view which the colored man as he grows more intelligent and gets farther from the fact of slavery, is likely to take of the assumptions of the dominant class at the South and his relations to it.

In this connection, it must be remembered that it is always easier and safer to hold a people in bondage where they have no rights, than to deprive a race of freemen of any right to which they believe themselves entitled. Almost every bloody revolution of the world has resulted not from continued oppression, but from an attempt to take away some right or privilege, very often a trivial one, which a people has previously enjoyed.

The Negro is human. One of the chief errors in the Southern views of the race and its relations has been the persistent effort to regard him as different from other men except in certain respects. Especially, is he not supposed to care anything about those rights of person, family and citizenship which the white man prizes more highly than life.

There is also the established notion that he has a sort of instinctive fear of the white man, so that one of the superior race is accounted able to hold in subjection a score of colored men, his equals in strength and perhaps in intelligence. The idea prevails also, that the fear and terror which were the sole means of restraint during slavery, will be equally efficient in a state of freedom. There is too a curious belief that Christianity, which was the right hand of Slavery, teaching as it did, that disobedience was a sin and that the Christian must endure all things rather than appeal to violence or resist with force, will always exert a like restraining influence.

As a matter of fact, all these assumptions are unfounded. The Negro is a man, affected by human motives, keenly alive to the implication of inferiority, jealous of the rights he has once possessed and which he never would have surrendered, but from an abiding faith the government of the United States would ultimately protect the secure him in their repossession and enjoyment.

Intelligen[ce] has the same influence on him as on other men. It enables him to see his wrongs more clearly, to penetrate shallow assumptions of his oppressors and to show him they may be resisted. It teaches him to know his rights, to feel his wrongs. The slave felt but dully the invasion of his family by the ravisher. That the woman he called his wife or daughter should become the victim of the master's lust was a common, every day fact in this world. To the freedman, the fact that his wife or his daughter is insulted, and that the law will afford no redress for the wrong, is a thought which lashes him to frenzy. So too, it is with every distinction of right or privilege between him and the white race. What the slave endured with sullen discontent, the intelligent freeman regards with flaming wrath.

The same is true of Christianity; hitherto it has restrained hereafter it will continually stimulate the sense of wrong and the impulse to resist injustice. They have learned that God is not unjust[,] that he has given the white race

no license to oppress. They do not believe that slavery was of divine ordain-
ment or that the white man has à right to define their rights and privileges
according to his own whim or interest. . . .

CHANGED CONDITIONS

Knowledge is power, whether for good or ill. Every colored man or woman
who has learned to read and write makes the race just so much harder to
control—so much the more dangerous to oppress.

The slave may be held, perhaps, for unnumbered generations by terror. The
habit of subjection is no doubt inherited as well as the impulse of mastery. It
is only with freedom that the real danger to the dominant class begins. What
the slave would endure as irremediable, the freeman resists as unendurable.

The slave, having no rights, thought little if anything of freedom of speech
and denial of political power; the freeman, seeing that all other rights and
privileges depend upon these, counts life not worth having without them.

Christianity, which was used as a weapon to induce the race to submit to
enslavement, impels the freeman to consider the defense of his rights, not
only as the highest duty, but his most exalted privilege.

These motives and impulses are sure to affect the colored man of the future, simply because he is a man and subject to human motives and aspirations. But above all, his relation to his environment will be colored by profound conviction that the philosophy, the political theories and the religious
dogmas on which the oppression of the past rested, are wholly false.

He will not believe that God created one race superior to another. He will
never admit that any accidental superiority gives one race the right to dominate and control another.

He will say that neither wealth nor intelligence gives their possessor the
right to deny to the poor or ignorant a voice in the direction of public affairs.

He will point to the fact that literacy is no guaranty of patriotism; that
the poor man has more need of the ballot than the rich, and that injustice,
oppression and evil come never from the weak and dependent elements of
society, but always from its best and most highly cultured classes.

As he studies history and notes its truths, he will perceive that the condition of no dependent people was ever improved by the voluntary action of the
dominant class; but that betterment has always come from resistance by the
oppressed, through the intervention of some external force or from the co-
operation of these two influences.

THE FUTURE

The precise consequences of an indefinite continuation of present conditions, it is, of course, impossible to predict. Some things may, however, be predicated of the future with the same certainty as if they had already occurred. Among these are the following:

The American people will not long permit a condition of affairs to exist by which free speech and free political action are denied to a great political party in one-third of the Union. The freeman of the North knows that his National Citizenship is of little value if it does not carry with it protection of his rights in every State.

The people of the North will not long submit to see 7,000,000 citizens deprived of political power and economic opportunity, because of "race, color, or previous condition of servitude." It smacks too strongly of that Slavery which it cost so much to overthrow.

Civilization will not permit the permanent subjection of a race once emancipated and enfranchised. The drift of human progress is all the other way, and the fact is beginning to be recognized that the ignorance and poverty of the colored race are neither the result of ethnic qualities nor of individual inclination on their part, but are ineradicable evidences of the reckless greed[,] injustice and neglect of duty of the white race in the past.

The world will not accept the shallow plea with which the dominant class of the South is seeking to excuse the enormities of the past, that they were not responsible for the original importation of the slaves from Africa. It matters not in what ships they came; it was the demand that brought them.

The world will hold the people of the North in a peculiar manner responsible for the future of the Negro in America.

1.—Because the Nation recognized and confirmed slavery by the provisions, limitations and evasions of the Federal Constitution.

2.—Because for eighty-five years it protected and maintained the institution with the full power of the National government.

3.—Because the people of the North denied the truth, paltered with conscience and bowed to the Slave Power of the South, for the sake of gain, finally moving only when necessity compelled, to abolish this most horrible of national infamies.

4.—Because in her hour of peril she appealed to the Negro for aid and without his assistance could not have vanquished her enemy.

5.—Because the people of the North are responsible for the emancipation of the slaves and it devolved upon them to secure to them such opportunity for personal and economic independence as the situation required.

6.—Because the people of the North, acting in the name and on the be-half of the Nation, guaranteed to the Negro the free and untrammeled exer-cise of the rights of National Citizenship and thus far have failed to afford him any protection or means of self-defense therein.

It may also be accepted as a fact that neither the American people nor the civilized world will permit the terrorization of a race by lynchings and barbarities unknown in any other civilized land to continue; nor can assas-sination and violence be recognized in any English-speaking community as legitimate political instrumentalities. Neither can authority, based on murder and intimidation of the citizens, be permanently maintained.

THE ULTIMATE

It does not require any special knowledge or sagacity to know that far as the colored man of the South is concerned, the ultimate result of present condi-tions must be one of two things:

Either the Negro will continue to submit to the unjust and unjustifiable rule of the whites or the time will come when he will in some way endeavor to secure the rights that have been wrested from him.

That he will continue tamely to submit to injustice is extremely improb-able. He is growing more and more sensitive to unjust discrimination and wholesale exaction. If he does continue to submit he will soon be practically reduced to serfdom and become a laborer wholly dependent on a class whose evident self-interest is evidently subserved by their hopeless subjection.

If he refuses to submit, he must either,

(1.) Appeal to the law for the assertion of his rights and the redress of his wrong.

(2.) Demand and secure the co-operation of such moral, political and eco-nomic forces as shall compel the dominant class of the South to accord him his inherent and constitutional rights.

(3.) If these methods fail or the pressure of unjust conditions becomes too great to be endured, there will be nothing left for him but an appeal to that great remedy of the oppressed—the divine law of retaliation which always obtains in favor of the weak and down-trodden when the later law of justice is denied them. Such an outbreak means no one can guess what of horror and devastation. No one can predict its outcome; no one should care to contem-plate it. Unfortunately, the dominant class think that in such an appeal the victory would rest with them. It is by no means certain that such would be the result. A race numbering 7,000,000 driven to desperation is a terrible force to confront, especially when it is so closely intermingled with the dominant race that it cannot be isolated from it. In such a conflict wealth and culture offer certain disadvantages. Property, as well as life, would be the object of attack. The torch, as well as the rifle, would be a chief instrument of offense. Cities may be burned, railroads destroyed, and civilization in all its forms be forced to do penance for injustice and oppression. Whatever the outcome of the strife an inconceivable injury to the country and to civilization would result. Even if it lasted a day the work of a decade might be destroyed and, in any event, a slaughter, unequalled in modern times, would ensue.

Can civilization afford such a result? Can the American people afford it? What can prevent such a consummation? There is but one remedy—one safeguard—JUSTICE!

WHAT THE NEGRO ASKS

The colored race does not demand reparation—thank Heaven for that—only justice, equality of civil privilege, political right and economic opportunity, properly guaranteed and secured for the future. If this is not accorded, resistance, wild and desperate, is as sure to be the final result as the days are to elapse.

Already thousands and tens of thousands of the more intelligent of the race see this and stand ready to demand justice or welcome extermination. The number and determination of these is sure to increase and the result which ordinary common sense sees to be inevitable, those who have watched the condition of affairs and the temper of the race most carefully and with the advantage of wide and unrestricted confidence on their part know it to be imminent.

We are living on a volcano—a volcano fed by the smoldering fires of two centuries and a half of oppression. When or where it may break out no one can tell. We only know that fresh injustice keeps it hourly in a state of probable eruption. It may be a massacre; it may spring from resentfulness at the "Jim Crow Car"; it may result from lynching a man who defends his wife's honor—the cause may be little or great—the result is sure to be one of inconceivable horror. Beside it, the terrors of the French Revolution and of St. Bartholemew's [*sic*] Eve are likely to sink into insignificance. The people of the United States have only to sit still and let this evil grow to its full magnitude as they did with slavery, to secure in the near future this result. Do we want it?

Can we afford it? Enforced ignorance and poverty are unpleasant facts. They are the fruits of oppression for which the penalty must be paid and that penalty is either JUSTICE OR WOE.

It is an inflexible and divine law of human nature that the oppressor must pay in kind for his wrong doing unless he consents to accord justice to the oppressed. That is the universal law of collective human relation. There is no statute of limitation—no excuse—no escape. Woe or justice, such is the inflexible historical alternative.

There are many thousands who believe that the time to avert such a calamity is past. They accept the words of the philosopher who wrote only half-conscious of the truth of the words he uttered: "Whenever violence usurps the place of law and terror becomes the sole reliance of power, the hope of voluntary amendment of conditions is at an end and revolution becomes the only resort of the oppressed."

MAGNITUDE OF THE PERIL

The consideration of these facts must convince any candid mind that the peril of the present situation is infinitely greater than was the apparent danger of slavery. Humanity, civilization, the national honor and sound policy alike demand that the 7,000,000 of our fellow citizens massed chiefly in the former locus of slavery, shall not be allowed to retrograde in development, manhood, or self-reliance. This it is impossible to avoid while they are subjected to the influence of legal discrimination or the assertion of white superiority and right to rule maintained by unlawful force and terror. Neither can we, as a Christian people, permit such a condition to ripen into strife and massacre. The fact that the dominant class belongs to the white race does not in any manner affect their rights as men or as citizens. The white man has a right to render and receive justice—nothing more. The white citizen has a right to equal power and privilege with the black citizen—nothing more. If he takes more he is an ursurper; if he is permitted to exercise more, the Nation endorses oppression and in effect re-establishes Slavery minus only the right to buy and sell. . . .

THE MEASURE OF JUSTICE

The world will not accept the silly plea that mere liberty to go withersoever he pleased, mere freedom of locomotion, was the only obligation due to the colored man, either from the Nation or the people of the South. The slave's labor, up to 1860, was a very large element of the Nation's wealth and almost the sole origin of the wealth of the South. Its staples were the product almost entirely of slave labor. A few white farmers worked the uplands in a slovenly, half-hearted way, winning a scanty self-support rather than adding any considerable amount to the aggregate of production. But the great mass of cotton, tobacco, sugar, rice and what were termed naval stores, were the direct product of slave labor. Southern civilization derived its sustenance almost entirely from slave labor. Its culture depended almost wholly upon the sweat which the lash wrung from dusky forms. It had no system of public schools, but its churches, academies, colleges, were not only built but supported by the proceeds of enforced toil.

The duty of a civilized people towards an uncivilized people—constituting a part of the population of a common country—consists of something more than merely permitting them to exist. Patriotism, elevation, opportunity, are essential elements of such obligation. The duty of the slaveholder and of the Nation which derived benefit from the slave's labor was, at least, to fit him for freedom. They had no right to allow him to remain in ignorance, to compel him to a life of immorality, and to close upon him the door of hope. Because they did these things the obligations resting upon them have been enhanced a thousand fold. While the colored man was forbidden to take or hold property, the white man became seized of all the lands of the South. The colored man cleared them, cultivated them and gave them value. All this as well as the value of the slave's person accrued only to the white man's advantage. The Southern man professes to be the especial friend of the colored man. It is not friendship that will discharge this obligation which accrued in the past. Only justice can wipe it out. The Southern man made exactly the same claim when he held the Negro as a slave. He was his "best friend," he said; treated him kindly and fed him well. Yet there was not one among all the white people of the South who would not rather have died a thousand deaths than have been a slave for a single day. Their kindness never reached to the height of justice. The colored man no longer asks the kindness of mere favor. He demands right, justice, equal opportunity, and stands before the world the most meritorious of creditors, holding a just and righteous claim for reparation which it would almost beggar the Nation to discharge, and asks in payment for past wrongs, only a citizen's right and a freeman's opportunity. The common sentiment of the civilized world will not permit either the Nation or the people of the South to ignore moral obligations of such weight in dealing with the colored race in the future.

ENCOURAGEMENT OF REVOLUTION

There is another view of this question which should not be neglected. The great danger of all republics has been the tendency to revolution. Every American citizen recognizes the fact that the Great Republic is not exempt from this peril. The bloodiest war of modern times has taught us that, if nothing more. But there is such a thing as revolution without warfare—revolution effected by preventing the expression of the popular will or the falsification of that will when expressed. In a republic such a state of affairs cannot long exist without stimulating ambition and leading to usurpation. Then must follow strife or submission.

The peril to be apprehended from present conditions is not restricted to the South alone. There the will of the majority was openly defied and finally overthrown by violence and terror. . . . The shot-gun, the bull-whack, the tissue ballot and laws made by an usurping minority, control and regulate the verdict of the ballot-box. What is the natural and evident deduction from such a state of facts? A child cannot help but draw the obvious inference. If revolution is possible by unlawful means in one State, why not in another? If it succeeds in a State, why not in the Nation? But it is said that "Southern methods" cannot succeed at the North? Possibly not; it is doubtful if any such resolute, determined, thoroughly compacted body of citizens as the dominant minority of the South exists at the North. It is not the methods, however, that are important; it is the fact that such a revolution once accomplished is submitted to, and may with proper care be indefinitely perpetuated. It is said there is no such ignorant and dependent class at the North as at the South. Very true; but it is just as easy to steal from a man who is asleep as from one who is blind. A neglectful citizen is just as easy to subjugate as an ignorant one. David B. Hill stole the State of New York much easier than Wade Hampton usurped the control of South Carolina. Suppose the Legislature should be authorized to choose the electors or the State gerrymandered and they be elected on the "Michigan Plan," what is the result? The National government in all probability, becomes the prize of revolutionary methods. The South, revolutionized by violence and fraud, joins hands with New York, revolutionized by fraud alone, to control the Nation.

Only the clear assertion of the rights of National Citizenship by National authority can prevent the American Nation from becoming the football of reckless revolutionary factions. A nation's life is never secure with an open sore of usurpation within its borders. The evil is sure to spread and blood-poisoning must ultimately ensue. . . .

FORCE OF PUBLIC OPINION

Today the voice of public opinion is more potent in shaping the action of peoples and nations than ever before. A million names upon our roll will command the attention of every phase of the world's thought. It will show the dominant class of the South that the sentiment of liberty, justice and equality of opportunity is not a mere evanescent whim on the part of the Northern people; it will show the colored citizen that he is not to be abandoned to the greed of a type who regard him as without any right which he is entitled to assert against their will and pleasure. It will encourage the "Silent South" to speak out and help avoid the peril which impends. One of the chief misfortunes of the situation, is that the dominant class of the South think, as they did in the days of slavery, that only "fanatics" and a few self-seeking political leaders of the North care anything about the condition or fate of the colored man. A chief purpose of the National Citizens' Rights Association, is to show beyond question the falsity of that notion and let them know that the army of those who love liberty is not less but greater than it was when it spurned the thought of revenge, and asked only obedience to law at Appomattox, and that it asks today only what it then required as the sole fruit of victory.

The National Citizens' Rights Association is composed of American citizens who believe that the power of the Nation is sufficient to avert the present evil as it was to destroy the viper Slavery from whose maw it crept. Whether it may be done without bloodshed or not, we do not know, but we believe that it is the duty of every citizen to see to it that all peaceful and lawful means are exhausted before such a terrible crisis shall occur, if occur it finally must.

They believe that it is the duty of every citizen who desires this to be remedied without bloodshed and who believes in justice, liberty and the free exercise of the rights of citizenship, to personally certify the same in order that the force of cumulated opinion may be brought to bear for the amendment of present conditions. The first object of the Association therefore is to form a roll of the liberty-lovers of the land. No fee is required beyond a two-cent stamp for the return of a certificate. No assessments are made, all contributions being purely voluntary.

At present the organization of the National Citizens' Rights Association is provisional in character, consisting of a President, a council of Administration and an Advisory Committee in each county having a sufficient membership to require it, usually when it reaches 500. The Provisional President makes a report to the Council of Administration each month of money received and work done. No officer has any salary or perquisites.

The only expense thus far has been for stationery, printing and a small sum for clerical work. A roll of the members is kept according to the numbers of the certificates of membership issued also, an autograph roll composed of the applications or membership arranged by state and counties. The first certificate of membership was sent out on November 6th, 1891; on the first of January, 1892, nearly 100 counties had been organized with active Advisory Committees in every State of the Union save one.

The Citizens' Rights Association has no specific remedy for the evils it desires to ameliorate. It recognizes the fact that the amendment of general conditions is always affected by the cooperation of multiform agencies. Its great purpose being to turn the force of cumulated public sentiment upon present evils, it will devote its attention first to ascertaining the extent of the sentiment by extending its membership. It is impossible to estimate the real force of such sentiment until we know how many liberty-lovers there are in the land, who they are, and where they are.

The means at present relied on for its extension, are the personal efforts of members. Application lists are sent to each one and as every one is able to obtain at least a few signatures, the enrollment of those favoring the movement goes on quietly, steadily and with the least possible expense.

When this work has proceeded to such a point as to justify it, it is the intention of the Council of Administration to give especial attention to serving and publishing reliable information in regard to political and economic conditions at the South; to aid in securing the adjudication of questions touching the rights of citizenship. It will use all lawful means to secure just legislation, and, in every way that may offer such to promote and protect the free, and equal exercise of the rights of American citizenship by all entitled thereto.

WHAT NEEDS TO BE DONE?

The need of this work will be appreciated at a glance.

1.—Since the suppression of free-speech at the South, just as in the days of Slavery, one of the most difficult things to do, has been to obtain a just and true idea of the condition of affairs in the various parts of the South, regarded from the standpoint of those who suffer injustice. A chief reason of this is the fear which citizens have of the consequences of giving information, should the fact become known. The National Citizens' Rights Association proposes to remedy this by protecting those who give it information from discovery. No member of the Association need fear disclosure of his identity. Indeed, he need not sign his name, the number of his certificate is sufficient. With

Advisory committees in each state and many counties, its opportunities for ascertaining the facts will be unrivalled. Indeed, the voluntary information already received is amazing.

2.—The mass of legislation which bears unjustly upon the colored man at the South, is but little comprehended by the people of the North. Some of the laws, like the Separate Car Act of various States are openly and professedly class legislation, which a colored minister with fine instinctive perception of true relations, has recently fitly termed, "the cradle of Slavery." Wherever such legislation is tolerated, some form of slavery is not very far away.

In other cases, as in the "amended" Mississippi constitution and election laws, what it is admitted could not lawfully be done directly is sought to be obtained by indirection. In other cases laws have been enacted or construed so as to be peculiarly burdensome to the laborer or that class of laborers who are mostly colored. And in still other cases the administration of the law is made unequal and unjust to their great wrong and oppression.

The National Citizens' Rights Association will encourage and aid, so far as it is authorized by the liberality of its members, the appeal to law and public opinion for the amendment of these evils.

3.—In addition to these, the National Citizens' Rights Association, while not distinctively partisan, will urge by every means in its power, the enactment and enforcement of National legislation intended to promote and secure to every citizen of the United States, the just and equal and untrammeled exercise of all the rights of citizenship in every State of the Union.

What results are possible no one can foretell, but certain things may be regarded as beyond question.

1.—Nothing desirable is ever accomplished without effort.

2.—No great cause is advanced without harmonious co-operation.

3.—If American citizenship is ever to be made less of a farce than American freedom was in the days of Slavery, it must be by the voluntary co-operation of American citizens.

4.—Parties and peoples yield to the force of public opinion, but public opinion can be made appreciable only by individual effort and demonstrable organization.

In this work the same plan will be pursued as in the work of extension, to wit, there will be no assessments. The organization is the voluntary action of its members and it will depend solely on gratuitous contributions to carry on its work, including such sums as may be received for publications made for its benefit. The extent of its work, therefore, depends on the liberality of its members. Whatever can be done with the funds contributed, that it will try to do:

when it is without means its work will cease. Thus far it has not lacked means for the actual work in hand. The contributions have not been large, but with every specific need, the money has been in hand to meet it. No one has been asked for a dollar, but many have been moved to give to help along the cause of liberty and justice.

The Association will not deal in promises but in work, and what it will do depends on the means which are provided to sustain its work.

But the most important duty of this Association will be to induce all citizens to give this terrible question their serious consideration, to impress upon all a clearer view of the peril it involves, and to endeavor to secure from all a recognition of the fundamental truth that JUSTICE is the only cure for wrong and only reliable basis of peace and prosperity. . . .

NATIONAL ORGANIZATION

The following are the officers of the National Citizens' Rights Association.
HON. ALBION W. TOURGEE, Provisional President[,] Mayville, Chautauqua Co., N.Y.
NATIONAL COUNCIL OF ADMINISTRATION.
Rev. J. Bates, Mayville, N.Y.
Prof. W. H. Pierce, Sec'y
Mr. V. A. Albro
Mr. E. A. SKINNER, Westfield, N.Y.
Rev. DAVID BEATON, Chicago, Ills.
Mr. GEORGE W. CABLE, Northampton, Mass.
Miss FLORENCE A. LEWIS, Philadelphia, Pa.
Mr. L. A. MARTINET, New Orleans, La.

It has been decided to increase the National Council of Administration to fifty members at an early day.

ADVISORY COMMITTEES. These are appointed from the most active members in each county, as soon as the membership in the country reaches 500. They are charged with the duty of appointing soliciting agents, and supervising and promoting the extension of the organization generally.

Form of Application for Membership
in the National Citizens' Rights Association.

I wish to enroll my name as a member of the National Citizens' Rights Association for the legal assertion and protection of the rights of American Citizenship, and hereby pledge my aid and support in extending its membership and promoting its patriotic purposes.

Name, ...

Post office, ...

County, ...

State, ...

Sign the above form and send, with two-cent stamp for return of certificate, to

ALBION W. TOURGEE,

Mayville, Chautauqua Co.,

New York.

26

Letter to Professor Jeremiah W. Jencks (1892)*

Tourgée used his new civil rights organization to send letters of protest or so-
licitation to politicians and other influential public figures on NCRA letter-
head. This letter to Cornell University professor Jeremiah W. Jencks (also spelled
"Jenks") provides a striking example of Tourgée's exhaustive effort to police
abuses of the historical memory of the Civil War and Reconstruction, as well
as to challenge the weak Darwinian logic of racial theorists. Despite Tourgée's
protests, Jencks, an influential political economist, nevertheless persisted in his
views, including his later advocacy of immigration restriction on racial grounds
after his appointment as a member of President Theodore Roosevelt's Immigration Commission in 1907.

The National Citizens' Rights Association.

Albion W. Tourgée, President
Mayville, NY   May 26, 1892
Prof. Jencks:

My dear Sir:
I find in several press dispatches of your lecture before the University Extension Society at Albany recently, the following:

"He said that history and science seem to show that the Negro is of an
inferior race and incapable of advanced civilization. When left to themselves,
experience showed that the Negroes rapidly retrograded from a higher civilization to a state of barbarism. In the Reconstruction period, the Negro governments of the South invariably ran the States heavily in debt and passed
shameful and oppressive laws against the whites. In places where they have
advanced, the advancement is so slight as to show them almost as careless and
improvident as the savage."

*Albion W. Tourgée to Professor Jencks, May 26, 1892, item 6273, Albion W. Tourgée Papers,
Chautauqua County Historical Society.

I would be glad to know whether this dispatch correctly represents you. It is as you are aware, radically opposed to the views I entertain after more than a quarter of a century devoted mainly to the investigation and study of current conditions of the race. Of course, you may be right and I may be wrong. I am old enough to have learned that the most careful and extended study, especially, of socio-political questions is very far from assuring any man's fallibility. I believe I wish to know the truth—God's truth—and am willing to accept it whatever it may be, but I cannot accept mere statements, however positive, nor can I believe that superficial study of unrelated phenomena is a secure basis for scientific conclusions.

I do not believe that it is scientifically decided that the Negro is inferior to the white man because I know of no scientific formula by which superiority and inferiority may be determined. Defective intellection may no doubt be often determined by scientific examination, but not intellectual quality.

Again, if it were true that the Negro was inferior to the white man originally, the peculiarity which distinguishes the human family from all other animals, is a capacity to outgrow initial attributes, not by the slow process of natural selection alone, but by reason of their moral and physical environments. The instances are numerous in which the offspring of the most degraded stocks, spring to the very front rank of intelligence and power in a single generation. The development of the Irish American from the bog-trotter is an instance in point.

If therefore, the fact of original inferiority was demonstrable what shall be said of the application of this doctrine to the American Negroes, nine-tenths of whom, according to the last census, show evident traces of white blood, and of whom a noted slave-trader declared that he "doubted if so many as a thousand pure blooded Africans were to be found in the whole country."

It must be remembered, too, that not a single indication of barbarous tendency has been shown by the colored man of the United States. He has kept the peace—no riot or bloodshed has been inaugurated by him since his emancipation, and during that time he has made far greater proportionate progress in civilization, in wealth, in education and in manhood, than the "poor-whites" of the same familiarity with the legislation of that period. For seven years (1868 to 1875) a Judge of the Courts of a Southern State; for three years engaged in the revision of her laws as Code Commissioner; during fifteen years (1865 to 1880) a careful student of my profession in one of those States; an active member of two Constitutional conventions (1868 and 1875); and the author of at least two standard works upon the laws of the State, I had entertained the impression that I had some knowledge of the legislation of the Reconstruction period. I am wholly unable to recall any shred of legislation of that time which was either "shameful" or "oppressive" to the whites, unless you consider the grant of equal privileges to colored citizens to be "shameful" and the taxation "oppressive." Nor do I know a single writer, newspaper editor or stump-speaker of that time who made such allegation.

It is quite true they did regard and allege as oppressive certain legislation —but I cannot conceive that a representative of Cornell University, engaged in lecturing for the sake of "University extension" in New York could lend himself to spread false impressions even to create political capital or seek the favor of the oppressor by falsely assailing the weak. That portion of the Southern people who were opposed to the equal citizenship of the colored man, did indeed denounce as "shameful and oppressive" certain legislation which was deemed not only just but absolutely essential to the establishment of free institutions.

The first of those laws which was deemed "shameful and oppressive" by them was that which permitted a colored man or woman to testify against a white man or woman in civil or criminal matters. One would hardly expect it, but this proposition met with the fiercest denunciation.

Another "shameful and oppressive" law was that which opened the jury-box to the colored man.

It was still worse to permit him to approach the ballot-box.

The rejection of the old presumption that impudent language from a colored man excused an assault by a white man was also considered very oppressive.

I do not recall, however, so much as a scrap of legislation drawing any distinction between the races or establishing any discrimination against the white people and in favor of the colored people in any of those States, and very much doubt if any such can be produced. If you know of any such, I shall be most happy to be cited to it.

It seems to me, that if you had intended to be quite fair in applying the test of racial capacity, you ought to have at least mentioned the legislation of that epoch which tends to reflect credit upon the "Negro" governments, as you call them, as well as discredit. I admit that so much injustice is hardly to be expected. The white man when he dismisses either the Negro's right or capacity, is sadly inclined to insist on all that militates against him and to preserve an impenetrable silence in regard to everything that makes in his favor. To my mind, the character of the legislation of that epoch is a very strong argument in favor of the civic capacity of the Negro who gave the same his assent and support in the first moment of his exercise of the powers of the citizen.

Among these acts of beneficent legislation, all of which were bitterly opposed by those who insisted on the Negro's incapacity for self-government, I might name:

1—The establishment of free public schools. Such a thing was never known in the law of any Southern State until put there by Negro-votes in 1868.

2—The abolition of whipping, branding, clipping, maiming and other barbarous forms of punishment.

3—The reduction of the number of capital crimes from SEVENTY to two or three.

4—The establishment of local elective township governments in stead of the appointive despotisms by which the people had previously been governed.

5—The abolition of property qualifications of voters and office-holders.

6—The abolition of property qualification for jurors, referees and special commissioners.

I might name many others but these were common to all the Stat[es] and establish beyond question this fact that never in her whole history under unmixed white rule, did the South or any single State of the South, advance so rapidly in that legislation which the world over has been the basis of free government, civilization and equal justice to all.

One thing more, I wish to state: as in the legislation, so in the administration and judicature of that era there was an absence of all spirit of revenge which is unprecedented in history and is all the more remarkable because the wrongs which for two hundred and fifty years had been heaped upon the subject race were of the most inconceivably atrocious character, as anyone may know who will read the Slave Codes of the Ante-bellum period and reflect that no people is ever as merciful to the oppressed as its laws enjoin them to be. No man was deprived of his life, liberty or property through oppressive laws or oppressive conduct of public officials. There was neither riot nor sedition instigated by the colored people, but the only violations of the public peace were those directed against the lives and persons and property of the colored citizenship and their friends. For every white man who has been killed by a colored man since the close of the war, at least ten colored men have falled [sic] victims to the white man's irrepressible desire to demonstrate the superiority of his race, to promote civilization and secure Christianity from peril of extinction by "killing a nigger."

In all those twenty-seven years but three[,] possibly four white men have been executed at the South for the murder of a colored person, and not one white man has been punished for the ravishment or seduction of a colored woman.

I do not think these things should be left out of the account when estimating the character and value of the Negro as a citizen. Industrially, he raises about all that is raised at the South except hell, and costs less to govern and maintain, than any other class of equal numbers in our population.

His morals are exactly what white Christian law taught him. They forbade him by law to have a wife or legitimate children; to defend his home, his person or any woman's honor. A white Christian civilization, which for two centuries and a half maintained by force of law a house of prostitution and enforced illegitimacy which at length amounted to five millions compelled to legal promiscuity and without defense or redress against the white man's added lust—such a people should at least have shame enough to be silent a century about the Negro's want of chastity.

One thing can be said in favor of his moral quality and Christian decency —he never enacted a law denying to any race or class the right of legal marriage nor mocked the Christian's God by making the marriage ordinance the cover for a union not intended to be permanent or valid.

I trust you will pardon this letter. The injustice of the utterances ascribed to you and the peculiar prominence that has been given them by reason of your position as an educator must be my excuse for troubling you with any words of mine.

I am too well aware how easy it is to be unjust to the weak and how unpopular it is to protest against a wrong done to an inferior to expect to secure justice from white Christianity who mocks at the pet theories of science, writes His immutable edicts in blood and writes them so large that even the American people cannot fail to read. A half century ago, Science, Christianity and the Constitution of the United States, were the three main pillars on which Slavery rested with all its horrors. Today, Science is voluntarily harnessing itself to the same Juggernaut car of oppression and declaring God's laws of life, of civilization, is merely that which rules the destiny of the brute—"the survival of the fittest." It would have us believe that Society, Government, Religion—even God himself, are powerless before man's inclination to oppress; before lust, brutality and barbarism. They would have the world believe that because the Negro is black, the white Caucasian has the right to rule over him and that it is his destiny to subject and destroy him. To such a doctrine you have done somewhat to link more closely the name of Cornell. God grant that they who teach our young men may learn that there is a truth more beautiful than that which governs the brute's existence and that, two elements of it are justice, equal right and equal opportunity for all the children of our common Father—not to be measured by race or color, but by the law of human conduct given by Mary's Son on Olivet.

Sincerely yours,

27

Letter to Louis A. Martinet (1893)*

Tourgée's letter of October 31, 1893, to New Orleans lawyer and civil rights activist Louis A. Martinet details a critical moment in the background planning for the *Plessy* v. *Ferguson* case. Moreover, it dramatically captures the challenges facing Tourgée and Martinet as they attempted to revitalize the interracial alliance between black southerners and middle-class northerners that had animated the old abolitionist movement. In the letter, Tourgée analyzes the likely disposition of each Supreme Court justice, and frankly warns his clients of the consequences of possible defeat in their case. With waning confidence in the court, Tourgée advises his clients to delay the case in order to mobilize public pressure—reaffirming his lifelong predilection for direct democratic action. Though Martinet and his associates would insist upon bringing the case to the Supreme Court despite its grim prospects, they assented to Tourgée's plan to stir up a public outcry in advance of the Supreme Court hearing. In the end, their efforts to mobilize public opinion failed, and the case was heard in April 1896 against a backdrop of seeming national indifference to African American civil rights.

My Dear Martinet:

I have been having some very serious thoughts in regard to Plessy's Case of late, as my preparation for the hearing has extended.

Shall we press for an early hearing or leave it to come up in its turn or even encourage delay?

I know you will be surprised to hear this from me, and I will explain the reason of it. When we started the fight there was a fair show of favor with the Justices of the Supreme Court. One, at least, had come to regret the "Civil Rights Cases" who had been most strenuously for them. There are now four

*Albion W. Tourgée to Louis A. Martinet, October 31, 1893, item 7438, Albion W. Tourgée Papers, Chautauqua County Historical Society.

men on the court who are not fully committed by participation in those cases. If Hornblower is confirmed there will be five.[1]

Of the whole number of Justices there is but one who is known to favor the view we must stand upon.

One is inclined to be with us legally but his political bias is strong the other way.

There are two who may be brought over by the argument.

There are five who are against us. Of these one may be reached, I think, if he "hears from the country" soon enough. The others will probably stay where they are until Gabriel blows his horn.

The court has always been the foe of liberty until forced to move on by public opinion. It moved on up to the level of the "Granger Cases" and the "Intoxicating Liquor Cases," because the general sentiment of the country was so unmistakably expressed as to have an *enlightening* effect.

It is of the utmost consequence that we should not have a decision *against* us as it is a matter of boast with the court that it has *never reversed itself* on a *constitutional* question.

Now, I do not wish to take the responsibility of deciding this matter without the knowledge of the committee.

I wish you would call them or have them called together and lay this letter before them.

My advice is:

1—To leave the case to come up when it will and not attempt to advance it.

2—To bend every possible energy to secure the discussion of the principle in such a way as to reach and awaken public sentiment.

Of course, we have nothing to hope for in any change that may be made in the court; but if we can get the ear of the Country, and argue the matter fully *before the people first,* we may incline the wavering to fall on our side when the matter comes up.

The prospects of the *National Citizen*[2] are beginning to show so unexpectedly well that I am strongly inclined to say, let the case go over and in the

1. William B. Hornblower, a New York Democrat, was nominated for a vacant seat on the United States Supreme Court by President Grover Cleveland shortly before Tourgée wrote this letter. Conservative Democratic senators, however, blocked his nomination, and Edward Douglass White, a white supremacist and Louisiana Democrat, eventually occupied the seat.

2. This refers to a proposed national journal to serve as the organ of the National Citizens' Rights Association. Tourgée's hopes for "reaching the country" rested largely on the successful launching of this journal, which never came to pass.

meantime array the sentiment of the country against Caste and against the Supreme Court as the ally of Slavery, Secession and Caste. The newspaper press worships the Supreme Court; the people do not. Such an attack would bring the press down upon the *Citizen* but would awaken attention and teach the Court—at any rate it could do no harm in comparison with an adverse decision.

The Kentucky people have been raising a lot of money to push a case from that state. Of course, they are a-way behind us. When they approached me to represent them I showed them the state of affairs and they are now consider- ing the question of asking to have their counsel associated with us and using the rest of the fund in subscriptions for the National Citizen. I think they will probably take 5,000 copies, I [will be?] serving in theirs as I do in yours without fee. If they do this with other indications, we shall be able to start the *Citizen* on a paying basis. If we do so, I have no fear but it will reach a very wide circulation within a year.

This will be of great advantage to the best of the colored papers, as it will bring them into many white homes where there is a desire to know the exact truth.

Please have the Committee advise me of their preference[,] not to relieve me of responsibility, but that I may know what is their view under the circum- stances. At least I do not wish them to be surprised or annoyed at what they might not otherwise understand. I have not written to Mr. Walker[3] about this; as he might not appreciate so keenly the ultimate purpose of the action. As soon as I can gather the inclination of the Committee I will write him fully.

Yours very truly,
Albion W. Tourgée

[Postscript]

The *Crusader*[4] was received last night. You are wrong about the matter of emigration: I doubted it before; now that I understand your view more clearly, I know it to be a mistake. The American Negro will have to make his con- test for equality of right and opportunity with the Negro-hating white man of the United Sates *wherever* he may be upon the planet. If a considerable number of the colored people should go to Mexico, a large white emigration would follow to make or seek opportunity for invasion through them. . . . The lust of conquest is only momentarily slumbering in the breast of our restless masses especially of the South whose people are born-filibusters. The habit of

3. James C. Walker, a white New Orleans attorney who served on the *Plessy* legal team.
4. Martinet edited the *New Orleans Crusader*.

spoiling the colored man has become too strong to be renounced. In a brief time the country would be embroiled in another war with Mexico and as a result the colored men who had fled there for refuge would have to begin the struggle for liberty and right over again with the hopeless condition of alien and discordant races weighing down their destiny. So too if they should go to Africa, the white American would go with them, and at first as a superintendent of emigration; then, as a merchant, a factor, a trader, a planter, and very soon the old contest would be renewed at a distance from the best influences among the American people, and with the power and flag of the Republic protecting and supporting the white man's wrong-doing.

There is no other way, my friend: the colored man must work out his deliverance here in the United States. It is his only hope. Before he can go securely on hopefully to another land, *he must become* an acknowledged equal factor of the American life. When he goes he must have the power of the United States behind him to protect his right, not to deliver him up to the white man's rapacity. There was never yet a Pharaoh in all the world history, who was willing to let a people he had wronged and oppressed go free, and there never will be. Every Israel must win its way to freedom by following God's guidance with courage and persistency, whether it lead through the Red Sea or through the desert towards a fixed and determined refuge, but they can never win by merely fleeing where the very evil they would avoid is sure to follow farther than they can fly. There is but one way: the battle of liberty, justice and equal opportunity must be fought out *here*. The colored man and those white men who believe in liberty and justice—who do not think Christ's teachings a sham—must join hands and hearts and win with brain and patience and wisdom and courage.

There are millions of the white people of the United States who believe in justice and equal right for the colored man. Who desire for him all that they would wish and pray for were they *in his conditions. You know this is true.* There are thousands who have attested it, by faithful service. Think of the millions of dollars they have freely given for the uplifting of the race! Think of that wonderful army of white-souled saints who went out of our Northern homes to face ostracism and ignominy to teach the way of life and self-respectful civilization!

All has not been wisely done. The people of the North did not know your conditions and could not then provide effective remedies. Perhaps you were not ready even for what ought to have been done.

Now, the time has come when both must work on sound, practical lines,

for the special good of your people and the general advancement of all that
American liberty professes and all that Christianity proclaims as its earthly
function. The will, the purpose, the means exist, and *may be reached and united*.
The appeal, and, in some sense, the initiative, must come from your people.
You must unite in making appeal to, and in demanding of the American people and of American Christians, *Justice*. Those of us who already believe must
join with you and echo this appeal so that it shall be heard by all the world.

It is a case in which in union there is strength, and without it weakness.
Without the voice of those white people who believe with you your demand
will pass, as it has heretofore, unheeded. Without both united, there is no
hope of success.

We must have two things: both practical, both difficult, both needing joint
action.

First we must have a *great journal* which shall voice the needs of your
people, the duty of mine and the obligations and interest of both with authority. It must be great enough to be heard by all the world and strong enough to
defy clamor and party. Such a journal should be in the control of both white
and colored men, in order that it may speak with confidence to work for both
races and illustrate the truth it advocates. Such a journal backed by the hearty
support of the colored people will find five white subscribers for every colored
one. It will bring those elements of both races which are in sympathy on these
great questions into substantial and intelligent harmony.

The trouble had been, heretofore, that there has been no way to reach the
intelligence of the North. They have had to take the testimony of the oppressors in relation to the oppressed. The mere race-journal, however well-
conducted, desirable, and brave it may be, is *necessarily restrictive* in its influence and circulation.

Such an organ of human right as is proposed would greatly enlarge the
circulation and enhance the influence of the colored press by sending its utterances into white homes they can never reach otherwise.

With such an organ of united sentiment, we must have also a great land
Exchange House and Trust Company—greater than any ever organized—
which shall enable the seekers for better conditions to shake off the dust of
the South from their feet and find secure liberty and self-support throughout the North. There are hundreds of thousands of small farms lying idle all
through the north waiting for just such willing workers. There are millions of
dollars ready for such an enterprise whenever it is put on a safe and practical
basis. There are millions more across the sea in the hands of people who are

tired of vain speculation and ready for solid, permanent investment, with a prospect of doing good instead of evil, united therewith.

What is required for success?

1—A Method—simple, secure, evidently practicable.

2—The men to manage and direct such a system.

3—The evidence of hearty co-operation and support on the part of the best elements of the colored people.

The last is by all odds, the most important. The two former may be supplied. Already a method that has been endorsed by the best practical brains of the country has been prepared. Men of long experience and special training in this very line, to put it into operation are not difficult to secure as they may be [presumed]. The great question with all investors is, Can the colored man be relied on to co-operate faithfully and truly in such an enterprise? His enemies say he cannot; his friends say he can. There is one way the doubt can be removed—by establishing such a journal as I have indicated. Within one year after that is done such an enterprise may be established which will every year provide scores of thousands of northern homes for self-supporting and self-respecting colored citizens.

It will be done, too—not because I have outlined this course—but because the logic of events shows it to be the only way. It saves the good of the past, minifies the results of its evil and opens the way for betterment in the future. The Southern white man cannot object to a movement which merely provides the colored man of the North the opportunity he desires and cannot have at the South; and the only way to convince the Northern Negro-phobist is to show tangible results.

You may not be willing to accept this method now. Your people may not be willing to give over the impracticable dreams of instantaneous relief from evils that oppress and begin the steady and tedious work of gradually overcoming them. I may not live to see these ideas put in practice, but if I do not I will leave them as my bequest to humanity and ask no other monument. The initiative in a sense rests with your people; but whenever you are ready to move I will guarantee that five white men will be ready to assist for every colored man who shows a readiness to act and a thousand dollars will be found ready to back the exertions of every colored man who can show a stable purpose, thrift, energy and a sober life as security for such favor.

Already the eastern holders of forfeited western mortgages are looking about for some safe method of dispensing of the properties they have been compelled unwillingly to take. Even now English investors are tired of being made the cats paw of unscrupulous American speculators. The opportunity is unprecedented. The main question is whether the colored man is ready to start, to move slowly in order to win surely. If he is, God has wonderfully opened the way for success before him.

Yours truly.

28

That Lynching: Judge Tourgée Writes Gov. McKinley and the Editor of "The Gazette" (1894)*

On January 22, 1894, Tourgée wrote to Ohio governor William McKinley urging him to support a plan for legislative action to combat lynching in Ohio. After failing in his efforts to mobilize Republicans in Washington to act on a national level, he shrewdly chose to target his native state, and to enlist the future president in demonstrating to the nation that lynching was a national crime, one that could be curbed through innovative legal measures. On February 17, Tourgée wrote to Harry C. Smith, a newly elected black congressman from Ohio and editor of the *Cleveland Gazette*, to secure his support for the measure. Representative Smith soon championed Tourgée's proposed legislation and published both letters in the *Gazette* on March 3, 1894, to publicize their efforts. Smith's article, entitled "That Lynching," appears here in its entirety. After an extended legislative battle led by Smith, a modified version of Tourgée's proposal passed the Ohio legislature and became a law in March 1896.

Columbus, Ohio—The letters given below were sent me last week by Judge Tourgée, who is too well-known to our readers to need further introduction. They (the letters) were drawn out by the (West Union) lynching of the 17 year-old Afro-American, Roscoe Parker, who was charged with the murder of an aged couple, residents of Adams county. It is a fact, generally known that no one person living has worked harder or more incessantly against the lynch disease than has Judge Tourgée. His fields of action have been and are the lecture platform and the press of the country. The letters:

*"That Lynching: Judge Tourgée Writes Gov. McKinley and the Editor of 'The Gazette,'" *Cleveland Gazette*, March 3, 1894.

Mayville, N.Y., Feb 17, 1894.

To Hon. H. C. Smith, Columbus, O.:

My Dear Sir—I recently addressed the enclosed letter to Gov. McKinley. I fear he does not realize how important a question this of protecting the life of the citizen really is. There is very little doubt that if Mr. Harrison had urged upon congress the grant of federal jurisdiction in such cases, and allowing the heirs of parties lynched to sue the county for a statutory recovery, it would have stirred the instinct of justice in the American people to an extent that would have assured his re-election. But, though he was urged to do so again and again he was unwilling to take such steps, chiefly because no one else had ever done so.[1]

Lynching is not the disease, but only the symptom of disease. The real evil is defiance of law and disregard for the rights of others. It is the most danger- ous form of anarchy, because it breaks down the safeguards of life and makes the worst of crimes an act consistent with the highest position in society and the church. Its spread throughout the country indicates a demoralization of public sentiment which, unless checked, will result in the most woeful con- sequences. In the south it is most frequent during the late summer and fall months when the crops are made, since the employer is then unrestrained by present interest in the laborer. In the north its steady progress is indicated both by its wide diffusion and contempt which is manifested by the mob for the officers of the law.

Such evils never cure themselves. On the contrary, they always grow worse and worse, until the law-abiding and the law-defying elements are ranged in express antagonism—law against anarchy. In any northern state the result of such conflict can never be in doubt. Governors and legislators, who have not nerve enough or sagacity enough, to apply the simple and effectual remedies which everyman knows will not only suppress lynching, but all the worst forms of disease from which it springs, are very short-sighted and neglectful of the welfare of those communities whose safety has been instructed to their keeping.

The evil is of especial interest to every colored citizen, because of the wide- spread sentiment that denies them, in almost every community, an equal right to the safeguards of the law, and they should be especially active in promoting the remedy.

You are at liberty to use the letter to Gov. McKinley in any way that seems fit.

Very truly yours,

Albion W. Tourgée

1. Both in private entreaties and through the NCRA, Tourgée unsuccessfully pressured Re- publican president Benjamin Harrison to denounce lynching.

THE LETTER TO THE GOVERNOR

Mayville, N.Y., Jan. 22, 1894

Hon. Wm. McKinley—Dear Sir: The attention which has been recently awakened by the failure of a grand jury in Ohio to indict parties well known to be guilty of lynching, must have called your attention to the remarkable spread of this alarming malady. In the decade 1882–1892 the increase of known fatal lynchings was more than 100 percent; in 1882, 117, in 1892, 236. Last year the aggregate was a little less, only 280; but taking into account the enormity and the publicity and general aggravated character of the acts, the record may be said to be very little, if any, improved.

Your excellency does not need to be informed of two things. First, that the fatal lynchings that are recorded constitute only a small part of those cases in which persons banded together under some more or less vague pretense of serving the public welfare, assault, beat, torture and otherwise invade the personal rights and liberties of the citizen; or second, that these acts are only symptoms of a much greater and more dread disease, to-wit, a general contempt for law and disregard for the personal rights of the citizen.

Side by side with lynching, murder has increased in even greater degree. In 1888 there were a trifle over 3,000 homicides known and recorded by the press; in 1893 this number was swelled to almost 7,000.

At the same time other crimes of violence have increased to an almost unprecedented extent. Train robberies, burglaries of the most daring and unexpected character abound in every portion of the land.

For these conditions there is but one sufficient reason—a widespread and constantly increasing lack of regard for the requirements of law and the legal rights of others. Even the churches and organizations professedly philanthropic and Christian in character, have not infrequently openly encouraged, promoted and excused such acts of violence.

As a result, the life and the personal rights of the citizen are less secure in the United States than in any other civilized country, save only Russia and Italy.

This indicates a disregard for law approaching very nearly to anarchy. Indeed, such conditions have always been the sure precursor of anarchistic outbreak. They are all the more dangerous when participated in by what are termed "the best elements" of the community. As soon as the law-breaker knows that the law is too weak to protect him from the anger of a mob, all restraint upon his every passion is removed. He knows that mere suspicion is equivalent to conviction and becomes, instead of a petty thief or simple tramp, a desperado. A law which does not punish is a farce; a law which does not protect is a mockery.

Of intermediate causes for this condition of affairs there is but one, to-wit: the disregard of the citizen for the rights of others and his consequent neglect of duty in securing the enforcement of law.

There is no method of stimulating this impulse to the performance of the prime duty of the citizen at all comparable with that of putting a pecuniary responsibility on the community in which such crimes as exist only by the connivance or condonement of the public, prevail.

If the present financial condition continues and the army of the unemployed, who are dependant on public charity for support, increases or even remains for any considerable period at its present dangerous rate of about one-twentieth of our population, we shall see within a brief time the same anarchistic spirit displaying itself in the destruction of property. The hungry and destitute will agree that if the rich and respectable are not punished for openly taking life they will be equally exempt from punishment from destroying the property which a large portion of our people already believe has been taken from them by legalized wrong. The law makes a community liable for the destruction of property by a mob. How much more ought it to be made liable for the destruction of life by a mob?

The meanest man's life is worth more than the richest man's wealth. The state which protects the property of the capitalist with a bomb-proof of steel and the lives of its citizens with a brush fence will have only its own folly and injustice to thank for the harvest of anarchy which is sure to spring from such seeding.

The question is not one touching any particular state or section, though more alarming in some than in others. The disease is national and the comparative virulence of its local manifestations merely show a somewhat greater lesion of moral fiber in one locality or another.

It is just as much a matter of national import as the protection of labor and much more important. Wages are a trifle thing compared with life, and opportunity is worth nothing without security.

"What shall it profit a man if he gain the whole world and lose his life?" What is the advantage of good wages and steady work if five, ten, a hundred, or a thousand of your fellow citizens may take your life with impunity? And if a hundred may do it, why not one?

If a grand jury will not indict the best citizens of a community for open and confessed murder, how can they indict the footpad or the burglar who slays his victim? A man may be poor, have no friends and be a criminal besides, but "A man's a man at that," and when the law punishes the poor and degraded for even trivial offenses and refuses to punish the rich and respectable for the blackest and foulest of crimes, it invites anarchy and appeals to barbarism.

In view of these things I have thought it might not be presumptuous on the part of a son of Ohio who has, perhaps, given more attention to the progress of mob rule in its various forms in our country than anyone else, to suggest whether the state of Ohio should not take the lead in prescribing an effective remedy for this American epidemic. If half as many people had fallen victims to cholera as have suffered from unlawful violence during the past ten years, every municipality in the country would be accounted criminally neglectful of its duty if it did not guard against it. Why should not the state protect its citizens against mobs as well as against cholera germs?

Every state in the Union protects the meanest of its citizens against the negligence of a railroad company by prescribing a statutory penalty to be recovered by his heirs in case of his death from failure of the company to provide every safeguard which the utmost care and the highest skill can furnish to secure safety of the traveler. In such cases it matters not what may be the character, status or purpose of the victim. The wife of the worst criminal in transit to the penitentiary would recover exactly the same amount as your excellency's widow should both be victims of a railway disaster. Why? Simply because the purpose of such enactment is to encourage diligence by touching the pocket nerve in case of negligence.

The law is based, too, on a clear recognition of the fallibility of juries and the ease with which "offense's gilded hand may shove by justice," knowing well that a jury would be slow to give an equal amount to the administrator of the "bum" killed in the smoking car and the executor of the millionaire killed in his private coach. Why should not the state do the same thing to stimulate the vigilance and sense of duty of the people?

Under our form of government the people are the prime conservators of the peace. Officers, policemen, justices, grand juries are only agencies which the law provides by which the people may act. Informers, spies, detectives are other agencies especially intended for tracing out criminals. But the great task of preserving the peace rests on the individual citizen. Churches and schools are its prime agencies and public opinion is a chief weapon.

Lynchings *never occur* except in a community whose cities favor and approve such outrage. The lyncher is always a coward who needs encouragement of others to screw his courage to the point of murder.

I would beg to suggest whether as governor of the great state of Ohio, you would not shed luster on her name by a special message to the legislature recommending:

First—That the legal representative of any person lynched in any county of the state shall be entitled to recover from the county the sum of $10,000, by action brought either in the county or where the victim resided, or, in case the plaintiff shall make affidavit that he is afraid to bring the action in the county where the crime was committed, then in any adjoining county.

Second—That such recovery shall be made a part of the next succeeding tax levy in the county, after judgment rendered against the same.

Third—That any person suffering violence or assault at the hands of a mob, if said violence amounts to serious personal injury, shall have a right of action against the city, town or community in which the same shall have been received and upon proof of such violence inflicted by a mob, shall be entitled to recover not less than $1,000 and more if the jury shall find the injury to be of greater pecuniary damage to such person by depriving him of capacity to earn a livelihood by his labor.

Fourth—That in case the injury is not serious, but amounts to a violent assault by such mob, the party injured may take his action against the city or town, and upon proof of such violence shall recover not less than $2,000 in any court having jurisdiction of an action for malicious damage to the person.

Fifth—That any compromise or agreement of any representative of a person who may have been lynched to take less than full amount of such penalty or recovery shall be void, and the parties to such pretended compromise and those seeking to procure it shall be liable to indictment and on conviction shall be imprisoned for one year.

I have suggested a very high penalty, $10,000, for lynching, double what a railroad generally has to pay for fatal negligence. For this there are two reasons:

First—Negligence is unavoidable with railroads—accidents must happen. The law only seeks to reduce their frequency. Lynchings are *wholly preventable*. The law seeks to wholly eliminate them.

Second—With a penalty of $10,000 there will probably not be more than one or two lynchings in Ohio in the next fifty years—perhaps not one. Put it down to $5,000 and its preventive power will be reduced at least one thousand percent.

Nothing, in my judgment, would add so much to the glory of the great commonwealth whose chief magistrate you are, as to take the lead in this most noble necessary and inevitable crusade against anarchy. I believe every northern state would follow such a lead, and this form of barbarism would be practically eliminated from them in a brief time.

Sincerely yours,
Albion W. Tourgée

29

Brief of Plaintiff in Error (1895)*

During the 1895 fall term, Tourgée and his legal team filed their briefs in *Plessy* v. *Ferguson* at the United States Supreme Court. Tourgée wrote the main argument of their case, reproduced below. In addition, a summary of their case (not reproduced here), jointly authored by Tourgée and James C. Walker, prefaced their materials. Two additional briefs, one authored by Walker, and another by Samuel F. Phillips and F. D. McKenney (also not reproduced here), completed the materials they submitted on Homer Plessy's behalf. Tourgée's brief, though often misconstrued, contains a straightforward explication of the law and history of the constitutional amendments as he interpreted them, accompanied by a host of legal interpretations and rhetorical strategies crafted for the sake of persuasion. As a guide to Tourgée's thinking on civil rights, the brief is best considered alongside his other writings and statements on these issues.

QUESTIONS ARISING

Some of the questions arising on this statement of facts and the decision of the court below, as we conceive, are as follows: Has the State the power under the provisions of the Constitution of the United States, to make a distinction based on color in the enjoyment of chartered privileges within the state?

Has it the power to require the officers of a railroad to assort its citizens by race, before permitting them to enjoy privileges dependent on public charter?

Is the officer of a railroad competent to decide the question of race?

Is it a question that *can* be determined in the absence of statutory definition and without evidence?

May not such decision reasonably result in serious pecuniary damage to a person compelled to ride in a car set apart for one particular race?

*Albion W. Tourgée, "Brief of Plaintiff in Error. In The Supreme Court of the United States," 5–36, item 8250, Albion W. Tourgée Papers, Chautauqua County Historical Society.

Has a State power to compel husband and wife, to ride in separate coaches, because they happen the one to be colored and the other white?

Has the State the power to exempt the railroad and its officers from an action for damages on the part of any person injured by the mistake of such officer?

Has the State the power under the Constitution to authorize any officer of a railroad to put a passenger off the train and refuse to carry him *because* he happens to differ with the officer as to the race to which he properly belongs?

Has the State the power under the Constitution, to declare a man guilty of misdemeanor and subject to fine and imprisonment, *because* he may differ with the officer of a railroad as to "the race to which he belongs"?

Has the State a right to declare a citizen of the United States guilty of a crime because he peacefully continues to occupy a seat in a car after being told by the conductor that it is not the one set apart for the race to which he belongs?

Is not the question of race, scientifically considered, very often impossible of determination?

Is not the question of race, legally considered, one impossible to be determined, in the absence of statutory definition?

Would any railway company venture to execute such a law unless secured against action for damage by having the courts of the state closed against such action?

Is not the provision exempting railway companies and their servants and officers, from action for damages in carrying into effect the provisions of this statute, of such importance as to be essential to the operation of the law in question?

Is not a statutory assortment of the people of a state on the line of race, such a perpetuation of the essential features of slavery as to come within the inhibition of the XIIIth Amendment?

Is it not the establishment of a statutory difference between the white and colored races in the enjoyment of chartered privileges, a badge of servitude which is prohibited by that amendment?

Is not *state* citizenship made an essential incident of *national* citizenship, by the XIVth Amendment, and if so are not the rights, privileges and immunities of the same within the scope of the national jurisdiction?

Can the rights of a citizen of the United States be protected and secured by the general government without securing his *personal* rights against invasion by the State?

Does not the exemption of nurses in attendance upon children, render this act obnoxious as class legislation and rebut the claim that it is *bona fide* a police regulation necessary to secure the health and morals of the community?

CONSTITUTIONAL PROVISIONS INVOLVED

The Plaintiff in Error relies on the following provisions of the Constitution of the United States in support of his contention that the said statute No. III, of the State of Louisiana, 1890, is null and void.

The Thirteenth Amendment

Section I.—Neither SLAVERY nor involuntary servitude except as a punishment for crime whereof the party shall have been duly convicted, shall exist within the United States or any place subject to its jurisdiction.

The Fourteenth Amendment

Section I.—*Affirmative Provisions.*

"All persons born or naturalized in the United States and subject to the jurisdiction thereof, are—

1—Citizens of the United States," and

2—(Citizens) "of the state in which they shall reside."

Restrictive Provisions.

1—"No State shall make or enforce any law which shall abridge the privileges and immunities of citizens of the United States."

2—"Nor shall any State deprive any citizen of life, liberty or property, without due process of law."

3—"Nor deny to any person within its jurisdiction, the equal protection of the laws."

This section has been separated into its constituent clauses, the more readily to show the construction for which the Plaintiff in Error contends.

POINTS OF PLAINTIFF'S CONTENTION

I—The exemption of officers and railway companies from suits for damage by persons aggrieved by their action under this law.

The Court below held that the language of this section did not exempt from damage resulting from *bona fide* exercise of the power conferred upon them by its provisions. The language of the act is explicit: "should any passenger refuse to occupy"—not the coach used for the race to which he belongs but—"the coach or compartment to which *he or she is assigned by the officer of such railway,* said officer shall have power to refuse to carry such passenger on his train and *for such refusal,* neither he nor the railway company he represents, shall be liable for damage, *in any of the courts of this state.*" Is not this a clear denial to the person thus put off the train, of any right of action? Is it not that very denial of the "equal protection of the laws" which is clearly contemplated by the third restrictive provision of the Fourteenth Amendment?

If so, is this provision of such importance as to be essential to the validity of the law as a whole? Our contention is that no individual or corporation could be expected or induced to carry into effect this law, in a community where race admixture is a frequent thing and where the hazard of damage resulting from such assignment is very great, unless they were protected by such exemption. The State very clearly says to the railway, "You go forward and enforce this system of assorting the citizens of the United States on the line of race, and we will see that you suffer no loss through prosecution in OUR courts." Relying on this assurance, the company is willing to undertake the risk. Without it they might well shrink from such liability. The denial of the *right to prosecute,* then, becomes essential to the operation of the act, and if such "denial" is in derogation of the restriction of the Fourteenth Amendment, the whole act is null and void. It is a question for the Court to determine upon its knowledge of human nature and the conditions affecting human conduct, in regard to which it would be idle to cite authorities. If it is NOT a violation of this provision it would be difficult to imagine a statutory provision which could be violative of it.

II—We shall also contend that, in any mixed community, the reputation of belonging to the dominant race, in this instance the white race, is *property,* in the same sense that a right of action or of inheritance is *property;* and that the provisions of the act in question which authorize an officer of a railroad company to assign a person to a car set apart for a particular race, enables such officer to deprive him, to a certain extent at least, of this property—this reputation which has an actual pecuniary value—"without due process of law," and are, therefore, in violation of the Second restrictive clause of the first section of the XIVth Amendment of the Constitution of the United States.

This provision authorizing and requiring the officer in charge of the train to pass upon and decide the question of race, is the very essence of the statute.

If this is repugnant to the Constitutional provision, all the rest must fall.

There is no question that the law which puts it in the power of a railway conductor, at his own discretion, to require a man to ride in a "Jim Crow" car, that is, in the car "set apart exclusively for persons of the colored race," confers upon such conductor the power to deprive one of the reputation of being a white man, or at least to impair that reputation. The man who rides in a car set apart for the colored race, will inevitably be regarded as a colored man or at least be suspected of being one. And the officer has undoubtedly the power to entail upon him such suspicion. To do so, is to deprive him of "property" if such reputation *is* "property." Whether it is or not, is for the court to determine from its knowledge of existing conditions. Perhaps it might not be inappropriate to suggest some questions which may aid in deciding this inquiry. How much would it be *worth* to a young man entering upon the practice of law, to be regarded as a *white* man rather than a colored one? Six-sevenths of the population are white. Nineteen-twentieths of the property of the country is owned by white people. Ninety-nine hundredths of the business opportunities are in the control of white people. These propositions are rendered even more startling by the intensity of feeling which excludes the colored man from the friendship and companionship of the white man. Probably most white persons if given a choice, would prefer death to life in the United States *as colored persons.* Under these conditions, is it possible to conclude that the *reputation of being white* is not property? Indeed, is it not the most valuable sort of property, being the master-key that unlocks the golden door of opportunity?

III—The Plaintiff in Error also contends that the provision of this act authorizing the conductor to "refuse to carry," *anglice* put off the train, any passenger who refuses to accept his decision as to "the race to which he belongs," is a deprivation of the *liberty* and *property* of the citizen "without due process of law," and as such is in conflict with the third restrictive clause of the XIVth Amendment.

The passenger is deprived of his liberty by being removed by the power with which the statute vests the conductor, from a place where he has a *right to be;* and of his property, by being refused and denied the enjoyment of that for which he has paid his money, to wit, the ticket purchased by him to the point of destination. This gave him the right to ride upon *that train* or any train, to the point designated. To take away that right, compel the passenger to go on foot or by other means to such point, is to seize, covert and destroy his property by pretended force of law. It is *pro tanto* an act of legalized spoliation—an act of forcible confiscation—a taking of property and interference with liberty under legalized forms and statutory methods, but without "*due* process of law."

IV—The plaintiff also contends that the provisions authorizing the officers of a train to require parties to occupy the particular cars or compartments set apart for distinct races, is a statutory grant of authority to interfere with natural domestic rights of the most sacred character.

A man may be white and his wife colored; a wife may be white and her children colored. Has the State the right to compel the husband to ride in one car and the wife in another? Or to assign the mother to one car and the children to another? Yet this is what the statute in question requires. In our case, it does not appear that the plaintiff may not have had with him a wife belonging to the other race, or children differing with him in the color of their skins? Has a State the right to order the mother to ride in one car and her young daughter, because her cheek may have a darker tinge, to ride alone in another? Yet such things as these, the act in question not only permits, but actually requires and commands to be done under penalty of fine and imprisonment, for failure or neglect. Are the courts of the United States to hold such things to be within the purview of a State's right to impose on citizens of the United States?

V—The plaintiff also insists that a wholesale assortment of the citizens of the United States, resident in the state of Louisiana, on the line of race, is a thing wholly impossible to be made equitably and justly by any tribunal, much less by the conductor of a train without evidence, investigation or responsibility.

The Court will take notice of the fact that, in all parts of the country, race-intermixture has proceeded to such an extent that there are great numbers of citizens in whom the preponderance of the blood of one race or another, is impossible of ascertainment, except by careful scrutiny of the pedigree. As slavery did not permit the marriage of the slave, in a majority of cases even an approximate determination of this preponderance is an actual impossibility, with the most careful and deliberate weighing of evidence, much less by the casual scrutiny of a busy conductor.

But even if it were possible to determine preponderance of blood and so determine racial character in certain cases, what should be said of those cases in which the race admixture is equal. Are they white or colored?

There is no law of the United States, or of the State of Louisiana defining the limits of race—who are white and who are "colored"? By what rule then shall any tribunal be guided in determining racial character? It may be said that all those should be classed as colored in whom appears a visible admixture of colored blood. By what law? With what justice? Why not count every one as white in whom is visible any trace of white blood? There is but one reason to wit, the domination of the white race. Slavery not only introduced the rule of caste but prescribed its conditions, in the interests of that institution. The trace of color raised the presumption of bondage and was a bar to citizenship. The law in question is an attempt to apply this rule to the establishment of legalized caste-distinction *among citizens.*

It is not consistent with reason that the United States, having granted and bestowed *one equal citizenship* of the United States and prescribed *one equal citizenship in each state,* for all, will permit a State to compel a railway conductor to assort them arbitrarily according to his ideas of race, in the enjoyment of chartered privileges.

VI—The Plaintiff in Error, also insists that, even if it be held that such an assortment of citizens by race in the enjoyment of public privileges, is not a deprivation of liberty or property without due process of law, it is still such an interference with the personal liberty of the individual as is impossible to be made consistently with his rights as an equal citizen of the United States and of the State in which he resides.

In construing the first section of the XIVth Amendment, there appears to have been, both on the part of the Courts and of textual writers, an inclination to overlook and neglect the force and effect of its affirmative provisions.

The evident effect of these provisions taken alone and construed according to the plain and universal meaning of the terms employed, is to confer upon every person born or naturalized in the United States, two things:

(1) National Citizenship.

(2) Statal Citizenship, as *an essential incident* of national citizenship.

This grant both of *national* and *statal* citizenship in the Constitution of the United States, is a guaranty not only of *equality* of right but *of all natural rights and the free enjoyment of all public privileges* attaching either to state or national citizenship. Its effect is (1) to make national citizenship expressly *paramount and universal;* (2) to make Statal citizenship expressly *subordinate and incidental* to national citizenship.

The State is thereby ousted of *all control over citizenship.* It cannot make any man a citizen nor deprive any one of the estate of citizenship or of any of its rights and privileges.

What are the rights, "privileges and immunities of a citizen of the United States"? Previous to the adoption of this section of the Constitution they were very vague and difficult of definition. Now they include all "the rights, privileges and immunities" of a citizen *of a State*, because that citizenship is made incidental to and coextensive with *national* citizenship in every State; and the United States guarantees the full enjoyment of both. It is evident that National citizenship *plus* State citizenship covers the whole field of individual relation, so far as the same is regulated or prescribed by law. All the rights, "privileges and immunities," which *can attach* to the individual as a part of the body-politic, are embraced either by the relation of "Citizen of the United States" or by the relation of *citizen* "of the *State* in which he may reside." The United States having granted *both* stands pledged to protect and defend both.

This provision of Section I of the Fourteenth Amendment, *creates* a *new* citizenship of the United States embracing new rights, privileges and immunities, derivable in a *new* manner, controlled by *new* authority, having a *new* scope and extent, dependent on national authority for its existence and looking to national power for its preservation.

VII—It may be urged against this construction that it ousts the exclusive control of the State over "its own citizens" by inference based on the effect of the grant of citizenship. That this is the real force of this provision of the Constitution would seem to be the only conclusion that can be reached from any reasonable interpretation of the language employed. The language of the affirmative provisions of the section, certainly includes everything that can be embraced by citizenship *of the United States* and citizenship of *the State of residence.* This leaves no room for any *exclusive State jurisdiction* of the personal rights of the citizen. If this provision means anything, it means that the government of the United States will not permit any legislation by the State which invades the *rights* of such citizens. These are fully covered by the grant of citizenship of the United States AND citizenship of the State. This construction is strengthened by the negative provisions which are supplemental of the positive ones. These prohibit the making or enforcement of any law "abridging the privileges and immunities of citizens of the United States"; provide that "life, liberty or property shall not be taken without due process of law"; and forbid the denial to any person of the equal protection of the law. All these are express restrictions of statal power already made subordinate and incidental to the national jurisdiction by the positive provisions of the same section.

These restrictive provisions were not intended to be construed by themselves, but in connection with and as supplemental to the affirmative provisions—taken together they constitute this section, the *magna charta* of the American citizen's rights.

VIII—Taken by themselves, however, and read in the light of the construction put upon Section 3 Article II of the Constitution, these negative provisions would seem quite sufficient to oust the exclusive jurisdiction of the State and establish the appellate or supervisory jurisdiction of the United States in all matters touching the personal rights of citizens.

It has no doubt occurred to every member of the Court, though no allusion seems hitherto to have been made to it, that the construction and phraseology of this section is strikingly similar to that of Section 3 of the IVth Article of the Constitution: "No person held to service or labour in one State under the laws thereof, escaping into another shall, in consequence of any law or regulation therein, be discharged from such service or labour, but shall be delivered up on the claim of the party to whom such service or labour may be due."

The celebrated case of Prigg *vs.* Pennsylvania; 16 Peters, 539, which finally determined the force of this section decided two things; (1) That the Courts of the United States had jurisdiction to consider and pass upon the validity of the acts of a State touching the rendition of fugitives from labour—to undo or invalidate all that might be done or attempted by virtue of State authority, in regard to the estate or condition of one claimed as a fugitive from labour; (2) That whenever the United States legislated upon the question, such legislation wholly ousted the State jurisdiction. What this section was to the fugitive from slavery, the provisions of the first section of the XIVth Amendment are to the rights and liberties of the citizen. In the former case, the Federal jurisdiction is inferred from the declaration "No person held to service, * * * shall be discharged therefrom"; in the other case, the jurisdiction is much more clearly indicated by the unqualified grant of national *and* state citizenship in the constitution. As the former gave jurisdiction concerning every matter relating to persons escaping from service or labour, so the latter gives jurisdiction of *all* matters pertaining to the rights of a citizen of the United States and the essential incident of such citizenship, his status as a citizen of any state. As in that case, state legislation was to be judged by its effect upon the acquired right of the master over the slave, so in this case, the statute is to be judged by its effect upon the *natural and legal rights* of the citizen. The Plaintiff in Error only asks that the rule of construction adopted by this Court *to perpetuate the interests of Slavery,* be now applied in *promotion of liberty* and for the protection of *the rights of the citizen.*

IX—The prime essential of all citizenship is *equality* of personal right and the *free* and secure enjoyment of all public privileges. These are the very essence of citizenship in all free governments.

A law assorting the citizens of a State in the enjoyment of a public franchise on the basis of race, is obnoxious to the spirit of republican institutions, because it is a legalization of *caste.* Slavery was the very essence of caste; the climax of unequal conditions. The citizen held the highest political rank attainable in the republic; the slave was the lowest grade of existence. ALL rights and privileges attached to the one; the other had *no legal rights,* either of person or property. Between them stood that strange nondescript, the "free person of color," who had such rights only as the white people of the state where he resided saw fit to confer upon him, but he could neither become a citizen of the United States nor *of any State.* The effect of the words of the XIVth Amendment, was to put *all* these classes on *the same level of right,* as *citizens;* and to make this Court the final arbiter and custodian of these rights. The effect of a law distinguishing between citizens as to race, in the enjoyment of a public franchise, is to legalize caste and restore, in part at least, the inequality of right which was an essential incident of slavery.

X—The power of the State to establish "police regulations."

The theory that the State governments had exclusive jurisdiction of certain specific areas of individual relation, which prevailed under our government up to the adoption of the XIVth Amendment, was so unique as to become a sort of fetish in our legal and political thought. The idea that certain phases of personal right were *wholly excluded* from the jurisdiction of the general government, was entirely correct. There was no definition of national citizenship in the constitution except in regard to naturalization, and so no relation was established between the individual and the general government requiring the latter to define or secure his natural rights or equal privileges and immunities. All the general government could do was to exercise the special jurisdiction conferred by the constitution. All outside of that was the *exclusive* domain of the States. The State might extend or withhold citizenship at its pleasure, the only check upon its power in this respect being that imposed by the Court in

Scott *vs.* Sandford, that the State could not make any colored person a citizen, so as to entitle him to any right as such, outside its own jurisdiction. Such exclusive jurisdiction still exists in regard to matters of political organization and control, and, indeed, in regard to all internal affairs, so long as the same do not conflict with the personal rights and privileges of the citizen. Of these, a final and corrective jurisdiction is reserved to the general government. It has the right, through its Courts, to inquire into and decide upon the force, tenor and justice of all provisions of State laws affecting the rights of the citizen. As in the case of fugitives from labor before the Congress had legislated upon the subject, the Federal Courts had jurisdiction to pass upon state laws and decide whether their purpose was to promote or to hinder such rendition, so now, the Court has jurisdiction to decide whether a State law is promotive of the citizen's right or intended to secure unjust restriction and limitation thereof.

It was natural that so great a change should prove a shock to established precedent. To avoid giving full and complete effect to the plain words of this amendment, the theory of exclusive state control over "police regulations" was formulated in what are known as the "Slaughter House Cases," 16 Wallace, 36.

In this case, an act of the legislature of Louisiana required all slaughter of food animals to be conducted at certain abattoirs to be erected by a company created by the act, during a period of twenty-five years. It was assailed on the ground that it deprived certain persons plying the trade of butcher, of the free exercise of their calling. The Court held that the law was a "police regulation" to promote the public health and that the state had the right to enact such legislation without being subject to the inhibition of the XIVth amendment unless it discriminated against the rights of colored citizens *as such.*

The demurring judges, Chief Justice Chase, Justices Field, Swayne and Bradley, concurring in the opinion of Mr. Justice Field, did not question the right of the State to make laws which should restrict individual right and privilege whenever the same were necessary for the promotion of public health and morals, but they contended that the XIVth Amendment conferred the jurisdiction to inquire whether this was the *real purpose* of the act, whether any discrimination against the colored citizen as such, was made by it or not. In other words, the Court held that the act was a police regulation intended to secure the public health and did not discriminate against colored citizens as such. The dissenting justices held that the promotion of the public health was a mere pretence for the grant of an exclusive privilege which impaired the rights of many for the benefit of the few, and that the XIVth Amendment by its express terms did embrace an assertion of *all citizens* without regard to race or color. Two things are noticeable in these opinions. (1) That the Court expressly refrains from asserting that cases may not arise which will be within the purview of this Amendment, which do not embrace any distinction against the colored citizen as such. (2) That so strong a dissenting portion of the Court concur in the construction of this Amendment given by Mr. Justice Field, found on pages 95 to 101, including these significant declarations:

"It recognizes, if it does not create, citizens of the United States and makes their citizenship depend upon the place of birth and not upon the laws of any State or the condition of their ancestry. A citizen of a State is now only a citizen of the United States residing in that State. The fundamental rights, privileges and immunities which belong to him as a free man and a free citizen, now belong to him as a citizen of the United States."

Speaking of the "privileges and immunities" of the first restrictive clause, he says: "The privileges and immunities designated are those which of right belong to the citizens of all free governments."

The opinion of the Court, p. 72 et seq., treats the affirmative provisions of this Amendment as a "definition of citizenship, not only citizenship of the United States but citizenship of the States," and regards the negative ones as restrictive only of discrimination directed against colored citizens, *as such*.

The opinion in Strauder *vs.* West Virginia, 100 U.S., 303, clearly shows, however, that the Court had, in the interval, advanced from the position held in the "Slaughter House Cases" to an unhesitating avowal of the conclusion that the Fourteenth Amendment was intended and would be effective, in preventing discrimination as to right. In this opinion *only* the prohibitive clauses of the Amendment are considered and the language of the Court is based upon the inference to be made from them without any regard for the positive endowing force of the affirmative provisions.

"It ordains," says the Court "that no state shall deprive any person of life, liberty or property, without due process of law, or to deny any person within its jurisdiction, the equal protection of the laws. What is this but declaring that the law in the States shall be the same for the black as for the white; that all persons, whether colored or white, shall stand equal before the laws of the States, and, in regard to the colored race for whose protection the Amendment was primarily designed, that no discrimination shall be made against them by law because of their color? The words of the Amendment are prohibitive but they contain a necessary implication of a most positive immunity or right most valuable to the colored man—the right to exemption from unfriendly legislation against them as colored—exemption from legal dis-crimination *implying inferiority in* civil society, lessening the enjoyment of the rights which others enjoy, and *discriminations which are steps towards reducing them to the condition of a subject race."*

In our case, the Plaintiff in Error contends that this is the precise purpose and intended and inevitable effect of the statute in question. It is a "step to-ward reducing the colored people and those allied with it, to the condition of a *subject race."*

XI—What an exclusive jurisdiction in the State to make and enforce "Police regulations" imports.

It is needless to cite authorities as to what constitute police regulations. All attempts at definition agree that they are regulations necessary to secure the physical health and moral welfare of society. No one questions the neces-sity of such regulations in any community or that they must to some extent interfere with the enjoyment of personal right and privilege. Every man must surrender something of his liberty for the well-being of the community of which he is a part. Two questions are of importance in regard to the jurisdic-tion of such regulations accorded to the State in the Slaughter House Cases. The one is, "How are the police regulations to be distinguished from other criminal or correctional legislation? Is there any distinctive form or character by which they may be distinguished?["]

The Court very properly declares that the term is "incapable of exact defi-nition." It even adopts the words of the decision in Thorpe *vs.* Rutland and Burlington Railroad, 27 Vermont 149, as indicating its character.

"It extends to the protection of the lives, limbs, health, comfort and quiet of all persons and the protection of all property; and persons and property are subjected to all kinds of restraints and burdens in order to secure the general comfort, health and prosperity. Of the perfect right of the legislature to do this, no question ever was, or upon acknowledged general principles, ever can be made so far as natural persons are concerned."

No one pretends to contravene this right of the State to enact police regu-lations that shall to a limited extent affect personal liberty. The question is whether this is an unrestricted right; whether the State has the right un-der the claim of protecting public health or regulating public morals, to re-strict the rights of the individual to *any extent* it may see fit? This seems to be the force of the decision in the Slaughter House Cases. I say seems because the Court very clearly intimates that if it had been a case of discrimination against *colored citizens* as such, it would have been within the jurisdiction of this Court to consider at least the intent and character of this discrimination. As near as I am able to state it, then, the Court's definition of the relation of the XIVth Amendment to the State's power to enact and enforce police regulations is, that it has the sole power and sovereignty to do so, as long as it does not distinguish against the rights of colored citizens as such. It may distinguish against white citizens or invade the rights of all to any extent and the general government has no right to intervene; but if it imposes a greater burden or any inequality of privilege, upon the colored citizen, the general government is thereby vested with power to prevent or correct this inequality. This position viewed analytically, is a strange one. As has already been indicated, it is difficult to see how this section can be held to protect a colored citizen's right and not secure the rights of white citizens. If it did, it would be obnoxious to the objection of being class legislation just as opprobious and unjust as that by which slavery was established.

But if the State has exclusive and final jurisdiction to make and enforce police regulations without question or review by the Federal Courts, why has it not sole sovereignty and exclusive jurisdiction over all the personal rights of the citizen in the same manner and to the same extent, as before the adoption of this Amendment? If this section means anything, it would seem that it must give authority to review the "police regulations" of the State just the same as any other legislation, to determine whether they unduly or unnecessarily interfere with the individual rights of the citizen or make unjust discrimination against any class; that if it gives the right to annul legislation inimical to one class, it must of necessity, give the same power as regards legislation injurious to any class.

In order to come within the scope of a "police regulation," even as defined in the "Slaughter House Cases," the act prohibited must be of a character to affect the general health or public morals of a whole community, not merely to minister to the wishes of one class or another. What is the act prohibited in the statute in question in this case? The sitting of a white man or woman in the car in which a colored man or woman sits or the sitting of a colored man or woman in the car in which white men or women are sitting, is this dangerous to the public health? Does this contaminate public morals? If it does from whence comes the contamination? Why does it contaminate any more than in the house or on the street? Is it the white who spreads the contagion or the black? And if color breeds contagion in a railway coach, why exempt nurses from the operation of the Act?

The title of an Act does not make it a "police provision" and a discrimination intended to humiliate or degrade one race in order to promote the pride of ascendancy in another, is not made a "police regulation" by insisting that the one will not be entirely happy unless the other is shut out of their presence. Haman was troubled with the same sort of unhappiness because he saw Mordecai the Jew sitting at the King's gate. He wanted a "police regulation" to prevent his being contaminated by the sight. He did not set out the real cause of his zeal for the public welfare: neither does this statute. He wanted to "down" the Jew; this act is intended to "keep the negro in his place." The exemption of nurses shows that the real evil lies not in the color of the skin but in the relation the colored person sustains to the white. If he is a dependent it may be endured; if he is not, his presence is insufferable. Instead of being intended to promote the general comfort and moral wellbeing, this act is plainly and evidently intended to promote the happiness of one class by asserting its supremacy and the inferiority of another class. Justice is pictured blind and her daughter, the Law, ought at least to be color-blind.

XII—The purpose and intent of the legislator as a rule of constitutional interpretation.

It is a remarkable fact connected with this decision (the Slaughter House Cases) and those which have followed it, that the rule that the purpose and intent of the lawmaker may be considered to explain doubt or ambiguity, seems in this case to have been used to *create* ambiguity and place upon this section a construction absolutely at variance with the plain and unquestioned purport of its words. No man can deny that the language employed is of the broadest and most universal character. "Every person," "no State," "any law," "any person" are the terms employed. The language has no more comprehensive or unmistakeable words. Yet in the face of these, the Court arrives at the conclusion that this section was intended *only to protect the rights of the colored citizen from infringement by State enactment!* This conclusion makes the "purpose and intent" inferred from external sources dominate and control the plain significance of the terms employed. Granting the assumption of the Court—which with deference, is only half-true—that the purpose of the section was to secure to the new-made colored citizen the same rights as white citizens had theretofore enjoyed, it does not follow that the language used should be wrested from its plain meaning to exclude all other force and consequence. One of the most common things in all corrective legislation is the use of terms including other acts than those it is sought specifically to restrain. A wrong done to specific individuals or classes is prohibited, not as to those classes alone, but as to *all;* or a specific offence calls attention to possible kindred offenses, and the whole class prohibited instead of the particular evil. Whatever may have been the special controlling motive of the people of the United States in enacting this section, or of the Congress which proposed it, one thing is certain, the language used is not particular but universal. If it protects the colored citizen from discriminating legislation, it protects also, in an equal degree, the rights of the white citizen. "All" can never be made to mean "some," nor "every person" be properly construed to be only one class or race, until the laws of English speech are overthrown.

This decision wholly neglects the fact that an amendment giving colored persons *exclusively* the protection it is admitted that this was intended to give them, would have been obnoxious to the severest opprobrium as *class legislation of the rankest sort.* It would have been giving to the colored citizen a security, a "privilege and immunity," not conferred on white citizens. It would have left the national citizenship of the whites dependent *on ancestry* while that of the blacks was *determined by the place of birth.* It would have protected the one from State aggression and oppression and left the other unprotected. Suppose the colored people to secure control of certain states as they ultimately will, for ten cannot always chase a thousand no matter how white the ten or how black the thousand may be, such a provision as has been supposed or such as the Court conceives this to have been intended to be; would leave the personal rights of a white minority wholly at the mercy of a colored majority, without possibility of national protection or redress. Indeed, if the construction which the Court puts upon it be the correct one, if only the rights of *colored* citizens are protected by this section from impairment by statal action or neglect, it is little wonder that the white people of the south declare themselves ready to resist even to the death, the domination of a colored majority in any state. If such is the law and *only colored* citizens are secured in their rights by this amendment, I do not hesitate to say that they are fully justified in anything they may have done or may hereafter do, to prevent control of the machinery of the state governments by colored citizens.

It was said above, that the assumption that this section was adopted for the protection of the colored citizen, was at best only half-true. The history of the times shows that exclusive state control over the persons and rights of the citizens of the state was not only the Gibraltar of slavery, but was the chief ingredient of that "paramount allegiance to the State," which was the twin of the doctrine of secession. Both rested on the same theory of the State's exclusive sovereignty over the inhabitance of the State. If slavery was one of the foundation stones of the Confederacy, as Mr. Stephens declared, the doctrine of "paramount allegiance" based on exclusive state-sovereignty over the personal rights of all inhabitants of the State, was certainly another. This exclusive sovereignty over the individual was well-founded, too, in the constitution. It came to be so fully accepted that Mr. Chief Justice Waite in Cruikshank's Case hereafter to be considered, even declares that it still exists. It was the nurse and secure defense of slavery and the excuse and justification of rebellion. A long and bloody war had just been concluded in which those in arms against the Union based the defense of their course wholly upon this theory. That the people of the United States should desire to eradicate this doctrine, is just as natural as that they should desire to secure the rights of the colored people they had freed. It was reasonable that they should seek to protect the nation against the recurrence of such peril. If they had such purpose, could they have effected it more fully than by the language of this section, creating a new and universal citizenship and making state-citizenship an incident of it? Thereby they would effect both ends with the same weapon. This they *meant* to do—and this they did, if the words of the constitution are to prevail, over a hypothetical limitation, based on a partial definition of the controlling purpose of the framers. It was the *real purpose* to destroy both "paramount allegiance" and discrimination based on race, at one blow; and this the section under consideration does, if the terms employed are given their usual and universal significance. The people of the United States were not building for today and its prejudices alone, but for justice, liberty and a nationality secure for all time.

XIII—The case of the United States *vs.* Cruikshank, 92 U.S. 542, proceeds upon the same, as we conceive, mistaken view, both of the character and effect of the XIVth Amendment. It wholly neglects the apparent effect of the affirmative clauses and dwells entirely upon the restrictive provisions. While admitting that all rights *granted or secured* by the Constitution of the United States, are within the protection of the general government, it entirely ignores the evident facts that the citizenship granted by this amendment differs *both in character and extent* from the citizenship of the United States, existing theretofore citizenship with all its incidents, is directly *granted and secured* to classes never before entitled thereunto, but expressly excluded therefrom. The opinion states, page 553, that it is the "duty of the States to protect all persons within their boundaries in the enjoyment of those inalienable rights with which they were endowed by their creator." And then, apparently oblivious of the fact that the States had failed to give such protection to the rights of their inhabitants and that their failure to do so in the past was *the sole reason* for the adoption of the XIIIth Amendment, and the apprehension that they might not do so in the future the sole reason for the adoption of the XIVth Amendment, the court proceeds to affirm that "sovereignty" for this purpose, (that is for the protection of the natural rights of the individual) "rests alone with the State." Truly, if this construction be the correct one, this section of the amendment is the absurdest piece of legislation ever written in a statute book. The States had many of them expressly denied a large portion of their population, not only liberty but *all natural rights.* The very definition of a slave was "a person without rights." (Code of Louisiana.) The nation conferred on more than half the population of this State liberty, national and state citizenship, embracing the inalienable rights of which they had been deprived and which were still denied by the State. Then, according to this construction, it said to the State; "The protection and security of these rights rests alone with you. I have made these people citizens and clothed them with the rights of citizens in the State and in the nation. You must not deny or impair these rights; *but if you do, it is your own affair.* I cannot prevent, restrain or hinder. Your sovereignty over them is paramount, exclusive and final. I cannot interfere to protect their rights or save their lives."

Does any man imagine—can any man believe when he recalls the heated war of words, the quarter-century of angry denunciation of this very theory, of the State's sole sovereignty over the lives and rights of its inhabitants, the years of bloody strife then just ended which resulted from this very theory, that the people of the United States meant to perpetuate this condition of affairs when they wrote these words in the Constitution which clothed these Ishmaels of our republic with the purple robe of citizenship? Does any one believe that they meant to restore *that very sovereignty* which was the excuse for resistance to national authority and which the bloody tide of war had only just overthrown? If that was their purpose, then Carlyle's grim designation of the people of Great Britain as "thirty millions of people—chiefly fools," should, when applied to the American people, be amended by leaving out the "chiefly" and saying "every last one a fool."

But the political aspect of these amendments was then to the fore and colored every man's thoughts. The old fetish of State-sovereignty which was essential to the stability of "a nation, half-free and half-slave," still blinded the eyes which could not see that the system which was the Gibraltar of Slavery must, *ex necessitate,* be perilous to equal rights and liberty—that the Moloch of Slavery would never be the true God of Liberty. What was good for slavery must be bad for freedom.

This court, indeed, in Strauder *vs.* West Virginia, 100 U.S. 303, distinctly recognized the inconsistency of the ruling in Cruikshank's Case and admit that the effect of the amendment is to prohibit legislation prejudicial to any class of citizens whether colored or not.

"If in those states where the colored people constitute a majority of the entire population a law should be enacted excluding all white men, from jury or service, thus denying to them the privilege of participating equally with the blacks in the administration of justice, we apprehend no one would be heard to claim that it would not be a denial to white men of the equal protection of the laws. Nor, if a law should be passed excluding all naturalized Celtic Irishmen, would there be any doubt of its inconsistency with the spirit of the amendment."

It is but a step farther to what the Plaintiff in Error insists is the true construction, to wit, that "equal protection of the laws," is not a *comparative* equality—not merely equal as between one race and another, but a just and universal equality whereby the rights of life, liberty, and property are secured to all—the rights which belong to a citizen in every free country and every republican government.

In our case, the presentment does not allege the color or race of the Plaintiff in Error, but merely that he refused to abide by the assignment of the conductor to a compartment set aside for *his race* and *persisted* in sitting in one set apart for another race. He was by this presentment either a white man in a colored compartment or a colored man in a white compartment. In either case, assuming that he had paid his fare which is not in question, he had a right to ride where he chose, any law of the State to the contrary notwithstanding; for such a law discriminates in the enjoyment of a public right *solely* on the ground of race. The court will take notice of the fact that in all ages and all lands, it is the weak who suffer from all class discriminations and all caste legislation, and that, in this country, it is the colored race which must always be the victim of such legislation. In this case, if we take the evidence of the State's witnesses on which the presentment was evidently based, and the self-description of the Plaintiff in Error who swears that he is seven-eighths white and that the colored intermixture is not visible, we have the case of a man who believed he had a right to the privilege and advantage of being esteemed a white man, asserting that right against the action of the conductor who for some reason, we know not what, was intent on putting upon him the indignity of belonging to the colored race. The mere statement of the fact shows, in the strongest possible light, the discrimination based on race which is the sole object of the statute.

XIV—The Civil Rights Case, 109 U.S. 3, while discussing at considerable length the provisions of this section of the XIVth Amendment is not applicable here, as it turns on the distinction between State acts and individual acts and considers only the effect of the prohibitive clauses of the section. It is to be noted, however, that although the learned justice who delivered the opinion of the Court, mindful no doubt of his own dissenting opinion in the "Slaughter House Cases," declares that "positive rights and privileges are undoubtedly secured by the XIVth Amendment," yet shows that he has not considered its affirmative clauses as *grants of right*, since he adds: "But they are secured by way of prohibition against State laws, and State proceedings affecting those rights and privileges."

Taken in its real significance, therefore, the opinion in the Civil Rights Cases, so far as it touches the question at issue in this case, is strongly and expressly in favor of the Plaintiff in Error. The act of which he makes complaint is a "State act" and a "State proceeding" in regard to the rights granted by the XIVth Amendment.

The dissenting opinion of Mr. Justice Harlan in these cases is especially notable from the fact that we here first find formally and distinctly set forth the view that the national jurisdiction to protect the rights of the citizen is based on the affirmative as well as the prohibitive clauses of this amendment. He says:

"The first clause of this act is of a distinctively affirmative character. In its application to the colored race, *it created and granted*, as well citizenship of the United States as citizenship of the State in which they reside. It introduced all that race any of whose ancestors were imported and sold as slaves, into the political community, known as "The people of the United States." They became instantly citizens of the United States and of their respective States.

Not only were five millions of freedmen transformed into *national* and *state* citizens by this amendment, but every citizen of the United States was endowed with a national citizenship determinable in a new manner and a state citizenship made an incident thereof and based wholly upon the national grant.

XV—The relation of the leading cases in which this section is construed, to the construction contended for by the Plaintiff in Error.

The decisions mentioned are really the only ones necessary to be considered in connection with the construction of this section. The others neither materially add to nor detract from what is there determined. In all these cases there is dissent which wisely leaves the door open for farther consideration. While the opinions in all of them enter into a general discussion of the legal effect of the section, it may be said that the Slaughter House Cases determine merely that the State has exclusive jurisdiction of such police regulations as are therein defined; that the Civil Rights Cases decide that Congress has no right to legislate in regard to the rights of citizens in places of amusement, &c., *until* the states have by legislation improperly restricted them; while the opinion in the case of the United States *vs.* Cruikshank, decides that the State has the same sole and exclusive jurisdiction over the lives, liberties and rights of all citizens residing in its borders that it had before the enactment of this amendment when slavery and its interests, not the liberties of the individual, were the objects the constitution was intended to secure.

Only by the most strained construction can this wholesale and compulsory racial assortment of passengers upon a railroad train, where all as citizens have an equal right as on a public highway, and where all pay an equal price for the accommodations received, be termed a police regulation. In the history of English jurisprudence only slavery has demanded that distinctions in civil rights or the enjoyment of public privilege be marked by race distinctions. To introduce them again into our jurisprudence is to reanimate in effect the institution which is denounced in form by the XIIIth Amendment, and the destruction of which threatened the nation's life. It is not a sort of legislation that ought to be helped by strained construction of the fundamental law. Even under the decision in the Slaughter House Cases this is not to be classed among those "police regulations" which are beyond the jurisdiction of the court.

It also comes squarely within the exception made in the Civil Rights Cases; it is a statute expressly ordained by State legislation and carried into effect by State agencies and tribunals.

The act in question is exactly such a one as these two cases assert to be within the purview of this court's jurisdiction to review. It is an act of race discrimination pure and simple. The experience of the civilized world proves that it is not a matter of public health or morals, but simply a matter intended to re-introduce the caste-ideal on which slavery rested. The court will take notice of a fact inseparable from human nature, that, when the law distinguishes between the civil rights or privileges of two classes, it always is and always must be, to the detriment of the weaker class or race. A dominant race or class does not demand or enact class-distinctions for the sake of the weaker but for their own pleasure or enjoyment. This is not an act to secure *equal* privileges; these were already enjoyed under the law as it previously existed. The object of such a law is simply to debase and distinguish against the inferior race. Its purpose has been properly interpreted by the general designation of "Jim Crow Car" law. Its object is to separate the Negroes from the whites in public conveyances for the gratification and recognition of the sentiment of white superiority and white supremacy of right and power.

It is freely admitted that Cruikshank's case is squarely against us. If the opinion in this case is to be held as law, the relation of the State to the personal rights of the citizens of the United States residing therein, is precisely what it was before the adoption States this section of the constitution, and there is nothing to prevent a State from re-enacting nearly all the caste-distinctions, which slavery created. If that is the law, what is there to prevent a State from enacting the old rule of slavery jurisprudence, that insulting words from a colored man justify an assault by a white man or negative the presumption of malice in homicide. See the State *vs.* Jowers, II, Iredell, N.C., 555: State *vs.* Davis, 7 Jones, N.C., 52, and State *vs.* Caesar, 9 Iredell, for a full discussion of this legal presumption of inequality. What is there, if the State's jurisdiction over personal rights is to remain as it was before this section was adopted, to prevent the State from adopting as "police regulations," laws requiring a colored man to remove his hat on meeting or addressing a white man? Compelling him to give way to his white superior on the highway and other acts of enforced inferiority?

Our contention is that the opinion in Cruikshank's Case cannot stand, because it is based on the false hypothesis that this section does not create or secure *new rights* to the individual but merely defines pre-existent rights and prohibits the States from impairing or denying them. We contend that it creates a *new citizenship*—new in character, new in extent, new in method of determination, new in essential incident. That it endowed five millions of people with all the rights of national and state citizenship, both of which they were before forbidden by law to enjoy; that for these hitherto excluded classes, it created, granted and proclaimed a citizenship which embraced the old citizenship and added to it the privileges and immunities of the new one. That it enlarged the privileges and immunities of pre-existing citizenship, by changing the method of determination and adding to it the right of State-citizenship to attach immediately upon residence obtained in the State, without regard to State legislation. We insist that the inference of right, obligation and power of the general government to enforce, maintain and secure the lives, liberties and personal rights of the citizenship created, granted and declared by this Amendment, is infinitely clearer, stronger and more imperative than the inference drawn from the assertion of the owner's right to regain control of his fugitive slave, set forth in Section 3 of Article IV. Upon the effect of such inference of right and power we adopt the whole of the argument of Judge Story in Prigg *vs.* Pennsylvania. The only difference in the cases is that in our case the inference is much stronger than in that and that the result to be attained, in that case, was in derogation of liberty, while in this, its maintenance and security is sought. In that case, the result was to deprive the slave even of the hope of escape; in this case, it would be to give the colored man a hope that some time in the future the promise of liberty and equality of civil right in the United States may be peacefully fulfilled. The one is a presumption in favor of justice and liberty as the other was presumption in favor of inconceivable wrong. Shall this court which was so ready to commit the government to the perpetuation of wrong, hesitate to apply the same rule to secure the rights of its citizens?

XVI—The construction insisted on by the Plaintiff in Error does not impair the "exclusive jurisdiction" of the State, except as to the personal rights of citizens. In other respects it still remains. Neither is it open to the common objection that it would require national legislation in regard to all the rights, privileges and immunities of citizens. It merely asserts the right of the Federal Courts to pass upon legislative acts of the States touching such rights and the power of Congress to legislate in regard thereto, whenever it becomes necessary.

There are other parts of the Constitution which illustrate this relation. The power to provide uniform laws on the subject of bankruptcy and the inhibition of the States to pass laws impairing the obligation of contracts, are instances. In the absence of such national legislation, the States may pass insolvent laws and even exempt within certain limits, the property of the debtor from execution; but the Federal Courts will inquire in regard to all such laws when presented to them, and determine how far they are consistent with the constitutional requirement. The enactment of a bankrupt law wipes them all away unless affirmed by it. So, too, in the absence of national regulation of inter-state commerce, statutes affecting it were passed by the State; the Federal Courts merely considering whether they were in obstruction of it or not. While laws taxing traders from other states more heavily than dealers resident within the state, no one questions the right of the state to tax them equally with its own citizens. The federal courts only inquire into the *equality* of such laws. So in the case of the rights of the citizen as provided in this Amendment; as long as the State protects and secures the rights of all citizens without injustice or discrimination, there is no need for legislative assertion of the national prerogative: the supervisory control of the Federal Courts over State legislation is sufficient. But suppose a State, say the State of Louisiana where the common law never prevailed, should repeal all statutes in regard to murder—all laws defining the crime, giving jurisdiction of its trial and prescribing its punishment—is there any doubt that the government of the United States would be able to provide for the security of its citizens resident in the State? The XIVth Amendment did not destroy the jurisdiction of the State over the rights of its citizens, nor even its exclusive jurisdiction in regard to other matters, but simply made its legislation in regard to the rights of citizens and its judicial action in relation thereto, reviewable by the courts of the United States and subject to restraint when found to be in derogation of the rights, privileges and immunities of the citizens to whom the nation has guaranteed the rights of equal citizenship in the State.

XVII—It has been decided in the case of the Louisville Railway Co. *vs.* Mississippi 133 U.S.R., 589, that the State may compel a railroad operated under its charter, to provide separate cars or compartments equal in character and accommodation, to be used by individuals of different races, if it sees fit to do so. But in this case the exception is expressly made that the right to compel individuals of different races to use these separate coaches is not thereby decided.

The act in question in our case, proceeds upon the hypothesis that the State has the right to authorize and require the officers of a railway to assort the citizens who engage passage on its lines, according to race, and *to punish the citizen if he refuses to submit to such assortment.*

The gist of our case is the unconstitutionality of the assortment; *not* the question of equal accommodation; that much, the decisions of the court give without a doubt. We insist that the State has no right to compel us to ride in a car "set apart" for a particular race, whether it is as good as another or not. Suppose the provisions were that one of these cars should be painted white and the other black; the invidiousness of the distinction would not be any greater than that provided by the act.

But if the State has a right to distinguish between citizens according to race in the enjoyment of public privilege, by compelling them to ride in separate coaches, what is to prevent the application of the same principle to other relations? Why may it not require all red-headed people to ride in a separate car? Why not require all colored people to walk on one side of the street and the whites on the other? Why may it not require every white man's house to be painted white and every colored man's black? Why may it not require every white man's vehicle to be of one color and compel the colored citizen to use one of different color on the highway? Why not require every white business man to use a white sign and every colored man who solicits customers a black one? One side of the street may be just as good as the other and the dark horses, coaches, clothes and signs may be as good or better than the white ones. The question is not as to the equality of the privileges enjoyed, *but the right of the State to label one citizen as white and another as colored* in the common enjoyment of a public highway as this court has often decided a railway to be.

Neither is it a question as to the right of the common-carrier to distinguish his patrons into first, second and third classes, according to the accommodation paid for. This statute is really a restriction on that right, since the carrier is thereby compelled to provide two cars for each class, and so prevented from making different rates of fares by the expense which would be incurred by a multiplicity of coaches. In fact, its plain purpose and effect is to provide the white passenger with an exclusive first class coach *without requiring him to pay an extra fare for it.*

XVIII—Has a state power to punish as a crime, an act done by a person of one race on a public highway, which if done by an individual of another race on the same highway is no offense?

This is exactly what the act in question does, what it was intended to do and *all* it does. A man of one race taking his seat in a car and refusing to surrender it, is guilty of a crime, while another person belonging to another race may occupy the same without fault. The crime assigned depends not on the equality of the act, but on *the color of the skin.*

XIX—The criminal liability of the individual is not affected by inequality of accommodations.

While the act requires the accommodations for the white and black races to be "equal but separate," it by no means follows as a fact that they always are so. But the man who should refuse to go out of a clean and comfortable car into one reeking with filth at the behest of the conductor, would under this act be equally guilty of misdemeanor as if both were of equal desirability. The question of equality of accommodation cannot arise on the trial of a presentment under this statute. Equal or not equal, the refusal to obey the conductor's behest constitutes a crime. There is no averment in this case of equality of accommodation, but merely that the Plaintiff in Error was assigned "to the coach reserved for the race to which he the said Homer A. Plessy belonged" and that he "did then and there, unlawfully insist on going into a coach to which by race he did not belong," (See copy of information, printed Record, page 14.)

It does not appear to what race he belonged or what coach he entered, but, in the questionable language of the information, it is asserted that he did not belong to the *same race as the coach*. It is not asserted that the coach to which he was assigned was equal in accommodation to the one which it is alleged he committed a crime in entering. In his petition for certiorari (Printed Record, page one) the Plaintiff in Error avers himself to be "of mixed Caucasian and African descent, in the proportion of seven-eighths Caucasian and one-eighth African blood. That the mixture of colored blood is not discernable in him, that he is entitled to every right, privilege and immunity secured to citizens of the United States of the white race by the constitution of the United States, and that such right, privilege, recognition and immunity are worth to him the sum of Ten Thousand Dollars if the same be at all susceptible of being estimated by the standard value of money."

The affidavits of the state's witnesses, before the Recorder who bound over the Plaintiff in Error to the criminal court, where the same was filed before the information was entered therein, one of whom was the conductor of the train (See printed Record, pages 4–5,) declare him to be "a person of the colored race" and that the car he entered and refused to leave was "assigned to passengers of the white race."

The crime, then, for which he became liable to imprisonment so far as the court can ascertain, was that a person of seven-eighths Caucasian blood insisted in sitting peacefully and quietly in a car the state of Louisiana had commanded the company to set aside exclusively for the white race. Where on earth should he have gone? Will the court hold that a single drop of African blood is sufficient to color a whole ocean of Caucasian whiteness?

XX—The exception which is made in section four of the Act in question should not be passed over without consideration: "Nothing in this act shall be

UNDAUNTED RADICAL

construed as applying to nurses attending children of the other race."

The court will take notice of the fact that if there are any cases in the state of Louisiana in which nurses of the white race are employed to take charge of children of the colored race, they are so few that it is not necessary to consider them as a class actually intended to be favored by this exception. Probably there is not a single instance of such relation in the state. What then is the force and effect of this provision? It simply secures to the white parent traveling on the railroads of the state, the right to take a colored person into the coach set apart for whites in a menial relation, in order to relieve the passenger of the care of the children making the journey with the parents. In other words, the act is simply intended to promote the comfort and sense of exclusiveness and superiority of the white race. They do not object to the colored person in an inferior or menial capacity—as a servant or dependent, ministering to the comfort of the white race—but only when as a man and a citizen he seeks to claim equal right and privilege on a public highway with the white citizens of the state. The act is not only class-legislation but class-legislation which is self-condemned by this provision, as intended for the comfort and advantage of one race and the discomfort and disadvantage of the other, thereby tending directly to constitute a "step toward reducing them to the condition of a subject race"—the tendency especially condemned in Strauder *vs.* West Virginia, supra.

XXI—There is another point to be considered. The plaintiff insists that Act III of the Legislature of 1890, of the State of Louisiana is null and void because in tendency and purport it is in conflict with the Thirteenth Amendment of the Constitution of the United States: "Neither Slavery nor involuntary servitude—shall exist, &c."

What is meant by the word "Slavery" in this Amendment[?] It is evidently intended to embrace something more than a state of "involuntary servitude," since it is used in contradistinction to that term. It is the estate or condition of *being a slave.* What was the estate or condition of a slave? We have a right to suppose that this term is used in the Amendment with relation to the estate or condition of those who had up to that moment been slaves in the United States. What was that legal condition? The slave as defined by the Code of Louisiana, by the courts of the various states, and by this court in Scott vs Sanford, was legally distinguished both from citizens and from "free persons of color," by one thing, he was a "person without rights." The fact that he was the property of another; that he was held in a state of involuntary servitude; that he might be bought and sold—these were indeed incidents of his condition, striking and notable incidents, but they were all the results of one striking and distinctive feature of his legal relation to the body politic, which is expressed by the all comprehensive statement that *he had no rights*. The master might grant him privilege, the State might restrain the master's brutality, but no right of person, of family, of marriage, of property, could attach to the slave. He was a person without rights before the law, and all the other distinctive facts of his status, flowed from this condition. He could not inherit, sue or be sued, marry, contract, or be seized of any estate, *because* he was a "person without rights."

The real distinction between the citizen and the slave was that the one was entitled to life, liberty, the pursuit of happiness and the protection of the law, while the other was beyond the domain of the law except when it took cognizance of his existence as the incident of another's right or as the violator of its behests. The law knew him only as a chattel or a malefactor.

This condition of utter helplessness and dependence came to be expressed in the public and private relations of the two classes. The slave was not only the property of his master, but he was also the defenseless and despised victim of the civil and political society to which he was subject as well as to his master. He could not resent words or blows from any citizen. Only in the last extremity was he permitted to defend his life. Impudent language from him was held the equivalent of a blow from one of the dominant class. He was in bondage to the whole white race as well as to his owner. This bondage was a more important feature of American slavery than chattelism—indeed it was the one feature which distinguished it from "involuntary servitude" which is the chief element of chattelism. Slavery was a caste, a legal condition of subjection to the dominant class, a bondage quite separable from the incident of ownership. The bondage of the Israelites in Egypt is a familiar instance of this. It was unquestionably "Slavery," but it was not chattelism. No single Egyptian owned any single Israelite. The political community of Egypt simply denied them the common rights of men. It did not go as far as American Slavery in this respect since it did not by law deprive them of all natural and personal rights. It left the family and unlike our Christian slavery did not condemn a whole race to illegitimacy and adultery. It was this subjection to the control of the dominant race individually and collectively, which was the especially distinctive feature of slavery as contra-distinguished from involuntary servitude. The slave was one who had no rights—one who differed from the citizen in that he had no *civil* or *political* rights and from the "free person of color" in that he had no *personal* rights.

The object of the XIIIth Amendment was to abolish this discrepancy of right, not only so far as the legal form of chattelism was concerned, but so far as civil rights and all that regulation of relation between individuals of specific race and descent which marked the slave's attitude to the dominant race both individually and collectively was concerned.

There were in all the slave states specific codes of law intended for the regulation and control of the slave-class. They marked and defined not only his relation to his master but to the white race. He was required to conduct himself, not only "respectfully," which term had a very different signification when applied to the slave than when applied to the white man, but was expected and required to demean himself "submissively" to them. His position was that of legal subjection and statutory inferiority to the dominant race.

It was this condition and all its incidents which the Amendment was intended to eradicate. It meant to restore to him the rights of person and property—the natural rights of man—of which he had been deprived by slavery. It meant to undo all that slavery had done in establishing race discrimination and collective as well as personal control of the enslaved race.

It is quite possible that the term "involuntary servitude" may have been employed to prevent that very form of personal subjection which, soon after the emancipation of the slave, manifested itself in the enactment of the "Black Codes" which assumed control on the part of the State of all colored laborers who did not contract within a certain time to labor for the coming year and hired them out by public outcry. At least, it is evident that the purpose of this Amendment was not merely to destroy chattelism and involuntary servitude, but the estate and condition of subjection and inferiority of personal right and privilege, which was the result and essential concomitant of slavery.

XXII—"Privileges and Immunities of citizens of the United States."

It has been suggested that the omission of the term "rights" from the category of things exempted from impairment by State authority, was an intended reservation of state control. We beg to suggest that exactly the contrary is true.

"Right" as defined by Chancellor Kent, "is that which anyone is entitled to have or do, or to require another to do, within the limits prescribed by law." Rights may be natural or conferred. The exercise of any right is a "privilege" in the legal sense. The distinction has been sought to be made between the exercise of natural and conferred rights, that the latter alone is the basis of privilege; but it does not rest on any solid ground. Privilege is the exercise of a legal right, however the same may attach.

"Immunity" is the legal guaranty of non-interference—either with "right" —that is the abstract title on which the claim that one may "have or do or require another to do," any specific thing rests—or with the "privilege," which is based upon or constitutes the exercise or enjoyment of such right.

"Right," which is the basis both of "privilege" and "immunity" is, therefore, expressly included by the use of these terms. No "right," of any citizen of the United States can be denied or contravened by the law of any State, without impairing the "privileges" and "immunities" of the citizen which correlatively depend thereon.

XXIII—The construction of the First Section of the Fourteenth Amendment contended for by the Plaintiff in Error, is in strict accord with the Declaration of Independence, which is not a fable as some of our modern theorists would have us believe, but the all-embracing formula of personal rights on which our government is based and toward which it is tending with a power that neither legislation nor judicial construction can prevent. Every obstacle which Congress or the Courts have put in its way has been brushed aside. Under its impulse, the Fugitive Slave Law and the Dred Scott decision, both specially designed to secure the perpetuation of slavery under the constitution, became active forces in the eradication of that institution. It has become the controlling genius of the American people and as such must always be taken into account in construing any expression of the sovereign will, more especially a constitutional provision which more closely reflects the popular mind. This instrument not only asserts that "All men are created equal and endowed with certain inalienable rights, among which are life, liberty and the pursuit of happiness," but it also declares that the one great purpose for which governments are instituted among men is to "secure these rights."

Applying this guiding principle to the case under consideration, what is it natural and reasonable to conclude was the purpose of the people of the United States, when in the most solemn manner, they ordered this broad, unmodified and supremely emphatic declaration to be enrolled among the mandates of our fundamental law? Were they thinking how to enlarge the power of the general government over individual rights so as to include all, or how to restrict it so as to include as few as possible? Were they thinking of State rights or human rights? Did they mean to perpetuate the caste-distinctions which had been injected into our law under a constitution expressly and avowedly intended to perpetuate slavery and prevent the spirit of liberty from growing so strong as to work its legal annihilation—were they seeking to maintain and preserve these discriminations, or to overthrow and destroy them?

The Declaration of Independence, with a far-reaching wisdom found in no other political utterance up to that time, makes the security of the individual's right to "the pursuit of happiness," a prime object of all government. This is the controlling idea of our institutions. It dominates the national as well as the state governments. In asserting national control over both state and national citizenship, in appointing the boundaries and distinctive qualities of each, in conferring on millions a status they had never before known and giving to every inhabitant of the country rights never before enjoyed and in restricting the rights of the states in regard thereto—in doing this were the people consciously and actually intending to protect this right of the individual to the pursuit of happiness or not? If they were, was it the pursuit of happiness by all or by part of the people which they sought to secure?

If the purpose was to secure the unrestricted pursuit of happiness by the four millions then just made free, now grown to nine millions, did they contemplate that they were leaving to the states the power to herd them away from her white citizens in the enjoyment of chartered privilege? Suppose a member of this court, nay, suppose every member of it, by some mysterious dispensation of providence should wake tomorrow with a black skin and curly hair—the two obvious and controlling indications of race—and in traveling through that portion of the country where the "Jim Crow Car" abounds, should be ordered into it by the conductor. It is easy to imagine what would be the result, the indignation, the protests, the assertion of pure Caucasian ancestry. But the conductor, the autocrat of Caste, armed with the power of the State conferred by this statute, will listen neither to denial or protest. "In you go or out you go," is his ultimatum.

What humiliation, what rage would then fill the judicial mind! How would the resources of language not be taxed in objurgation! Why would this sentiment prevail in your minds? Simply because you would then feel and know that such assortment of the citizens on the line of race was a discrimination intended to humiliate and degrade the former subject and dependent class— an attempt to perpetuate the caste distinctions on which slavery rested—a statute in the words of the Court "tending to reduce the colored people of the country to the condition of a subject race."

Because it does this the statute is a violation of the fundamental principles of all free government and the Fourteenth Amendment should be given that construction which will remedy such tendency and which is in plain accord with its words. Legal refinement is out of place when it seeks to find a way both to avoid the plain purport of the terms employed, the fundamental principle of our government and the controlling impulse and tendency of the American people.

ALBION W. TOURGÉE,
of counsel for Plaintiff in Error.

30

Oral Argument of A. W. Tourgée (1896)*

In addition to his written brief, Tourgée appeared before the U.S. Supreme Court on April 13, 1896, accompanied by co-counsel Samuel F. Phillips, to present his case. Tourgée's planned remarks were typed onto forty-five large note cards which bore the heading "Argument of A. W. Tourgee." Expanding upon key points from his brief, this document provides further insight into Tourgée's legal strategy in *Plessy* v. *Ferguson*, particularly in regard to the ambiguities of Homer A. Plessy's racial classification.

If the court please:

I wish to call the attention of the Court to certain points connected especially with the "Federal Question" involved in this case.

The first of these is that stated in the brief filed by Mr. Walker and myself as the 1st Point of Plaintiff's Contention, page 7.—The exemption of railway companies and officers from prosecution in the courts of the state by persons excluded from the cars by the train officers under the provisions of section 11 of this act.

The court below practically admitted the unconstitutionality of the Section by claiming that it did *not* protect either railway or official, if they *wrongfully* excluded a passenger, that is, if they excluded a passenger for insisting upon his right to ride in one car when in fact he belonged to the race assigned to another car (See page 12 of record).

This construction deprives this provision of all significance and leaves the section precisely the same effect it would have were the last member of the sentence "and for such refusal, &c," had not been written.

Our contention is that this provision is a plain denial of the right to sue in

*"Argument of A. W. Tourgée," item 6472, Albion W. Tourgée Papers, Chautauqua County Historical Society.

the courts of the state for an injury received and as such is a clear legislative violation of the restrictive provisions of the XIV Amendment.

Also that this provision is such an intimate and essential provision of the statute, that under the rule laid down by Chief Justice Shaw, in Warren vs. Wayon and Alderman of Charlestown vs. Gray 84 and cited with emphatic approval by this Court in Allen vs. Louisiana 103 U.S. page 84, "If they are so mutually connected with and dependent on each other, as conditions, considerations, or compensations, as to warrent [*sic*] a belief that the legislature intended them as a whole and that, if all could not be carried into effect the legislature would not pass the residue independently, and some parts are unconstitutional, *all* the provisions which are thus connected or dependent must fall with them."

We think this rule applies to the present statute with a nicety that almost implies that it was *made for it*. That this provision is an essential part of the whole idea of the statute it seems to us cannot for a moment be questioned. What is the purpose of this act? Evidently to assort passengers on the railroads of the state according to color. They are called "races," it is true, but the only racial distinctions recognized by the act are "white" and "colored." The statute does not use the ordinary scientific terms, Caucasian, Mongolian, Indian, Negro, &c. Why? Evidently, because the legislature recognized the fact that by this act they were imposing a greatly added expense on the railroad companies of the state in requiring them to provide separate accommodations for each race. So, in the first place, they reduce the whole human family to two grand divisions which they term "races," the "white race" and the "colored race." It is a new ethnology by prejudice based on the lessons of slavery, does not stop at trifles. In effect, the legislature says to the railways, you must have on all trains two grand divisions of humanity.

To this it was evidently expected that the railway companies would make two objections:

1—"It will greatly add to the expense of running our trains to provide duplicate accommodations."

2—"We cannot distinguish between 'white' and 'colored' men and women. Our officers will have to act on the spur of the moment, judging by inspection only, and it is impossible to distinguish some 'white' men from 'colored' at a glance. We shall be subject to innumerable suits for damage, if we obey this law."

They were evidently correct in these conclusions. A once noted Senator from Ohio used to tell with great glee of his experience on a visit to New Orleans, that once finding time hanging heavy on his hands, he determined to attend a public assemblage and was met at the door with the emphatic statement: "Colored men are not allowed here."

Some of the Court may have heard this story as I did, from the lips of Tom Corwin,[1] who traced his descent to a noted English ancestry, of which he was justly proud.

To obviate such apparent difficulty the legislature says in the second section, in effect:

"You are hereby authorized and required to make such assortment according to color and to prevent such loss and annoyance from suits for damages from those aggrieved by your action, we hereby authorize you to put off your trains and refuse to carry any one who declines to accept the assortment according to race, of your officials. And in order to relieve you from damage and annoyance we hereby assure you that neither you nor your officials shall be liable for damages resulting from such action in any of the courts of this state."

This promise, is also coupled with a threat in the fourth section, where the legislature declares:

"That any railways company which refuses or neglects, to carry out its provisions shall be deemed guilty of a misdemeanor. And that any employee who neglects or refuses to make such assortment of passengers shall be fined, for each offence."

The whole statue is but a machine to effect the compulsory assortment of passengers on the line of color; and in the chain of related forces relied upon to effect this result, the two chief links are the railway companies who have to provide the extra cars and the railway conductors who have to do the sorting. Both are liable to suits for damage for thrusting the passenger into the wrong compartment or putting them off the train for an insufficient cause. The denial of the right to recover damages is one of the essential means by which the co-operation of these forces is to be secured. It is evident that this legislature would not have passed this law had not this exemption from liability been embraced in it to secure the co-operation of the roads here in. It is a clear denial to such excluded persons of the equal protection of the law—the denial of remedy for wrong—of a right of action for damage done. This

1. Thomas Corwin was governor of Ohio (1840–42), U.S. senator (1845–50), and U.S. minister to Mexico (1861–64).

is a "federal question" because it is a violation of the restrictive clauses of the XIVth Amendment. . . .

I also desire to submit to the court a proposition not alluded to in any of the briefs for the relator, to wit:

THAT IF IT APPEAR TO THE COURT THAT THIS STATUTE IS INTENDED AND DESIGNED TO DISCRIMINATE AGAINST COLORED CITIZENS AND IN ITS NATURAL AND EVIDENT OPERATION DOES SO DISCRIMINATE, TENDING TO REDUCE THEM TO A DEPENDENT AND SERVILE CONDITION, WE ARE ENTITLED TO A REVERSAL OF THE JUDGEMENT BELOW, NO MATTER WHETHER THE RELATOR IS WHITE OR BLACK.

Every decision and every dissenting opinion in this court, from the Slaughter House Cases to the present term, in which the force of the XIVth Amendment has been considered has admitted and affirmed one principle, to wit: that state legislation having such object and purpose is unconstitutional.

But our friends upon the other side will say, it does not appear whether Plessy is a colored man or a white one. We submit that it is entirely immaterial which he may be.

The act with which he is charged, whether white or black is one changed with one single purpose. The machinery of the statute is intended only to promote one object. If that object is an unconstitutional one, no man can be held guilty of crime for its violation.

The object of the act is to prevent white and colored citizens from occupying the same car. This is sought to be effected by two means: (1) By making it criminal for a "white" man to occupy a "colored" car and (2) by making it criminal for a "colored" man to sit in a "white" car. Both are parts of the same general purpose and if this purpose is an unlawful one, a white man can no more be held liable for violating its provisions than a colored man.

In order to carry out its purpose the law professes to create two criminal offences, two distinct crimes one of which can only be committed by a white citizen and the other only by a colored citizen. One consists of a white citizen refusing to go into a car assigned to the "white" race or refusing to leave the car assigned to the "colored" race, at the command of the conductor. No colored man can commit this crime. The one crime which the "colored" citizen can commit against the provisions of this statute, is exactly the converse of this, to wit: refusing to go into the car assigned to the "colored" race or to leave the car assigned to the "white" race at the command of the conductor. These crimes are not identical and cannot be made identical by mere vagueness of statement.

UNCERTAINTY

We contend that THE PRESENTMENT ITSELF IS VOID FOR UNCERTAINTY. It is precisely equivalent to an allegation of trespass which fails to give the ownership or description of the land entered upon, but merely says that the defendant entered upon land not his own. This is an objection not taken in the court below but it is fundamental and can neither be cured by neglect nor by subsequent proceedings. It is like the omission of the word "heirs" in a conveyance or the term "malice prepense" in an indictment for murder—a defect that goes to the very root of the prosecution.

The presentment is an "artful dodger" hung on a distributed middle. It is an attempt to shift the burden of proof upon the defendant, and hold a person to answer a charge not described with sufficient certainty to enable one to define its elements. It is true it follows the "*words*" of the statute; but these words comprehend two crimes, the one a "white" man may commit and the other only a "colored" man may commit. They are alternative in character and "color" is not only an ingredient but the chief ingredient in both.

The Statute itself is a skillful attempt to confuse and conceal its real purpose. It assumes impartiality. It fulminates apparently against white and black alike. Its real object is to keep negroes out of one car for the gratification of the whites—not only to keep whites out of another car for the comfort and satisfaction of the colored passenger. It is simply an attempt to evade the constitutional requirement of equality of right and legal privilege to all citizens and to avoid the decisions of this court in regard to legislation intended to discriminate against the colored citizen by professing to discriminate against both.

The court must take notice of human nature and universal conditions. A class or race claiming superiority always insists on special privilege. A class or race to whom is imputed inferiority always resists discrimination or special privilege based on the assumption of superiority by other class. This is the universal law of human nature. On it is based all progress toward equal right. It is the hope of humanity the keynote of progress everywhere. To it we owe all that has been accomplished toward the overthrow of rank and caste in the past and the establishment of free institutions. It is a divine impulse by which the eternal struggle for equality of right and privilege for all is carried on from generation to generation, from century to century, in every land and nation under heaven. When it is relaxed caste and inequality of condition increase. When it is overcome oppression abounds and becomes irremediable except through social convulsion.

A noted divine said in his sermon two weeks ago, that he "thanked God for the French Revolution." So should we all. It was the great lesson of history, the infallible teacher, against legalized inequality—restricted right and unequal privilege.

A race or class claiming superiority naturally desires to see its exclusiveness crystallized into law—and is forever demanding such recognition of its demand. In all history, there cannot be found an instance of the poorer, the weaker, the class stigmatized as inferior, asking or demanding that such disparagement be legalized or perpetuated. A class whether weak or strong may voluntarily withdraw itself from association with others, but it would be contrary to all human nature for it ask or desire such separation to be made a matter of law. Even the Jew who boasts of his exclusiveness fought for centuries against legal exclusion from public right and equal privilege.

The claim that this act is for the common advantage of both races or was so intended and accepted, is simply farcical.

The universal instinct is true in this respect. Whatever emphasizes the distinction between a class claiming superiority and one branded with inferiority is of necessity detrimental to the inferior. Whenever the class claiming to be superior sets legal bounds to the privilege of the inferior, these bounds are always intended to accentuate the difference between them; and that difference is intended to exalt the one and debase the other.

Suppose in one of our northern states or in England a law should be passed requiring one set of cars for "ladies and gentleman" and other for "working people"; should require them to be so labeled; should authorize and command the conductor to assort passengers into these two classes and make it an indictable offence for any one to refuse to obey his direction.

The "Ladies and Gentlemen" would have no ground for complaint. The best is good enough for any one. But those who were thus by law classified as non-gentlemen—the clerk, the working man, the "dinner pail brigade" what would they say? Perhaps not one of them would claim to be a "gentleman." Hardly one in a thousand would care to enter the car from which he was thus excluded, but to be legally labeled "not a gentlemen" would arouse his inextinguishable wrath. No railroad could run such cars. They would be mobbed at every station. And the fact that "gentlemen" were excluded from the "working peoples" cars as well as working people from the "gentlemen's" cars, would be justly hooted as a subterfuge too cheap to deceive a child.

If such is the character of this act, then according to every decision, according to every dictum uttered by any justice of this court such a law is in violation of the XIVth Amendment and void in consequence. If such is the case, every iota of the machinery of the statute calculated to effect this purpose is unlawful and cannot be made to bind, hamper or restrict the liberty of any man black or white, nor make any man's act in violation of its criminal.

Therefore, we say that it makes no difference in the world whether the relator is "white" or "colored," an immaculate Caucasian or an indistinguishable compound of all the races of the world. When he is charged with crime, his liberty invaded, arrested and imprisoned for violating an act whose very essence is to establish an unconstitutional distinction, it makes no difference whether he was a "white" man in the "Jim Crow" car or a colored man in a white car, he has a clear and unmistakable right to appeal to this court for protection. It is just as much an act of derogation to the colored citizen to force a white man to ride in a "white" car as to compel a "colored" man to ride in a "colored" car. Both acts are part and parcel of the same general purpose and design and any man charged with crime for refusal to comply with it is protected by its unlawful purpose and character—its essential unconstitutionality. No man can be hanged with a rotten rope. . . .

It may be said that every man knows to which race he belongs and whether the car he was in was a "white" or "colored" one.

It does not follow. He may have been unable to read. One third and more of the people of the state are and so [may] not have known the distinction between the cars. He may have been the only passenger on the train and so have had no other means of information.

Again, he may not know whether he is a white man or colored. It is a question which the law of Louisiana has not decided, and which science is totally unable to solve. See the very able argument on this question in the brief of Mr. Walker, page 37 et seq. How shall a man who may have one-eighth or one-sixteenth colored blood know to which race he belongs? The law does not tell him; science decides perhaps one way and common repute may decide the other. If the law charges him with being in the wrong car, is it not bound to set out the facts that constitute it the wrong one? The statement, "in a car to which he did not by race belong," is a conclusion, *not a fact.*

The Federal Courts claim the right to adopt their own interpretation of the law, although a different interpretation may be adopted by the state courts. . . .

If he has made a mistake the court says he is liable to an action for damages subject to "defenses for good faith and probable cause." But in the meantime, he has a right to punish summarily the person who refuses to occupy a particular coach by refusing to carry him upon the train. We submit that this is in itself a deprivation of the liberty and property of the citizen without due process of law, whether the conductor is right or wrong in his assignment; that it is unlawful punishment for the crime of presuming to disagree with the conductor upon an important and difficult question of race. The passenger must submit to the conductor's judgment or lose his right to ride upon the train. It gives the conductor authority to eject for mere disagreement with him upon one of the most abstruse questions of physics and of law. This is an interference with his liberty. If he has paid for his ticket he loses his money. As the act is mandatory only nominal damages could be recovered even if the conductor was in error; if he should happen to be right none at all. We submit that an act that requires a man to carry a certified copy of his pedigree in order to satisfy a conductor of his right to ride in a car, or entitle him to substantial damages if refused, is clearly a denial of justice that is in conflict with the XIVth Amendment. And without such pedigree stuck into his face, a conductor compelled by fear of indictment to act, would be liable only for nominal damages for any false assignment he might make. The construction of the court below, even if accepted, serves only to show the real character and purpose of the act to relieve the railway and its officers from liability for acts which once committed, are practically irremediable. Many can oppress as well as one and such oppression is perhaps even more hopeless.

Contemplating this fact, we are forced to ask the question why is it true? Why was this Court once simply a policeman forever saying to the sufferer from stated injustice—"Pass on?"

There is one simple, sufficient yet painful answer. The constitution of the United States was intended and designed to perpetuate Slavery—to put it beyond all power of control or attack by the spirit of individual liberty and equality which the principles of the Declaration of Independence were sure to germinate.

This object was accomplished by giving to the states an absolute exclusive and final jurisdiction over the lives, persons, liberties and rights of all those who lived within borders, except two classes, viz:

1—Citizens of other states, and

2—Fugitives from labor.

How serious and how irremediable is the evil that may be wrought by this power is evident from a moment's consideration. The fact that a man rides, even thought it may be against his will, in a "colored" car, has a tending to create a belief that he is a colored man. Frequently repeated, it would no doubt establish such a reputation for him. And such reputation is the greatest misfortune that can befall any man or woman in this United States. Death is a trivial matter in comparison with it. There is not a man in this room who would not prefer death to the lasting evil of such general reputation. A man might well prefer leprosy as an alternative, for that at least dies with its victim. The blight of color lives on and on. It clouds the hearth, blasts the home, curses the loved ones, debases the child and sends its taint along the family line—not only until all trace is lost but until even the tradition of it has died out of human memory. The most precious of all inheritances is the reputation of being white. This is true from every point of view socially, politically, professionally, even religiously. No word can paint the injury that may accrue from the reputation of being "colored" or the advantage that may result from the reputation of being "white."

Your honors can easily perceive how a white man's reputation may easily become clouded by the action of a conductor, or the opportunity of one of those who stand upon the border-land of the two races be lost through the exercise of this power in law which puts such power to do immeasurable evil in the hands of one man, without adequate remedy, can be held consistent with the equal right of American citizenship. Its only effect is to perpetuate the stigma of color—to make the curse immortal, incurable, inevitable.

But it may be answered that if a man does not like the laws of one state he can move to another. One of the marvels of our American citizenship is that such barbarous evasion should ever have come to find utterance even in popular discussion, much less to have escaped the lips of men holding such exalted positions as Justices of this court. It is the most cowardly and infamous of all arguments by which injustice has sought to excuse itself. "If you don't like the laws of the state where you live, get out of it." It is the world-wide alternative of tyranny. It is what Spain said to the Jews; what England said to the Puritans and the Irish; what Russia says to the Jews, when she offers the choice between apostasy and exile. Turkey is more merciful when she offers the alternative —circumcision or death.

One can only feel pity for the noble men who sat upon this bench and were forced to formulate this principle as the only hope of escape for the citizen of the United States who suffered from the injustice and oppression of any State. And our history shows that states *can* oppress. A republican form of government is no guaranty against injustice.

Because of this, citizenship of the United States became a limited, indefinite and inferential relation. No personal rights could be considered by this court, except in a few restricted relations. The State had exclusive jurisdiction

of the rights, lives and persons of all her inhabitants. The citizen of the United
States has no rights, privileges or immunities that could be asserted against
the state.

On this rested not only the security of Slavery but the doctrine of "State
Sovereignty" and of the "paramount allegiance" of the citizen to the state.

WHAT WAS THE EFFECT ON THESE CONDITIONS OF THE FIRST SECTION OF
THE XIVTH AMENDMENT OF THE CONSTITUTION OF THE UNITED STATES?

The course of decision upon this most important constitutional provision
ever made, has been most remarkable. In every one of the cases in which it has
been considered there has been earnest, sometimes almost passionate dissent.
There is a lack of harmony in the reasoning by which they are supported and
the limitations assigned to the provisions of this act which would seem to be
sufficient excuse for asking the court to consider a line of thought in regard
to it which seems, not unnaturally, to have escaped at least express notice and
construction hitherto.

THROUGH ALL THESE OPINIONS THERE SEEMS TO RUN ONE GENERAL LINE
OF THOUGHT, TO WIT: THAT THIS SECTION MUST BE HELD TO PROTECT THE
COLORED CITIZENS OF A STATE FROM HARMFUL DISCRIMINATION AS RE-
GARDS LEGISLATIVE OR JUDICIAL INFRINGEMENT OF THEIR RIGHTS; AND A
HALF EXPRESSED CONCLUSION THAT IT DOES NOT IN LIKE MANNER PROTECT
THE WHITE CITIZEN OF THE UNITED STATES FROM THE IMPAIRMENT OF HIS
RIGHTS BY STATE ACTION.

I cannot believe this construction correct or that it can ever conclusively
remain as an accepted construction of this section.

Such a construction makes the Constitution class legislation of the most
obnoxious character. It gives the colored citizen a right of the most exalted
character which is denied to the white man—a right to the Federal courts to
intervene between him and the State in which he dwells, whenever the laws of
said state shall be of a character to end to the disparagement of his equality
of right as a citizen of said state. According to this construction, if the laws
of any state should harmfully distinguish against the white citizens of the
United States resident in her borders, they would have no legal remedy. Suppose a colored majority in any state should levy a poll-tax upon white polls
only. According to this theory there would be no remedy for them. If the state
courts should sustain it they could not come here and lay upon this court the
duty of protecting them. The court would have to say that this section was
intended only for the protection of the colored citizens and the white ones
must look out for themselves. I cannot believe that this was the purpose of the

people of the United States in making this change in the organic law—or that this court in the exercise of its final jurisdiction will so ordain.

The underlying idea of the court, no doubt, has been that the Amendment was intended to secure equality of right for all citizens without regard to color, but this CANNOT BE DONE BY DECLARING THAT IT APPLIES ONLY to discrimination AGAINST the colored citizen. Inequality may also arise from DISCRIMINATION IN HIS FAVOR. . . .

The NEW citizenship of the United States, has nothing to do with race or descent, but is determined solely by the place of birth, "Born or naturalized in the United States."

In the NEW, state citizenship is an essential and inseparable incident of national citizenship. The Citizen of the United States, ex vi termini,[2] becomes a citizen of the state in which he may reside.

The OLD state-citizenship was determined wholly by the action of the State itself. It decided the terms, conditions and limitations of its own citizenship. The United States, could neither make nor unmake a citizen of any state. A man might be a citizen of any state and not a citizen of the United States. Under the XIVth Amendment, the state has nothing to do with constituting any man a citizen. The general government has defined, limited and prescribed state-citizenship. Every citizen of the United States is thereby constituted a citizen of the state in which he resides.

Under the pre-existing law no man having a drop of colored blood in his veins, could become a citizen of the United States. It was in all literalness a "white man's government." No colored man could sue or be sued, plead or be impleaded as a citizen in her courts. In the NEW citizenship color is expressly ignored and the sole condition of citizenship is birth in the United States. . . .

What then did the XIVth Amendment effect?

1—It created a new national citizenship, differing in scope, derivation, rights and manner of determination from any that had previous existed.

2—It lifted one-eighth of the population of the United States from a position of legal inferiority—free persons of color—to the plane of citizenship.

3—It made STATE-CITIZENSHIP an incident of NATIONAL citizenship.

4—By this grant of a NEW citizenship of the United States the constitution guaranteed to every person thus endowed protection in the secure enjoyment of all the rights, privileges and immunities attaching thereto.

5—By attaching STATE-Citizenship, as an essential and universal incident, to this grant of NATIONAL citizenship, the United States became the guaran-

2. Latin, "by the force of the term."

tor to every citizen of the secure enjoyment of all [the rights, privileges and immunities attaching thereto]. . . .

As the final and exclusive jurisdiction over the rights of all the inhabitants of a state was intended solely to protect and perpetuate slavery, it is fit and proper that is should disappear with slavery. As it was intended to promote inequality of right it is proper that it should disappear with the dawn of the epoch of equality in our government. As it was intended to promote injustice it should not be perpetuated in the hope of establishing justice. As it has been the seed of strife its elimination is the guarantee of peace.

. . . . . .

V

CODA:
LETTERS FROM BORDEAUX

31

Letter to President William Mckinley (1898)*

In 1897, President William McKinley appointed Tourgée the United States consul to Bordeaux, France. With this appointment Tourgée began a self-imposed
public silence on the "race problem," but he nevertheless maintained a regular
private correspondence with McKinley offering unsolicited advice on a variety
of controversial topics that included racial strife. In this letter, written on November 23, 1898, Tourgée reflects upon the Wilmington riot in North Carolina,
in which white supremacists killed at least twenty-two blacks in an armed uprising against the city's biracial Republican majority, forcing Republican leaders to
resign from office and scores of African Americans to flee for their lives. This
successful coup d'état left Tourgée stunned and demoralized.

Hon. William McKinley, President.
Washington, D.C.
Dear Sir:
I doubt if even the almost unprecedented approval of your administration on
an off year at the polls, which marked the election of two weeks ago, would
have impressed me with the duty of dictating my congratulations from a sick
bed, because I think it should be assumed that every patriotic American endorsed the verdict of the people, whether he speaks or keeps silent. At least
such would be the fact in my case, though every day since last April, has added
to my wonder and approval of the amazing tact and ability which you have
displayed in the remarkable crisis of our history, the first chapter of which is
about closing. It is only the fact that its last few days have been marked by a
revival of that most dangerous and horrible feature of American life, a display
of race antagonism at the South, that compels me to express to you my sincer-
est sympathy and keenest apprehension.

*Albion W. Tourgée to William McKinley, November 23, 1898, William McKinley Papers,
Library of Congress.

As you are aware this has been the subject of my special and unremitting investigation and study for more than a quarter of a century. Every day of that time, I have grown less and less hopeful with regard to the outcome. For a time I believed that American Christianity and the inherent love of liberty and justice of the American people, would find a way to solve this problem without any of that wholesale slaughter which has marked the progress of personal liberty and individual opinion in the Old World, but that soothing theory I have long since abandoned. I believed that the United States would just as readily approve the massacre of the colored race throughout her borders, as France would approve by the verdict of her masses, the slaughter of the Jews. There was time when we had a conscience upon this subject; when the American people believed that Liberty and Justice were essential elements of republican freedom and prosperity. That time has passed away. The pulpit is silent; the press regards such manifestations as these in North and South Carolina, only with a sort of vague disfavor. If a thousand voters had been killed at Wilmington, I doubt if there would have been any public manifestation of any great extent, to express disapproval.

I had entertained the hope, perhaps a foolish one, that the bravery of the colored troops as manifested in the late war [the Spanish-American War] and known disinclination of the white people of the United States to military service in time of peace, might have opened the way for the organization of new colored regiments, of which the line officers would also be colored men, for service in our new possessions. I have thought that this might be secured by providing that the field and staff of such regiments should always be graduates of West Point, leaving the line officers to be appointed from existing regiments or from civil life, as the case might be. If the North Carolina ebullition had not occurred, I should have ventured to address you, expressing this view, but now, I fear it is useless to hope for any legislation which may open the door, even the least, to the colored man, who has again been placed under the heel of race prejudice in the United States.

The more I have studied the question, the less I seem to know how it may or ought to be handled—how with existing elements it can be handled successfully. I was one time in hopes that the colored people would settle down to a grim determination to make it a religious question; that they would take one day in each year, make it a day of Supplication for justice, in all their churches, and so appeal fervently and submissively to the religious sentiment of the world—to man as well as to God, or rather to man though supplication to the Almighty. Such a "Supplication Day," I have urged upon the colored people for many years. I am afraid they are not large enough or strong enough to appreciate its scope, or realize the necessity for such an appeal when political remedy seems hopeless. It is possible that such a suggestion from you might be more effective.

For myself, I confess that I am quite unable to advise in regard to the steps necessary or desirable to ameliorate the present condition. Indeed, I have little hope that it ever will be, or can be ameliorated by any party or political tendency. It seems to me one of those questions which are beyond remedy by any human means, that it has so cankered the political and moral sentiment of the American people, that no organized resistance to it is possible. It seems to be one of those questions which only God can handle. I have no doubt that He will sometime take it in hand, its own injustice, by finding in the Race Problem the end of its liberties and the destruction of its organic character. It seems to me not unlikely that the next great outbreak of barbaric slaughter, such as followed St. Bartholomew's Eve, may occur in the United States of America, and that when it has passed by, the Republic which has so long boasted of Liberty, Justice and Equality, will be only a blood-drenched theater on which inflamed factions will struggle for mastery.

I hoped that this hideous monster would not show his head again during my time. This outbreak in North Carolina appeals to me very closely. I fought this matter all over there twenty-odd years ago, and cannot help attributing the fact that this is the last of the Southern States to yield to the disfranchisement and degradation of its colored citizens, to the good seed which I then sowed with earnestness and prayer, without fear, favor or affection, through many a hard fought struggle. However it has come again, alike in all its essential features, with the conscience of the North weakened and that of the South—the white South—hopelessly debauched that God will pity our country and aid you upon whom the task and trial will most sorely fall, is my sincere and constant prayer.

Very Respectfully,
Albion W. Tourgée

32

Letter to Ferdinand L. Barnett (1900)*

In this letter, written on August 6, 1900, Tourgée replied to his friend Ferdinand L. Barnett, who had asked for Tourgée's analysis of the motives of white lynch mobs. Barnett, editor of the *Chicago Conservator,* and his wife, Ida B. Wells-Barnett, were prominent black leaders with whom Tourgée had had a long association. This letter conveys Tourgée's deep sense of despair and powerlessness as he criticizes the accommodationism of black ministers and predicts that it will require "martyrs by the thousand" to overcome the current wave of reaction.

My Dear Sir:

I am in receipt of your letter of July 1, 1900, and am truly glad to learn of your promotion which has been well-deserved.

Upon the subject in regard to which you write, I must ask you to excuse me from making any statement or argument. All my life, since arriving, at manhood, the study of the relations of the Anglo-Saxon to the colored races of the world, especially in the United States, has been the chief and most absorbing of that life. I have not contented myself with discussing theories, but have observed for myself. Not a condition which had developed since I first sat with amazement and horror [to witness], Christian Slavery on American soil, has escaped my personal scrutiny. I was one of those who believed that the fall of slavery was the end of the discordant race relations. I was amazed that it did not. . . .

Yesterday there came to me the adoption of the constitutional amendment in North Carolina.[1] For a few days there will be seen here and there a little quiver of excitement at its gross injustice. There will be some newspaper law

*Albion W. Tourgée to Ferdinand L. Barnett, August 6, 1900, item 9665, Albion W. Tourgée Papers, Chautauqua County Historical Society.

1. This 1900 amendment added a literacy test and poll tax as requirements for voting.

exploiting its violation of the Federal constitution. The editorial Wiseacres do not realize three things:

1—That the Supreme Court of the United States, consistent with all its history as opposed to the liberty of the individual and filled with blind devotion to the supremacy of State control and delineation of the right of the citizen, has already gnawed away the substance of these amendments inspired by the rude experience of war leaving only the small shell to blight the hope of those who looked to the [Federal government] for liberty and equal rights for all.

2—That there is now considerable element of the white people of the United States who desire the civil, political or industrial liberty and equality of the colored race in the United States.

3—That there is no such community or intensity of sentiment among the colored people of the United States as is absolutely essential to impress any considerable element of the white people with the duty or policy of doing justice to them.

Without such sentiment no legislation or executive action of any national party can improve present conditions. Indeed, it is doubtful if judicial construction has not so tied the hands of Congress that no majority however great and however desirous of doing justice could improve present conditions. . . .

The colored man has been disfranchised throughout the Southern States.

He has been deprived, in one way and another of that protection of person and property which constitute liberty.

Not one out of ten thousand white murderers who kill colored men suffers the penalty of the law.

Not one white man who violates colored womanhood, suffers any punishment therefore.

Christianity has separated the Church into "White" and "Black."

Instead of trial by jury, lynch-law has become the rule.

The "Jim Crow Car" has become an established institution in all the states of the South.

That this will be followed by other more oppressive and restrictive institutions, no reasonable man who studies the course of repressive legislation since the close of the War of Secession can doubt.

Against these tendencies what reactionary or reformatory force exists in any part of the country?

A few churches or rather a few ministers—do a little, a very little feeble protesting. Others do some vigorous and impassioned justification. Christianity is on both sides as it has always been since the black man came to disturb the peace of the church by his absurd demand for the application of the Christian ethic to the "colored brother."

The colored people—dazed, blinded, confused, deceived, is it any wonder that they have lost heart and hope? That they have not thus far developed that passionate love for freedom which makes liberty the central thought of religion and is the only impulse yet known by which a people secures equal liberty with others[?]

"Science," that form of self-inflated thought which degrades manhood, and conditions of the Almighty by formulating all powerful material conditions, has formulated a "gold-cure" for injustice as well as drunkenness. The trouble with it is that it applies only to the victim of wrong, not to his oppressors. . . .

I have no doubt that God will find a way to cure this woeful wrong—the worst offshoot of slavery. How will it be done? I know not.

When? Certainly not until the colored people of the United States have developed the same passion for Justice that their fathers displayed for Liberty. Not until every service in every "colored church," palpitates with the impassionate demand for Justice before the law, equal rights as men and equal opportunity as doers of the world's work—not until that time and it may be long afterwards—will the power that rules on earth, through human instrumentalities and by the operation of human motives, find a way to do what the dominant ideal of my generation was too weak to accomplish and which your race has, thus far, proved itself incapable of rightly demanding.

Apparently, it must come whenever it does come, through some effective appeal to the brain and conscience either of ALL the white people of the United States or of a portion of them united with practically all the colored people, in some supreme effort for justice. What will move to such action, no man knoweth. But this we do know—that in all history no forward step has been taken towards justice or liberty along the lines the Wise Men of any age have marked out, but only in answer to the cry of the weak, the poor and the oppressed.

God found a way to overthrow Christian Slavery in the United States. . . . I will not say God heard. But a way was found, a way no man had looked for, a way no wisdom had marked out. It was not the result of argument or theory. It did not come through legislation. No court ordered it. No President declared in its favor. Only the madness of those who sought to perpetuate slavery based on race distinctions—on the color of the skin alone—only their madness made possible the overthrow of the institution they sought to perpetuate as a part of American civilization and American Christianity. No man laid the plans; no man foretold or could have foretold the method of its execution.

Who did it? We say it was God. There are thousands who do not doubt it was the devil's work. There are millions more who do not care whether God or devil did it. One truth remains at the bottom of it all. Had it not been that by some mysterious influence slavery was made the enemy of the Nation and millions thereby moved to work its destruction, there is no reason to believe it would not have been today the dominating power of the Republic. As it was the madness of those who sought to perpetuate "the sum of all villainess" that worked its destruction, so perhaps the horror of what is done, the woefulness of what is suffered and the fear of what may be attempted, will some day wring the American Negro's withers until the hope of liberty shall fill his soul and echo in his prayer as did the longing for the day of "Justice" in the untaught worship of his fathers whom the Christian master kept soul-blind and starved with whip and brand lest he should read the word of God.

When that time shall come, Civilization will hear; Christianity will hear; God's will again be done and the Negro, the Freedom, in the United States of America will be free, equal in Right and Opportunity. There may be rich negroes; there may be learned Negroes, but until some enlightening miracle or some soul-thrilling horror shall again stir the heart of the Christiandom and shame the pretensions of Civilization, the colored man as a component part of American life will be no better than it is today and there is every prospect that it will be indefinitely worse. There is no instance in history where oppression has cured itself or a people who have been thrown down from the pinnacle of self-ruling citizens, to the level of unrepresented serfs, been restored to the position they have lost. The power that debases a people, a race, a type, never willingly lifts it up again. Oppression is an evil which is never self-curing. Slavery grew worse, harsher, more devilish and hopeless every day until the Dred Scott Case declared it irremediable, indestructible, part and parcel of the Constitution on which the Nation's existence depended. Then its doom was sealed. The counter-currents of human nature bore it to swift destruction. . . .

In my opinion, the condition of the American Negro will not improve until for years the world and God have heard his agonizing cry for justice, liberty, equal right and a freeman's opportunity—until the race has furnished martyrs by the thousand perhaps by the hundred thousand dying for liberty of action, as cheerfully as Cranmer[2] for freedom of belief, unless God works a miracle in their behalf. He did it once but he waited two hundred and forty-seven years before putting forth His hand. The world moves fast today. Perhaps when the year two thousand dawns, the colored man in the United States will have regained the rights of person, the civil and political status so many thousand died to confer upon him, and which the people by the enactment of those amendments which have been nullified by legal construction, thought they were giving him. Today is in God's hands as was Yesterday, but there is no instance in the past of his intervening for an oppressed people until they have sweat drops of blood and uttered groans of agony that have thrilled the heart of the world with pity for their woe.

   Believing this, I have no more heart to argue the motives of the lyncher than I have to go back and discuss the motives of the slave-master. I do not believe that the slave-owner acted from love of the slave nor that the mob-murderer acts from apprehension of the Negro power. Both hypotheses are equally absurd, both are formulated to furnish an excuse for incalculable evil, not to repress, cure or mitigate it.

   I am, dear Sir,

Very respectfully,
Albion W. Tourgée

2. Here Tourgée refers to the Protestant martyr Thomas Cranmer, archbishop of Canterbury, who in 1556 was burned at the stake for heresy by the Catholic monarch Queen Mary.

33

Letter to President Theodore Roosevelt (1901)*

On October 16, 1901, President Theodore Roosevelt inadvertently made international headlines when he entertained black leader Booker T. Washington at the White House. Harshly criticized, especially by the southern press, Roosevelt welcomed this letter of support, dated October 21, 1901, from Tourgée in Bordeaux. Tourgée hoped that Roosevelt would stand up to the criticism and lead a new challenge to segregation. Alarmed by the negative response to his meeting with Washington, however, Roosevelt afterwards carefully adhered to the conventions of the "color line." For Roosevelt's response to Tourgée's letter, see Theodore Roosevelt to Albion Tourgée, November 8, 1901, in *The Letters of Theodore Roosevelt*, vol. 4, *The Square Deal, 1901–1905,* ed. Elting Morison et al. (Cambridge: Harvard University Press, 1951), 190.

Honorable Theodore Roosevelt, President
Dear Sir:
On Friday the 18th instant the Paris Herald brought the astounding information that Mr. Booker T. Washington had dined with you at the White House.

On Saturday the 19th instant, the same journal gave the first installment of the denunciation of your act.

It would be hard for me to give any idea of the emotions I have experienced in contemplating this momentous incident. To say that I have been thoroughly dazed is not too much. For more than thirty years my chief thought and study has been the relation of the white and colored races to each other, to the United States, to other nations, to Christianity and to civilization. It is beyond all doubt the most momentous question that has ever presented itself to the statesman and the Christian, to civilized men and nations, for solution.

*Albion W. Tourgée to President Theodore Roosevelt, October 21, 1901, Theodore Roosevelt Papers, Library of Congress.

Twenty one years ago I thought I knew the remedy and wrote it in "A Fool's Errand":

"The remedy for Darkness is light; for Wrong Righteousness; .... Make the spelling-book the scepter of National Power."

It was a genuine fool's notion. I sincerely believed at that time that education and Christianity were infallible solvents of all the evils which have resulted from the white man's claim of individual superiority and collective right to rule, regulate and subordinate the colored man and colored peoples to his will and pleasure.

Today, I am ashamed to have been that sort of a fool. I realized now, that if all the people of the United States black and white alike, were saints of the most approved quality and all of them endowed with the highest educational qualifications, the question of color would not be a whit less difficult than it now is.

Why? Because education does not eradicate prejudice, but intensifies it. Because Christianity does not condemn or prevent injustice done to the weak by the strong, but encourages and excuses it. Civilization has small regard for justice, but the highest reverence for success and power.

The question has had two phases in our national history, to wit:

1st-   The first, a great moral and political conflict for the perpetuation of slavery; that is, the right of the individual white man to own, possess, dominate and control the individual colored man. In this struggle, liberty won, and slavery—the ownership of one man by another and involuntary servitude—was destroyed. AS A LEGAL ESTATE, it can never again exist in a Christian country. It may be simulated but can have no legal force or form.

2nd-   The second phase of this struggle was based, not on the right of the white individual to own and control the colored individual, but upon the right of the collective white population of a State to dominate, control, debase and degrade the colored population of the same—to deprive them of personal and political right and equal opportunity. In this struggle the victory has been overwhelmingly with the advocates of oppression, inequality of right and opportunity. For the first time in history a people endowed with political rights have been disfranchised by millions. This has been done wholly on account of race and color. This victory has been accomplished by violence—by organized force, nullifying the laws and pledges of the United States—by assassination, by fraud, by mob-murder and burning at the stake.

To this revolution of savagery, there has been for years no considerable moral antagonism. Hardly a newspaper, a college president, a church speaks in condemnation of the end sought to be obtained. Only now and then one feebly protests against the barbarous character of the methods employed.

There seems to be no present prospect of amelioration of these conditions. No party is willing to attempt the protection of the colored man, because he has no vote with which to repay its guardianship of his interests. No church stands by him as a man, lest some other denomination should take offense or they should themselves incur opprobrium.

No social sentiment demands justice and equal opportunity for him, because he is both poor and black. If Christ should make a second coming in the form of a NEGRO, I candidly believe it would disintegrate and destroy the Christian churches of the United States. Then, indeed, might it be written, "He came to His own and His own received Him not."

If I had ever any doubt as to this, it was put to rest by an experience of my own at the White House. I was invited to dine with a President for the purpose of claims which had been more than half promised me and which I greatly desired, because of the special opportunity it offered for independent literary work. It chanced that a colored man was also an applicant for the place—for which he was fairly competent. In the after-dinner colloquy upon the subject, I remarked to the President, that although I greatly desired the place, if he was inclined to nominate the colored aspirant, I would cheerfully withdraw as I felt that a competent colored man had claims to recognition by the party and the government which no one else could possess.

There was an impressive silence. Then the President said, "Do you think I would appoint a NEGRO to the bench?"

"Why not if competent?"

"Because, I would never require my brethren of the bar to recognize a man as judge whom I would not practice before myself."

"And you would not practice before a judge having colored blood in his veins?"

"No more than I would invite him to my table."

That settled the matter; the colored man was not appointed nor I either—probably because of my folly in broaching this subject.

Yet this man was a Republican, a patriot and stood very near the head of a great Christian sect.[1] If such a man could not deal justly with a fellow-citizen

1. Here Tourgée refers to President James A. Garfield, a minister and elder in the Christian Church (Disciples of Christ), who passed Tourgée over for an appointment on the U.S. Court of Claims in the spring of 1881.

and fellow-Christian, how many are there who would; and how can one expect education of knowledge to incline the white man to deal justly with a
colored race?

These were my convictions until two days ago I learned that the President
of the United States had broken bread at his own table with a person of this
race, thus doomed to oppression and infamy by the dominant forces of our
American Christian civilization.

I thank you—I congratulate you—I pity you. It was the bravest thing ever
done by an American. It has no parallel for downright pluck in all history,
save Latimer's greeting to his fellow-sufferer:

> "Be of good cheer, Brother Ridley, for with God's help we shall this day light
> such a fire in this realm of England that none shall ever put it out."[2]

This is the best piece of wit as well as the most profound forecast, that ever
fell from human lips.

It may not be comforting to say so, but I think you have done an act as
brave as Latimer's and of the same sort. You will be roasted like him, too, and
like him ultimately justified with a personal earthly immortality.

Whether you so intended or not, or whether you now desire or not, you
have written your name large across the future in which a new civilization and
a new Christianity lie hidden which shall establish of all time on earth the divine decree that, "white is not always right," and that whoever, man or nation,
would make color the test of right or righteousness, can no longer be counted
a servant of Jesus Christ, but must stand an enemy alike of God and Man.

You have lightened the fire and may be consumed therein; but when future
Ages turn back the pages which bear the record of the great struggle for equality of right and equal opportunity for all, they will find your name recorded
on them as the first and bravest of the champions of a righteousness in your
day even more inconceivable than Cranmer's [i.e., Latimer's] prophetic jest.

I thank God that I have lived in marvelous times. That I saw the love of
liberty spring up after the staggering blow of the "Dred Scot Case" had killed
hope in almost every heart; that I witnessed the overthrow of slavery and a
means none dreamed of, until God showed the way and prepared the instrument; that I heard with mine own ears that "glad refrain of falling bolt and
rended chain" which echoed around the world. And especially I am glad that
I have lived to know that an American President is brave enough to ask a col-

2. A Protestant martyr, Hugh Latimer, made this statement before being burned in 1555 for
heresy alongside Nicholas Ridley.

ored gentleman to his table. Whatever may hap, it is a brave man's act, a true Christian's act which the world can never forget. In my opinion, it is one of the momentous acts of history, the effect of which no man can measure and only the future reveal.

You may have noticed that God has a queer fashion of doing things in His own way. In what you have done may be found the key to your dying predecessor's utterance: "This is God's way." God grant you may have opened the door to a newer and diviner progress.

With the most sincere Admiration, and profound regard, I am,

Your Obedient Servant,
Albion W. Tourgée

34

Letter to E. H. Johnson (1902)*

In 1902, the Reverend Thomas Dixon published *The Leopard's Spots*, a novel about Reconstruction infused by conservative Lost Cause mythology and virulent anti-black racism. Though controversial in its day, this novel enjoyed tremendous commercial success. In this letter to his former classmate, E. H. Johnson, Tourgée responds to Dixon's book in an extraordinary thirty-eight-page analysis that constitutes one of the most penetrating commentaries on the history and memory of Reconstruction of the early twentieth century. Fearing that his opinions might jeopardize his position at the consulate, Tourgée marked each page "Personal & Confidential," and left it unsigned.[1]

My dear Johnson,

I have your pleasant letter and the article from *Watchman*.[2] It was kind of you to write the article and especially thoughtful to send it to me.

Dixon's book "*The Leopard's Spots*," was sent to me when it first came out, by the publishers. I have read it carefully. It is a most remarkable book—perhaps the most remarkable ever written, not in style or subject but in the truths it unconsciously reveals. I would not have written it for all the wealth of our rich land or all the glory the world can give; yet after a fashion I am glad another has done it.

The book is entirely worthless as a narration of events or an analysis of causes. It bears not the remotest similitude to anything that ever happened. As a picture of the times, it is not worth discussing; but as a delineation of the

---

*Albion W. Tourgée to Prof. E. H. Johnson, item 969, May 15, 1902, Albion W. Tourgée Papers, Chautauqua County Historical Society.

1. These headings have been removed for this volume.

2. Johnson published an article in *The Watchman*, included with his letter to Tourgée, in which he compared *The Leopard's Spots* with Tourgée's *A Fool's Errand*. Prof. E. H. Johnson, "'The Leopard's Spots' and 'The Fool's Errand,'" *The Watchman*, April 24, 1902.

dominant thought of the southern white man of yesterday and today, it is of inestimable value. I have known Dixon almost from his boyhood—know his type and the influence by which he and those like him have been shaped. There are many admirable things about these people. But their view of events is colored wholly by the prejudices of the class and section and their ideal of God is simply a being endowed with the impulses and sentiments of the southern white man. If one of them could be convinced that this ideal was incorrect he would simply think it so much the worse for God. Like all his type he has a most admirable sense of self-sufficiency. He is not self-assertive in the sense of persistently declaring his inerrancy. It would be derogatory to his unquestioning self-confidence to do so. He is right, indubitably right not because he has studied a matter, but because he cannot be wrong. Doubt is a thing wholly unknown to his class. If others question their conclusions so much the worse for them. There may be merely speculative questions of how much or how far—questions of degree among them. But whatever dissents from their conclusions upon vital points is simply insignificant or incurably wrong.

The old minister is a perfect type; announcing God's will in accordance with his own wishes; kind to the colored man as long as he is the submissive instrument of the white; hating him as an independent creature; believing God to be a partial and inequitable ruler rather than a just Father of all His children; whose mouth is full of cursing and his heart bent on murder as soon as one whom he hates gives him occasion to put in practice the murderous tendencies of his class.

This is what Slavery and the isolation of plantation life made the white man of the South. I have studied him closely from the outbreak of the War of Rebellion until my departure from the United States. I lived among them for 15 years (1865–1880), after that I visited and observed year by year their development—what we call the "New South." Long ago, I ceased to write or speak upon the subject; not that I do not consider it of prime importance, but because I did not wish to be the one whose voice should loose the avalanche.

I have learned something since I wrote "*A Fool's Errand.*" I believed in many things then, such as the Fatherhood of God and the Brotherhood of Men. I believed in Christianity (the modern article measured and prescribed by those who know and declare its function)—I believed in the United States as the flower of liberty, security and equal right for all. I believed the abolition of Slavery was all that was required to establish ultimate equality for and in right, opportunity and security before the law. I was so proud of our government and civilization that I could not endure the thought that it should be stained with injustice and oppression. I believed in that curious fetich of our modern thought "Education" as a remedy for wrong. When I wrote "the remedy for Wrong is Righteousness; for Darkness, Light. Make the spelling-book the scepter of national power!"—I believed every word of this Fool's Gospel.

Now, I realize its folly, though I am glad that I then believed. Now, I realize the terrible truth that neither Education, Christianity nor Civilization, mean justice or equality between man and man, when one is white and the other is colored. White Christianity twists with enthusiasm and Master's words to excuse wrong to the colored man individually and collectively. There has never been a white Christian people who were willing to give a colored people equal opportunity, equal right and security to enjoy "life, liberty and the pursuit of happiness." Even our American Christian slavery was the worst ever known on earth. We gave the master the power of life and death over his servant. We gave him the right to compel his female slave to his will and made the issue of the master's loins also a slave. We forbade the slave to learn to read or write and made it a felony to teach him. We denied him the right of marriage, legitimacy or a family name. We denied him the right of appeal to any court against his master and would not allow him to testify against any white person. It was not the Legrees who made slavery horrible, but the Christian people who stripped the slave of any right, destroyed his opportunity and taught him that Christianity was the religion of the white man, that the earth and the colored peoples were made for the white man's enjoyment and control and the colored races created to submit to his direction and to administer to his pleasure and enjoyment.

This is what Dixon's book teaches and luminously shows to be the animating and dominant impulse of the southern whites of the best class—of the perfect, inerrant, impeccable type. Annihilation, deportation or eternal and unresisting subjection to the will and pleasure of the white people—these are the only alternatives which a Christian minister offers to the colored people of the United States.

And he is right. Unless God intervenes there is no other fate before the colored American whom the Nation made a citizen, but whom neither the courts nor Christian sentiment will grant protection in his rights as a man or as a citizen. To have made the name of slavery anathema, but have sanctified its most degrading and debasing element, the subjection of one race to the will of another, as part of our civilization. For slavery to have substituted caste, for individual ownership, subjection to the will of another race; for the enormities of chattel-slavery, lynch law and the stake; for the lash, the control of wages and general immunity from punishment for the master's right to kill.

How many white men have been punished for killing colored persons in the southern states during the past quarter of a century?

Do you think a white man has been or ever will be punished in those states for rape of a colored woman?

Or do you perhaps believe that the killing of a colored man for "impudence" to a white person—or jostling him on the street or failing to give the whole sidewalk to a lady and stand cap in hand while she passed by, is a crime?

It is the very highest form of blasphemy to claim that the idea of "white supremacy" and the later barbarian which demands race-subjection or extermination is pleasing to God or conformable to the religion of the Man of Nazareth. Modern Christianity in its name and those who suffer them are colored peoples in whom the Church has no interest except in their salvation. We are willing to punish them with unlimited promises of heavenly delights, but not willing to accord them equal rights and opportunities on earth.

It is because of this ineradicable and almost universal attribute of the southern whites that neither education nor Christianity nor birth combined offer the slightest hope for the solution of this problem—a problem the most important by all odds, that Civilization and Christianity have been called upon the face. If Civilization and Christianity cannot furnish a public opinion— a general impulse—which will compel the southern whites to loosen the grip they are tightening year by year on the manhood and equal right of the colored American, Christianity will certainly lose its hold upon humanity as a religion of Justice and Truth—let alone all consideration of the love it boast to have for others. Men who utter such sentiments as Dixon puts into the mouth of Dr. Durham and himself endorses and approves, are the worst enemies Christianity has or can have. Ten thousand unbelievers are less potent than one such degrading the name of Christ. God cannot approve such hellish venom towards a people whose mental and moral conditions we have been responsible for 300 years. Such a Christian ideal drives of necessity, men who believe in liberty, justice and equality of right into opposition with any religion, creed or cult which approves or excuses such tendencies.

We have somewhat gotten the idea that our Christian civilization compels the endorsement and approval of God. For that reason perhaps, we find His will and purpose as to all things human, unhesitatingly declared as a justification for acts which would make the most barbaric and savage of pagan peoples ashamed. The defense of slavery by the Church was a hard strain on the conscience of its best adherents. The approval of the New Barbarism will be much worse. It is no longer a mere national question but a world-question—the question whether Christianity is a white man's religion or the expression of the All-Father's will.

The attribution of Divine approval to the theory of white supremacy and colored subjection, is just as absurd as the claim of Divine authority for Christian Slavery. Thousands of true believers not only maintained this doctrine, but accounted as "infidels" those who would not stain the nave of God by attributing to him the sanction of such infamy—a barbarism Bael even would never have sanctioned. It became a sort of bluff to the Almighty. Yet I do not think He was frightened. The Christian Church—no matter how confident its declarations in support of evil, has never yet been able to command His support for injustice. He is a good accountant who never shrinks from balancing his book with *red ink*. He finds a way too, of causing events to pass without the aid of human advice. He found a way to destroy Slavery—that is the legal estate of which had never been advocated by any writer, statesman or thinker on either side of the great question. Dixon claims it was "*Uncle Tom's Cabin*" that induced the people of the North to defy God's will and destroy the "patriarchal institution." It was God, not Mrs. Stowe who did it and the instrument he used was that inspired lunatic, John Brown. God threw him into the face of the over-confident South and rushed on to the destruction of that institution which they attributed to God and with a curious intensity of faith defied Him to refuse to support their views. "If God does not give victory to the South and maintain our institutions founded on His word," said a well-known divine, "I will renounce my belief and tear up my commission as a Christian minister." His bluff did not win, and when he learned that there were still some printed copies of his sermon in existence ten years afterwards, he publicly retracted his declaration. I heard his retraction and have one of the few printed copied of his defiance which is still extant.

The disease of which Dixon and his creature Durham most suffer, is a super-abundant knowledge of God's purposes, past, present and to come. Not to a poor fool like me who cares nothing for any cult and does not believe God has given anyone a right to prescribe or declare His purpose towards my race or people, but to whom His will is only justice, equality and helpfulness for the weak, the Miracle of the overthrow of Slavery is one great and indubitable demonstration that God rules in the affairs of men and over-rules the wisdom of the wisest. It is the one Miracle which I have seen with my mine own eyes.

To excuse this insane frenzy which dare no longer appeal to the Scriptures for support, the slave-theory of the master's right and the slave's helplessness having received such a terrible rebuttal that all the world had to admit its falsity and infamy, Dixon does not hesitate to draw on a super-heated imagination for incidents which he puts forth as palliating facts. Take for instance chapters XX and XVI—the election of 1867 was held under military authority and was conducted with that strict regard for regularity which characterized military discipline as administered by one of the gentlest and most irreproachable of our Regular Army officers. I know all its details for I con[d]ucted the registration and elections in one of the largest colored counties in North Carolina myself, and was familiar with all that was done in that State. These are facts:

I.—No officer of the Freedmen's Bureau had anything to do with the registration or election, nor was any registration held at any "Agency" of such Bureau. The Freedmen's Bureau was entirely distinct from the Army and its officers could not perform functions imposed on the Army. Any one having the slightest knowledge of the organization of either should have known this. As a matter of fact, nearly all the agents of this Bureau in North Carolina were either Northern ministers, teachers or wounded officers of our Army. Any sane man can easily judge whether such a man were likely to be guilty of the atrocities charged against them. Most of them were fools who thought justice to the weak was part of their duty to God and their country. As a rule they were self-sacrificing Christian men.

II.—Instead of an election held without notice, justice was given by publication and by posting printed placards in each precinct more than 30 days before the election. It is probable that some of these were torn down by the opponents of Reconstruction, who thought thereby to prevent an election; but no man of the Reconstruction party could have had any motive to prevent the fullest notice.

III.—It is enough to make a cast-iron dog laugh to read the tales of atrocities committed by the "Union League" as it was called. I suppose I know as much of it and its workings as man ever did. It was the most harmless of voluntary associations. It was organized in Philadelphia early in the war and was intended simply as a means of rallying the loyal people in case of Confederate invasion. It was extended through the South as for the purpose of enabling the loyal people of that section to make themselves known to our soldiers. Colored people were afterwards admitted to it for the purpose of enabling them to give notice to each other of Ku-Klux raids. It tolled bells and lighted beacon fires when the ghostly horsemen appeared. I canvassed the whole State in the spring of 1868, and know I suppose all there was to be known of such an organization. I never heard in any of its meetings anything but the mere expression of patriotic sentiment. The proof that it was thoroughly harmless is found in the fact that no such thing as a crime was ever charged against such organization or an indictment found for any offence traceable to it. You must remember that the courts were always open and the Grand Juries, composed almost entirely of white men were free to make any presentments they choose. The records of the courts show no such presentments they choose, and a white Southern Grand Jury has never been a bashful body. The whole idea is farcical. The organization extended over a large part of the State and was entirely disbanded and all meetings prohibited because the white people, being accustomed to laws which forbade the assembling of more then three colored men even for prayer, unless a white man was present to see that they did not ask anything of the Almighty prejudicial to the interests of the whites, could with difficulty be induced to prevent even colored schools and churches to exist. Very many, indeed, were burned and we who were leaders of Republican policy thought it not wise to encourage any unnecessary assemblages. It was in fact, a sort of supplementary Sunday school teaching the duty of patriotism. It was intended to stimulate the individual manhood of the colored citizen and inspire him with a sense of responsibility in his new relationship. This was what made it so obnoxious to the white people to whom the mere fact that the Negro was allowed to testify against any of the superior race was the most grievous fact of reconstruction, unless it was that as judge, I would not allow a witness or defendant to be called "Nigger." This was regarded as an absolute denial of the vested divine right. I had to use the power of commitment for contempt several times before I could put an end to this gross violation of law.

The recently emancipated slave needed every possible encouragement to enable him to stand upright before his recent master. I have no doubt that the singing of patriotic songs of the League—the "Star Spangled Banner," the "Red, White and Blue" and that noblest of all national anthems "The Battle Hymn of the Republic" and some others regarding education, etc., which constituted a chief element of these meetings, were of the utmost value in fitting the new citizen for his duties. Its chief function was to teach this man whom for two centuries and a half all knowledge had been forbidden by law, how to conduct in orderly and respectful fashion, a public meeting—and education for which they had special need. When a Supreme Court judge, who had come up from the "poor white" class, could say to me: "I have never yet got so that I could stand exactly straight before a man who used to own 'twenty niggers,'" you may imagine that was the burden of apprehension which rested on the recent slave, who for generations has been forbidden by law to leave the plantation or walk the highway without a written pass from the master. The colored school houses, built by Northern charity were burned down almost as fast as put up for a while. They were regarded with a universal hate which you have found it hard to conceive if you had not read Dixon's book. Such encouragement as was afforded by these instrumentalities, was necessary to implant in the colored man's mind that appreciation of citizenship which made it so difficult a task for the "Ku Klux" and "Red Shirts," armed and disguised as they were, to prevent him from going to the ballot-box in which he knew the hope of liberty was enshrined. That there were controversies between members of the League and those who could not realize that they were no longer masters, was no doubt true. The "League" was used to distribute political information. The former pastors were not above lying about election-day and giving out Democratic tickets as Republican. It was absolutely necessary to find some means of disseminating such information and preventing the voter from being deceived by studied misinformation. That members of the League as well as of the Sunday school were sometimes criminals, I do not doubt, but that crime came from the one is as absurd as to suppose it was taught in the other.*

IV.—In his rage to blacken and defile all things, all classes and all forces which tended to antagonize the white ideal of the destiny and duty of the colored people, Dixon has not hesitated to fall foul of that marvelously devoted class of self-sacrificing missionaries, the teachers of the colored schools established and maintained by Northern charity. I have known hundreds of them and because of my known sympathy with their work had a certain familiarity with this class. They were accomplished and devoted women—the very best types—the daughters of college professors, doctors, ministers, farmers and teachers—the pick of the flower of our Northern life. Not one of them within

*[Tourgée's note] The Union League was embraced in the Act of Amnesty granted to the Ku-Klux, when they began to feel the halter draw and scores of them were in jail under indictment for murder and other most infamous acts of violence. This was done against the protest of every Republican in the State merely for the purpose of blinding the eyes of the North to make them believe that members of the Union League required amnesty for acts performed under its investigation. Not a single instance of such crime was known, and no member of the League ever plead this Act in bar of prosecution. On the other hand, hundreds of Ku-Klux were released from indictment by this Act. If I were at home, I could give you from my dockets, the names of more than 500 thus released. The inclusion of the Union League was merely a pretence which the North swallowed like a hungry pike taking a fly and was thereby led to a conclusion as false as it was absurd.

my knowledge was ever charged with any impropriety, though they were subjected to the most rigorous ostracism by the white Christians of the South. It
is an insult to the memory of this noblest army of missionaries our Northern
life ever sent forth, to defend them from the innuendoes of a man whom
civilizations and Christianity have only fitted for the cowardly aspersion of
the most notable exemplars of Christian charity. He does not count truth as a
matter of any consequence in comparison with the hate-inspired prejudices of
class which he worships as more than God-like.

V.—So too, with the outrages imputed to our troops during this epoch.
The discipline of the troops stationed in the State was especially severe; and
the conduct of the troops particularly fine. The charges of any violations of
the peace or invasion of the rights of citizens were so rare as not to be worth
considering. While the State was nominally under military rule (from 1867 to
1868) you should know that it was conducted under the forms of civil law, the
courts enforcing the laws of the State except as their barbarity was modified
by the orders of the military chief and capital punishments were allowed only
after reviewed by the general commanding. Whipping, branding and crop-
ping being entirely forbidden. Otherwise, former laws, except those regulating Slavery remained in force and were administered by the State Judiciary.
The colored troops were especially noted for their good discipline, and at any
time such an inconceivable event as that narrated would have cost the life of
every man engaged in it. Soldiers did not wander about the country without
their officer. But the fact that a colored man should be a soldier at all, it mat-
tered not how well-behaved or submissive to discipline, was of itself a mortal
offense to the white man of that time as it is today.

A curious thing is that Dixon represents troops as collecting taxes as a
prelude to one of his impossible outrages. There were no taxes derived under
the Reconstruction Act until the autumn of 1868 and none collected until the
autumn of 1869. Now, the military control of the State ended in 1868 and no
United States troops could possibly have been concerned in any act of the
State government except on the constitutional demand of the Governor upon
the President. In short, the sales for taxes, etc., are a pure myth.

From 1869 until 1872, the forced sales of land in North Carolina were
amazing in number, but they were not in any considerable amount for taxes,
and if for taxes, the lands were redeemable upon very favorable terms, and
no dispossession was possible except after suit brought and judgment in the
regular course, occupying at least one year. The great sales of land of that
period were due to debts contracted before the end of the war on which no

judgments could be rendered from 1861 to 1869. Because of the "stay-laws" enacted by the Confederate legislature at the outset of the war, no judgments or even trials were permitted in actions for debt. Parties were required to plead at the Spring term 1869 and judgements began to be rendered at the Spring term 1870. The confederacy had ruined the South. All its accumulations were swept away. All the wealth it had consisted of the profits of crops raised after 1865. Its lands were encumbered far above their value. This condition induced the general Government to pass the Bankrupt Law in 1867. But for this the people of the South would have been ruined by what were called "Old Debts." Judgment sales and bankrupt sales prevailed by thousands in every country. They had noting to do with Reconstruction any more than a contemporaneous eclipse of the sun. Taxes were light; so were assessments. As a fact, the so-called political thefts of this period hardly cost the state a cent. The legislature did indeed etc., authorize the issue of railroad bonds in immense quantities. But no taxes were levied to pay the interest on them and when the Democrat[s] came into power, they were repudiated. So that neither the State nor the people of the State actually lost any money and not a cent of taxes was ever levied or collected to pay them.

Dixon says the "School Fund" was squandered. The State never had any School Fund except money loaned it by the United States in the distribution of the "Surplus of 1868." This went into the maw of the Confederacy in exchange for Confederate bond. What the Republicans did do was to issue school fund bonds. These were sold on the State's account and the proceeds applied to current expenses. It was not regular but it was a thing often done and hardly possible to be avoided when there is an empty treasury. You must remember that the "Johnson regime" which controlled the State from 1865 to 1868, left no funds available for those acting under the Reconstructions Acts of 1867. They paid out the last cent, and the first Republican legislature had to furnish some means to pay its members and other expenses of government. There was never and could never have been any order for a thirty percent tax levy. The whole story is not only false, but absurdly and impossibly false in its reason and detail. Nobody was sold out for taxes during that time much less was a levy for tribute made on any town.

"In a suite of rooms in the Capitol they established a brothel," writes Mr. Dixon.

The Capitol of North Carolina is a pretentious structure, or cruciform in shape, of amazingly few rooms for such a building hardly enough for its State officers. For four years, 1868 to 1872, I had a desk in one of these and knew every man who occupied the others. During that time I never knew of such a thing as is charged by Mr. Dixon, and cannot see how it could have existed. There were, no doubt dissolute men in the Republican Party. There were unquestionably dissolute women in Raleigh, but from what I have heard of the facilities offered by the city in that line, both before and since that epoch, I can see no reason for "a brothel in the Capitol" even if it were possible. As, however, I had no part or lot in any such matters, it is possible there may have been instances of individual impropriety in some of the offices of the Capitol. Such things are by no means infrequent among the classes which Dixon so highly extols, and the legal prohibition of marriage between slaves, which had existed for more than a hundred years, naturally weakened the obligations of morality among the colored people. The records of bastardy and illegitimacy in Southern States show that such violations of the moral law are not confined to any race or people. For many years I was required officially to know these records in several counties, but Wake County in which Raleigh is situated was not in my district. If there were sometimes prostitutes in the legislative galleries I could not have known it as I never had any acquaintances in that class.

I note these things, not as matters of importance, but merely to show the lack of restraint which Dixon puts on a perfervid imagination. His conclusions are by no means unfamiliar, but his facts are very largely original—the only original things in his book.

What was thirty years ago is of little consequence in comparison with what will be tomorrow. The financial evils of the Reconstruction days were bad enough, but all combined they do not equal in amount the frauds of Tammany Hall, nor would the actual cash loss in any State equal that sustained by the State of New York in the single matter of building the Capitol at Albany, which is said to have cost $18,000,000, could be duplicated for half that sum and a better one built for $5,000,000. Yet no one has proposed murder as remedy—yet!

You say, "The South sees the North self-converted to the Southern political faith." In a sense this is quite correct. The love of "killing a nigger" has spread very widely through the North, I suppose we are all murderers at heart and lynching offers the only method of gratifying our lust for blood without fear of the law and without apprehension of rendering one obnoxious to the Christian sentiment of the country. The anti-Negro mobs of the North are so far mere cyclones, which resemble those of the South only in immunity from punishment and the absence of serious and earnest protest against them. Thus far, they have not reached the point of general approval. It is by no means certain however, that it will not yet come.

Your citation of the Philippines, Porto Rico, and Hawaii as instances of approval of the Southern policy is very far from correct. There is a world-wide difference between refusing a man the right to vote and taking it away from him after it has once been conferred upon him. This has never been done in the United States except at the South. Other states have refused to give the ballot to certain of their citizens who are unable to read or write, but they have always conserved the rights of those who are already voters. I am not aware of any instance in history in which the right to share in the function of government has been taken away from any considerable number of people unless it was with an entire suppression of the ballotorial right as in Poland and Finland.

But even if justifiable at all, it can never be justifiable when it is affected by fraud, by terrorism, by murder. Read Senator Tillman's recent speech, a true statement of the means by which the disfranchisement of the Negroes has been effected in the South. There is not in all the world's history so great a retrogressive movement in the field of personal liberty as has taken place in the United States since 1875. With the Negro's right to vote, has gone as a matter of course, all his other rights. Is a white man ever punished in those States for killing a Negro? He is so rarely even indicted that such a fact is almost incredible, and as for conviction and punishment, you would be amazed to know that your two hands have fingers enough on them to count the execution of white men for the murder of colored men in all these States for 25 years.

When a man knows that his life is not secured by law he has no other rights. If you were a Negro working on a plantation and there was a difference as to the amount due you and you knew your employer would be in no danger of the law if he killed you, do you think you would dispute his claim? It is a safer thing for a Southern white man to kill a Negro than for him to kill another white man's dog.

It is not a strange thing that the sense of justice toward the colored man should grow dull at the North. American Christianity and our commercial civilization have always rested under a peculiar domination from the South. Four-fifths of the northern people, if not in favor of Slavery, were up to thirty years ago opposed to any interference with it notwithstanding its inconceivable enormities. They were anti-Negro. Only when the South threatened the Nation's life, were they willing to use the Slave as an instrument for its salvation. As soon as the new rebellion against the act of the Government in granting citizenship to the Negro became successful and the colored race was deprived of legal protection and rendered hopelessly subject to the collective action of the whites, the North resumed its old position of subservency to Southern opinion upon all subjects touching the colored citizen. These influences have been peculiarly potent in effecting this result:

1—The fact that the southern white man is individually and collectively stronger than the Northern man as a social force. He cares nothing for the public opinion of the North or other countries. He may take the trouble to denounce it, but it never influences his thought or action. There are no actions or doubtful elements. There are practically no Southern men who believe that the Negro has any rights at all, but only such privileges as the whites may accord them. Everything, the land, the State, the present and the future belongs to the white man and he has a divine right to do with it all just what he chooses. The very positiveness of his conviction paralyzes the conscience of the North and induces it to accept as ultimate truths the bald assertions made upon this and kindred subjects. We accepted their views of Slavery and now we accept their views on the results of Slavery. They made us then believe that the Slave was a brute, and now that the Negro-citizen is a monster.

2—The Southern whites control the sources of information. A colored man who reveals the facts in regard to the real treatment of his race, is already assured of short life. I was fully convinced of this from the results of an attempt I made to secure the facts as to the killing of colored men in each State. From mere mercy, I had to abandon the idea. For instance you do not probably know that in these States, a contract of hire upon a plantation is by the year unless otherwise stated in writing; that a man who leaves the employer's service before the end of his term or while the employer claims a balance against him, is guilty of the statutory crime of "obtaining money under false pretenses;" that for this he may be sentenced to State prison for two or more years. The mere fact, may be known but our Northern Christian conscience does not realize that this makes the colored hireling practically the slave of the white man. He has only to claim a dollar of debt to convict him of a felony, and he must either serve another year or face a Southern penitentiary.

3—The confidence which the white Christians of the North have in the white Christians of the South causes every one who contravenes in the least degree their acts and statements to be branded as a falsifier. A Northern man who dares to face ostracism, threats and imperil his life to tell the truth, is counted by the North as a calumniator. Except in a few cases he cannot get a hearing. The press, especially the religious press, is closed to him if he makes appeal for justice or to any one who speaks for him. I do not blame the press. Journals are published to make money and to do so they must follow the inclination not only of their readers, but of those they hope to secure as readers. I do not think there is any considerable proportion of our people who desire that the colored people of the United States should have any rights or enjoy any privileges except such as the white people to whom they are not subject, are willing to give them.

It will no doubt shock you to have me say that education is no better guaranty of the liberty of a people who are subject to the control of another class, than Christianity. If every white and colored person of the South was not only able to read and write but fit for an A.B. at any college, and in addition thereto was an acceptable member of an orthodox Christian church the race question instead of being solved would be infinitely more dangerous and terrible than it is today. Caste starts always from the top and oppresses those beneath. The Negro has never dreamed of injuring or oppressing the white people; but the white lash themselves into fury at the very idea that a colored man even thinks himself as good as a white man. The colored people were killed some few weeks ago, as I am informed, at a "colored camp-meeting" in a Southern State. Seven of these were men and three were women. One of the men was charged with having "insulted" a white man. Their friends were forbidden to remove their bodies. A day or so afterwards a trench was dug and the bodies thrown into it. There were no religious services, but a white minister made "a brief talk to the colored people present advising them to go to their homes, behave themselves and *remember to raise their hats whenever they met a white person on the roads.*"

Education teaches the dominant class how to make the subjection of the class it is inclined by temperament and interest to oppress, more complete. It was the most intelligent of the whites who organized and commanded the Ku-klux and the "Red Shirts."

Education can do nothing for the colored man except to make him more sensible of his wrongs and render him desperate in longings to ameliorate the evils which beset him. Being deprived of all political power, having not a legislator, not a judge, not a magistrate, not an officer and hardly a juror of their own race or who is inclined to give them justice—what aid can education give them? It may teach them to fight or it may incline them to submit to whatever fate may await them. It is the boast of the Dutch government in the East Indies, first, that it is profitable; second, that it is peaceful. The reasons are plain: no colored man is allowed to own or lease land, and he is never permitted to speak to a Dutchman in Dutch unless he has at least one knee on the ground. They are not slaves—only caste-inferiors. They are *permitted* to be Christians but not encouraged to be. Christianity is a bad religion for slaves and caste-inferiors. We made it serve for slaves by preaching to them always, "Servants . . . obey your masters." When the law permitted them to read the Scriptures for themselves and they became mere caste-inferiors, Christianity did not have the same effect upon them. On the contrary, there is no doubt that such pernicious dogma as "OUR FATHER who art in Heaven," "OF ONE BLOOD are all nations of the earth," and other similar absurdities, have inclined the colored people of the United States that "all men are born equal," and if they are not permitted to remain equal in right and privilege before the law of our free Republic [*sic*]. I think the greatest miracle the world has ever seen is that any free colored people should accept Christianity. Of course the slaves had to believe—it was their only chance to secure favor. But judged by our own acts individually and collectively, I cannot see how any one can suppose that the Christian world believes that "Do unto others so ye would that they should do to you," applies to the relations between a white Christian peoples [*sic*] and the colored races over which they claim dominion. It is evidently taken to mean that a white man should treat a colored man as he believes a "nigger ought to be treated." That is no doubt the way Dixon and Dr. Durham would render that measure of Christian ethics.

Do not think that I am soured or desire to advocate any change in present conditions. I have learned that God sets in human affairs by human agencies and prepares his tools in His own way. Science has foolishly tried to declare human qualities by noting the racial and physical conditions of environment. The mistake lies in counting man as an animal only, subject to material influences. The truth is, that man is more a moral and intellectual being than a brute. The most potent influence in sharing his character and quality is the public opinion which surrounds him—the quality of the collective life during his impressionable years. This is not only the most potent of formative forces, but more potent than all others. It is through these general impulses that God has acted in pushing humanity up from the caveman to the civilized perfectibility which does not hesitate to regard itself as the finished product of civilization. The general impulse of today is the sure measure of tomorrow's tendencies. The desire to equal yesterday's warlike achievements inspire the individual activities which have resulted in the marvelous wealth accumulation of today. This had dwarfed yesterday's sentiment as regards personal rights. The North is blind to everything else. The South is still imbued with its old impulse of "white supremacy," and the "God-like excellence of the Anglo-Saxon." Only God can change these conditions. He can as he always has, at the crises of history, wholly modify the general impulse. He does it in a thousand ways—never twice alike. When Isabella signed the same day the decree expelling the Jews and the charter for Columbus' voyage, He opened two ways for a better future. Had the Jews been of finer nettle they would have resisted and at least have sold the hundreds of thousands of lives they lost in a way to make other nations shy of such infamies. But the Jews were trained by centuries of submission, non-resistance and mercenary accumulation to secrecy, evasion and chicanery. They thought they could buy their peace. Booker T. Washington is teaching the same doctrine to the colored people of today. So are our white people, "Abandon your Rights! Submit to all the white man requires! Get riches but never resist oppression!"

This is the course our white Christianity of the South preaches. Dixon and Dr. Durham are wiser and more sincere. They say that if you give the Negro an academic education you put him on a level with the white man. If you give him the industrial education you make him the successful rival of the "poor white"—the only Southern white laborer—and this will be a moral offense to the white race. God punished Spain for the horror of the Jewish expulsion and the Inquisition by the very glory and weakening wealth of her discoveries and conquests. I have no doubt that He will either change by some means the existing impulse of our Nation to oppress long suffering people to whom we owe so much of good-will and Christian charity, or punish us as no other nation has ever been punished since none has sinned so grossly against such light.

If I feel so keenly why do I not raise my voice in protest?

I have learned that man may not choose God's instruments. While my heart had burned with inexpressible agony at the woe and shame which I believe awaits our people in the near future and even now stains our Nation's glory, I have not been able to devise any way by which it has seemed possible for me to avert the destiny that impends. I suppose I have not the true spirit of the martyr nor the exalting confidence of the "reformer" that the methods I may choose to advocate are the prophet-nerve to decry all else but my own convictions and write regardless of consequences, of the truths which I have seen and studied. If I believed that anything I could do or say would awaken the slumbering sense of justice in the white Christian world, I do not think I would hesitate to do the best in my power.

But I have learned that the utmost sincerity of conviction and the utmost forgetfulness of self do not make one even an obscure instrument in the per-

formance of God's will. I had a neighbor in Western New York, who in the
old days, devoted himself with the utmost self-forgetfulness to demonstrating
to our self-blinded people of the North the inconceivable infamies of Slavery.
He did not appeal to arms or violence, and had not one drop of blood on his
soul. But he liberated scores of slaves in Kentucky by the marvelous adroit-
ness of his plans and was finally sentenced to life-imprisonment in her penitentiary. He received, I do not know how many lashes at different times, and
was released by the thoughtful sagacity of Abraham Lincoln, when the end
seemed near at hand. In all his woes he answered not wailing with railing, but
after each new torture prayed:

"Oh, Lord, I pray Thee only that Thou wilt make my suffering the means
of opening the eyes of the people of my country to the enormities of the institution of Slavery!"

And when it was over and he was free to tell his story, Slavery was doomed
and he had not even the poor consolation that his woes and sufferings had
even helped to produce the result!

It was pitiable, but it is the common lot of those who are not chosen as the
pivots of events. John Brown's insane effort to destroy Slavery by an attempt
fore-doomed to failure to even a child's apprehension, had accomplished what
the more beautiful, sweet and self-forgetful sacrifice of my old friend never
have effected. You do not even know his name—yet one would have thought
him a better instrument for the miracle God had in mind to perform than
"Brown of Ossawattamie."

While I have never lacked confidence in my own conviction, I have never
thought it in the scope of my duty to do or say things that in all probability
might lead to the horrors of greater strife and bring on others the woes of
fresh bloodshed. I realize that this weakness was that of a Fool and not the
unreckoning hardihood of the undoubting Wise Man who is given to prescribe limits and methods to the Almighty. But I have pursued this course
so long that I have even developed a sort of pride in the belief that what I
have written has been "with charity for all" and cannot have done harm to
any. This is, of course, a Fool's notion and I quite admire the intrepidity with
which Dixon hurls his torch into the magazine of dynamite which under-
lies the social fabric of the South. "Perpetual submission to White control,"
"deportation" from their native land, or "Annihilation." These are the terrible
alternatives which he, in God's name and for the gratification of the White
man's pleasure, pronounces against ten millions of American citizens. Heavens! What a pronunciamento to issue in encouragement of that flame of in-

justice which three centuries of the most infamous oppression has lighted in the heart of the southern white man! It is quite possible that it may create an explosion more terrible than the eruption of Mt. Pelee. More convulsions are often of a character to dwarf the most fearful of Nature's phenomena. Not since the Deluge—if that was as extensive as its narrators imagined—has there been so wide-spread destruction and general woe as followed on the preaching of one insane monk who appealed in God's name to every lustful passion to induce the parents of Europe to give their children to be lead to death in the "Children's Crusade." A man who has nerve enough to appeal to a universal murderous prejudice is the most terrible of human forces. What is it to him how deep the stream of blood may flow, so long as the Southern white man's pride of race is satiated?

Of course, everyone knows that the deportation of ten million of American citizens is a physical impossibility. We have (1) No right to remove them; (2) We have no place to which they might be sent; (3) The cost is an insuperable obstacle; (4) The barbarities of the slave-trade were trivial to the infamies which attend enforced deportation of such a vast number subject to the cruelty the white man always visits on the colored in his power. Probably, one-fifth would go to feed the sharks, perhaps more. The horrors of the "Middle Passage" would be outdone.

I suppose Dixon thinks the general threat of "deportation" or "extermination" will induce the colored people to submit themselves forever to deprivation of right and permit the whites always to enjoy undisturbed the delights of the "nigger-hunt" with every now and then the luxury of roasting a "big buck nigger" alive. I have studied the colored man since he became a citizen in every state and under every condition of life. Perhaps no man living has made himself so familiar with the colored people of all classes, in every State between the Potomac and the Rio Grande as I have done. The old slave masters and those who inherit his ideas think they know the Negro. Nothing could be more delusive indeed, it is a general rule of human nature that the dominant class know little of that which they control and oppress. The Negro is above all things secretive and in a sense unconscious of his own nature. His ideas of his future and destiny are inchoate. But "au fond" as the French say, at bottom, he has a love of liberty which centuries of Slavery have only served to emphasize. He is gentle and inaggressive. No people in the world's history every endured such wrongs as they with so few acts of violence and so few crimes of retribution chargeable to their account. *Three-fourths* of those who have been lynched have been charged with "insolence to a white man" or larceny. Crimes of violence have been very rare except against each other or when set upon by white assailants. Yet I do not think they have the oriental fatalism which makes them willing to endure forever. Neither have they that love of accumulation which would make them, like the Jew, willing to submit to anything for gain. The time is sure to come when the Negro's enhanced sense of personal and collective rights and wrongs of his race will develop the martyr-spirit and he will cease to submit to the dominant will regardless of consequences. Lynchings and burnings are sure seedlings of slaughter. The more mob-murders there are the more there must be. Not only does the vampire appetite for blood increase by what it feeds on, but the victims of such barbarity grow desperate, and knowing that they can expect neither justice nor mercy at the hands of their white rulers who are more than masters-murderers when they choose—they naturally elect to make their deaths costly to those they are now coming to regard as their enemies. They have lost confidence in the government of the United States[,] never had any confidence in the Southern people and have now wonderingly arrived at a just estimate of the indifference of the North.

The great danger is that they will turn to God as their fathers did and pray for release and vengeance with that fervor with which the slave prayed for "Jubilee," which was for him simply another name for Liberty. Whenever a wronged people get in the habit of thus appealing to God against their oppressors, it cannot be denied that He has a most inconvenient habit of listening. When that point is reached, the crop of martyrs will increase and some Christian's conscience will be fired with the impulse to do justice.

Mr. Dixon probably thinks the Negro not enough of a man to do this. Let him not be too sure. Martyrs are not a product of mere culture. Those who die for ideas and peoples and liberty are very rarely the rich and cultivated. In our war of Rebellion it is true, the best culture died for the most object and degraded—the product of centuries of Christian slave-degradation. But that was after the strange masonry of Slavery has passed from lip to lip the terrible message of the "Dred Scott Case," and the bondsman despairing of human aid had turned to God as his only hope. I have heard the story from hundreds, of the great change in the slave after he first began to pray for "Jubilee." Intelligent Southerners used to attribute it to the "John Brown Raid" which I have heard many say "spoiled all the slave-labor of the South." But the best observers among the colored people of that epoch declared that "atter the las' court went agin us, there warn't nothin' else ter do but ax the Lord ter take our matter in hand." It is indeed, the universal conviction among the colored people that the destruction of chattel-slavery was an answer to prayer, which had made them submit so patiently to the evils they have since suffered from the hands of whites. This restraint will not last always. The members of the South Carolina legislature who said it would be "necessary to kill about two thousand niggers to counteract the effect of the President's action in inviting Booker T. Washington do dine at the White House" was probably correct, and the killing of these two thousand will make necessary the killing of other thousands to keep this optimistic and forgiving race from appealing to God against their murderers.

If the colored people were like you and me in their moral development, there would be no such submission to present conditions. We have neither the faith nor the long-suffering patience with wrong which Slavery taught. We would fight—not merely to obtain justice but for revenge for injustice. We would rather die for a thousands deaths than wear colored skins in Christian America. If Christ should come down in a black hide and we could not escape admitting His identity, I suppose the better part of the Christian church in America would renounce their faith. If you could suddenly become a Negro and experience one single week of Negro's hopelessness as a part of American life, I fancy you would curse God and die when the Sabbath came or else become a "bad nigger" fit only for a rope or the stake for the "insulting language" you would use toward the "superior race."

But there is another thing which had kept me silent on this subject. I not only feared to be the one whose words might start the avalanche, but I was a coward as well. It was necessary—or I thought it was—that I should live, and the American people have little use for the work of one who ever spoke a word for justice to a colored race. How long do you suppose I would hold my present position or any other under the government if this letter should get into print or even an inkling of my views should become known? I can tell you—just as long as it would take the machinery of government to project another into my place. We are a very tolerant people as long as one does not differ with us. In sending this to you, I am really putting the daily bread of myself and family into your hands. This is why I have marked every page *Personal and Confidential.*" The Southern white man's antipathy for the Negro is nothing in comparison with his burning hate for the white man who has ever dared advocate justice for the colored man, and whatever the South demands the North accords. You do not realize how far this sentiment extends. A New York publisher wanted my work on his journal, but would only take it on condition that I would not allow my connection with it to be known, saying, "The people are tired of the Negro and it might do us great harm to have it made public that one of your pronounced views wrote editorials for us." He was quite right. I fancy that if it was left to a secret ballot whether the Negro should be deported at a cost of 5 billion dollars—or "exterminated" by the Southern whites free of cost, there would be a big majority in favor of "extermination."

I have written this letter at odd times in the brief intervals of official duty at an over-worked and under-paid consulate. Why, I hardly know, except that I desired someone outside of my own family might know my views. Hundreds of colored people and some whites have written me on the same subject wondering why they do not hear from me upon this question. I have had to put them off with some evasive reply, because I dare not say to them that in my opinion caste-supremacy established and maintained by unlawful violence, is a far more dangerous condition than Slavery ordained and regulated by law. Yet it is literally true that Slavery was a more hopeful state than the present. Whatever exists by law may be remedied by law, but that which exists in defiance of law rests upon a public sentiment which no law can control.

I cannot help thinking or writing upon these things because it was burned into my soul in the wonderful speech to which we were exposed, that the chief purpose of what we call Christian civilization, was to create conditions favorable to the uplifting and development of the weak—to lead humanity upwards not downwards. A civilization which gluts power with cruelty and shames the boast of peace with a policy of murder must be abhorrent to a God of any sweeter qualities than Bael, and should stir Christianity to its core. That it does not show how thoroughly the tendency to excuse any evil which may contribute to the power and/or pride of greed of the white race, has paralyzed the brain and conscience of Christianity.

I unfortunately believed Ben Adhem's meek request when denied a place among "those who love the Lord,"

"Write me then
As one who loves his fellow men,"[3]

to be the very brightest, sweetest, truest expression of the central thought of Christianity. The "selfishness of salvation" never appealed to me. I was willing to leave all that comes after this life to the power which controls the future

---

3. Tourgée chose this couplet, from James Leigh Hunt's "Abou Ben Adhem" (1838), as his own epitaph. It appears on his gravestone in Mayville, New York.

which our eyes cannot penetrate. But the idea of being a co-worker in the betterment of humanity has always kept me struggling for what I know to be impossible under present conditions and may be delayed for ages. Because of this I felt myself to have been a Fool in having tried to graft freedom and justice on the seared stump of Slavery, and now know that I was never more a Fool than when I thought knowledge and Christian civilizations would peacefully reconcile the new barbarism with the Christ-idea of justice between man and man and race and race, or our national ideals of equal rights, security, justice and opportunity for all. Milk may do for babies, but it is useless as a remedy for collective wrongs or the healing of evils which have come to dominate Christian thought and color the tendency of civilization. When barbarism is entrenched in civilization and Christianity smiles a placid approval of policy of Murder the time for argument and reason is past and only He who is able to control the general impulse by events which appeal to every heart, can find a remedy or avert the inexpressible horror which impends.

I hope you will pardon me for this great screed. I never wrote such a letter before and am never likely to do it again. Indeed, I would destroy it now, but for Mrs. Tourgée, who has gravely decided that I ought to send it. If you live to read it through you are at liberty to drop it in the fire.

I am glad you are coming over for the trip you outline, and do not doubt it will furnish you a needed rest and refreshment. I wish you could include Bordeaux on your route, but this is a peculiarly isolated part of Europe owing to the lines of travel which have been inflexibly established by the use of storm and submission of all the world to the mercantile demands of England.

I am not much of a traveler owing to the fettering disability of the old spinal wound, which ties me to my chair and thereby no doubt secures the performances of some duties I might otherwise neglect. In almost five years I have not been out of my Consular District but once—for seven days which I passed in London. I shall often think of you and wish you a good time. I have often thought I would like to visit Norway, not so much for the "Midnight Sun" as to take a few trout and perhaps a salmon in her icy waters. I suppose I might as well lay away the hope in lavender as one of the pleasant yearnings not to be fulfilled unless by proxy. If you get a chance, make a cast for me even if you never touched a rod before.

We are very pleasantly located here at Bordeaux. It is a busy Consulate, almost wholly commercial. The work is varied, but I have enjoyed getting the routine machinery in shape, and take no little pride in having perhaps the best ordered Consulate in the service. My health is now much better than it has been in many years. The climate is very soft with frequent rains but mostly light so the aggregate amount is not as much as with us. The spring has been cool and damp which has made the vegetation very lush, so that just now southwest France is probably nearly as beautiful as you may have fancied it. On the whole I find it a most excellent place in which to pass the last days of an ill-spent life. I hardly expect ever to return to the United States again unless ordered there from some grave infraction of curiously framed rules which give about equal pleasure and annoyance.

With kindest regards and warmest wishes, I remain,

Most sincerely yours,

BIBLIOGRAPHY

WORKS OF ALBION W. TOURGÉE

Unpublished Letters and Private Papers

Albion Winegar Tourgée Papers. Chautauqua County Historical Society, McClurg Museum, Westfield, NY. 11,167 items. Available on UMI microfilm, 60 reels.

Fiction

The Lagby Papers. *Greensboro Union Register,* ca. January 1867. [Regular series.]

God's Anynted Phue. *New Berne Republican Courier,* ca. February 1872. [Regular series.]

[Henry Churton]. *'Toinette: A Tale of the South.* New York: Fords, Howard, & Hulbert, 1874.

[Henry Churton]. Mamelon. *Christian Union* 13 (April 19–June 14, 1876). [Regular series.]

Figs and Thistles: A Romance of the Western Reserve. New York: Fords, Howard, & Hulbert, 1879.

[Anonymous]. *A Fool's Errand; By One of the Fools.* New York: Fords, Howard, & Hulbert, 1879.

A Fool's Errand, By One of the Fools; The Famous Romance of American History. New, Enlarged, and Illustrated Edition. To Which is Added, By the Same Author, Part II. The Invisible Empire: A Concise Review of the Epoch on Which the Tale is Based. New York: Fords, Howard, & Hulbert, 1880.

Bricks Without Straw: A Novel. New York: Fords, Howard, & Hulbert, 1880.

A Royal Gentleman and Zouri's Christmas. New York: Fords, Howard, & Hulbert, 1881.

[With Steele McKay]. *A Fool's Errand* [1881 Philadelphia stage production]. Ed. with an introduction by Dean Keller. Metuchen, NJ: Scarecrow, 1969.

John Eax and Mamelon; or, the South without the Shadow. New York: Fords, Howard, & Hulbert, 1882.

"Hot Plowshares." *Our Continent* 2–3 (July 12, 1882–May 23, 1883). [Regular series.]

Hot Plowshares. A Novel. New York: Fords, Howard, & Hulbert, 1883.

[Anonymous]. "With Gauge and Swallow, Attorneys." *Our Continent* 5, no. 23 (1884): 706–12.

379

[Anonymous]. The Veteran and His Pipe. *Chicago Daily Inter-Ocean,* April 25, 1885–September 19, 1885. [Regular series.]

[Anonymous]. *The Veteran and His Pipe.* Chicago: Belford, Clark & Co., 1885.

Button's Inn. *Chicago Inter-Ocean,* December 12, 1886–January 23, 1887, and *Buffalo Sunday Express,* December 19, 1886–January 30, 1887. [Regular series.]

Button's Inn. Boston: Roberts Brothers, 1887.

"Professor Cadmus's Great Case." *Lippincott's Monthly Magazine* 40 (December 1887): 890–908.

"Christmas Eve in a Palace Car." *Chicago Daily Inter-Ocean,* December 25, 1887, 18.

Black Ice. New York: Fords, Howard, & Hulbert, 1888.

[Edgar Henry]. *Eighty-Nine; or, the Grand Master's Secret.* New York: Fords, Howard, & Hulbert, 1888.

"An Unlawful Honor." *Lippincott's Monthly Magazine* 41 (January 1888): 103–18.

"A Retainer in Cupid's Court." *Lippincott's Monthly Magazine* 41 (March 1888): 400–15.

"The Letter and the Spirit." *Lippincott's Monthly Magazine* 41 (April 1888): 537–58.

"A Shattered Idol." *Lippincott's Monthly Magazine* 41 (June 1888): 826–38.

"A Bill of Discovery." *Lippincott's Monthly Magazine* 42 (July 1888): 112–24.

"A Conflict Between Church and State." *Lippincott's Monthly Magazine* 42 (September 1888): 395–406.

"How I Became the Widow's Attorney." *Lippincott's Monthly Magazine* 42 (October 1888): 532–43.

"'Missionary Joe.'" *Lippincott's Monthly Magazine* 43 (February 1889): 236–49.

"A Legal Impressionist." *Lippincott's Monthly Magazine* 43 (June 1889): 871–85.

"A Dissolving View." *Lippincott's Monthly Magazine* 44 (July 1889): 79–93.

"The 'Long Vacation.'" *Lippincott's Monthly Magazine* 44 (August 1889): 252–67.

With Gauge and Swallow, Attorneys. Philadelphia: J. B. Lippincott, 1889.

Pactolus Prime, or the White Christ. *The Advance* (Chicago) 22–23 (December 13, 1888–March 14, 1889). [Regular series.]

Pactolus Prime. New York: Cassell Publishing Co., 1890.

Nazirema or the "Church of the Golden Lilies." *The Advance* (Chicago) 23 (October 3, 1889–July 3, 1890). [Regular series.]

Murvale Eastman, Christian Socialist. New York: Fords, Howard, & Hulbert, 1890.

A Son of Old Harry. *New York Ledger* 47 (April 4, 1891–August 29, 1891). [Regular series.]

A Son of Old Harry: A Novel. New York: Robert Bonner's Sons, 1891.

"Corporate Billee." *Cosmopolitan* 11 (May 1891): 96–108.

Out of the Sunset Sea. *Chicago Daily Inter-Ocean,* December 18, 1892–March 26, 1893. [Regular series.]

Out of the Sunset Sea. New York: Merrill & Baker, 1893.

"An Astral Partner." *Green Bag* 7 (July–August, 1896).

The Mortgage on the Hip-Roof House. Cincinnati: Curts & Jennings; New York: Eaton and Mains, 1896.

"The Man Who Outlived Himself." *Washington National Tribune,* September 30–November 4, 1897. [Regular series.]

The Man Who Outlived Himself. New York: Fords, Howard, & Hulbert, 1898.
"The Summerdale Brabble." *Washington National Tribune,* March 7, 1901–May 2, 1901. [Regular series.]

Poetry

"Poll Tax Song." *National Anti-Slavery Standard,* November 9, 1867.
"Bring Flowers—Bright Flowers." *Greensboro Patriot,* May 14, 1873.
"John Workman's Notions." *Greensboro North State,* September 26, 1878.
"Monumentum in Aere." *Our Continent* 1 (May 31, 1882): 249.
"Yesterday and To-Day." *Our Continent* 1 (July 5, 1882): 328–29.
"Duplessis Mornay." *Our Continent* 2 (November 29, 1882): 656–57.
"A Dirge." *Chicago Daily Inter-Ocean.* August 4, 1888.
"Childe Rob, of Lincoln." *Chicago Daily Inter-Ocean.* June 22, 1888.
"The Ballad of Gettysburg." *Chicago Daily Inter-Ocean,* July 4, 1888.
"Daniel Periton's Ride." *Independent* 41 (June 27, 1889): 1.
"The Christ." *The Basis* 2 (December 1895): 34.
"Tho He Slay!" *The Independent* 48 (December 10, 1896): 37.

Nonfiction: Books, Articles, Essays, Broadsides, and Published Speeches

"To the Voters of Guilford." Broadside. N.p.: n.p., October 21, 1867.
[With Victor C. Barringer and William B. Rodman]. *Book of Forms.* Prepared by Commissioners of the Code. Raleigh, NC: n.p., 1868.
[With Victor C. Barringer and William B. Rodman]. *The Code of Civil Procedure of North Carolina, To Special Proceedings.* Raleigh, NC: N. Paige, State Printer, 1868.
A Plan for the Organization of the Judiciary Department, Proposed by A. W. Tourgée, of Guilford, as a Section of the Constitution. Raleigh, NC: n.p., 1868.
"National Education." *Washington Chronicle,* January 17, 1871.
[Henry Churton]. "Why Reconstruction was a Failure." *Northampton (MA) Free Press and Journal* (c.1876).
"One of Three Things." N.p.: n.p., ca. 1876.
"Root, Hog, or Die." N.p.: n.p., ca. 1876.
["C"]. "The Southern Question." *Rochester (NY) Democrat and Chronicle,* September 16, 1876.
The Code of Civil Procedure of North Carolina, With Notes and Decisions. Raleigh, NC: John Nichols, 1878.
A Digest of Cited Cases in the North Carolina Reports, Containing a Syllabus of Each Case Cited, To the End of the 79th Volume, a List of the Cases in Which it is Cited, and a Careful Synopsis of Each Modification, Extension or Reversal. Raleigh, NC: Alfred Williams, 1879.
Statutory Adjudications in the North Carolina Reports, with a Supplement to "The Code with Notes and Decisions," and an Index of Parallel References. Raleigh, NC: Alfred Williams, 1879.

"Aaron's Rod in Politics." *North American Review* 132 (February 1881): 139–62.

"Reform versus Reformation." *North American Review* 132 (April 1881): 305–19.

"The Education of the Negro." *Congregationalist* 33 (November 1881): 389.

"The Christian Citizen." *The Chautauquan* 2 (November 1881): 86–91.

The Invisible Empire: A Concise Review of the Epoch. New York: Fords, Howard, & Hulbert, 1883.

"Give Us a Rest." *Chautauqua (NY) Assembly Herald,* August 6, 1883.

"The Negro's View of the Destiny of His Race." N.p.: n.p., 1883.

An Appeal to Caesar. New York: Fords, Howard, & Hulbert, 1884.

"National Aid to Education." *New York Tribune,* April 12, 1884.

"A Summer University." *The Day Star,* June 24, 1886, 1–2.

"A Study in Civilization." *North American Review* 143 (September 1886): 246–61.

"The Renaissance of Nationalism." *North American Review* 144 (January 1887): 1–11.

[The Veteran]. "Logan, the Loyal." *Chicago Daily Inter-Ocean,* February 10, 1887, 4–5.

[The Veteran]. "Old Abe's Son." *Chicago Daily Inter-Ocean,* August 20, 1887, 9.

"Catching the Viper." *Chicago Daily Inter-Ocean,* September 28, 1888, 9.

"The South as a Field for Fiction." *Forum* 6 (December 1888): 404–13.

"The Claim of Realism." *North American Review* 148 (March 1889): 386–88.

"Shall White Minorities Rule?" *Forum* 7 (April 1889): 143–55.

"A Tide Watcher's Thoughts." *Philadelphia Press,* June 2, 1889.

"A Queer 'Comedy of Errors.'" *Congregationalist* 51 (June 27, 1889).

"Our Semi-Citizens." *Frank Leslie's Illustrated Weekly* 69 (September 28, 1889): 122–23.

"Shall We Re-Barbarize the Negro?" *Congregationalist* 41 (December 5, 1889): 411–16.

"The Negro's View of the Race Problem." In *First Mohonk Conference on the Negro Question. Held at Lake Mohonk, Ulster County New York, June 4, 5, 6,* ed. Isabel C. Barrows. Boston: G. H. Ellis, 1890. Reprint, New York: Negro Universities Press, 1969.

"The American Negro: What Are His Rights and What Must Be Done to Secure Them?" *New York Tribune,* February 16, 1890.

"The Right to Vote." *Forum* 9 (March 1890): 78–92.

"The Rehabilitation of the 4th of July." *Independent* 42 (July 3, 1890): 8–9.

Introduction to *Wealth and Civilization,* by N. B. Ashby. Chicago: Howard and Wilson, 1891.

Is Liberty Worth Preserving? Chicago: Inter-Ocean, 1892.

"Christian Citizenship." *The Golden Rule* 7 (August 1892).

"The Anti-Trust Campaign." *North American Review* 157 (July 1893): 30–41.

An Outing with the Queen of Hearts. New York: Merrill & Baker, 1894.

"As A Public Man." In *Martin B. Anderson, LL.D. A Biography,* ed. A. C. Kendrick. Philadelphia: American Baptist Publication Society, 1895.

"Yesterday's Duty and How It Was Done." *Boston Globe,* May 31, 1896.

"The Reversal of Malthus." *American Journal of Sociology* 2 (July 1896): 13–24.

"The Literary Quality of Uncle Tom's Cabin." *Independent* 48 (August 20,1896): 3–4.

"The Best Currency." *North American Review* 163 (October 1896): 416–26.

"Some Advice to Young Voters." *The Golden Rule* 11 (October 1, 1896): 4–5.

A Memorial of Frederick Douglass from the City of Boston. Boston: City Council, 1896.

"The Story of a Thousand." *Cosmopolitan* 18 (November 1894–April 1895) and *The Basis* (May 25, 1895–November 2, 1895). [Regular series.]

The Story of a Thousand. Being a History of the Service of the 105th Ohio Volunteer Infantry, in the War for the Union. Buffalo, NY: McGerald & Son, 1896.

The War of the Standards, Coin and Credit, versus Coin without Credit. Question of the Day, vol. 88. New York: G. P. Putnam's Sons, 1986.

"Pending Problems." *North American Review* 164 (January 1897): 38–49.

"The Twentieth Century Peacemakers." *Contemporary Review* 75 (June 1899): 886–908.

"The Unwritten Law and Why It Remains Unwritten." *Green Bag* 20 (January 1908): 8–17.

Nonfiction: Newspaper Editorials and Published Letters

"Kingsville Boys at Bull Run: Albion Tourgée to Valentine Tourgée and Albion Tourgée to Emma Kilbourne." *Conneaut [Ohio] Reporter,* August 8, 1861.

"Lieutenant Albion Tourgée of Kingsville to Valentine Tourgée." *Conneaut Reporter,* February 18, 1863.

"Lieutenant Albion Tourgée of Kingsville to Valentine Tourgée." *Conneaut Reporter,* February 25, 1863.

"Albion W. Tourgée to Editor." *Greensboro Patriot,* September 14, 1866.

The Union Register. Greensboro, NC, December 1, 1866–June 14, 1867. [Edited and contributed regular editorials.]

[Signed "Wenckar" and "Winegar"]. "North Carolina Correspondence." *National Anti-Slavery Standard,* October 19, November 9, December 14, 1867, and January 4, 1868.

"Albion W. Tourgée to Editor." *North Carolina Standard,* January 28, 1870.

"Albion W. Tourgée to Senator Joseph C. Abbott." *New York Tribune,* August 3, 1870.

"Albion W. Tourgée to E. S. Parker." *Greensboro New North State,* June 18, 1875.

"What the Pew Thinks. No. 2." *Greensboro New North State,* August 6, 1875.

["C"]. Letters signed "C." *Greensboro North State,* March–May, 1878. [Weekly series.]

["C"]. *The "C" Letters as Published in the "North State."* Greensboro, N.C.: North State Book and Job Printing Office, 1878.

["C"]. Letters signed "C." Second series. *Greensboro North State,* June–July 1878. [Weekly series.]

"About Carpet-Baggers." *New York Tribune,* January 31, 1881.

"To the Readers of the Chautauquan." *The Chautauquan* 2 (December 1881): 182.

Our Continent [and *The Continent*]. Vols. 1–6. February 15, 1882–August 20, 1884. [Edited and contributed regular editorials.]

National Education. *Our Continent* 4–5 (October 3, 1883–November 15, 1884). [Regular series.]

[Siva]. A Man of Destiny. *Chicago Daily Inter-Ocean,* April 25, 1885–September 19, 1885. [Weekly series.]

[Siva]. *A Man of Destiny.* Chicago: Belford, Clarke & Co., 1886.

[Trueman Joyce]. Letters to a Mugwump. *Chicago Daily Inter-Ocean,* September 26, 1885–December 12, 1885. [Weekly series.]

[Siva]. "A Child of Luck." *Chicago Daily Inter-Ocean,* March 20, 1886–December 4, 1886. [Weekly series.]

Letter to a King. *Northwestern Christian Advocate* 35 (January 5, 1887–September 28, 1887). [Weekly series.]

"Tourgée on Beecher." *Chicago Daily Inter-Ocean,* March 13, 1887.

"Tourgée on Tuley." *Chicago Daily Inter-Ocean,* May 15, 1888.

A Bystander's Notes. *Chicago Daily Inter-Ocean,* April 21, 1888–August 12, 1893; May 5, 1894–January 5, 1895. [Weekly series.]

[John Workman]. John Workman's Notions. *Chicago Daily Inter-Ocean,* July 1, 1891–January 20, 1892. [Weekly series.]

[John Workman]. John Workman's Notions. Second series. *Chicago Daily Inter-Ocean,* January 27–April 20, 1892. [Weekly series.]

[Siva]. A Man of Destiny. Second Series. *Chicago Daily Inter-Ocean,* January 13, 1894–April 28, 1894. [Weekly series.]

"That Lynching: Judge Tourgée Writes Gov. McKinley and the Editor of 'The Gazette.'" *Cleveland Gazette,* March 3, 1894.

Letter on the writing of *Button's Inn. Dunkirk (NY) Grape Belt,* June 29, 1895.

The Basis. Vols. 1–2 (March 20, 1895–November 9, 1895 [weekly], and December 1895–April 1896 [monthly]). [Edited and contributed regular editorials.]

The Science of Self-Government. *The Basis* [1] (August 3–November 2, 1895). [Regular series.]

A Bystander's Notes. *The Basis* [1]–2 (April 13, 1895–March, 1896). [Weekly series.]

A Bystander's Notes. New series. *Chicago Inter-Ocean,* August 7, 1897–October 2, 1898. [Weekly series.]

SECONDARY WORKS

Aaron, Daniel. *The Unwritten War: American Writers and the Civil War.* New York: Alfred A. Knopf, 1973.

Becker, George J. "Albion W. Tourgée: Pioneer in Social Criticism." *American Literature* 19 (March 1947): 59–72.

Blight, David W. *Race and Reunion: The Civil War in American Memory.* Cambridge: Harvard University Press, 2001.

Bowman, Sylvia E. "Judge Tourgée's Fictional Representation of the Reconstruction." *Journal of Popular Culture* 3 (Fall 1969): 307–23.

Brown, Sterling. *The Negro in American Fiction.* Washington, D.C.: Associates in Negro Folk Education, 1937.

Buck, Paul H. *The Road to Reunion, 1865–1900*. Boston: Little, Brown and Company, 1937.

Caccavari, Peter J. "Reconstructing Reconstruction: Region and Nation in the Work of Albion Tourgée." In *Regionalism Reconsidered: New Approaches to the Field*, ed. David Jordan, 119–38. New York: Garland Publishing, 1994.

———. "A Trick of Mediation: Charles Chesnutt's Conflicted Literary Relationship with Albion Tourgée." In *Literary Influences and African-American Writers*, ed. Tracy Mishkin, 129–53. New York: Garland Publishing, 1996.

Carter, Everett. "Edmund Wilson Refights the Civil War: The Revision of Albion Tourgée's Novels." *American Literary Realism 1870–1910* 29 (Winter 1997): 68–75.

Cooper, Anna Julia. *A Voice from the South*. Xenia, OH: Aldine Printing House, 1892.

Cowie, Alexander. *The Rise of the American Novel*. New York: American Book Co., 1948.

Current, Richard Nelson. *Those Terrible Carpetbaggers: A Reinterpretation*. New York: Oxford University Press, 1988.

Curtis, Michael Kent. "Albion Tourgée: Remembering Plessy's Lawyer on the 100th Anniversary of Plessy v. Ferguson." *Constitutional Commentary* 13 (Summer 1996): 187–99.

Devin, William A. "Footprints of a Carpetbagger." *The Torch* 17 (April 1944): 16–19, 21.

Dibble, Roy. *Albion W. Tourgée*. New York, Lemcke & Buechner, 1921.

Douglass, J. Allen. "The 'Most Valuable Sort of Property': Constructing White Identity in American Law, 1880–1940." *San Diego Law Review* 40, no. 3 (Fall 2003): 881–946.

Du Bois, W. E. B. *Black Reconstruction in America, 1860–1880*. New York: Harcourt, Brace and Company, 1935.

Ealy, Marguerite, and Sanford E. Marovitz. "Albion Winegar Tourgée (1838–1905)." *American Literary Realism, 1870–1910* 8 (Winter 1975): 53–80.

Elliott, Mark. *Color-Blind Justice: Albion W. Tourgée and the Quest for Racial Equality from the Civil War to Plessy v. Ferguson*. New York: Oxford University Press, 2006.

———. "The Question of Color-Blind Citizenship: Albion Tourgée, W. E. B. Du Bois and the Principles of the Niagara Movement." *Afro-Americans in New York Life and History* 32.2 (July 2008): 23–49.

———. "Race, Color Blindness, and the Democratic Public: Albion W. Tourgée's Radical Principles in Plessy v. Ferguson." *Journal of Southern History* 67 (May 2001): 287–330.

Firestone, Harvey. *Separate and Unequal: Homer Plessy and the Supreme Court Decision That Legalized Racism*. New York: Carroll & Graf, 2004.

Fishel, Leslie H., Jr. "The 'Negro Question' at Mohonk: Microcosm, Mirage, and Message." *New York History* 74 (July 1993): 277–314.

Franklin, John Hope. "Albion Tourgée, Social Critic: An Editor's Introduction." In *A Fool's Errand*, Harvard Library Edition, vii–xxviii. Cambridge: Belknap Press of Harvard University Press, 1961.

Fredrickson, George M. *The Black Image in the White Mind: The Debate on Afro-American Character and Destiny, 1817–1914.* Middletown, CT: Wesleyan University Press, 1971.

———. "The Travail of a Radical Republican: Albion W. Tourgée and Reconstruction." In *The Arrogance of Race: Historical Perspectives on Slavery, Racism, and Social Inequality,* 94–106. Middletown, CT: Wesleyan University Press, 1988.

Gerber, David. "Lynching and Law and Order." *Ohio History* 83 (Winter 1974): 33–50.

Gloster, Hugh. *Negro Voices in American Fiction.* Washington, DC: Associates in Negro Folk Education, 1937.

Golub, Mark. "*Plessy* as 'Passing': Judicial Responses to the Ambiguously Raced Bodies in *Plessy v. Ferguson.*" *Law & Society Review* 39 (September 2005): 563–600.

Gross, Theodore L. *Albion W. Tourgée.* New York: Twayne, 1963.

———. "The Fool's Errand of Albion W. Tourgée." *Phylon* 24 (3rd Qtr. 1963): 240–54.

Hardwig, Bill. "Who Owns the Whip? Chesnutt, Tourgée, and Reconstruction Justice." *African American Review* 36 (Spring 2002): 5–20.

Hubbell, Jay B. *The South in American Literature, 1607–1900.* Durham: Duke University Press, 1954.

Kaplan, Sidney. "Albion W. Tourgée: Attorney for the Segregated." *Journal of Negro History* 49 (April 1964): 128–33.

Karcher, Carolyn L. "Ida B. Wells and Her Allies against Lynching: A Transnational Perspective." *Comparative American Studies* 3 (2005): 131–51.

———. Introduction. In Albion W. Tourgée, *Bricks Without Straw: A Novel.* Durham: Duke University Press, 2009.

———. "'Men are Burned at the Stake in Our Free Country:' Albion W. Tourgée's Antilynching Journalism.'" *Resources for American Literary Study* 30 (2006): 178–215.

———. "The White 'Bystander' and the Black Journalist 'Abroad': Albion W. Tourgée and Ida B. Wells as Allies against Lynching." *Prospects* 29 (2004): 85–119.

Keller, Dean H., ed. "Albion Tourgée and a National Educational Program." *Peabody Journal of Education* 41 (November 1963): 131–35.

———. "Albion Tourgée as Editor of THE BASIS." *Niagara Frontier* 12 (Spring 1965): 24–28.

———. "A Checklist of Writings of Albion W. Tourgée (1838–1905)." *Studies in Bibliography* 18 (1965): 269–79.

———, ed. "A Civil War Diary of Albion Tourgée." *Ohio History* 74 (Spring 1965): 99–131.

———. "Tourgée's Ohio Days." *Ohioana* 5 (Winter 1962): 98–100, 110.

Lively, Robert A. *Fiction Fights the Civil War: An Unfinished Chapter in the Literary History of the American People.* Chapel Hill: University of North Carolina Press, 1957.

Lofgren, Charles A. *The Plessy Case: A Legal-Historical Interpretation.* New York: Oxford University Press, 1987.

Luker, Ralph E. *The Social Gospel in Black and White: American Racial Reform, 1885–1912*. Chapel Hill: University of North Carolina Press, 1991.

Magdol, Edward. "A Note on Authenticity: Eliab Hill and Nimbus Ware in *Bricks Without Straw*." *American Quarterly* 22 (Winter 1970): 907–11.

McAfee, Ward M. "Reconstruction Revisited: The Republican Public Education Crusade of the 1870s." *Civil War History* 42 (June 1996): 133–53.

McDaniel, Ruth. "Courtship and Marriage in the 19th Century: Albion and Emma Tourgée." *North Carolina Historical Review* 61 (July 1984): 285–310.

Medley, Keith Weldon. *We as Freemen: Plessy v. Ferguson*. Gretna, LA: Pelican, 2003.

Morris, Robert C. *Reading, 'Riting, and Reconstruction: The Education of Freedmen in the South, 1861–1870*. Chicago: University of Chicago Press, 1981.

Nye, Russell B. "Judge Tourgée and Reconstruction." *Ohio State Archaeological and Historical Quarterly* 50 (July 1941): 101–14.

O'Connor, Leo. *Religion and the American Novel: The Search for Belief, 1860–1920*. New York: University Press of America, 1984.

Olenick, Monte M. "Albion W. Tourgée: Radical Republican Spokesman of the Civil War Crusade." *Phylon* 23 (4th Qtr. 1962): 332–45.

Olsen, Otto H. "Albion W. Tourgée and Negro Militants of the 1890's: A Documentary Selection." *Science and Society* 28 (Spring 1964): 183–207.

———. "Albion W. Tourgée: Carpetbagger." *North Carolina Historical Review* 40 (Autumn 1963): 434–54.

———. *Carpetbagger's Crusade: The Life of Albion Winegar Tourgée*. Baltimore: Johns Hopkins University Press, 1965.

———, ed. *The Thin Disguise: Plessy v. Ferguson, A Documentary Presentation*. New York: Humanities Press, 1967.

———. "Tourgée on Reconstruction: A Revisionist Document of 1892." *Sherif* 2 (September 1965): 21–29.

Scott, Rebecca J. "'There is No Caste Here': Public Rights, Social Equality and the Conceptual Roots of the *Plessy* Challenge." *Michigan Law Review* 106 (March 2008): 777–804.

Simms, L. Moody. "Albion Tourgée and the Fictional Use of the Post–Civil War South." *Southern Studies* 17 (Winter 1978): 399–409.

Smith, Mark M. *How Race Is Made: Slavery, Segregation, and the Senses*. Chapel Hill: University of North Carolina Press, 2006.

Sobieraj, Jerzy. "Albion W. Tourgée and the Ku Klux Klan." *American Studies* 17 (1999): 29–34.

Stephens, Robert. "Tourgée's Bricks Without Straw." *Southern Quarterly* 27 (Summer 1989): 101–10.

Sundquist, Eric J. *To Wake the Nations: Race in the Making of American Literature*. Cambridge: Harvard University Press, 1993.

Thomas, Brook. *American Literary Realism and the Failed Promise of Contract*. Berkeley: University of California Press, 1997.

————, ed. *Plessy v. Ferguson: A Brief History with Documents*. Boston: Bedford Books, 1997.

————. "Tragedies of Race, Training, Birth, and Communities of Competent Pudd'nheads." *American Literary History* 1 (Winter 1989): 754–85.

Thomas, Clarence. "The Virtue of Defeat: *Plessy* v. *Ferguson* in Retrospect." *Journal of Supreme Court History* 2 (1997): 15–24.

Weissbuch, Ted N. "Albion W. Tourgée: Propagandist and Critic of Reconstruction." *Ohio Historical Quarterly* 70 (January 1961): 27–44.

White, Ronald C., Jr. *Liberty and Justice for All: Racial Reform and the Social Gospel (1877–1925)*. San Francisco: Harper & Row, 1990.

Wilson, Edmund. *Patriotic Gore: Studies in the Literature of the American Civil War.* New York: Farrar, Straus, and Giroux, 1962.

Woodward, C. Vann. "The Birth of Jim Crow." *American Heritage* 15 (April 1964): 52–55, 100–103.

INDEX

Slavery *(continued)*

Civil War, 39, 40, 60, 80, 194, 199, 260, 367; and day of Jubilee for slaves, 101, 374–75; definition of slave, 313; and Democratic Party, 37; as domestic institution, 101–2; emancipation of slaves, 60, 80, 101, 194, 224–26, 259, 265–66, 352; end of, due to Thirteenth Amendment, 225, 297, 298, 313, 316, 322–24; and end of slave trade, 119; evil of, 80, 216–17, 228, 231–34, 259, 349; exclusion of, from Northwest Territory, 217; fear of masters by slaves, 263, 264; fugitive slaves, 3, 250, 304, 318, 325; God's will for end of, 348–49, 354, 360, 374–75; illiteracy of slaves, 101, 116, 117, 119, 135–36, 358; justification of, 56, 107–8, 109, 112–13, 160–61, 220–21, 255, 260, 357–61; in Kentucky, 3; laws on, 119; legal protection for, 113, 138, 170, 265; legal status of slaves, 154, 257, 264, 322–23; marriage prohibited to slaves, 154, 158, 166, 257, 280, 323, 358, 366; and master-slave relationship generally, 157, 169, 360–61, 370; names of slaves, 154, 257; need for black authors' perspectives on, 13; and planter aristocracy, 39; religion of slaves, 103; reparations to blacks for, 10, 41, 123–39, 267, 269; and Republican Party, 31–33, 66; in Rome, 109; southern literature on, 12–13, 203–11; and southern view of separation of races, 97–102, 109–10; and state sovereignty, 311–14, 337; statistics on, 132, 226; in Stowe's *Uncle Tom's Cabin*, 13, 229–34, 360; Tourgée's opposition to generally, 3, 217, 228, 346; and treatment of slaves, 115–16, 119, 263, 269, 279; and U.S. Constitution, 113, 138, 170, 225, 258–59, 265, 280, 335. *See also* Abolitionism

Smiley, Albert K., 152

Smith, Garret, 218

Smith, Harry C., 14, 289–95

Smith, Mark M., 20

Social Gospel movement, 2, 3, 10

"Solid South," 71–73, 82–84, 86, 117. *See also* South and Southerners

South and Southerners: advantages of slavery for, 79–80, 158, 169, 268–69; black population of southern states, 114–15, 120; and blacks as laborers, 103, 115, 120, 152–54, 242–43, 257, 258, 261–62, 368; and blacks' struggles for equality leading to conflict, 103–4, 121–22; and Civil Rights Bill (1875), 7, 53; Civil War's impact

on, 206; collection of information on, by National Citizens' Rights Association, 272–73, 368; disfranchisement of, after Civil War, 34, 42; and divine order of white supremacy, 108–10; domination of northern civilization and Christianity by, 367–69, 375–76; education of, 55; and financial worth of freedmen, 120, 159–60, 277; and gradual approach to rights for freedmen, 7, 53, 62; illiteracy of, 55–56, 69–74, 79, 117–18, 167, 206; and isolation of races, 95–104; and literature on slavery and Civil War, 12–13, 203–11; losses of, due to emancipation of slaves, 80; and Lost Cause mythology, 12–13, 20, 84–85, 194–95, 199, 356–78; and Memorial Day, 199–201; New South, 357; poor whites of South, 153–54; and public school system, 162, 169–70; and purported inferiority of freedmen, 8, 96–99, 107–10, 160–61, 220–21, 263; and race question, 160–61; and racism, 95–96; reconciliation between North and, 3, 58, 93–94; representation of, in Congress based on slave population, 258–59; in Republican Party, 72, 73, 86, 258; and rule of white minorities, 112–22; secession by, 59, 77, 83–84, 113, 118, 311–12; and "solid South," 71–73, 82–84, 86, 117; and states rights, 86; treatment of freedmen by, 40–42; as Unionists, 34, 41–42. *See also* Blacks; Confederacy; Lynching; Race question; Racism; Reconstruction; Segregation; Slave owners; Slavery

"The South as a Field for Fiction" (Tourgée), 12–13, 203–11

South Carolina: black population of, 114; illiteracy in, 70, 73, 118; literacy of blacks and whites in, 118; white minority rule in, 118

Southern Loyalist Convention (1866), 31, 31*m*, 32

Spain, 336, 371

Spanish-American War, 344

"Speech on Elective Franchise" (Tourgée), 6, 35–42

Spencer, Herbert, 211

State v. Caesar, 317

State v. Davis, 317

State v. Dennis Haines, 44

State v. Jowers, 317

"States' rights" theories, 86

Stephens, John Walter, 7, 47–48, 51, 312